SAVING
—— THE ——
WORLD
ONE CASE
AT A TIME

Kenneth Foard McCallion

Also by Kenneth Foard McCallion

Profiles in Courage in the Trump Era

Profiles in Cowardice in the Trump Era

COVID-19: The Virus that Changed America and the World

Treason & Betrayal: The Rise and Fall of Individual-1

The Essential Guide to Donald Trump

Shoreham and the Rise and Fall of the Nuclear Power Industry

SAVING
—THE—
WORLD
ONE CASE
AT A TIME

Kenneth Foard McCallion

Bryant Park Press

Bryant Park Press

Published by Bryant Park Press

An imprint of HHI Media, Inc.

Copyright © 2022 by Kenneth Foard McCallion

Jacket and Book Design by Christopher Klaich

Manufactured in the United States of America

Hardback ISBN: 978-1-7371492-5-5 Paperback ISBN: 978-1-7371492-6-2

DEDICATION

This book is dedicated to my father, Harry J. McCallion, an accomplished trial lawyer and guiding light throughout my formative years and the early part of my law career. He taught me that the law is a noble profession and that a lawyer can make a significant contribution to the ongoing fight for truth, fairness, and justice, even when the odds seem to be permanently stacked against them.

This book is also dedicated to the love of my life, my wife Susan, without whose encouragement and assistance I never would have been able to take on many of the most challenging legal cases – and in some cases legal crusades - of my career. She steadfastly stood by my side not only during the long legal battles in U.S. courts, but also during my lengthy sojourns throughout Europe and Africa.

Finally, the book is dedicated to the plaintiffs, friends and colleagues who joined me down the less travelled and perilous paths of environmental, human rights and other plaintiff's litigation.

ACKNOWLEGEMENTS

My deepest and heartfelt thanks goes to Aaron Jerome, and the rest of a small army of researchers, fact-checkers, editors, proof-readers, colleagues and clients who have contributed countless hours to this project, and without whose assistance this book would not have been possible. Especially a big thanks to Christopher Klaich for his always inspiring design and has put up with my endless changes with grace and good spirit.

Table Contents

Lawyers have their duties as citizens, but they also have special duties as lawyers. Their obligations go far deeper than earning a living as specialists in corporation or tax law. They have a continuing responsibility to uphold the fundamental principles of justice from which the law cannot depart.

– Robert F. Kennedy

Preface

In the years since I graduated from law school in 1972, there have been significant developments in virtually every area of law, just as there has been in society in general. As medicine strives to provide a cure for every illness, the ideal of the law is to provide a legal remedy for every wrong. Unfortunately, however, neither the fields of medicine nor law will ever fully accomplish these aspirational goals. Disease and illness are an inevitable fact of life, although they continue to fall disproportionately on the poor and powerless, while the rich and powerful – not coincidentally – manage on average to live longer and healthier lives than the rest of us. Similarly, the platonic ideal of equal access to justice seems like an ever-receding mirage, both in criminal and civil cases. Civil litigation in both state and federal courts continues to be primarily an instrument of rich and powerful individuals and corporations, at the expense of the poor and powerless.

However, this does not suggest that dedicated plaintiffs' attorneys and trial lawyers – what my father preferred to call "lawyers for the people" – cannot make a real difference in evening up the scales of justice. At least in America, where a contingent fee system is both allowed and encouraged, ordinary people can be given more of a fighting chance to have their day in court and to recover the monetary damages they have suffered.

The United States may be considered litigious compared to almost every other country. Some conservative politicians and political pundits promote the false narrative that a large number of civil cases filed in the U.S. by the average American – urged on by avaricious plaintiffs' lawyers – have created mountains of unnecessary and frivolous complaints in the hopes of getting a large settlement or money judgment that they don't deserve. This is untrue. Instead, more lawsuits are filed in American courts than in other countries' courts because our legal system permits attorneys to work on a contingent fee basis, which requires that the attorney carefully evaluate and vet a case's merits before it is filed. If and only if the case is successful, a plaintiff's attorney may recover a percentage (usually one-third) of any settlement, award, or judgment. Each case must be carefully evaluated since the dismissal of the case by way of motion or otherwise leaves the plaintiff's lawyer – as well as the plaintiff – with nothing. American attorneys are also permitted to advance litigation expenses out of their pocket on behalf of a client. As a result, anyone residing in the U.S. – and even some foreign clients in special circumstances – can access justice in state or federal court if they convince a plaintiff's lawyer to take their case.

This contingent fee provision, which is contained in most retainer agreements between trial lawyers and their clients, is vital to the American justice system. It allows all citizens, regardless of their financial resources, the ability to bring their case before a court of law. Most people in other countries cannot afford to hire a lawyer to represent them, even when they have been seriously injured as a result of someone else's negligence or have some other meritorious claim. Also, other countries, such as the United Kingdom, have a "loser pays" rule regarding attorneys' fees. This means that a plaintiff who brings a lawsuit outside the U.S. must not only pay an attorney on a "pay as you go" basis but must also run the risk of having to pay the defendant's attorneys' fees if the case is unsuccessful. This rule has a decidedly chilling effect on civil litigation, even when a claim is well-founded or when the law is unclear or unsettled, and the case is brought in a "cutting edge" area of the law.

Obviously, no one with any common sense will bring a test case on a legal issue that needs clarification if the result of a loss will lead to financial ruin. In contrast, the free enterprise system in the U.S. has generally co-existed, at least for the past several decades, with a remarkably open and accessible civil justice system. While our economic system has produced wide disparities in income and wealth between the rich and the poor, the judicial branch of government and legal system in the United States has helped – to some small degree – to level the playing field between the haves and the have-nots.

The American legal system's ability to give ordinary people access to justice and protect our Constitutional rights and fundamental democratic principles is especially important now. Rising authoritarianism and a disregard for the Rule of Law and for truth nearly succeeded in silencing the moderate and progressive voices in Congress, the White House, and the federal government's executive departments during the

Trump presidency. With political campaigns requiring millions of dollars to be considered even "competitive," and the country in the midst of a seemingly endless war on terrorism, where any person or group who questions aggressive interrogation techniques and detention without a trial are labeled as "un-American," it is essential for lawyers and other concerned citizens to focus on protecting and exercising the rights and remedies that are recognized under the U.S. Constitution and ingrained in our judicial system.

At least on the far right side of the political spectrum, it is fashionable to portray most lawsuits as frivolous claims brought by opportunistic plaintiffs looking for a way to "get rich quick" by extorting large sums of money from innocent corporations. The reality, however, is that filing a civil complaint on behalf of a plaintiff in this country is a precarious business – both for the plaintiff and the plaintiff's attorney. Large pharmaceutical or chemical companies and other large corporations who find themselves named as defendants in civil damage cases have almost unlimited financial resources. Consequently, their strategy is to delay any lawsuit brought against them for as long as possible and to use every means available to exhaust the patience and financial resources of the plaintiff and attorney so that the case never even gets to trial. Then, even when the plaintiff's case defies the odds by surviving, going to trial and succeeding with a jury verdict and damages award in favor of the plaintiff, the well-financed defendant often appeals any verdict rendered against it, further stretching out the litigation process for an additional few months to years. As a result, the reality is that, while a few plaintiffs succeed in hitting the "jackpot" and collect significant settlements or damage awards, the vast majority of "successful" civil lawsuits filed each year lead to only minimal damage settlements. Many more are dismissed without the plaintiff or the attorney receiving a dime. In many cases, the person bringing the lawsuit – rather than becoming an instant millionaire or getting an undeserved "windfall"– ends up losing significant time, energy, and money, and the lawyers who have championed and financed the case are left empty-handed.

In the waning decade of the 20th Century and the first two decades of the 21st Century, it became the mantra of conservative politicians and prominent business executives and their P.R. firms to divert attention from widespread corporate abuse and excess by blaming most of the ills in the United States on the "trial lawyer." The bankruptcy of companies in the asbestos business, the rising cost of health care, and the lowering of confidence in Wall Street were all being laid at the feet of the plaintiffs' lawyer. However, this was like shooting the messenger who reports the bad news. Plaintiffs' lawyers do not create corporate negligence and abuse any more than the investigative reporters who first exposed the Enron corporate scandal "created" the underlying facts they were reporting. Instead, plaintiff lawyers try to make corporate defendants pay for the damages caused to others due to those corporate abuses once they are exposed. And if companies are forced to pay large sums of money for their negligence and wrongdoing, it is less likely that they will do it again. Thus, when successful, civil litigation can be a strong deterrent.

However, there is no doubt that some of the criticism leveled against some trial lawyers is justified. As in any business or profession, a small percentage of rogue lawyers who manufacture frivolous or completely bogus cases are usually hoping for a quick and lucrative settlement before the weaknesses of the case are fully disclosed during the discovery process. Sometimes companies that are being sued are willing to settle for the "nuisance value" of the case to avoid the expense or negative publicity resulting from the filing of a lawsuit. But these are the rare exceptions. Nine out of ten weak cases are either dismissed before trial or end up in a jury verdict favoring the defendant.

Over the last decade or so, the medical insurers, drug companies, and other special interests in the United States who have felt threatened by the civil litigation process have mounted a massive public relations campaign to vilify plaintiff's lawyers. This campaign, which has been waged under benign-sounding slogans like "tort reform," has largely succeeded in distorting the truth regarding the vital role trial lawyers play in protecting society from self-interested, unregulated companies. These companies improperly try to enhance their profit margin by cutting corners on safety, manufacturing defective products, or polluting the environment.

Following his re-election in 2004, President George W. Bush (my former college classmate) announced that "tort reform" was at the very top of his conservative agenda. The avowed strategy was to demonize plaintiffs' attorneys, who are portrayed, not as the champion of those injured due to the negligence and medical malpractice of corporate pirates and unqualified doctors, but as blood-sucking leeches who have driven up medical costs and malpractice insurance premiums through frivolous lawsuits. Never mind that barely 2% of the cost of malpractice premiums can be linked to the cost of malpractice verdicts. Awards related to the number of lawsuits filed in the United States have remained relatively steady for at least the last decade, and only about 2% of the civil cases filed ever get to trial.

This book attempts to set the record straight on all aspects of the civil litigation process through a detailed examination of specific cases I have been personally and professionally involved in. Each one of these cases was brought on behalf of the U.S. or the New York State government (when I was a prosecutor) or - when I was in private practice - individual plaintiffs seeking justice in American courts.

So, you may ask, how did it come about that I had the opportunity to work on so many significant and, in some cases, landmark cases? The short answer is that I always sought out exciting job opportunities, even if they did not pay the top salaries offered by large New York law firms. Rather, I sought out job opportunities that would offer me the greatest challenges and where I felt I could work on important cases that made a difference, no matter how abysmal the pay. I always proudly maintained two licenses throughout my life – one was my law license, and the second was my "hack license," which allowed me to drive a yellow taxicab in New York City. My law license, of course, was the one that permitted me to pursue a career in the law, but my hack license was also important in that it provided me with a continued reminder of how I started out making a living in New York and that my background was firmly rooted in the working class from which my grandparents had sprung since they first arrived here as immigrants.

After graduating from Yale College in 1968 and Fordham Law School in 1972, and after a brief stint at a large New York law firm, I served as a prosecutor for about the next 15 years. During that time, I served as an Assistant U.S. Attorney, a Special Assistant Attorney General with the Organized Crime Section of the U.S. Department of Justice, and a New York State prosecutor with the Attorney General's Office and the New York State Special Prosecutor's Office.

For the last 35 years, I have primarily worked in private practice as an environmental and human rights attorney, specializing in international human rights cases. I worked on several Holocaust restitution cases, particularly those that led to the settlement with the French Banks and another with the German government and German industry. I spent a fair amount of time in Russia since I represented many Russian survivors of World War II who had been transported to Germany against their will and then used as forced laborers under abysmal conditions. These Russian forced laborers were finally able to receive some compensation from Germany due to a settlement reached in Berlin after protracted negotiations. Much of my legal work on behalf of these Russian clients took place in St. Petersburg, Russia, where President Vladimir Putin got his start.

I spent several years representing the former Prime Minister of Ukraine, Yulia Tymoshenko, and other Ukraine opposition leaders, who were arbitrarily jailed and prosecuted on trumped up charges by the previous Ukraine President Viktor Yanukovich. In February 2014, after a series of prolonged and often bloody public demonstrations, this pro-Russian and autocratic president was forced to flee Kyiv for the Moscow safe haven offered by his patron, Vladimir Putin. With this regime change, Ms. Tymoshenko and other political prisoners were immediately released from prison. Also, this regime change meant that U.S. citizens such as Paul Manafort, Rick Gates, and other consultants working for the pro-Russian Ukrainian regime lost their jobs. But they quickly landed on their feet by offering their money-laundering services to Ukrainian and Russian oligarchs who were looking to stash their ill-gotten millions and billions in real estate projects in the U.S., including some of Donald J. Trump's condominium projects in New York and Florida. Manafort and Gates then went on to serve as the Chairman and Vice-Chairman of the Trump 2016 presidential campaign, where they used their close connections with the Russian power elite and intelligence services to forge important connections that advanced the cause of the Trump campaign.

This book is also meant to be a primer for the uninitiated – those not familiar with all the elements of a civil lawsuit but have a gnawing feeling that they are not always getting the whole story when they read about a case in the newspaper or hear about it on T.V. The actual cases discussed run the full gamut from well-publicized cases – such as the Exxon Valdez oil spill and the World Trade Center attack on September 11, 2001 – to the largely unknown but typical cases of a family that was poisoned and driven from their home by the improper application of pesticides. It is also a book about real people: the victims, the lawyers, the judges, and other participants in the legal system. In the end, it is a book about how the justice system works, how the right of both citizens and non-citizens to bring a lawsuit in the United States is one of the most cherished rights available to ordinary people, and how that right is worth fighting for.

Introduction

I suppose I was destined to be a trial lawyer. It was the family trade. My father was a lawyer who had grown up in the Hunts Point section of the South Bronx and then worked his way through the City College of New York and Fordham Law School. My father would always tell us about the cases he was working on at the dinner table, describing his cross-examinations and closing arguments in colorful detail. As we grew older, he would give my three brothers and me the facts of a case and ask us what arguments we would make on both sides. He would then give us comments and suggestions but rarely declared a winner. We thought it was a great game. The greatest compliment was when he exclaimed: "Now you are thinking like a lawyer!"

The law wasn't just a way of making a living or even just a profession to my father. Instead, he viewed our legal system, inherited initially from England and then refined here for over two hundred years, as an imperfect yet elegant instrument for providing equal justice to all, no matter their circumstances or position in society. As he saw it, the legal system was not just a mechanism for fairly resolving disputes between parties; it was also a means of empowering the otherwise powerless, which my father referred to generically as "the people." The scales of justice were never even, he warned us, because large corporations, the rich and the powerful always had plenty of money and the best lawyers that money could buy. But sometimes --just sometimes-- a "people's lawyer," who represented just ordinary people, was able to take on the special interests and use the legal system to beat them at their own game.

Both my father and my uncle, who had been a union organizer for many years, inherited their sense of social justice from their father, a New York City transit worker. My grandfather emigrated from Ireland during the 1930s. He had three photographs on his mantlepiece. One was of Jesus, the second was of President Franklin D. Roosevelt, and the third was of Mike Quill, the feisty president of the Transit Workers Union

(TWU). All three of the photos were about the same size as if no one should take precedence over the others.

My father and uncle often regaled us with tales of the fledgling American labor movement, many of whose leaders were Irish-Americans, including colorful stories of pitched battles with "Pinkertons," scabs, and other union busters. These tales of good versus evil made for exciting bed-time stories and dinner table conversations. As I grew older, my public library card gave me access to dozens of books on U.S. labor history. I soon realized that almost none of this critical – and often violent – era in American history was covered by any of the social studies or American History courses to which America's children were exposed. By the age of thirteen, I had read the biographies of Eugene V. Debs and most of the other icons of the American labor movement. I had also devoured several books on FDR and the New Deal. I was delighted to learn that many of the stories I had heard from older family members were based on historical events. However, in the grand tradition of Irish storytelling, the details were often embellished and nuances erased in order to create a more compelling tale.

As the McCarthy hearings unfolded before our eyes on television during the mid-1950s, my parents took turns explaining who the "good guys" and the "bad guys" were. Of course, from their perspective, there was no doubt that the red-baiting and union-busting Senator Joseph McCarthy was the "bad guy," and Edward R. Morrow was one of the "good guys." When the Senator finally self-destructed, it was as important an event in our house as when the Yankees clinched the World Series.

As the civil rights movement began to grow in the early 1960s, my father and uncle drew parallels between the struggle for labor rights in the 1930s and 1940s and blacks' struggle for civil rights in this country. We were constantly reminded that prejudice and discrimination were not just racially motivated. Not long ago, the Irish who arrived in this country were met with businesses signs that read: "No Irish Need Apply." We didn't attend the March on Washington or hear Dr. King speak in person, much to my regret. Still, we watched the speeches on T.V., including the now-famous "I Have A Dream" speech. We attended several peaceful civil rights rallies in the New York area, including one in memory of a local Pelham High School graduate, Michael Schwerner, who was killed along with two other civil rights workers in Mississippi.

Our family was also staunchly Catholic, but the faith we practiced was not just of the conservative variety taught in catechism class and at Sunday mass. It was not enough to "keep the faith" or have the "right" set of beliefs and principles. We were taught that we must also "live the faith," which required us to accept the radical message of the gospels and apply it to our own lives. This meant regular visits to the soup kitchens of the Catholic Worker Movement in lower Manhattan and regular attendance at various meetings, rallies, and discussion groups dealing with a wide variety of issues, including housing for the poor and civil rights.

Needless to say, my parents were a bit out of step with the conservative orthodoxy of our local parish. Eventually, our family, like that of many others similarly inclined, gravitated to other more socially active Catholic communities affiliated with certain local colleges, such as the College of New Rochelle, or the Jesuit community near Columbia University in Manhattan, where Father Daniel Berrigan and others often led discussion groups on the merits of "liberation theology" and other contemporary topics.

My father often had his own "take" on the gospels when he wanted to make a point. While the gospels instructed the importance of "comforting the afflicted," my father - with a sly grin and glint in his eye - also noted the importance of "afflicting the comfortable." Just so there was no doubt as to who he was referring to, he used the term "the comfortable" and "the upper crust" interchangeably, which he defined as "a bunch of crumbs held together by their own dough."

My father was a bit suspicious when I decided to go to an Ivy League school and become a "Yalie." City College was a lot closer and had provided him with an excellent education at a substantially reduced cost. So he couldn't completely understand why I wanted to go to an "Ivy League" school. In the 1960s, Yale still had a reputation of a finishing school for rich kids from prep schools, or "preppies," as they were called. In the Class of '68 at Yale, the public high school graduates such as myself generally tended to gravitate to one another, just as George W. Bush and the other prep school graduates tended to do the same by joining the fraternities on campus and the secret societies, such as "Skull and Bones." Although George Bush and I were both members of Davenport College, one of the thirteen residential colleges at Yale, and saw each other nearly every day at the dining hall, we were on different paths. I naturally turned out for the local civil rights marches and anti-war rallies in downtown New Haven. As the dynamic Yale Chaplain, William Sloane Coffin, emerged as one of the leaders of the Vietnam anti-war movement, I often attended his lectures and sermons at Battell Chapel on the Old Campus. As for George W. Bush, he was saving much of his energy for greater things later in his life, such as the U.S. Presidency, but as far as I could tell at the time, it appeared that the only "revolution" he was enthusiastic about, or even aware of in the turbulent mid-1960s, was the sexual one.

I later had the opportunity to know and respect him more during my years at various U.S. government agencies. In my view, he deserves much more credit than he has been given for turning his life around, sobering up, and following in his father's footsteps to become President of the United States. Of course, the disastrous invasion of Iraq that Bush plotted with the help of Defense Secretary Donald Rumsfeld and Vice President Dick Chaney was one of the biggest blunders in American history, but no one is perfect.

Thanks to George W, we had one of our class reunions at the White House shortly after U.S. troops had taken Baghdad in Operation Desert Storm. I congratulated him on the swift success of the military operation but questioned whether he had a plan in place to "win the peace." He assured me and the others present that he did, in fact, have a fully developed plan that could successfully convert Iraq into a peaceful, capitalistic, and democratic state. As it turned out, and as we all now know, his administration had absolutely no idea what to do after it had defeated the Iraqi forces and occupied the country. We are still paying the price for that debacle.

As my June 1972 graduation approached, I soon began searching for some alternative means of public service, other than joining the military and getting shipped out to Vietnam. Although my father and older brother had been in the military, they supported my decision to join the "war on poverty" instead. Although I was opposed to the war and knew it was a terrible mistake, I would have never considered dodging the draft or moving to Canada, like many of my contemporaries. However, I was not about to volunteer to fight in a war that I believed to be morally wrong.

I ended up enlisting in one of the "Great Society" programs enacted during President Johnson's administration shortly after the assassination of John F. Kennedy. One of these programs was called "Volunteers In

Service to America," or VISTA, a domestic version of the better-known "Peace Corps." I was assigned to a VISTA training camp at the University of Oregon in Eugene. I spent the next few months working to help organize migrant farmworkers, bringing me into contact with the charismatic Caesar Chavez and other leaders of the United Farm Workers. From there, I did a tour of duty as a community organizer and tenant advocate in a West Seattle housing project run by the Seattle Housing Authority. I quickly learned that every time there was a confrontation on a picket line or the living conditions in a housing project needed to be challenged, we had to try to find a lawyer who would represent us. I began to learn how to draft up papers for Temporary Restraining Orders and Preliminary Injunctions, but we still needed to find a lawyer to go to court. Not surprisingly, there were not enough lawyers available who were willing to work in this kind of high-stress job for subsistence wages. It soon became clear to me that I needed to start attending law school as quickly as possible if I was going to continue in this line of work.

Fortunately, Fordham Law School offered me a scholarship. I had done quite well academically in college. Also, the fact that my father was teaching legal writing there at the time probably helped. So I went back east to New York to attend Fordham Law at its relatively new campus at Lincoln Center on the West Side of Manhattan. I also started working part-time at a legal services office on Eleventh Avenue in Manhattan known as Mobilization for Youth ("MFY"), and I drove a taxicab at night. The cab driving paid my share of the rent for a small West Side apartment off Columbus Avenue that I shared with two other Fordham Law students.

During the spring of 1970, many law schools across the country, including Fordham, were beset by student strikes, boycotts, and heated debates over the Vietnam War and the lawyer's role in promoting social justice. In addition to the traditional law school courses, such as business law, contracts, and torts, there was a demand for courses on more "relevant" subjects, such as environmental, human rights, and civil rights law. Given my background, and after having spent a year as a VISTA volunteer, it was inevitable that I would take a vocal role in this debate.

At the time, every law school had a "law review," which was published several times a year and contained scholarly articles on various legal topics, but with an emphasis on business law topics. Very few law schools had more than one law review at the time, and Fordham Law School had only the Fordham Law Review. By my second year, due to our efforts, the Fordham Urban Law Journal was established, and I was one of its first editors. The focus of this new law journal was housing, zoning, and other legal issues confronting the community lawyer in an urban environment. Now Fordham and most other law schools have several law journals focusing on environmental law, consumer rights, international law, and a host of other legal specialties. Establishing the Urban Law Journal at Fordham was an important first step in this development.

After graduating from Fordham Law School in 1972, I worked at a prominent New York law firm, Rosenman & Colin, for a couple of years, during which time I was able to pay off most of my student loans while honing my legal research and writing skills. I learned a great deal about antitrust, contract, and securities law, which are three of the major litigation areas for large law firms that handle cases involving large corporations and high net worth individuals.

However, given my background and upbringing, it was difficult for me to be passionate about the cases that I was assigned to work on. Nor was I being allowed actually to go to court very often. This was not unusual since associates at large law firms don't get to see the inside of a courtroom with any degree of frequency, and when they do, it is usually strictly in a supporting role. A partner in the law firm usually gets to argue the motions and conduct witnesses' depositions. Very few large civil cases actually go to trial. They are typically resolved by motion practice or settlement. So although the law firm provided me with some excellent experience, it was not conducive to fulfilling my ambition to become a trial lawyer. Since I was told that criminal prosecutors and defense lawyers generally get more trial experience than civil practice attorneys, I decided that it was time for me to become a prosecutor.

As fate would have it, a Special Prosecutor's Office was being established around 1975 by the New York State Legislature and Governor's Office to address the burgeoning nursing home scandal. Nursing home owners and operators, such as Bernard Bergman, were alleged to have illegally siphoned off millions of dollars in Medicaid funds intended for the care of elderly nursing home patients. Originally established in January 1975 in response to reports of nursing home abuse as the Office of the New York State Special Prosecutor for Nursing Homes, Health and Social Services, this office later underwent a name change to the "Special Prosecutor's Office for Medicaid Fraud" in recognition of its broadened mandate to Medicaid fraud throughout the health care industry. The nursing home scandal had been first exposed in late 1974 by the Temporary State Commission on Living Costs and the Economy, and by the media, with extensive investigative reports being published by the New York Times, the Village Voice, and WNEW-TV. The first Special Prosecutor I served under was Charles J. ("Joe") Hynes, who later served six terms as the Brooklyn District Attorney. I then worked under Joe Hynes' successor, Edward J. Kuriansky.

The Special Prosecutor's office gave me invaluable investigative, grand jury, and prosecutorial experience, and the Office itself was generally considered a successful model on a nationwide scale. In October 1977, for example, Congress, citing the success of New York's Medicaid fraud program, created the federally funded Medicaid Fraud Control Unit Program to encourage other states to "help establish Medicaid Fraud Control Units patterned after the successful unit in New York." This led to the establishment of the Medicaid fraud control units in 47 other states, which collectively have obtained thousands of convictions, recovered hundreds of millions of dollars in restitution, and prevented the loss of many more billions of dollars in Medicaid overpayments. In 1982, the U.S. House of Representatives' Select Committee on Aging, in an extensive study of the various states' Medicaid fraud control efforts, found that New York's Medicaid-fraud program had "changed New York from the least effective to the most effective state in terms of Medicaid (fraud) detection and prosecution."

After spending a few years as a Special Assistant Attorney General with the Special Prosecutor's Office, I received a call from Tom Puccio, who was then the Chief of the U.S. Department of Justice's Brooklyn Organized Crime Strike Force. Based upon a string of high-profile, successful prosecutions of several Mafia bosses, the Brooklyn Strike Force was authorized to hire several new prosecutors, and someone must have recommended me for the job.

After a couple of hours of interviews with Tom Puccio and others at the Brooklyn Strike Force, I was offered the position on the spot. When I asked when they wanted me to start, I was told, "Yesterday." With the permission of the two offices, I then spent a few weeks basically working two jobs. I wrapped up the aspects of the investigations I was handling at the Special Prosecutors Office while, at the same time, getting familiar with a couple of the organized crime cases that I was assigned to handle at the Brooklyn Strike Force.

The Organized Crime Strike Force program was created within the U.S. Department of Justice in the late 1960s to find and prosecute the Mafia and traditional organized crime, as well as labor racketeering and other illegal racketeering conspiracies. The congressional effort to form the Strike Forces was led by then-Senator Robert Kennedy of New York, who emphasized the importance of encouraging coordination between the various U.S. agencies involved in organized crime and racketeering investigations – including the FBI, DEA, Postal Service, Labor Dept. and ATF – with state and local law enforcement agencies. There were 14 strike forces around the country, including Boston, Cleveland, Chicago, Denver, Kansas City, Los Angeles, and Philadelphia, but it was the Brooklyn Strike Force, with high-profile prosecutions of "Fat" Tony Salerno of the Genovese Crime Family, Paul Castellano of the Gambino Crime Family, the Abscam investigation and the Lufthansa Heist investigation that was immortalized in the movie "Goodfellas," that gave the Brooklyn Strike Force its pre-eminent position in the federal prosecutorial galaxy during this era.

Since all of the major cases that I had the good fortune to work on during my career seemed to come my way by pure luck or serendipity, I developed a rather fatalistic attitude towards the practice of law. Working on consequential cases on the side of the public interest, or on behalf of the powerless and the disenfranchised seemed to be my fate – which I wholeheartedly welcomed. As one legal crusade ended, it seemed that the next one would always find me. I was never able to resist a good fight or a quixotic quest for justice, no matter what the sacrifice involved or the personal price that had to be paid. Maybe it was the challenge against all odds that was irresistible. Or maybe it was the adrenaline rush. Or perhaps it was the look of gratitude on the face of a client who had been turned down by other qualified attorneys. Or maybe I am just crazy enough to take on one after another seemingly impossible cause. Whatever the reason, I have chosen a path (or, more accurately, the path has chosen me) that few attorneys have successfully traveled for five decades, and at least it can be said that I have had an interesting career. It is not for everyone, and I am definitely not recommending it for the faint at heart. You must be consumed by passion for a cause before you can even begin to think about taking this path.

A young lawyer recently called me to say that he was taking a leave of absence from his major, well-paying law firm and had a few months to devote to public interest work before he started a federal clerkship. I told him I would get back to him and arrange to get together, but as usual I was running to court or somewhere else and forgot to take down his number, or I wrote it down and misplaced it. Typical of me. Sure enough, he called me back a couple of days later, and after one or two more of these episodes, I realized that he was very serious about working on a human rights and genocide case against Germany I had recently filed on behalf of two African indigenous groups. He quickly became obsessed with the case as I was, a true kindred spirit. The start of a beautiful friendship and colleague-ship.

People ask me how it came about that I ended up as lead counsel in several Holocaust litigation cases. I often ask myself the same question. As an Irish Catholic, it might seem unusual that I would spend much of my life representing Jewish victims of the Holocaust and their families. But not really. When you labor in the international human rights field, most of the U.S. case law has revolved around the resolution of Holocaust cases, so it was almost inevitable that I would end up working on cases that resulted in substantial settlements with the French Government and the French Banks in Holocaust restitution cases. I was also at the signing of the settlement with the German government and German industry in Berlin, where I represented both Jewish groups as well as the Russian forced laborers who were finally able to receive some compensation from Germany as a result of their unpaid labor during World War II.

After that, I spent several years representing the former Prime Minister of Ukraine, Yulia Tymoshenko, and other Ukraine opposition leaders, who were arbitrarily jailed and prosecuted on trumped up charges by the previous Ukraine President Viktor Yanukovich. In February 2014, after a series of prolonged and often bloody public demonstrations, this pro-Russian and autocratic president was forced to flee Kyiv for the Moscow safe haven offered by his patron, Vladimir Putin. I had the good fortune to be in Kyiv at around the time that these meaningful and historical events were taking place, although I ended up in a medical clinic for part of the time following a scuffle with some state security officers who were shadowing me and some of the opposition M.P.s that I was with. My right shoulder became badly separated when I fell, requiring surgery to reset it.

With the regime change in Kyiv and in their haste to flee the country, the pro-Russian regime left behind some damning evidence linking Paul Manafort, one of Yanukovich's top advisors, to more than $12 million in cash payments from the pro-Russian Party of Regions. I and others used this and other evidence on Ms. Tymoshenko's legal team to file a civil RICO case on her behalf against Manafort, Rick Gates, and others in the U.S. District Court for the Southern District of New York. The money laundering and other evidence that we had gathered attracted the interest of the FBI and the U.S. Attorney's Office for the Southern District of New York, which launched a criminal investigation of Manafort, Gates, and others. Special Counsel Robert Mueller's office later took over this investigation after his appointment on May 17, 2017.

The rest, as they say, is history....

Chapter 1
The New York Nursing Home Investigation

In 1975, a nursing home scandal erupted in New York State that radically altered the course of my law career. Fresh out of Fordham Law School, I worked as an associate in the prestigious mid-town Manhattan law firm of Rosenman & Colin, where I had an opportunity to work on a wide variety of complex civil cases, particularly in the antitrust and mergers-and-acquisitions areas. However, if I continued down the private practice path towards a possible partnership, it was doubtful that I would get the kind of courtroom and trial experience that I so desperately craved. I knew that criminal law, either as a prosecutor or defense attorney, was the only sure-fire route to gaining the trial experience where attorneys could call themselves "trial lawyers." The unfolding state nursing home investigation seemed like a good opportunity for a young, ambitious lawyer like me to get into the courtroom on a regular basis.

I carefully followed the press reports of widespread abuse of nursing home patients around the State, as well as the swirling allegations of financial fraud by nursing homeowners, who were accused of bilking millions of dollars from Medicaid, the relatively new federal and State-funded program. Then, in 1975, Governor Hugh Carey and New York State Attorney General Louis Lefkowitz appointed Charles J. "Joe" Hynes as Special State Prosecutor for Nursing Homes, Health and Social Services. Hynes, a Brooklyn native who had risen through the Brooklyn District Attorney's Office ranks to become the First Assistant D.A., was generally perceived as an excellent choice for the job in the New York legal community. Although a hard-nosed prosecutor, he was also affable and could turn on his considerable Irish charm at press conferences or whenever the occasion called for it.

Joe Hynes quickly set about putting together a first-rate legal and investigative team of lawyers and accountants. Almost all of them already had experience in various District Attorney's offices or as federal prosecutors. Fortunately for me, he also opened the ranks to a few young "green" attorneys without any prosecutorial experience but seemed to be quick learners and hard workers. It may also have caught his eye that I had worked during the summers while still in high school for the New York City Department of Health, helping organize the fledgling Medicaid system. One of the most significant issues that New York City and State faced was setting up a Medicaid program that was "self-administered," instead of turning over the administration of this vast new program to Blue Cross/Blue Shield.

Blue Cross was the largest private insurance program at the time. I recall going to Blue Cross/Blue Shield's offices and being ushered into a large conference room with a table that seemed to extend about half the distance of a football field. Other members of the NYC Health Department team and I were then given a presentation on how efficient and cost-effective Blue Cross was in administering their programs, as they made a serious pitch to take over the administration of New York City's Medicaid program. Ultimately, the decision was made (I think wisely) that New York City and State could effectively administer the program "in-house" without the need to contract it out to a private company. A press conference announcing this decision was held at the Health Department's main offices at 125 Worth Street in lower Manhattan. The Department's leadership called on me to make a brief report on a phone survey of doctors in New York City to get their views on the direction of the Medicaid program. The press seemed less interested in the survey results than in the fact that I was still in high school.

I am not sure if my brief experience working for the NYC Health Department tipped the scales in my favor, but shortly after applying for a legal job with the Special Prosecutor's Office, I got a letter accepting my application and asking when I could start. I was ecstatic! Here finally was my chance to get out of the law library, where I was spending most of my time at the law firm and get into real investigative and prosecutorial work. I gave Rosenman & Colin two weeks notice and read up as much as I could on the nursing home scandals in New York and the possible violations of relevant civil and criminal laws that were being investigated.

However, my first taste of prosecutorial experience had nothing to do with courtroom dramas. Instead, my primary task as a young prosecutor in the office was to churn out dozens of subpoenas to nursing home owners and operators, seeking the production of their financial and patient records so that we could do an in-depth investigation of the fraud charges that were loudly reverberating in the press and in the public hearing in the State Assembly and Senate.

All of the nursing homes targeted in our investigation quickly "lawyered up" with some of the City's most experienced defense attorneys and law firms. It soon became apparent that they were not going to roll over easily. They were going to try to make it as difficult as possible to collect the evidence we needed to introduce to the grand juries being convened.

For example, when Margaret Klein Moscowitz, a former employee of Bernard Bergman's Towers Nursing Home, was subpoenaed and questioned about the housekeeping contract she had with the nursing home, she declined to appear before the special grand jury on the frivolous ground that the Talmud forbade her to testify against another Jew. The argument was rejected in State Supreme Court in Manhattan, but every legal challenge such as this one was another obstacle that took time and resources to overcome.

Mrs. Moscowitz's husband, Emil, a butcher supplying several Bergman nursing homes, also fought a subpoena of his records and succeeded in reducing the scope of the documents sought by the subpoena. Both sides then appealed the ruling, which, even when expedited, took at least a couple of weeks to complete and to get an order from the Appellate Division of the State Supreme Court.

In addition, one of Bergman's wholly-owned companies, Scientific Environmental Inc., challenged a subpoena for its records as "arbitrary, capricious and burdensome." Other challenges to our subpoenas alleged that they violated the Fifth Amendment rights of nursing home operators, owners, and employees against self-incrimination. Some even challenged the special prosecutor's legislative and statutory authority to investigate specific crimes.

Another major target was Albert Schwartzberg, a promoter and builder of several nursing homes. A subpoena of his company, Di-Corn Corporation, led to a motion to quash as irrelevant and "unduly burdensome." We attempted to determine whether any of Schwartzberg's records would shed some light on allegations that he was closely associated with several state and local politicians.

The Bernard Bergman Case

One of the Special Prosecutor's Office's first and most prominent indictments was that of Bernard Bergman. An Orthodox rabbi who turned a $25,000 inheritance into a $24 million real-estate and nursing-home empire, Bergman first acquired the Towers Nursing Home on Central Park West and 106th Street in 1955. However, soon after it became eligible for Medicaid reimbursement of its nursing home expenses, this and other nursing homes owned by Bergman became the epicenter of state and federal fraud charges. Claims started pouring in about residents in the nursing homes being abused and neglected. Some residents reported that they had not been given adequate heat, that the facilities in which they were housed were infested with mice and other vermin, and that they had been subjected to physical abuse by the staff.

The Towers Nursing Home was closed in 1974 as a nursing home, but a New York State Senate investigation in 1975 still heard from witnesses about the Towers. These witnesses testified that patients at the nursing home had been left to lapse into comas due to untreated dehydration, bedsores caused by coarse bedsheets and lack of nursing attention, and failure to notify health authorities of an epidemic of diarrhea in the facility. Shortly before the facility was closed, an unannounced inspection of the nursing home found unsanitary conditions, including milk being used a week past its expiration date and excrement on the floors of patients' rooms.

After an extensive investigation by the Special Prosecutor's Office and federal prosecutors, Bergman was sentenced in 1976 to serve a four-month sentence in a federal correction center after pleading guilty to Medicaid and tax fraud charges. Before being sentenced by Judge Marvin E. Frankel in Federal District Court in Manhattan, Bergman said that, although he had allowed his business "to be conducted in a manner that violated the law," he had "intended no evil." He added, "I am not the monster I was portrayed as being."

Special Prosecutor Hynes publicly complained that Bergman's sentence was too lenient and constituted "special justice for the privileged." Hynes eventually got his way by forcing Bergman to plead to additional state charges. Bergman ended up serving an eight-month sentence in state prison after completing his federal sentence.[11]

In February 1989, the Special Prosecutor's office received almost $1.4 million in penalties and interest that Bergman was obligated to pay New York State under his plea agreement.[12] Hynes appointed former U.S. Attorney General Ramsey Clark as receiver of the Bergman assets. According to Clark, Bergman repaid $1.8 million to the Medicaid program during his lifetime and reported paying back "several hundred thousand more" at his death[13] Bergman died of a heart attack at Mount Sinai Medical Center in Manhattan on June 16, 1984.[14]

The Charles Sigety Case

The Special Prosecutor's thorough investigation, as well as that of our federal partners who coordinated their investigation with us, led to a $1 million settlement in November 1975 of a Medicare overpayment claim against Charles E. Sigety, the owner of the Florence Nightingale Nursing Home.[15] This was the largest such recovery from a nursing home up to that time.[16]

Most of the overpayment by Medicare to Sigety occurred in 1968, the first year the nursing home participated in the Medicare program. At that time, the Social Security Administration had almost a "blank check" policy for nursing homes, uncritically accepting the cost estimates of medical providers for reimbursement, subject to later audit.[17]

When an audit was later begun in 1970, it was found that Medicare had overpaid Florence Nightingale Nursing Home by $730,028 in the first year. Sigety countersued in the U.S. District Court in Manhattan, challenging the accounting procedures and claiming that he had been underpaid. However, when the federal government started withholding payments from Sigety, he finally settled the claim in 1975, acknowledging the $1 million overpayments. Sigety also consented to a $15,000 fine for State Health Department violations at Florence Nightingale.[18]

Sigety received some additional adverse publicity in January 1975. The New York Times reported that a draft report of the State Welfare Inspector General's office alleged that the Florence Nightingale Nursing Home had billed Medicaid in 1972 for $40,571 for his foreign travel, club dues, opera tickets, wine, and liquor, and other personal items.[19]

The Metropolitan New York Nursing Home Association Investigation

Another aspect of the Special Prosecutor's investigation involved specific allegations that Medicaid funds were improperly used to make thousands of dollars of contributions to charitable organizations, particularly the United Jewish Appeal.[20] The investigation focused on contributions of $6000 to $20,000 a year per nursing home from 1969 through 1974. The donations were channeled through the Metropolitan New York Nursing Home Association.[21]

What distinguished a legitimate contribution to an association from a crime was that legitimate contributions as dues were eligible for Medicaid reimbursement. Conversely, if the payments were being made to the association to disguise non-reimbursable charitable contributions, then it was a crime.[22] The Metropolitan Nursing Home Association appears to have received these substantial checks from nursing homeowners and then turned around and disbursed the funds to the various charitable organizations, including United Jewish Appeal, the American Parkinson Disease Association, and the Synagogue America the Brooklyn Histadrut Council.[23]

Evolution of the Special Prosecutor's Office to the Medicaid Fraud Control Unit

The Special Prosecutor's Office soon became the model for similar investigative and prosecutorial units throughout the country. The office, renamed the Medicaid Fraud Control Unit ("MFCU"), was cited in a 1977 report by the House Select Committee on Aging as the best in the country.[24] Joe Hynes testified before the U. S. Congress in 1976, advocating legislation establishing fraud control units in every State with federal funding. The legislation became law in 1977, and soon there were 48 states with Medicaid Fraud Control Units.[25]

In 1995, the MFCU was incorporated more directly into the Attorney General's Office and placed within its Criminal Division. The MFCU continued to successfully prosecute some of the largest and most sophisticated frauds committed against the Medicaid program. It charged nearly 3,000 defendants for Medicaid fraud and related crimes and achieved over a 91% conviction rate. The office was responsible for the recovery of more than $326 million in overpayments, fines, and restitution.

Joe Hynes and many of his fellow prosecutors and staff members later distinguished themselves in other government positions and judges. Hynes himself was elected as the Brooklyn District Attorney and served eight terms. His successor, Edward J. Kuriansky, was later named the New York City Department of Investigation Commissioner. Richard D. Carruthers became an Acting New York State Supreme Court Justice. Howard Wilson, Hynes' Chief Assistant, who had previously served as a federal prosecutor in the U.S. Attorney's Office for the Southern District of New York, also served in senior executive positions in the New York City government. My immediate supervisor, Alain M. Bourgeois, later served as First Deputy Commissioner with the New York City Department of Investigation.

As for me, I had finally found my "calling" in the law, as an investigative attorney and as a prosecutor. My strong Christian upbringing and belief that the ongoing battle of good versus evil in the world forces us all to take sides eventually made it virtually inevitable that I would become a prosecutor. As a prosecutor for New York State, I would proudly identify myself in the courtroom as "Kenneth McCallion, For the People." Technically, but also genuinely, we did not represent just the government or New York State. We represented "the People of the State of New York," which was a subtle but important distinction that I always kept in mind throughout the years.

As the initial batch of high-profile nursing home cases was winding down, I got a call from a fellow prosecutor I knew joining the U.S. Department of Justice's famed Brooklyn Strike Force, located across the East River in downtown Brooklyn. I was told that Tom Puccio, the head of the Strike Force, was looking to expand the office's small staff of prosecutors, and I was urged to submit my resume. I had worked on several "white collar" nursing home cases by then, but they all ended in settlements and guilty pleas, not trials. I still hungered for the chance to prove myself in court in an actual trial, not just the usual motion practice and oral arguments before a judge. The Strike Force seemed like a golden opportunity for me, which I immediately jumped on. Fortunately, Tom Puccio was willing to overlook my lack of trial experience, explaining that 90% of their work involved investigations, and only 10% involved actual trials. I gratefully accepted his offer, and with Joe Hynes' blessing, I immediately moved over with the title of "Special Prosecutor, Organized Crime Section, U.S. Department of Justice."

Chapter 2

The Brooklyn Organized Crime Strike Force

The creation of the Organized Crime Strike Force program within the U.S. Department of Justice was the brainchild of Robert F. Kennedy in the early 1960s. He was the U.S. Attorney General for his older brother, President John F. Kennedy. At 35-years old, Bobby Kennedy had no experience that qualified him for this powerful position, and J.F.K. acknowledged this by saying, only half-jokingly, that his brother "needs some solid legal experience and this job should provide it."

Attorney General R.F.K., however, rose to the challenge, boldly deciding to take on organized crime in the U.S. even though the FBI, under the leadership of Director J. Edgar Hoover, had pretended for decades that it didn't really exist. Hoover was more interested in investigating home-grown communists and in pursuing bank robbers, auto thefts and other high-profile and relatively easy targets. That way he could go to Congress each year with an impressive record of victories, as he sought ever increasing budget allocations. According to Ronald Goldfarb, a lawyer who worked at the Department of Justice at the time,[1] the Department of Justice's Organized Crime and Racketeering Section traditionally consisted of "just two or three lawyers reading files." Under Kennedy, however, the Section quickly grew to about 60 lawyers, and the Mafia and other organized crime groups became one of the DOJ's top priorities. By this time, the Mafia had an estimated 5,000 members and thousands of associates across the country. Kennedy encouraged all of the federal Government's investigative agencies – the DOJ, the FBI, the IRS and others – to work together to investigate large-scale crimes and national crime syndicates. The DOJ also went after crooked union officials, such as Jimmy Hoffa of the United Brotherhood of Teamsters, who were controlled by organized crime so that the mob could gain access to the hundreds of millions of dollars in the union pension and welfare funds.

R.F.K. and the DOJ's Organized Crime Section were relentless in their pursuit of Teamsters Union president James "Jimmy" Hoffa. The hostility between Robert Kennedy and Hoffa was intense, with Hoffa accusing Kennedy of conducting a personal vendetta - what Hoffa called a "blood feud" - against him .[2] On July 7, 1961, after Hoffa was reelected as Teamster president, R.F.K. told reporters the Government's case against Hoffa was not weakened merely because what he called "a small group of teamsters" were supporting their union's president.[3] The following year, it was leaked that Hoffa had bragged to a Teamster local official that Kennedy had been "bodily" removed from his office. A Teamster press agent confirmed the statement, saying that Hoffa had physically ejected Kennedy from his office.[4]

On March 4, 1964, Hoffa was convicted in Chattanooga, Tennessee, of attempted bribery of a grand juror during his 1962 conspiracy trial in Nashville, and sentenced to eight years in prison and a $10,000 fine.[5] After learning of Hoffa's conviction by telephone, Kennedy issued congratulatory messages to the three prosecutors.[6]

After President Kennedy's assassination on November 22, 1963, at the hands of Lee Harvey Oswald, R.F.K. stayed on as Attorney General for some time under President Lyndon B. Johnson, but left in 1964 to pursue a successful run for a Senate seat in New York. However, the Organized Crime Section of the Justice Department continued to receive the enthusiastic support of Nicholas Katzenbach, the incoming Attorney General, and under his successor, Ramsey Clark, new Strike Force field offices were established around the country, including the one in Brooklyn where I was hired.

At the time I joined the Brooklyn Strike Force, Tom Puccio was the chief of the unit, leading a team of about a dozen prosecutors. While Puccio headed the office, the Strike Force handled some important and, now, legendary cases. Among them was the Abscam political corruption investigation that toppled scores of politicians. This case was featured in the film *American Hustle*, with an undercover FBI agent posing as a wealthy Arab sheik, ready to hand out large sums of cash to virtually any politician who would meet with him and other undercover FBI agents. The Lufthansa Kennedy Airport heist dramatized in the movie *Goodfellas* was also handled by our office.

And then there was the investigation and prosecution of John Cody, the President of the powerful and mob-dominated Teamster Local 282. This local union controlled most of the cement and construction trucks going in and out of the major construction sites in the New York area. Included among those construction projects was Trump Tower and other sites owned by young developer Donald J. Trump.

I had already compiled a reasonably solid record of grand jury indictments and convictions (but no trials) of several nursing home operators while with the State Special Prosecutor's Office. All of the cases I worked on ended in plea bargains and guilty pleas to reduced charges. In return for hefty fines and Consent Decrees, the nursing homes in question and their owners promised to correct their accounting practices that had led to the Medicaid fraud charges, and to cease and desist from any further neglect or abuse of nursing home patients in their facilities.

When I started working at the Brooklyn Strike Force, I was probably the youngest and least experienced prosecutor there. I was surrounded by seasoned attorneys who had spent many years prosecuting and trying cases in District Attorneys' Offices throughout New York City. So, I was a bit taken aback when Tom Puccio told me on my first day on the job that I should start preparing for a trial scheduled to begin in just a few weeks. I was immediately gripped by terror. However, I tried my best to maintain my composure, replying, "OK, I'll get on it right away."

The Fatico Cases

At first look, the trial I was assigned to handle was a seemingly run-of-the-mill illegal gambling case against several mobsters. FBI agents had raided an unlawful gaming site in Queens and rounded up a dozen or so organized crime members, or "wiseguys" as they preferred to be called. The principal defendant in the case was Daniel "Danny" Fatico, a member, or "button man," in the Gambino crime family.

As it turned out, however, the case ended up being anything but ordinary. This case and related prosecutions of Danny Fatico and his brother Carmine, a reputed "capo" in the Gambino family, proved to be of monumental and lasting legal significance, even to this day. Federal judges now continue to hold what is known as a pre-sentencing "Fatico Hearing," where hearsay testimony by federal agents and others as to a defendant's organized crime affiliations and other criminal activities may be introduced at a sentencing hearing. The first such hearings took place in connection with the sentencing of Danny and Carmine Fatico in the federal courthouse in Brooklyn, in connection with two related cases tried by myself and other prosecutors from the Brooklyn Strike Force.

We didn't know at the time that these prosecutions before the legendary Judge Jack B. Weinstein would have such lasting significance. All we knew was that this would perhaps be the last federal criminal prosecution for illegal gambling. Organized crime groups were getting out of the unlawful gaming business, as states started issuing casino licenses and narcotics trafficking was becoming much more profitable. As the legal gaming industry grew, the smaller illegal operations became less profitable.

FBI agents had been after Danny and Carmine "Charley Wagons" Fatico for some time. They had already put a lot of time and resources into building a case against them. This effort included seemingly countless hours of surveillance of the Fatico brothers' headquarters in the East New York section of Brooklyn, at a social club named the Bergin Hunt & Fish Club. John Gotti was a frequent visitor there as he climbed his way up the ranks of the Gambino family organization. Through the prosecution of Danny Fatico and his brother on gambling and related charges, the FBI was making a concerted and perhaps last-ditch effort to crack organized crime's vice-like grip on New York.

Al Capone had been brought down on tax evasion charges, despite a long history of murders and violent crimes. So, the FBI and the Strike Force were hoping that by throwing gambling and every other possible charge against the Fatico brothers and their associates, they could be convicted on at least some charges that would justify lengthy prison terms.

I knew that I was in for a rough ride when Roy M. Cohn and his partner, Michael Rosen, showed up in federal court for the arraignment of the Fatico brothers. Cohn was a legend by then, having gained fame in 1954 as Senator Joseph McCarthy's chief counsel during the Army–McCarthy hearings of suspected communists in the Federal Government and the military. After that, Cohn became a successful "mob lawyer" in New York and a top political fixer. One of his proteges was the young developer, Donald J. Trump, who Cohn introduced to key mob-controlled union bosses, such as John Cody. If he ordered a general strike, Teamster boss Cody had the power to shut down any real estate construction project in the New York area. He controlled the delivery of all construction materials, including steel, lumber, and ready-mix cement. If Cody ordered a strike, construction sites would be shut down immediately. Through corrupt deals arranged through Cohn, New York developers such as Donald Trump and Sigmund Sommers could buy "labor peace" with the Teamsters and other mob-controlled unions by agreeing to put phantom, no-show "teamster foremen" on their payrolls. The salaries for those non-existent employees went directly to the mob bosses who controlled the local teamster union and other construction unions, such as the International Brotherhood of Electrical Workers (IBEW) and the local laborers' unions. Once Trump, Sommers, and other developers made these "sweetheart" labor contracts with Teamster Local 282 and other unions, they never had to worry about their construction sites being shut down, even if the teamsters ordered a City-wide general strike.

If we were successful in these prosecutions of the Fatico brothers, it was hoped that the corrupt bonds between the local labor unions, the mob, and developers such as Trump and Sommers could be broken, or at least strained. At the very least, we hoped that the construction unions and the developers would start thinking twice about continuing to make their corrupt deals with the Faticos and other mob members if they knew that the FBI and the Brooklyn Strike Force were looking into their every move and ready to indict and prosecute whenever the opportunity arose.

In addition to the gambling case that we successfully prosecuted against Danny Fatico, both Carmine and Daniel Fatico were indicted in a related case connected to a series of truck hijackings. After a mistrial was declared due to a jury deadlock, they pleaded guilty and were convicted of one count of conspiracy to possess a quantity of furs stolen from a foreign shipment. They faced maximum sentences of five years' imprisonment and $10,000 fines.[7] However, before Danny Fatico and other mob members could be given substantial penalties for illegal gambling and additional minor federal charges, the sentencing judge conducted a factual finding to determine the sentence. Assuming the judge found that the defendant was affiliated with an organized criminal organization and regularly engaged in a pattern of criminal conduct, the sentence imposed on the mob defendant could be "enhanced" or increased by a substantial number of years of imprisonment.

Judge Weinstein initially rejected the proposed hearsay testimony as to Danny Fatico's organized crime affiliations and history, finding that reliance on "such untested evidence in a situation such as the one before us would violate the Fifth Amendment right to Due Process and the Sixth Amendment right of Confrontation."[8] Unless reversed, such a ruling would have virtually prevented federal agents to testify to information provided them by confidential informants or other sources who could not themselves be called to testify in open federal court, without the risk of severely shortening their life spans.

Fortunately for us prosecutors, and also for the general public, the Second Circuit Court of Appeals, however, reversed, "holding that . . . neither the Confrontation nor the Due Process Clause is violated by use in the sentencing of information supplied by an unidentified informant, where there is good cause for not disclosing his identity, and the information he furnishes is subject to corroboration by other means."[9] In other words, the court permitted the introduction of "hearsay" evidence, as long as the testimony of the federal agents had a high degree of reliability.

At the sentencing hearing of the Fatico brothers, government witnesses painted a detailed portrait of the extensive organized crime activity going on in the New York City area.[10] They testified that five active, organized crime families were operating in the greater metropolitan area: The Colombo family, the Lucchese family, the Genovese family, the Bonanno family, and the Gambino family. At the top of each family was the Boss; directly underneath the Boss was the Underboss, who acted much like the company's executive officer. Next in line was the Counselor, or "Consiglieri," who helped "keep the peace." Each organization also had numerous "Capos," or "lieutenants," at the next level, and each capo directed a substantial network of "soldiers," numbering in the hundreds, depending upon the size of the family. The soldiers, all of whom were officially initiated, full-fledged members of the crime family, were variously referred to as "buttons," "made-men," "nice fellows," or "goodfellas." Beneath the "soldiers" were the "non-member associates," who were affiliated with the family, but not "made," that is, initiated into the family. Each capo has a social club or headquarters, which served as a meeting place for family members and associates in a particular territory.

According to one federal expert witness, Aniello Dellacroce was the Boss of the Gambino family at the time; Paul Castellano was the

Underboss, and Joseph N. Gallo was the consiglieri. The Gambino family had at least twenty capos, including Carmine Fatico. The organization, spread across the Eastern seaboard from Rhode Island to Florida and inland as far as Detroit, had about 1100 soldiers. The principal activities of the Gambino family were loan sharking, hijacking, narcotics, gambling, and extortion. Danny Fatico was identified at the sentencing hearing as a "made" soldier in the Gambino organization.

One agent who was a member of the federal Organized Crime Task Force - Robert John - testified that Danny and Carmine Fatico operated out of the Bergen Hunt and Fish Club in Ozone Park, Queens, New York. Detective John P. Capobianco of the Brooklyn County District Attorney's Office testified that he had observed Carmine Fatico in front of the Ravenite Social Club on Mulberry Street talking with Joseph N. Gallo and Gambino Family Boss Aniello Dellacroce. The Ravenite Social Club was reputedly the criminal headquarters of Dellacroce. Other law enforcement agents testified at the hearing that Carmine and Danny Fatico were frequently seen outside the Ravenite Club, with Dellacroce doing "walk and talk" meetings to make sure they were not being bugged.

Kenneth McCabe, Detective Capobianco's partner, also gave vital testimony at the sentencing hearing of Danny Fatico. With ten years in the New York City Police Department and nine years working in the Kings County Organized Crime Unit, McCabe had been a critical witness in the gambling case against Danny Fatico that I tried. "Kenny" McCabe, a large, beefy Irish-American cop with a strong Brooklyn accent, was a legend among law enforcement agents and prosecutors long before I joined the Strike Force. He was known for his near-photographic memory and marathon stakeouts of Mafia chieftains at their social clubs, weddings, and funerals. He testified at their trials in such detail that few defense lawyers even dared to cross-examine him for fear that he would surprise them with even more incriminating testimony about their clients. He took so many pictures - including those of mobsters' children's weddings - that he came to be known as "La Cosa Nostra's unofficial photographer." He was a master of surveillance, with the patience to watch a mob social club for hours, studying the behavior of those going in and out, sorting out bosses, capos, and soldiers from the "wannabe" mob pretenders who often hung around the clubs where the real "wiseguys" conducted their business. McCabe contributed critical evidence to the multiple trials of Paul Castellano, the head of the Gambino family, who was gunned down in 1985. Through his surveillance work, McCabe then established that Castellano had been succeeded as head of the family by the notorious John Gotti.

The testimony of these reliable and professional law enforcement officers was necessary at the sentencing hearing. The only first-hand evidence of Danny Fatico's position in the Gambino family came from Salvatore Montello and Manuel Llauget, two unindicted co-conspirators in the fur hijacking cases against Fatico, which were separate from the illegal gambling case. Although Montello was not a "made man" himself, he was a known associate of Carmine and Danny Fatico. He was in a position to testify first-hand about their criminal activities. However, both Montello and Llauget had extensive criminal records. They were subjected to devastating attacks on their credibility in cases where they had testified, with the juries in those cases failing to convict based on their testimony. Llauget's record included a conviction for murdering his wife, which did not go over well with either the women or the men on the juries in the trials where he testified. When they testified at the first "Fatico Hearing," both men and their families were in the Government's witness protection program.

Montello and Llauget testified that in March of 1971, when a dispute arose concerning the quantity and quality of some 7,000 hijacked furs delivered to the Faticos, a "sit-down" was arranged with boss Aniello Dellacroce. Daniel Fatico took Llauget to a "social club" on Mulberry Street in Manhattan, where Fatico and Llauget met with Dellacroce and the disgruntled "buyer" of the furs. Dellacroce arbitrated the dispute and, after questioning Llauget about furs, decided that Llauget was telling the truth and would be paid the agreed price for the stolen furs. This was one of those rare examples of how "justice" was meted out in the mobster's world without someone getting killed or at least seriously injured.

After the sentencing hearing, Judge Weinstein found that the Government had met its burden of proof to establish that Danny Fatico was an active member of an organized crime family by "clear, unequivocal and convincing evidence."[11] Judge Weinstein noted that Fatico had recently been sentenced to three years on a federal gambling charge in the jury trial I had prosecuted. This sentence was independent of the hijacking case that had ended in a hung jury, after which Carmine and Danny Fatico had pleaded guilty.

Judge Weinstein explained that if he could not take the organized crime issue into account in sentencing, Daniel Fatico would have been sentenced in the hijacking case to no more than a three-year term, concurrent with the gambling sentence. These sentences were Fatico's first significant taste of incarceration in his long criminal career. Based upon the evidence presented at the sentencing hearing, the court concluded that the defendant was a member of the Gambino crime family. Judge Weinstein sentenced him to a prison term of four years to be served consecutively with the three-year sentence for gambling. The judge found that this new sentence was necessary for purposes of "incapacitation" to keep the defendant in prison for a prolonged period. Thus, the public was protected from further criminal conduct by the defendant, and the prolonged prison term also prevented him from acting in concert with other members of this dangerous group of well-organized criminals. Instead of being eligible for early release and parole within one year, the finding of Fatico's organized crime affiliations meant that Fatico would have to spend a minimum of six years in a federal prison before being eligible for release.

Since the original Fatico Hearings in 1978, this kind of sentencing hearing has become a mainstay of criminal prosecution and sentencing in federal courts throughout the country. This has been true in both traditional organized crime cases as well as in other non-mob criminal conspiracies. For example, on August 18, 2020, federal prosecutors in the U.S. District Court for the Southern District of New York asked the court for permission to hold a Fatico Hearing as part of their attempt to secure the imposition of an enhanced sentence on Clare Bronfman. Bronfman - the heiress to the Seagram's liquor empire – was charged with having bankrolled an upstate New York sex slave ring run by NXIVM cult leader Keith Raniere.[12] Bronfman had previously pleaded guilty in April 2019 to charges of conspiracy to conceal and harbor illegal aliens for financial gain, and fraudulent use of identification. Bronfman's lawyers tried to distinguish the conduct of her plea counts from the lurid aspects of the NXIVM (pronounced Nexium) conspiracy detailed in the Government's presentence report. However, the federal prosecutors wanted to tie her as closely as possible to the core of the conspiracy, which involved shocking examples of degradation and exploitation of numerous vulnerable young women. The prosecution argued that this dispute could only be sorted out for the judge through the taking of sworn testimony from witnesses in a Fatico Hearing.

Other Strike Force Successes Against Traditional Organized Crime Groups

By the early 1980s, the DOJ's Organized Crime Section had made significant inroads into traditional La Cosa Nostra (LCN) organized crime groups in the U.S. In fact, for career law enforcement agents and federal prosecutors who enjoyed their work, despite the long hours and relatively low pay, the Strike Forces were perhaps *too* successful. The Strike Forces eventually worked themselves out of a job by decimating the ranks of the Mafia's traditional organized crime groups. By 1999, jokes began circulating that the only Mafia organization that federal agents had not infiltrated was *The Sopranos*. Originating on HBO, the T.V. show featured a fictional New Jersey-based organized crime group headed by Tony Soprano (played by James Gandolfini).

In order to win many hard-fought prosecutions, the Strike Forces used all the traditional investigative tools at the disposal of law enforcement, but they especially relied on the use of informants, undercover operations, and Title III electronic surveillances. As a result, most of the "bosses" of the major LCN families across the United States were indicted and/or convicted. The entire leadership of the Bonanno Family was indicted and convicted for violations of the relatively new RICO criminal statute, which was designed to convict entire criminal organizations and their members for having engaged in a pattern of racketeering activity over an extended time. We no longer had to prosecute career criminals like Carmine and Danny Fatico on isolated illegal gambling and hijacking charges. Now, with the RICO statute, they could be prosecuted on a wide range of criminal activities in one criminal prosecution.

Enacted in 1970, the Racketeer Influenced and Corrupt Organizations Act, better known as RICO, made it a federal crime for any person who is employed by or associated with an enterprise that is engaged in or affects interstate or foreign commerce, to conduct or to participate in the conduct of the affairs of that enterprise through a pattern of racketeering activity.[13] As long as we were able to prove that a defendant was associated with an ongoing criminal enterprise and committed two or more specified federal crimes within a specified time period, we could bring a federal RICO indictment against him, which after conviction or guilty plea, would almost always result in a substantial prison sentence.

Very soon, the Strike Forces were racking up so many impressive RICO victories over organized crime that we began referring to it as "the nuclear option." As a result of a series of undercover investigations conducted in New York and Florida, as well as some strategically placed wiretaps, the Boss of the Colombo family, Alphonse Persico, was indicted and convicted, although he fled the jurisdiction, forfeiting a $250,000 bond. The "acting boss" of the family, Carmine Persico, was then convicted of parole violation and was incarcerated at Danbury Federal Prison in Connecticut. The "boss" of the Genovese family, Frank Tieri, was convicted on four counts of RICO violation and sentenced to 20 years in prison. A principal Genovese family member, John Russo - renowned for his extreme violence to anyone or anything in his path - was found guilty and sentenced to three years imprisonment. A central Gambino family member, Robert DiBernardo, was convicted after a long-term undercover investigation directed at organized crime's control of the pornography industry in the United States.

The ABSCAM Case

During the late 1970s and early 1980s, one of the Brooklyn Strike Force's most successful series of prosecutions and racketeering convictions arose from the so-called ABSCAM investigation. The two-year investigation initially targeted trafficking in stolen art and forgeries, but later evolved into a public corruption investigation. The FBI was aided by a convicted con-man and swindler, Melvin Weinberg, and his girlfriend Evelyn Knight, who helped plan and conduct the operation. They were facing prison sentences at the time, and in exchange for their help, the FBI agreed to recommend that they be released on probation.

The sting operation was as straightforward as it was audacious: videotape politicians accepting bribes from a fictitious Arabian company in return for various political favors. The operation was directed by FBI Special Agent John Good and originally staffed by other agents from the

FBI's Long Island office in Hauppauge. This team of FBI agents – which numbered as high as 100 at the peak of the investigation - worked under the supervision of Assistant Director Neil J. Welch, who headed the bureau's New York Division, and Tom Puccio, the head of the Brooklyn Strike Force.

As part of the undercover operation, a "front company" was formed, called Abdul Enterprises, in which F.B.I. employees posed as fictional Arab sheiks led by owners Kambir Abdul Rahman and Yassir Habib. They supposedly had millions of dollars to invest in the United States. The FBI funded a $1 million account with the Chase Manhattan Bank in the name of the fictional company, giving Abdul Enterprises the credibility it needed to further its operation.

The public corruption part of the investigation began when a forger under investigation suggested to the "sheiks" that they invest in casinos in New Jersey and that licensing could be obtained for a price. The undercover operation was immediately re-targeted toward political corruption. Each Congressman approached would be given a large sum of money in exchange for "private immigration bills" to allow foreigners associated with Abdul Enterprises into the country, as well as for building permits and licenses for casinos in Atlantic City. Among the casino projects involved were the Ritz-Carlton Atlantic City, the Dunes Hotel and Casino (Atlantic City), the Penthouse Boardwalk Hotel and Casino, and the sheik's fictional casino.

The first political figure who became ensnared in this phony investment scheme was Camden mayor Angelo Errichetti. In a secretly recorded conversation, he told the sheiks' representatives, "I'll give you Atlantic City in exchange for monetary kickbacks." Errichetti helped recruit several government officials and United States congressmen who were willing to grant political favors in exchange for monetary bribes of between $50,000 and $100,000.

As the FBI had always done in their investigation, they tape-recorded each of the money exchanges; however, this was the first time in American history that there were secret videotapes of government officials accepting bribes. The meeting places included a house in the Foxhall neighborhood of Washington, D.C., owned by Lee Lescaze, an editor of The Washington Post. There were also meetings on a luxury yacht in Florida, and hotel rooms in Pennsylvania and New Jersey.

In addition to the Mayor of Camden, the investigation led to the arrest and prosecution of six Congressmen and U.S. Senator Harrison A. "Pete" Williams of New Jersey, a New Jersey State Senate member, Philadelphia City Council members, and an inspector for the United States Immigration and Naturalization Service. This sting operation derived its code name from the term "Arab Scam," since the informants and undercover FBI agents were posing as wealthy Arab sheiks seeking to bribe U.S. Senators and Congressmen. However, when the Arab communities in Brooklyn and elsewhere objected to the term "Arab" in connection with the word "scam," the Government changed the explanation of the acronym. The new story was that the investigation's name was short for "Abdul Scam," the fictitious name of the company providing the funding for the bribes.

This massive FBI anti-corruption operation captured the media's attention and public imagination when the first prosecutions were handed down in 1980. It had the full array of characters that any good cinematographer would want to work into a gripping action film: there were phony Arab sheiks, real mobsters, corrupt local politicians, U.S. members of Congress on the take, and it was all orchestrated by a cigar-chomping con artist paid by the feds to set up the stings. In fact, the Abscam investigation provided the core material for *American Hustle*, a popular movie released in late 2013.

At first, the undercover agents seeking political "favors" in return for stacks of $100 bills wore the fancy suits and improvised headdresses that made them appear to be at least the Hollywood version of some wealthy Arab "sheiks," but none of them could actually speak Arabic if necessary. This oversight nearly proved disastrous, and the agents' "cover" was nearly blown. An FBI agent who was of Lebanese descent and fluent in Arabic was quickly located, and he took over the leading role in the sting operation. After that, it worked smoothly without a hitch.

FBI undercover agent Tony Amoroso also played a significant supporting role throughout the ABSCAM operation, and I had an opportunity to work closely with both Amoroso as well as FBI special agent John Good during my tenue at the Strike Force. Many of my cases were out in Long Island, which we referred to as "the Wild East," since it was directly east of Brooklyn on Long Island. Organized crime's corrupt political grip seemed to increase as you got further away from New York City.

During the ABSCAM investigation, everything was videotaped. Having a tape was both good and bad news for those of us in law enforcement at the time. The good news was that when played in a packed courtroom before a jury, a videotape of a Congressman taking a bribe is hard – if not possible – to cross-examine. One Congressman could be seen on video stuffing $100 bills in his suit pockets, patting them down, and then saying, "How do I look?" Another target of the investigation admitted on videotape: "I've got larceny in my blood." Yet another tape showed Rep. Michael "Ozzie" Myers, a Philadelphia Democrat, famously saying: "Money talks in this business and bullshit walks." Priceless. Based upon the airtight case against him provided by the videotapes and testimony of the FBI undercover agents, Myers was expelled from Congress and served 21 months in prison for taking a $50,000 bribe.

The bad news about the ABSCAM videos was that from that time on, every time a federal prosecutor appeared before a jury, the jurors were expecting the prosecution to show them a film of the crime as it took place, which, of course, was impossible in most cases. The testimony of witnesses and documentary evidence continued to be the mainstay of law enforcement investigations and prosecutions. But such evidence was not necessarily as compelling as the videotapes of the in-progress crimes of the ABSCAM investigation, so some jurors would give federal prosecutors such as myself quizzical looks as if to ask: "So where are the tapes?"

Each indicted politician was given a separate trial. During these trials, controversy arose regarding the prosecutorial ethics of the operation. Many of the lawyers defending the politicians and other defendants who were charged accused the FBI of "entrapment." However, the law generally does not prevent law enforcement officers from offering a supposed bribe to an elected official, or anyone else for that matter, as long as the agents do not go to great extremes to overcome any genuine reluctance of the target to participate in an illegal scheme. Since "entrapment" as a legal defense was very hard to prove, and would almost require proof of duress by the agents, every judge assigned to preside over an ABSCAM prosecution overruled this claim, and each politician was convicted.[14]

However, following widespread criticism that the ABSCAM sting operation was too close to the line of entrapment, Attorney General Benjamin Civiletti issued The Attorney General Guidelines for FBI Undercover Operations ("Civiletti Undercover Guidelines") on January

5, 1981. These were the first Attorney General Guidelines for undercover operations and formalized procedures necessary to conduct covert operations to avoid future controversy.

Following the initial press accounts about the investigation, Congress also held a series of hearings to examine FBI undercover operations in general, and the ABSCAM investigation in particular. The House Subcommittee on Civil and Constitutional Rights began hearings on FBI covert operations in March 1980, and concluded with a report in April 1984. Among the concerns expressed during the hearings were the undercover agents' involvement in illegal activity, the possibility of entrapping individuals, the prospect of damaging the reputations of innocent civilians, and the opportunity to undermine legitimate privacy rights.

The Lufthansa Airlines Heist

On December 11, 1978, half a dozen masked robbers raided the Lufthansa Airlines cargo building at J.F.K. Airport in New York, making off with more than $5 million in cash ($21 million in today's dollars) and almost $1 million in jewelry. To this day, the Lufthansa heist is one of the largest in U.S. history. The plan's origins came from Peter Gruenewald, a Lufthansa cargo worker at J.F.K. Airport, who knew that Lufthansa regularly flew large amounts of unmarked cash from Europe to J.F.K. The U.S. currency was primarily exchanged overseas by U.S. tourists and service members. Typically, the money would be transferred to U.S. banks via Brink's armored vehicles. However, sometimes the cash had to be stored at the airport over the weekend or until the next business day, creating an opening for an "inside heist."

Gruenewald discussed the plan with a fellow cargo worker and friend, Louis Werner - his first mistake. Werner had a substantial personal gambling debt with a bookmaker, Martin Krugman, so he shared this plan with Krugman in the hopes that Krugman would go easy on him about the collection of the gambling debt. Krugman, in turn, discussed it with the associate mobster Henry Hill. As depicted in the movie *Goodfellas*, Hill was associated with James "Jimmy the Gent" Burke, who had connections with Lucchese crime family members. Burke and Hill were already quite familiar with the inner working of J.F.K. Airport, having hijacked trucks regularly from there, often taking two or three trucks per week to fund their expensive lifestyles, as well as to generate money to take care of their organized crime family contacts.

The Lufthansa heist was carried out at 3 a.m. on December 11th, when a black van loaded with masked men pulled up outside the Lufthansa storage area. The men burst in waving their guns, enough to get the night-shift employees to submit to being handcuffed in the break room. The cash and jewels were loaded in the van, and the crew silently made their getaway.

Then the trouble started. Rather than taking the van to be crushed at a mob-controlled junkyard, getaway driver Parnell "Stacks" Edwards got drunk and left it illegally parked on the street in Brooklyn. His fingerprints and a footprint were found in the interior of the van. Edwards quickly became the first suspect in the heist to be murdered at Burke's direction. But Burke's paranoia, mixed with greed, did not let the killing end there. Krugman was the next to go, disappearing on January 6, 1979. By the summer of that year, eight men associated with the robbery were dead.

The FBI caught a break when Gruenewald started cooperating, and with his testimony, Louis Werner was convicted for his role in the heist. However, Werner refused to cooperate and to give up his co-conspirators, so the case stalled again. "These 'goodfellas' thought they had a license to steal, a license to kill, and a license to do whatever they wanted," commented George Venizelos, FBI assistant director-in-charge of the New York field office.

The biggest break in the investigation finally came in the spring of 1980, when Hill was arrested on six drug-related counts. He was also held as a material witness in the Lufthansa robbery. It wasn't long before he "flipped," convinced by the FBI and by Strike Force attorney Ed McDonald to testify against not only Burke, but also Lucchese family underboss Paul Vario. Although I was not actually present in the conference room where Hill was being grilled, I could clearly hear Hill being told over and over again by McDonald, who headed up the Strike Force at the time: "You have everything to gain and nothing to lose." As with other career criminals who got "jammed up" facing lengthy prison terms unless they cooperated, Hill's resistance finally broke when a surveillance tape was played for him in which Burke could be heard clearly saying that Hill needed to be "whacked."

After hearing the tape, Hill entered into a cooperation agreement with the FBI and the Strike Force on May 27, 1980. The deal included a stay-out-of-jail card and a free pass for himself, his wife Karen, and their two sons, courtesy of the federal Witness Protection Program run by the U.S. Marshal Service.

Hill told the FBI agents and prosecutors assigned to his case that he and two Pittsburgh gamblers set up the 1978–79 Boston College basketball point-shaving scheme by convincing Boston College center Rick Kuhn to participate. Kuhn, a high school friend of one of the gamblers, encouraged teammates to join in the scheme. Hill also claimed to have an N.B.A. referee in his pocket who worked games at Madison Square Garden during the 1970s. The referee had apparently incurred gambling debts on horse races.

Hill's testimony led to 50 convictions, including Burke's conviction on two separate counts: the basketball point-shaving scheme and an unrelated murder of scam artist Richard Eaton. Burke was sentenced to a 12-year prison term, where he died in 1996. Paul Vario, who was convicted of racketeering, also died in prison in 1988.

Even though Hill was in the Witness Protection Program, this did not deter him from continuing with his life of crime. In 1987, Hill was convicted of cocaine trafficking in a federal court in Seattle and expelled from the witness protection program. In August 2004, he was arrested at North Platte Regional Airport in Nebraska after he had left behind his luggage containing drug paraphernalia. On June 13, 2012, Hill died in a Los Angeles hospital, one day after his 69th birthday.

John Cody, the Teamsters, and Donald J. Trump

When I was working with the Brooklyn Strike Force, the most notorious New York union leader and racketeer was John A. Cody, the President of Teamsters Local 282. Cody used strikes, extortion, and old-fashioned intimidation to dominate the New York construction business and strike fear into the hearts of every New York developer, including the young Donald J. Trump, who was building his signature Trump Tower at the time.

Cody's union delivered cement and other building materials to virtually every major building site and development project in New York City and Long Island. To win " labor peace " for developers like Trump and Sigmund Sommers, who was building North Shore Towers on the Queens-Nassau border, they had to sign a "sweetheart" union contract with Teamster Local 282. The terms were simple: the developer would agree to put several teamster union foremen on the payroll as "no-show" employees. Their salaries would then go to Cody, who, in turn, would pass at least several hundred thousand dollars on to Paul Castellano, the Boss of the Gambino crime family. Cody also made millions of dollars in loans to various mobsters from the Teamster Local 282 Pension and Welfare Fund.

The major challenge we had during the Strike Force's investigation of John Cody and Teamster Local 282 was securing the cooperation of witnesses who were willing to testify against Cody and the mob bosses. Legitimate contractors and honest employees feared economic or physical reprisals if they spoke out. Dissident union members saw that other union members and employees who cooperated with law enforcement agencies were often blacklisted from jobs. Fourteen members of Cody's union who publicly raised charges of corruption against Cody soon found themselves unemployed. "Everyone in construction in New York knows that if you complain, you lose your job," said Herman Benson, executive director of the Association for Union Democracy.[15]

As for the developers in the New York area, we were finally able to get Sigmund Sommers to cooperate with our federal investigation after we learned that, at Cody's insistence, Sommers had given a penthouse apartment in the North Shore Towers building complex on the Queens-Nassau County border to Marilyn Taggert, Cody's girlfriend. In return, Cody agreed not to shut down the construction site at this development project. Sommers was also forced to agree to a corrupt labor contract with Cody, whereby Sommers was required to put several "phantom" union shop stewards and teamster foremen on the payroll so that money could be generated for payments to Cody and his mob bosses.

Donald Trump, who was then an up-and-coming young developer in Manhattan, ostensibly agreed to cooperate with the Strike Force investigation, through his lawyer Roy M. Cohn. When he came into the federal building to be interviewed about his dealings with Cody, however, he adamantly insisted that the labor contract he had signed with Local 282 was "legitimate." He swore he didn't know whether or not the teamster shop stewards and foremen were showing up for work at the

Trump Tower construction site. In other words, Trump "stonewalled" our investigation. Since our orders from Washington were to only prosecute organized crime members and corrupt labor leaders, we could not pursue a prosecution against Trump for lying to federal agents. Nor could we charge him for participation in a conspiracy with Cody and others to violate various labor and racketeering laws. These limitations on who we could pursue with criminal charges made our investigation much harder. But with the assistance of Sommers and other witnesses, we finally built a solid criminal case against Cody.

Trump also refused to give federal prosecutors information about the relationship between Cody and Verina Hixon, the former wife of a Texas billionaire. Hixon lived in a luxurious apartment with a swimming pool on the floor directly below Trump's penthouse apartment in Trump Tower. The apartment was a combination of two apartments that together were worth upwards of $10 million. It was strongly suspected the apartment had been put in Hixon's name at Cody's request as part of a deal to buy labor peace for the construction of Trump Tower. Likewise, Sigmund Sommers had given a penthouse apartment at North Shore Towers to Cody's other girlfriend, Marilyn Taggert.

On October 8, 1982, Teamster President Cody was convicted of having engaged in a pattern of racketeering activity since 1968 in violation of the federal racketeering statute and for evading federal income taxes on a $150,000 kickback. He was also found guilty of violating the Taft-Hartley Law by accepting gifts from contractors who did business with his union.

On December 2, 1982, Cody was sentenced in federal district court in Brooklyn to five years in prison for labor racketeering and tax evasion. The courtroom was packed as Judge Jacob A. Mishler imposed the prison sentence and a fine of $80,000. Cody was required to serve one-third of his sentence, or 20 months, before being eligible for parole. Although I handled most of the investigation of the case, it was tried by another federal prosecutor, Michael A. Guadagno. By then, I had already left the Strike Force to take an executive position with the New York State Attorney General's Office, working under Attorney General Robert Abrams. At the sentencing, Mike Guadagno noted that Cody had close links with "high-echelon members of organized crime," further telling Judge Mishler that Cody was concerned not with "the good of his union members, but only with lining his own pockets."

When Cody eventually went to jail for racketeering, Robert Sasso, Local 282's Treasurer, took control of the union. In a desperate attempt to regain power, Cody hired a former jailhouse inmate to assassinate Sasso. Unfortunately for Cody, however, the inmate was an informant for the FBI and recorded conversations about the plot, including Cody discussing the "relative merits of using explosives or a gun with a silencer" to kill Sasso. Cody served a longer prison term for attempted murder as a result.

The Suffolk County Southwest Sewer District Investigation

The construction of the Southwest Sewer District (SWSD) on Long Island, at the cost of almost $1 billion in the late 1970s and early 1980s, turned into a cesspool of graft and corruption of unprecedented size and scope. The 57-square-mile sewer district, situated in the southwest portions of Islip and Babylon Townships, was still not in operation when we started our federal investigation in 1979. However, the 250,000 residents had already begun paying taxes on it at the beginning of 1978.

The SWSD project was way behind schedule, since mob-controlled cement and construction companies working with corrupt local politicians were less interested in actually completing this massive project than they were in siphoning off as much of the money as possible. At the same time, they were cutting corners on the construction of the pipe, so the entire system was in danger of leaking from day one it went operational. Perhaps we should not have been surprised. "Pork barreling" and graft have been a part of almost every public works project since time immemorial. However, the graft involved in this project was so massive that it might even make Boss Tweed blush.

The consulting engineer on the project – Charles Walsh of Bowe, Walsh, and Associates – seemed to be the linchpin to the corruption puzzle on Long Island relating to the sewer district. Charles Walsh and his company were the most prominent political contributors to both parties in Suffolk County. Charles Walsh acknowledged making substantial contributions and hiring relatives of county politicians and leaders, including the son of a former county executive, H. Lee Dennison.

A federal grand jury that I and other Strike Force attorneys empaneled on Long Island issued dozens of subpoenas to elected officials and construction companies throughout the area for records relating to campaign contributions and business records. With the help of accounting-savvy FBI agents, we were trying to unravel at least part of the intricate web of corruption that had engulfed the project from its start.[16]

One of the first indictments of a corrupt politician related to this federal-state probe was issued by our local counterparts from the Suffolk County District Attorney's Office in 1979. This was an indictment of one of the most powerful political figures on Long Island, Smithtown Leader Nicholas Barbato.[17] The indictment on grand larceny and extortion charges issued by a special county grand jury investigating the sewer project, did not directly relate to the SWSD project itself. However, Barbato has been an influential, behind-the-scenes advocate of the sewer project, and it was believed that his cooperation would be instrumental in advancing the investigation. At the very least, Barbato was in a position to shed a great deal of light on how Long Island taxpayers ended up being saddled with so many inflated contracts and costs relating to the project, and why it was constructed so poorly that it was already leaking like a sieve.

Early in the investigation, we learned that Suffolk County politicians who had pushed the sewer project ahead had received heavy contributions and patronage jobs from contractors. Despite overwhelming criticism that the project was excessively costly and ill-conceived, Barbato had urged county legislators to support the project as proof of their loyalty to Republican County Executive John V. N. Klein. Barbato was known to have extensive business dealings with sewer contractors and had already admitted getting $200 a week plus benefits from Twin County Transit Mix, which has provided hundreds of millions of dollars of concrete to the sewer district. Barbato had also admitted being on the payroll of the George P. Tobler Insurance Agency, which was the county's insurance agent for nearly ten years. His indictment charged that he extorted his salary by threatening to have the county insurance contract terminated.

The linchpin of the entire sewer project appeared to be Charles T. Walsh, the principal partner and 98 percent owner of Bowe, Walsh & Associates, the consulting engineer for the whole project. Not surprisingly, when Walsh and his company were awarded this lucrative consulting contract, he and his firm were the major political contributors to Suffolk County politicians of both parties. As a consulting engineer, it was Walsh's responsibility to be sure that prospective bidders on sewer construction work knew and understood the requirements of the specifications, and that bids were proper. Walsh's company was also responsible for ensuring that only qualified contractors were awarded contracts, that contractors were paid only for work performed, and that the materials used were in accordance with the specifications. However, one of the unwritten requirements that Walsh imposed on contractors selected on the SWSD projects was to be closely affiliated with one or more of the Suffolk County politicians who backed Walsh's selection as the project's consulting engineer.

The federal trial relating to the SWSD lasted for five weeks in late April and May 1979. It was prosecuted on behalf of the Dept. of Justice and the Brooklyn Strike Force by John Jacobs and me. The presiding Judge was John Thomas C Pratt, and the trial was held in a makeshift federal courtroom set up in the motor vehicle building in Westbury, Long Island. It wasn't until several years later that Long Island got its own official federal courthouse, so we had to make do with temporary space borrowed or rented in state or local government buildings.

The corporate defendant in the case was the Clearview Concrete Company. This mob-connected concrete company had supplied approximately 97% of the concrete pipe needed for constructing the SWSD project, at the cost of roughly $20 million. The individual criminal defendants were Vincent DeLillo, the former president of Clearview, and David Francis, the plant superintendent. They were charged with having conspired to defraud the Government by making and supplying substandard concrete.[18]

Over thirty government witnesses testified during the trial. Witnesses included civil engineering experts who presented evidence that the main pipe leading to the sewer-treatment plant and smaller-diameter pipe used throughout the district were so poorly designed and constructed that leaks were inevitable. Because of this evidence, the U.S. Environmental Protection Agency authorized an additional $500,000 for an exhaustive examination and repair of pipe already in the ground.

The defense strategy at trial was fairly unusual. Instead of denying the massive fraud, the defendants admitted that it had occurred, including conducting rigged tests of the pipe it manufactured, the bribery of inspectors hired by consulting engineers, and the improper repair of pipes previously installed. However, the defendants argued that they did not have any knowledge or involvement in the fraud themselves but that it was completely the brainchild of the company supervisor, Walter Gorman, who was the Government's chief witness at trial.

One of the most dramatic parts of the trial was when the FBI agents working with us brought a three-edged bearing test machine into the courtroom. An expert showed how the defendants falsified the test results and made it look like the concrete met the necessary specifications, when it clearly did not. Most of the concrete wouldn't have passed the test without the tampering.

Testimony presented at trial established that the three-edged bearing machine used by Clearview at its premises included the addition of a mysterious "yellow valve." This valve meant that the actual amount of pressure applied to the pipe under examination could be secretly reduced without any reduction in the reading on the gauges visible to the inspectors. Defendant Francis had the job of operating the yellow valve whenever an inspector was present, so that they would be sure that all of the concrete being tested passed the inspection with flying colors. Just to make sure that this fraudulent scheme was successful, other Clearview employees were ordered to position their bodies during the tests in such a way as to block the inspectors' view of the yellow valve.

Expert testimony also showed that the metal supports used for the piping were more like chicken wire than the strong metal "rebar" (reinforced bar) that the engineering specifications required. However, during our demonstration for the jury of how the phony tests were conducted, the FBI agents assisting us at the trial accidently ended up spilling a few gallons of oil on the courtroom floor, which greatly annoyed the meticulous Judge Pratt. We all pitched in during an emergency break at the trial in order to clean it up.

Although not as dramatic - but very professionally satisfying for me - was that when we got to cross-examine DeLillo, we used a transcript from a civil deposition in a case I had found. DeLillo apparently had forgotten about this prior civil testimony sworn under oath, since his testimony in that prior case was diametrically opposed to what he was testifying to about in the federal criminal trial. In his prior civil deposition, he had testified in great detail about the testing procedures that were being used, while in the federal criminal trial he professed to being completely clueless as to how the testing of the concrete had been conducted.

As a result of this conflicting sworn testimony, we were able to persuade the judge to give a jury charge at the end of the case stating that the jury did not have to decide whether DeLillo was testifying truthfully or not in the federal trial. All they had to find was that the discrepancies between his federal trial testimony and his prior civil deposition were so inconsistent that they could conclude that he perjured himself in one case or the other. This testimony tipped the scales decidedly in the Government's favor, leading the eight men and four women on the jury to quickly conclude on July 31, 1979, that we had proven our case beyond a reasonable doubt.

Another highpoint in the trial was when one of the prosecution witnesses testified that Andrew DeLillo – the father of defendant Vincent DeLillo – warned that "whoever this guy [the FBI informant] is, if he hurts my son he will be looking over his shoulder for the rest of his life." The defense objected to this testimony about the threat as unduly prejudicial, and that it should be excluded under Rule 403 of the Federal Rules of Evidence. However, Judge Pratt let this powerful testimony in anyway, and the Second Circuit Court of Appeals affirmed the trial court's ruling on this issue after all the defendants were convicted.[19]

In the Government's summation to the jury at the end of the case, we argued that the Government and Long Island taxpayers had "wanted a Cadillac" when it came to the quality of the pipe that they had expected and paid for, while what they got was "a broken-down Ford."

Although it was exhilarating to have won a favorable jury verdict after five long weeks of trial, the grueling schedule that we maintained during that time period left me in a state of near exhaustion. Not only did we have to prepare and try the case, which regularly led to 16 hour work days, but I had to commute from Manhattan to Mineola, Long Island and back each day. On one of my daily morning commutes, I got a flat tire and replaced it with a temporary "inner tube" tire I had in my trunk, thinking that I would get the flat tire repaired later in the day, or replace it with a new tire. However, I was so singularly focused on the trial that I forgot about the replacement tire that was only supposed to be driven a few miles at most, and then replaced with a real tire. Inevitably, the temporary tire exploded while I was driving on the highway several days later, and the car had to be towed. Fortunately, my inadvertence did not cause a major accident or injury to myself or anyone else. But it was certainly a reminder that life must go on even when you are on trial, and that the ordinary details of daily living cannot be neglected without suffering the consequences.

I also came to learn that, win or lose, there was inevitably an emotional let down after a trial. It was not necessarily a real depression, but when the daily adrenaline dose stops pumping through your system when you are continually in front of a judge and jury, it is hard to go "cold turkey" when the trial is over. As a result, I tried as best I could to move quickly into my next big investigation and trial, seeking the "rush" that envelops you when you are involved in something significant, something big. I suppose it was an addiction of sorts, but at least it was a positive addiction (although my marriage and family life undoubtedly suffered from my obsession with my cases).

"Big" Tom DiDonato

Although those of us in federal law enforcement certainly viewed the organized crime families as "the enemy," there were some benefits to dealing with an organization with a clear-cut leadership structure. For example, I handled a Strike Force prosecution against Thomas "Big Tom" DiDonato and some of his organized crime associates. We had very little direct evidence of loansharking, illegal gambling, hijackings, extortion, and other criminal activities against DiDonato himself. Still, we had a great deal of evidence he was directing all of these illegal operations and that his "crew" were reporting to him, either directly or indirectly. So I had the FBI agents working with me on the case draw up a large pyramid chart showing DiDonato at the top of the chart and the other defendants filling out the pyramid below him. In my summation of the case, I asked the jury (rhetorically, of course) why he was known as "Big Tom" when he was of average or even slightly diminutive stature. I then answered my question by suggesting that his nickname was derived from his status in the criminal organization as its "Big Man." He had insulated himself and did not have to get his own hands dirty since he had "button men." The jury must have accepted my arguments since they returned a guilty verdict against DiDonato and his other "crew" members in less than one hour.

The problem was that one of DiDonato's close family members thought that I had "crossed the line" and had unfairly overreached in my arguments to the jury in getting a conviction against DiDonato on admittedly thin evidence. An FBI informant told the Bureau that this disgruntled family member had angrily ordered a "hit" on me. The FBI assigned some of its SWAT team members to accompany me to and from my apartment on the Upper West Side of Manhattan to the Strike Force offices at the federal court in downtown Brooklyn. I was also to told not to accompany FBI and DEA agents on any of their investigative "field trips." I had often done so to get out of the office and to see with my own eyes the social clubs and other venues where our organized crime targets hung out and conducted their business.

However, this "protective detail" for me only lasted a couple of weeks since an FBI supervisor arranged a "sit down" with DiDonato. He was still out on bail awaiting sentencing. The FBI supervisor strongly suggested his cooperation in getting the "contract" on me withdrawn would be considered in the FBI's sentencing recommendation. DiDonato, of course, agreed, and we could rely on his ability to control the actions of his family members. While we had made some progress in breaking down the code of silence of the traditional mafioso, the leadership still had substantial control over their members. An organized crime member could not carry out a "hit" or "contract" without the express authorization of higher-ups in the hierarchy.

As a further "reward" for DiDonato and to smooth over some still ruffled feathers in his family, we also told DiDonato that we would recommend to the Bureau of Prisons that he be sent to the minimum federal correction facility at Allenwood, Pennsylvania. It did not quite live up to its "country club" reputation, but it did provide fairly pleasant living quarters and excellent recreational facilities. When we gave DiDonato a brochure with photos of the facility, I felt more like a travel agent than a federal prosecutor, but if that was what was necessary to keep the peace between the five mafia families and federal law enforcement, so be it.

Daniel Cunningham and the Security Guards Union

Another prominent case that I worked on while I was at the Strike Force was the investigation and prosecution of Daniel M. ("Danny") Cunningham. He was the President of two affiliated unions: the Federation of Special

Police and Law Enforcement Officers and the Allied International Union of Security Guards and Special Police.

By the late 1970s, the private security guard industry had grown 10 to 15% each year and was a $12 billion industry.[20] Even as the U.S. and the world economy were experiencing a recession, the private security industry was booming. Businesses and communities grew increasingly concerned about the rise in crime and saw the need to supplement their municipal law enforcement with private security contracts. Many residential communities started investing in 24-hour private security vehicle patrols in their neighborhoods. On July 24, 1980, the Business Bulletin of the *Wall Street Journal* announced that the "[s]ilver lining of the recession is apparent at private security firms."[21] In addition, the large casinos opening in Atlantic City, New Jersey, and elsewhere, created unprecedented opportunities for security companies to expand their businesses. By the early 1980s, it was estimated that there were over 1 million private security guards employed throughout the U.S., which meant that there were more security guards in the country than law enforcement officers.

Never missing an opportunity to infiltrate any legitimate business they could, several mafia organizations in the greater New York area started exerting their leverage to take control of several security guard companies and the unions that represented the guards themselves. The most successful of the security guard union locals in the New York area and at the Atlantic City casinos were the two unions established by Cunningham, who ran these unions from their headquarters in Great Neck, Long Island.

During the extensive investigation of Cunningham and his organized crime connections, we established that Cunningham was fronting for John "Sonny" Franzese, a member of the Colombo crime family. Cunningham also had business dealings with members of the Gambino, Genovese, and Bonanno crime families. At the trial of the case that I prosecuted for the Government, Cunningham was convicted in June 1982 on federal charges of embezzling money from his two labor organizations and bribing a Department of Labor investigator.[22] The embezzlement charges were based on the evidence we presented at trial showing that he paid thousands of dollars in union funds to his wife, Susan, for a no-show job. We also established that he was dispersing union funds to other fictitious union employees. In addition to the embezzlement charges, Cunningham was also convicted for Obstruction of Justice.

The defense lawyer in the case – Ivan Fisher – was one of the best criminal trial lawyers in New York at the time, so waiting for the jury to come back with a verdict seemed endless and excruciating to me. As we waited for the jury to come back, I tortured myself with doubts about the outcome. Did I make any mistakes during the trial that would cause the jurors to have reasonable doubts about Cunningham's guilt? Had I been forceful enough to summarize the evidence and ask the jury to return a guilty verdict during my closing argument? As a perfectionist, I experienced the tortures of the damned until the jury finally returned a guilty verdict on all 13 counts.

Maybe we were just lucky, or perhaps we had the combination of investigative and trial skills necessary to be effective prosecutors, but we were able to secure convictions in well over 90% of the cases that we tried while I was with the Brooklyn Strike Force.

To obtain an enhanced sentence of Cunningham, we presented information to Judge I. Leo Glasser concerning Cunningham's organized criminal associations, as well as evidence that he was a co-conspirator in a 1977 plot to murders two men.[23] The victims of the murders to which Mr. Cunningham was linked were Ruben Gonzalez and Raymond Aponte, Long Island men whose bodies were found in December 1977 in a car trunk in the J.F.K. Airport "long term" parking lot. For the victims, it was the "eternity" parking lot. Each had been shot in the head. In the letter that I sent to Judge Glasser, I explained that Cunningham had "assisted" in their murders "by luring them to a meeting at a diner," where they were "grabbed" by several individuals by prearrangement with Cunningham. The murders stemmed from a falling out between Cunningham and the victims over efforts of the three men to organize the employees of private carting companies.

On July 29, 1982, Cunningham was sentenced to five years in prison and a fine of $80,000.[24] He was released from jail on bail pending his appeal of the racketeering charges. However, on September 28, 1982, Cunningham's bail was revoked, and he was ordered to begin serving his five-year prison sentence even though his appeal was still pending.[25] The reason for this was that Cunningham had arranged for the placement of two incendiary devices at the Nesconset, Long Island home of a prosecution witness who had testified at his trial. This witness was William Wachholder, Cunningham's father-in-law. The assumed motive was revenge. Fortunately for Wachholder, both incendiary devices – one a flare grenade and the other fireworks combined with gasoline – malfunctioned. Had they worked, it is likely that they would have burned down the home. Although there was not enough evidence yet to charge Cunningham with responsibility for these incidents, I successfully argued to Judge Glasser at a hastily called hearing that "it really strains credulity that anyone other than Mr. Cunningham could have been behind these two attempts."

My interest in Wachholder's continued good health extended far beyond normal humanitarian impulses. Wachholder was a crucial witness in a continuing investigation that I was heading up into Cunningham's attempts to infiltrate and expand his interests into nuclear power plants, which created a potential national security threat. Cunningham handpicked Wachholder to head a division of the union, which was named "Local 1, Power Plant Police and Security Officers." This new division was formed for the specific purpose of organizing security guards at nuclear power facilities and construction sites on the East Coast. Included in this group was the Shoreham Nuclear Power Plant in eastern Long Island. The idea that Cunningham and his organized crime associates would have access to Shoreham and other nuclear power plants was terrifying. Under the watchful eyes of the Strike Force leadership in Brooklyn and Washington, D.C., I and some FBI agents assigned to work with me embarked on an intensive investigation to determine whether any of the security guards in Cunningham's union had access to confidential information or fissionable nuclear material at any of the country's nuclear power plants.

On February 14, 1983, Forbes magazine ran a cover story entitled: "Brother Cunningham and the Guards." It detailed Cunningham's efforts to organize security guards at nuclear facilities. The frightening prospect that crime-controlled labor unions might gain access to nuclear fuel at power plants also attracted the attention of Ed Bradley of CBS's "Sixty Minutes." Since the Cunningham trial was completed and Cunningham had been sentenced to his 5-year prison term, the Justice Department authorized me to discuss matters of public record regarding our investigation with Bradley and others at CBS. Of particular interest to them was the information that we had gathered during the investigation about the formation of the security guard unions by Cunningham and his organized crime associates.

Because of my work with the Strike Force on this subject, Ed Bradley requested an interview with me. My superiors at Justice OK'd it, and Bradley met me at a hotel room at Dulles Airport in northern Virginia, which was near the FBI Academy where I was teaching a class on white-collar crime investigations. During the program, Bradley pointed out that many of the same contractors delivering concrete to Shoreham had previously supplied defective concrete for Suffolk County's sewer district, the case that I am other Strike Force attorneys had successfully prosecuted.

On the same "Sixty Minutes" show that I was on, Lt. Remo Franceschini of the New York City Police Department discussed the organized crime influence of the Lucchese crime family over Local 66 of the Laborers' Union and its President, Peter Vario. Lt Franceschini also mentioned Teamster Local 282, which played a prominent role at the Shoreham Nuclear Power Plant construction site. He alluded to the investigation that I had been working on that established the organized crime connections between Cody and members of the Gambino organized crime family. He vividly described Shoreham as a "perfect pork barrel for organized crime to reap money out of . . . on no-show jobs, on kickbacks, on being able to get rid of stolen merchandise."

Also interviewed for the "Sixty Minutes" program was Wayne Prospect, a Suffolk County legislator and anti-Shoreham activist. He had been elected primarily based on his opposition to the Shoreham Nuclear Power Plant. Prospect was quoted as stating that "LILCO should have posted a sign outside the plant saying, "Hail, hail the gang's all here." Following the Sixty Minutes program, Prospect introduced a resolution in the Suffolk County Legislature "to determine the extent to which the infiltration of organized crime at Shoreham contributed to the exorbitant cost overruns of the Shoreham facility."

The Russian Mob Comes to Brooklyn

My tenure with the Brooklyn Strike Force and other assignments for the U.S. Department of Justice coincided with the emergence of major Russian organized crime groups in the U.S., particularly in the Brighton Beach section of Brooklyn.

With the fall of the Soviet Union, there was a dramatic increase in the size and influence of traditional organized crime groups in Russia. Mikhail Gorbachev loosened the restrictions on private enterprise, opening up new opportunities for criminal gangs. It is estimated that, at one point, the Russian Mafia controlled up to two-thirds of Russia's economy, with many ex-KGB agents joining up and becoming criminal bosses. During the dissolution of the USSR from 1989 to 1991, there were formal meetings among Russian organized crime syndicates to carve up control of post-Communist Russia. With the privatization of state-owned businesses, many organized crime leaders, joined by ex-government officials, rebranded themselves as legitimate "oligarchs" with one foot in legitimate companies and the other in illegal activities, such as money laundering. Many of these oligarchs had their own private security forces, primarily drawn from the criminal gangs.

Over time, there was a merger between the Kremlin leadership under Vladimir Putin and Russian organized crime under the unifying leadership of Semion Mogilevich. He was considered by Western European and U.S. law enforcement and intelligence agencies to be the "boss of bosses" of a vast criminal empire controlled by Russian Mafia syndicates around the globe. The FBI and U.S. Department of Justice considered him to be "the most dangerous mobster in the world," with his hand in almost every form of illegal activity – including weapons trafficking, contract murders, extortion, drug trafficking, and the international trafficking of women for prostitution – as well as many legitimate businesses. Mogilevich's nickname was "The Brainy Don," due to his business acumen. According to U.S. diplomatic cables, he controlled RosUkrEnergo (RUE), a company actively involved in Russia–Ukraine natural gas transmissions to Western Europe by pipeline. He was also believed to have a substantial hidden interest in Raiffeisen Bank.

Between the 1970s and mid-1990s, about 300,000 Russian immigrants settled in the New York area, many in the Brighton Beach and Sheepshead sections of Brooklyn, which became known as "Little Odessa."

Donald J. Trump - then a brash young New York developer - saw Russian organized crime as a means to meet the growing financing needs for his various real estate projects. Trump properties also met the requirements of Russian criminal syndicates to find legitimate business operations willing to serve as "laundromats" for the laundering of illegally obtained cash. A large percentage of the original purchases of Trump Tower co-ops came from Russian-Americans affiliated with organized crime. Over 13 Trump Tower owners in early 1980 were either full-fledged members of Russian organized crime or had strong affiliations with it. In 1984, for example, Russian organized crime affiliate David Bogatin, who had arrived from Russia seven years earlier, bought five luxury condos in Trump Towers for $6 million. Trump was one of the few developers willing to sell co-op units to anonymous buyers. Hence, his projects became magnets for Russians and Ukrainians with the need to launder tens and hundreds of millions of dollars in dirty money. In 1987, Bogatin pleaded guilty to his role in a vast gasoline-bootlegging scheme run by Russian mobsters Marat Balagula and his associate Igor Roizman. After Bogatin fled the country, the Government seized his five Trump Tower condos, based on an investigation that concluded he had bought them to launder money and hide assets.

Then, when Trump's Atlantic City casinos started falling like a house of cards, with one bankruptcy after another, Trump was able to land on his feet by leaving legitimate U.S. banks holding the bag for about $4 billion in losses. Trump just moved on to new luxury real estate projects financed with Russian-Ukrainian "grey" money. The buyers of Trump's co-ops were willing to pay the price – the more inflated the better – since they only wanted to hold onto them for a couple of years before reselling them, thereby converting "dirty" money into squeaky clean funds.

Although we successfully prosecuted several of the Russian mob figures who used the purchase and sale of Trump's co-ops for money laundering purposes, I and other Strike Force attorneys were never given the green light to develop conspiracy or racketeering cases directly against Donald Trump and other developers. If we had been permitted to do so, Trump's career may have turned out to be much different.

The Disbanding of the Strike Forces

Despite the overwhelming success of the Strike Forces around the country, everything changed when President Ronald Reagan appointed Richard "Dick" Thornburg as his Attorney General in 1988. Thornburg, who had served as the U.S. Attorney for the Western District of Pennsylvania in Pittsburg and then elected as the Governor of Pennsylvania from 1979 until 1987, had gotten into a significant jurisdictional dispute over cases with the head of the Pittsburg Strike Force in 1974. Thornburg apparently never got over it. His bad experience with the Pittsburg Strike Force must have been a festering sore because one of the first decisions he made after being sworn in as U.S. Attorney General was to announce that the Strike Forces would be disbanded. Instead of being run by the Organized Crime Section of the Justice Department from Washington, the strike force prosecutors would report to their respective U.S. Attorneys in the federal judicial district where they worked.

Within a few months, about one-fourth of the strike force attorneys around the country "voted with their feet" and left government service for private practice or, like me, stayed on for a while as Assistant U.S. Attorneys before leaving federal service. I tried my best to transition to working at the U.S. Attorney's Office for the Eastern District of New York, which covered Brooklyn, Queens, and the rest of Long Island. But the Government's War on Drugs was ramping up then, and soon the only cases that I was allowed to work on involved the prosecution of relatively low-level "mules" and other drug distributors. I was willing to pitch in to help with drug prosecutions in south Florida, where the Miami and Fort Lauderdale offices of the U.S. Attorney were overwhelmed with drug prosecutions. Cases were referred to them by the relatively new Drug Enforcement Administration (DEA), which was seeing a massive spike in the distribution of cocaine and other narcotics into the U.S. by Colombian, Cuban, and other Latin American organizations. The violence of these groups was exponentially greater than that of the traditional Mafia families that we were used to dealing with in Brooklyn and Long Island.

When my Strike Force superiors asked me to help out the DEA with drug prosecutions, I quickly realized that the Colombian, Cuban and other Latin American drug cartels had a code very different from that of the L.C.N. families I was used to working with. Although the drug cartels dealt harshly with anyone they suspected of acting as an informant for the DEA or the FBI, just as the traditional organized crime families did, they did not consider federal agents or prosecutors to be "off limits." As a result, given the high-profile nature of the narcotics trafficking investigations and prosecutions that I was working on, I had DEA agents accompanying me almost everywhere I went. I had to wear a bulletproof vest when I went out in public or travel to Colombia to meet with informants, witnesses, and law enforcement agents there from the U.S. and the host country (Colombia). Once, when I was returning to the U.S. on a commercial flight from Cali, Colombia, the Avianca Airlines plane I was on was suddenly diverted to Cartagena, supposedly to repair its radar unit. It had to be fully operational before the plane (or any plane) could be cleared to enter U.S. air space.

The DEA agents I was with were understandably very nervous. They suspected that the Colombian drug cartel had arranged for the plane to be diverted. The agents saw the action as possibly a "message" or "warning" to U.S. law enforcement. Diverting a plane would show us that their tentacles reached everywhere in the country, including the national airline. Worse, this could be a trap to isolate and eliminate us in a city where the U.S. had no significant law enforcement presence and the Colombia authorities we dealt with and could trust were not given enough time to provide us with a security net. Although getting shot and killed was always a realistic fear, our most significant fear was of being kidnapped. The U.S. had a declared policy at the time that it would not pay ransoms, even for U.S. law enforcement personnel. Hence, the prognosis in the event of capture by the cartels was always a bleak one. As it turned out, our layover in Cartagena for about a day until we could arrange for alternative air transport back to the U.S. was uneventful. Still, the anxiety level of the DEA agents (and mine) was always at a boiling point whenever we were "in country" in generally hostile environments as we found in Colombia.

After about a year of working primarily on drug cases, I was offered – and accepted – an executive position with New York State Attorney General Robert Abrams. As New York State Deputy First Assistant Attorney General under R. Scott Greathead, the chief of the Division, I was able to continue to work on the Shoreham Nuclear Power Plant investigation. In addition to the labor racketeering and organized crime aspects of this massive construction project, I added other major complex investigations where I was able to bring to bear the skills that I had developed as a nursing home fraud prosecutor and with the Brooklyn Strike Force.

Chapter 3

Shoreham and the South Carolina Nuclear Power Plant Cases

Fraud on the Rate Payers

Throughout the early part of my law career, it seemed like every position I held - either with the government or in private practice – had something to do with the Shoreham Nuclear Power Plant. I had become very familiar with the construction of the Shoreham plant by the Long Island Lighting Company (LILCO) while I was a prosecutor with the Brooklyn Organized Crime Strike Force of the U.S. Department of Justice. As discussed in the previous chapter, I headed up the investigation and prosecution of Daniel Cunningham. As President of the Security Guard Union, Cunningham and his associates had carried out their labor racketeering activities while closely linked to several prominent organized crime members in the New York area. Even after we convicted Cunningham in 1982 of various labor racketeering, bribery, embezzlement, and other charges, the Department of Justice and other government agencies continued to consider this encroachment of organized crime into a nuclear power facility to be a priority national security issue. There was a danger that organized criminal elements could get their hands on fissionable nuclear material that would be a valuable commodity on the international black market or a means of extorting money from the utility or the U.S. government to guarantee its safe return.

The concerns about organized crime reaching its powerful tentacles into the growing nuclear power industry extended far beyond the Department of Justice and the FBI. During the 1980s, long before Al-Qaeda and other terrorist networks burst onto the international scene, the greatest threat to our country's security by non-state actors was posed by organized criminal groups, particularly the Mafia and Russian organized crime. Our task was to keep them as far away from nuclear power plant projects as possible and investigate the massive cost overruns that these construction projects were experiencing. These overruns were a tell-tale solid sign of the presence of organized crime-controlled unions and construction companies. The mob "skimmed" millions off the top of labor and construction projects to pay bribes to corrupt officials and keep vast amounts of cash flowing upward to the Mafia bosses.

When I joined the New York State Attorney General's Office as Deputy First Assistant Attorney General, I was asked to launch a state investigation to determine whether the infiltration of organized crime at Shoreham contributed to the plant's excessive cost overruns. On behalf of New York State and its Attorney General's Office, I coordinated our efforts with the continuing federal investigation and the civil and criminal investigation of the Shoreham project being conducted by Suffolk County and the Suffolk County District Attorney's Office. Eventually, the Suffolk County Legislature and the Suffolk County Executive asked me to head up the County's plans to bring a civil racketeering suit in federal court against LILCO and some of its executives. With State Attorney General Abram's blessing, I then became Special Counsel to Suffolk County, with the full support of the private law firm I joined as a partner – Hill, Betts & Nash.

During the 1970s, New York State and the residents of Long Island generally welcomed the idea of a nuclear plant in eastern Long Island, which they were promised would generate almost limitless amounts of "clean energy" at law cost. By the 1980s, however, the American public in general, and the residents of Long Island in particular, had soured on nuclear power as a solution to their growing energy needs. In order to fully appreciate this dramatic shift in public opinion, however, it is necessary to understand the dual traumatic nuclear disasters of Chernobyl in 1978 and the Three Mile Island accident in 1979. These two nuclear disasters shook public confidence in the safety of nuclear power as a reliable energy source, and it laid the groundwork for the decision by Suffolk County on Long Island to retain the law firm where I was a partner – Hill, Betts & Nash - to investigate and prosecute fraud allegations relating to the construction and financing of the Shoreham Plant. But first, a summary of the Chernobyl disaster and the Three Mile Island accident is appropriate since they set the stage for the Shoreham litigation.

Shoreham Nuclear Power Plant, decommissioned after protests at the height of the No Nukes movement, Long Island, New York.
Wendy Connett / Alamy Stock Photo BHJH87.

The Chernobyl Disaster

The Chernobyl disaster was caused by a nuclear accident on April 26, 1986, at the No. 4 reactor in the Chernobyl Nuclear Power Plant, near the city of Pripyat in the north of Ukraine.[1] It was the worst nuclear disaster in history, rivaled only by the later 2011 Fukushima Daiichi nuclear disaster in Japan. The Chernobyl accident ironically started during a safety test, where there was a planned decrease of reactor power in preparation for an electrical test. However, the power unexpectedly dropped to a near-zero level. When the operators triggered a reactor shutdown, a combination of unstable conditions and reactor design flaws caused an uncontrolled nuclear chain reaction.[2] A large amount of energy was suddenly released, vaporizing superheated cooling water and rupturing the reactor core in a highly destructive steam explosion. This energy release was followed by an open-air reactor core fire that released considerable airborne radioactive contamination for about nine days.[3] Rapidly rising radiation levels in the area led to establishing a 10-kilometer (6.2 mile) radius exclusion zone. About 49,000 people were initially evacuated from the site. The exclusion zone was later increased to a 30-kilometer (19 miles) radius, leading to 68,000 more people from the wider area being evacuated. By December 1986, a protective sarcophagus was built around the reactor, reducing the spread of radioactive contamination.

The Chernobyl reactor explosion first killed two of the reactor operating staff. In the emergency response that followed, 134 station staff and firefighters were hospitalized with acute radiation syndrome after absorbing high doses of ionizing radiation. Of these, 28 died in the days to months afterward and approximately 14 suspected radiation-induced cancer deaths followed within the next ten years.[4] Estimates of the eventual total death toll from the Chernobyl incident vary widely, but there were at least 4,000 fatalities in Ukraine alone. In addition, there were most probably between 9,000 to 16,000 fatalities when assessing all of Europe, where radioactive contamination was detected in the atmosphere thousands of miles away from ground zero.[5]

After Chernobyl, U.S. officials were quick to try to reassure the American public that "it couldn't happen here," only to have to later "walk back" these reassurances by admitting that nine U.S. facilities had characteristics similar to those of that runaway Soviet plant.

The Three Mile Island Accident

On March 28, 1979, the worst accident in the history of the U.S. nuclear power industry began when a pressure valve in the Unit 2 reactor at Three Mile Island failed to close. Cooling water, contaminated with radiation, drained from the open valve into adjoining buildings, and the core began to overheat dangerously. Built-in 1974 on a sandbar on Pennsylvania's Susquehanna River, the TMI power plant was just 10 miles downstream from the state capitol in Harrisburg. A second reactor began operating in 1978.

On March 28th, as cooling water drained out of the broken pressure valve at TMI, the emergency cooling pumps automatically went into operation. If the operators had done nothing, these safety devices would have prevented any major crisis. However, human operators in the control room misread the confusing and contradictory readings and shut off the emergency water system. The reactor was shut down, but operators in the control room also shut off the emergency water system. As residual heat from the fission process was still being released, the core had heated to over 4,000 degrees, just 1,000 degrees short of a meltdown. If the core had melted down, there would be nothing to stop its downward trajectory, meaning that the core could theoretically keep melting downward until it reached the other side of the earth. Hence the term "China Syndrome." Fortunately, the TMI core did not completely melt down, although trace amounts of radioactive material were released into the atmosphere.

While no one was injured, the TMI accident – coming so soon on the heels of the Chernobyl disaster - graphically demonstrated the lack of preparedness of utility companies and power plant operators to deal with fundamental safety issues. As a result, TMI proved to be a public relations disaster that spilled over into the Shoreham debate and eventually sounded the death knell of nuclear power in this country. In addition, following TMI, there were over 34,000 other mishaps reported by the nation's nuclear utilities to the Nuclear Regulatory Commission (NRC) between 1980 and 1988. There was an increase in the number of workers contaminated with radiation. Eventually, a growing public consensus emerged that the nuclear genie released during the Manhattan Project at the end of World War II should be returned to its bottle.

The Shoreham Nuclear Power Plant Case

The Shoreham project had been in the works for at least a decade by the time I got involved with the investigations and litigation surrounding it. In 1969, LILCO – the utility serving approximately 1 million customers on Long Island – announced a plan to build an 820-megawatt nuclear power plant at Shoreham, a rural area in eastern Long Island. At first, Suffolk County and the local towns and villages were generally supportive of the project. If it would eventually provide reliable electrical power to eastern Long Island at a reasonable cost, it would give a much-needed boost to the Long Island economy and increase the tax base for the local towns. However, severe safety concerns were raised, and as the plant's costs rapidly mounted, the tide shifted, and Suffolk County became one of the project's most vocal opponents.

Over the years, the Suffolk County Legislature served as an incubator for some of Long Island's best and brightest political lights. Two county executives – John Klein and Patrick Halpin – got their start as legislators. Congressmen Thomas Downey and Robert Mrazek also used the legislature as a springboard for their political careers. In 1984, the Legislature not only withdrew its support for the near-completed Shoreham plant but actively opposed the licensing of Shoreham by the NRC, advocating the abandonment of the facility. On December 23, 1985, the County Legislature introduced a resolution, known as Local Law 2-86, making it a crime, punishable by both fine and imprisonment, for any person, without prior county approval, from conducting any "test or exercise" such as that planned by LILCO for the Shoreham plant. However, federal district court Judge Leonard Wexler enjoined Suffolk County from interfering with LILCO's planned tests, finding that it interfered with the exclusive right of the NRC and the federal government to regulate the testing of radiological hazards.[6] As it turned out, however, LILCO's drill turned into a fiasco. On September 11, 1987, the NRC staff filed a report concluding that LILCO's February 1986 drill of its emergency evacuation plan for Shoreham was so deficient that it was "fundamentally flawed."[7]

Although LILCO was permitted to go along with its testing and safety exercises, the problem of developing an effective evacuation plan in the event of a nuclear disaster at Shoreham became a virtually insurmountable hurdle for LILCO and other pro-Shoreham advocates. Most Long Islanders already knew from painful experience that, even in the best of times, trying to drive from Point A to Point B on Long Island during rush hour or on Sunday afternoon during the summer holidays was an excruciating ordeal. The Long Island Expressway has a well-deserved reputation of being "the longest parking lot in the world," so it would not be of much help if the Shoreham plant experienced a nuclear incident. Moreover, since Long Island's road network runs primarily east-west, this road system would make it impossible for Suffolk County residents living *east* of Shoreham to evacuate without first driving *towards* the plant – in other words, into the danger zone.

When a LILCO official was asked how people living to the east of the plant – or anywhere on Long Island - would evacuate in the event of an emergency, he thought for a long moment and then answered, trying to keep a straight face: "Boats and planes." Where these boats and planes would come from, he did not say. Perhaps an armada of small craft from the Connecticut side of Long Island Sound could help evacuate a few hundred people from Long Island in a Dunkirk-type operation, but that would leave a few million people still trapped on the island.

The impossibility of developing an effective evacuation plan in the event of a nuclear accident at Shoreham was later dramatically confirmed. An Avianca Flight 52 - on a regularly scheduled flight from Bogotá, Colombia to New York - crashed on January 25, 1990, in an area near Cove Neck on the north shore of Long Island, killing 40 of the 158 passengers. As the *Los Angeles Times* reported:

> The chaos at the site created by the narrow roads and conges-
> tion meant that victims did not arrive at hospitals for an hour
> following the crash at the earliest. Some rescuers were forced
> to abandon their vehicles which could not make it through the
> traffic and raced to the scene on foot.[8]

Given the chaos caused by one plane crash, LILCO had no honest answer to the question of what would happen if two or three million people living on all of Long Island suddenly had to evacuate in the event of a major disaster at Shoreham.

LILCO Seeks A Bailout from the Ratepayers for the Cost Overruns At Shoreham

In addition to safety concerns, the rising costs of the project eventually doomed Shoreham. At first, the cost of the Shoreham plant's construction was estimated by LILCO at $217 million, and commercial operation of the plant was projected for May 1975. Both of these predictions – as to cost and construction time - proved to be not just exceedingly optimistic, but downright fraudulent. As we later established at trial, LILCO offi-cials knew when they made those projections that there was no way they could complete the project in that relatively short time frame for the bar-gain-basement costs they were estimating. But they were afraid that the New York State Public Service Commission ("PSC") would not approve the "pass along" of the construction costs to the ratepayers if they candidly gave realistic cost and timetable projections. So they lied. Eventually, as the project's costs mushroomed to over $3 billion, the LILCO ratepayers found themselves paying hundreds of millions of dollars in construction costs for a nuclear power plant that seemed doomed from the start.

Initially, the costs of the Shoreham plant were not factored into the rates LILCO charged its customers. According to expert testimony at the trial in federal court in Brooklyn, the standard practice for utilities - as dictated by each state's regulatory agency that set the rates – is that the customers should only be charged for power generating plants currently producing energy. Charging ratepayers for a power plant not yet in operation was highly unusual.

Beginning in 1974, however, and notwithstanding Shoreham's incomplete status, LILCO sought rate increases based, in part, upon Shoreham's construction costs. The procedure for accomplishing a rate increase based upon Shoreham's ongoing construction costs required LILCO to file a detailed application for a rate increase with the PSC. The PSC - a commission consisting of from five to seven members appointed by the state's governor, with the advice and consent of the Senate[9] - is authorized to approve such applications to the extent they are "just and reasonable."[10] In determining whether a rate increase is justified, public hearings are held. Interested parties submit written briefs and testify under oath as to the appropriateness of the proposed rate increase. After that, an Administrative Law Judge ("ALJ") files a written opinion addressing the matter. Additional briefs may be submitted in response to the ALJ's opinion. Finally, the PSC itself renders a decision. Utilizing this process, which involved a series of false and fraudulent representations as to projected construction costs and timetable for the plant, LILCO applied for and received numerous rate increases from 1974 onward.

Suffolk County's Civil RICO Case Against LILCO

On March 3, 1987, I and other attorneys working with me at Hill, Betts & Nash filed a class action suit against LILCO and some of its former officers. The case was filed in Brooklyn federal court on behalf of Suffolk County, five individual ratepayers, and one business corporation. The proposed class consisted of LILCO ratepayers from 1974 to 1987. During the rate-making process, we claimed that the LILCO defendants repeatedly testified falsely to the PSC about Shoreham's construction status and anticipated commercial operation date, thereby causing the PSC to grant LILCO unwarranted and excessive rate increases.[11]

On May 1, 1987, we filed an amended complaint on behalf of Suffolk County and other LICO ratepayers. We were asserting that the conduct of the LILCO defendants violated the federal Racketeer Influenced and Corrupt Organizations Act ("RICO"),[12] as well as New York State common law, under theories of implied contract and unjust enrichment.

The PSC proceeding that we primarily focused on was the so-called PSC "Prudence Proceeding" ordered by the PSC in 1978. The Prudence Proceeding was a part of a PSC investigation to determine why the Shoreham plant had such exorbitant cost overruns and delays. The PSC hearings were also a means for the PSC to decide if all or part of the high construction costs were attributable to mismanagement on the part of LILCO, such that these costs should not be passed along to the Long Island ratepayers. During that investigation, the PSC demanded that LILCO turn over documents that would shed light on the internal decision-making process at Shoreham, thereby aiding the Commission in reaching a decision.

During our investigation, we contacted a former Shoreham manager who had worked for the engineering company Stone & Webster Engineering Corp. The Shoreham manager – John Daly - provided us with a wealth of information, including the fact that LILCO, in order to impede the PSC investigation and proceedings, literally loaded thousands of documents onto a truck in a deliberately haphazard fashion and dumped this mountain of documents on the PSC staff. LILCO's hope was that this huge "document dump" would prevent or delay the discovery of the few relevant documents, strategically distributed throughout this paper morass like needles in a haystack. John Daly told us (and later testified), that his boss, William Museler - the Shoreham assistant project engineer who was later named a LILCO vice president – directed him to inundate the PSC with written material and to do so in a way that would make the discovery of pertinent information as difficult as possible. Daly also testified at trial that Museler told him to produce only those Shoreham schedules "that looked real good" to be passed on to the PSC, and to "deep six" the actual plans that would make LILCO look bad.[13]

Gordon Dick was another whistleblower who lost his job when he refused to go along with the fraudulent scheme concocted by LILCO and Stone & Webster to mislead the PSC into agreeing to pass on millions of dollars in costs onto the ratepayers during construction. He had grown up in Scotland and had extensive experience as a manager in the nuclear industry. At Shoreham, Dick worked as a special assistant to LILCO Vice-President Andrew Wofford. From the start, Wofford made it clear to Dick that his study of Shoreham construction management practices and schedules should not reach any conclusions that would be harmful to LILCO's defense against allegations that the project had been mismanaged.

Despite this warning, Dick completed an interim report in January 1980 on the Reactor Core Isolation Cooling System, which became known as the RCIC report. He concluded that there were severe deficiencies in Shoreham's engineering and construction management and that these deficiencies affected the completion schedules. Alarmed, LILCO immediately moved to suppress the RCIC report and ordered Dick to distribute only four copies. Shortly after that, J.P. Novarro, LILCO project manager, advised Dick not to issue a final report on his findings and then reassigned him to other duties.

Dick further told us that Robert Wiesel, a Stone & Webster structural engineer assigned to conduct critical component tests to be reported to the NRC, was ordered in about April 1983 to falsify a Shoreham safety document. These documents dealt with the severity of vibrations that the nuclear plant could withstand from any seismic activity, such as an earthquake. The altered Wiesel Report was filed with the NRC and, shortly after that, LILCO received its low-level power license from the NRC.

However, despite weeks of searching, we could not find a copy of the altered Wiesel Report submitted to the NRC after the negative test information had been deleted. We searched all of the documents produced by LILCO and Stone & Webster as part of the "discovery" materials they produced in response to our document demands. We then resorted to the rather cumbersome technique of finding the Wiesel Report by using the Freedom of Information Act (FOIA), which gives citizens the right to petition a government agency for information that has not been made public. The procedure is a simple one, though it does not always produce the desired result.

We finally received a copy of the Wiesel Report from the NRC after conducting a FOIL search of their records in response to our request. As expected, this final report by Wiesel's team appeared to give LILCO a clean bill of health on the seismic adequacy of the components. But we couldn't be sure that there wasn't a draft report with damning language in it. So we renewed our detailed document demands to Stone & Webster and LILCO for all drafts of the Wiesel Report. Lo and behold, within the thousands of relatively worthless documents produced by Stone & Webster, there was the draft report! The draft Wiesel Report included the deleted portion of the "conclusion" section critical of Shoreham's ability to withstand an earthquake. The final document was thus whitewashed to falsely suggest that the plant was fully capable of withstanding an earthquake without being damaged.

Greg Minor, a California-based nuclear engineer, testified for Suffolk County at trial as an expert witness. After reviewing the draft and final versions of the Wiesel Report, he concluded that the final report had materially altered Wiesel's findings, which was that half of every piece of equipment and component he looked at had a problem. Instead of providing the NRC with an accurate negative assessment, the final document submitted to the NRC mischaracterized the problems as insignificant.

Another "smoking gun" document that we found was one of LILCO's internal documents that had been haphazardly loaded on a truck and dumped on the PSC. One of the documents that eventually surfaced was a LILCO memorandum dated December 4, 1975, from A.T. Jorgenson, a LILCO senior vice president, to J.J. Tuohy, chairman of the board. This two-page document outlined a plan to give the PSC some optimistic cost data and completion dates since "it is quite easy to slip a construction date one year following the issuance of construction license." We now had a document in which a senior vice-president appeared to be telling the LILCO chairman of the board that they should lie to state and federal regulators and get away with it by "slipping" the date. The utility got the approval.

As we further dug into the mountain of LILCO documents, my office began to resemble an archaeological dig, with piles of papers covering almost every square inch of floor space. But after weeks of work, the outlines of intentional fraud by LILCO on the regulators started coming more clearly into focus. Time after time, it appeared that LILCO and its engineer, Stone & Webster, were telling each other internally that they were anywhere from a few months to two years behind the announced schedule, and making up that lost time was impossible. And yet, LILCO executives continued telling the PSC that the company could keep its previously announced schedules until, inevitably, at the last minute, they would have to admit they were not yet done and that the schedule had to be reset. If the PSC had known the truth, it would have either denied LILCO its requests to pass the plant costs onto the ratepayers or, at the very least, have ordered that those "pass-alongs" should be spread out over a more extended time period.

The Federal Prosecutors Try to Jump On the Anti-Shoreham Bandwagon

It eventually became publicly known that two high-level whistleblowers – Gordon Dick and John Daly – were cooperating with our investigation. Shortly after that, we received requests from Rudolph Giuliani, the U.S. Attorney for the Southern District of New York, and Andrew Maloney, the U.S. Attorney for the Eastern District of New York covering Brooklyn, Queens and Long Island, to speak with these two key witnesses. For advice on how to proceed, I recommended that Dick and Daly retain separate counsel, and I recommended that they retain Jim Harmon, a former Brooklyn Strike Force prosecutor with whom I had closely worked. Upon analyzing the case, Harmon quickly filed a claim by Dick and Daly under the False Claims Act, a statute enacted during the Civil War to encourage citizens to blow the whistle on contractors defrauding the government by awarding them a "bounty" if the wrongdoing was proven in court. Harmon sought payment from LILCO to both Dick and Daly for the "wrongdoings" they had disclosed, which were alleged in Suffolk County's RICO complaint. Upon review by the U.S. Attorney for the Eastern District of New York, Andrew Maloney's office decided to permit Harmon to civilly prosecute LILCO and Stone & Webster under the False Claims Act on behalf of the government for falsification of safety documents.

Meanwhile, a turf war and power struggle had broken out between these two U.S. Attorneys' Offices. The FBI sided with the U.S. Attorney's Office for the Eastern District of New York, declining to assign agents to Rudy Giuliani's Shoreham investigation because this was a Long Island matter. It correctly concluded that the case belonged in the Eastern

District.[14] However, no federal criminal charges were brought against LILCO or its executives despite a lengthy federal investigation. The absence of criminal charges left it entirely to Suffolk County and my firm's legal team to fight on alone on behalf of the ratepayers.

A Few Words About RICO

The federal court complaint and the amended complaints we eventually filed against LILCO and some of its executives were brought under the civil RICO statute.[15] The criminal RICO statute passed by Congress in 1970 was primarily designed as a means of prosecuting individuals involved in organized crime. In fact, as a prosecutor with the Brooklyn Strike Force, I had successfully used the criminal provisions of RICO against government officials accused of various white-collar crimes.

While the criminal provisions of RICO were only available to federal prosecutors, Congress had wisely included civil RICO provisions in the statute. The civil provisions permitted private parties, as well as state and local governments, to recover money damages from those who engaged in extortion or fraudulent schemes that rose to the level of a "pattern of racketeering activity."[16] Recognizing that government prosecutors, with their limited staff and budgets, could not alone stem the rising tide of white-collar crime, the civil provisions of the RICO law were designed to encourage private parties to supplement government efforts. The statute permitted fraud victims to sue for three times the amount of the damages they had suffered due to fraudulent schemes and to recover their attorneys' fees, if successful.

Since I was among the first federal prosecutors to successfully use the RICO statute in criminal prosecutions, I had been asked by a Congressional Committee and my superiors within the U.S. Department of Justice to testify more than once about the statute. These hearings were often called by pro-business Congressmen who were concerned that the Justice Department was overusing this powerful law enforcement tool against companies that broke the law, rather than just organized crime. However, each time that Congress considered narrowing the statute's scope, it ended up leaving it fully intact or expanding its scope to make it even more powerful. At these hearings, I had the opportunity to meet and work with G.

Robert Blakey, a professor at Notre Dame Law School, who is generally considered the "father" and original draftsperson of the RICO statute.

The private enforcement provisions of the civil RICO statute were modeled after those outlined in the antitrust laws, which resulted in the vast majority (more than 84 percent) of treble damage antitrust enforcement actions being brought in federal courts by private parties rather than by the federal government. We successfully argued before Congress that to deprive consumers of an opportunity to recover considerable damages for patterns of fraud under the RICO statute, while permitting businesses to sue for treble damages under the antitrust laws, would be patently unjust. Without the incentive of treble damages, the federal courthouse door would be effectively barred to all but the wealthiest consumers – precisely those who needed help the least. We argued that eliminating the treble damage provision would create a loophole for wrongdoers who had received billions of dollars of fraudulently stolen money. The civil provisions of the RICO statute were used successfully as a follow-up to criminal prosecutions so that injured parties could collect money damages from those who had engaged in corrupt practices.

Even though the utility industry and most other significant corporations bitterly objected to being labeled as "racketeers" when civil RICO suits were filed against them, they were not reluctant to use this controversial statute when it served their purposes. For example, in February 1988, LILCO filed a civil RICO suit against General Electric Company, accusing it of selling LILCO an inadequately tested and unsafe design for the containment system, a critical safety system in the Shoreham plant. In this action, LILCO accused GE of fraud, breach of contract, and intentional malicious behavior related to the alleged concealment of flaws in the Mark II containment system LILCO purchased for the Shoreham plan.

The RICO Conspiracy By LILCO and Stone & Webster

Our RICO complaint charged LILCO with conspiring with its executives and Stone & Webster to deceive the PSC and the public. For each of the PSC rate proceedings that included requested rate charges for Shoreham's construction, we carefully assembled documents showing that LILCO's officers told the PSC one thing while at the same time knowing they were lying. They would never be able to complete the project for the relatively small additional sums they were projecting. They also knew that there was no way to complete the project within the time they were telling the PSC it would take.

LILCO was very successful in its fraudulent scheme to deceive the PSC and the public since about 30 cents of every dollar that the ratepayers were being charged was attributable to the construction costs of the Shoreham plant. Over 14 years, an estimated $2.9 billion in increased rates were passed on to LILCO's ratepayers due to these fraudulent representations to the PSC. If our case succeeded at trial, the damages would be tripled under the civil RICO statute, for a total award of $8.7 billion.

The Shoreham case was assigned to the legendary Judge Jack B. Weinstein, who had been appointed United States District Court judge for the Eastern District of New York by President Lyndon B. Johnson in 1967 and served as chief judge in that court from 1980 to 1988. Judge Weinstein and I knew each other well since I had tried my first jury trial before him eleven years earlier when I was a fledgling federal prosecutor with the Brooklyn Strike Force. I also had several other trials before Judge Weinstein, but at least for me, the first one was the most memorable.

Judge Weinstein made it a practice of never raising his voice in his courtroom, but he never needed to. At six feet two inches tall and in excellent physical condition due, in part, to his practice of playing a vigorous game of squash several times a week, the 67-year old jurist was always in unquestioned control of the proceedings. He had a no-nonsense and often stern demeanor, often leavened by his quick wit and flashing smile.

During trials, Judge Weinstein also knew how to move his cases along. He prodded lawyers from both sides to streamline their cases, and he even cautioned witnesses who were not answering pointed questions put to them. At one point in the LILCO trial, when a junior LILCO lawyer asked a witness a seemingly endless series of questions on his professional background, the judge interjected: "Ask him the question [relevant to the case] and get him off the stand."[17] The witness was off the stand within minutes. When LILCO lead attorney Michael Lesch tried to get some complex charts into evidence, and Weinstein sustained our objection to them, Lesch attempted to get the judge to change his mind by commenting, "This next one is particularly fascinating to me." "Not to me," Weinstein retorted. "Life is too short."[18]

Often getting to work at the courthouse before sunrise, Judge Weinstein maintained a pace that would quickly break lesser mortals. In addition to his full-time court schedule, he taught at Columbia University Law School one afternoon a week. He authored several major legal works, including the authoritative *Weinstein's Federal Evidence*.[19]

Judge Weinstein, who was already in his sixties when we tried the Shoreham case, continued his distinguished judicial career for several more decades, which spanned an incredible 53 years. He assumed senior status as a judge on March 1, 1993, but maintained a full docket of cases until he retired on February 10, 2020, at the age of 98. But let's not get too far ahead of ourselves. Back to the late 1980s and the Shoreham RICO case.

Although the rest of the Suffolk County litigation team and I were anxious to get our civil RICO case to trial before a jury, LILCO tried to throw every conceivable roadblock in our way to prevent or at least delay a trial. It must have known it would be facing a legal blizzard of incriminating evidence at trial, as well as a possible jury award that would bankrupt the company. As a part of its defense strategy, LILCO tried to lay off some of the blame for the delays in completing the plant by filing a civil RICO action against GE, as previously discussed. LILCO also moved to dismiss Suffolk County's civil RICO suit, but Judge Weinstein refused to do so in a written opinion he handed down in early March 1988. A trial date was set for September 26, 1988. In comments from the bench, Judge Weinstein cryptically expressed the view that the case looked to be either "a relatively simple documentary case" or "nothing."[20]

But our civil RICO trial did not go forward as a class action, as we had expected. We had hoped that Judge Weinstein would let our named plaintiffs represent the interests of the tens of thousands of other LILCO ratepayers whose utility rates had been fraudulently increased through LILCO's misrepresentations to the PSC. However, Judge Weinstein had other ideas. Before the RICO trial began, on September 6, 1988, Judge Weinstein denied our motion for class certification on the ground that Suffolk County and the other named plaintiffs were not proper class representatives.[21] Suffolk County was, by far, the largest LILCO ratepayer with governmental interests that were a far cry from the concerns of typical ratepaying families, who were primarily concerned that the lights worked and that the electric rates were reasonable. On the other hand, Suffolk County was also concerned about safety issues and a host of other political and governmental issues.

Even though Judge Weinstein did not permit Suffolk County from representing the interests of all LILCO ratepayers, he allowed the County and the other plaintiffs to continue to prosecute the action in their individual capacities, with Suffolk County's RICO case serving as a first "test case" against LILCO to be tried before a jury. The ruling meant that other lawyers from the law firm and I would be serving as lead counsel since we represented LILCO's largest ratepayer: Suffolk County.

On September 19, 1988, to simplify and expedite the upcoming trial, Judge Weinstein dismissed Suffolk County's state law claims without prejudice. He made it clear that he only wanted to try the civil RICO claims, and he also severed the trial of Suffolk's RICO claims from the prosecution of the RICO claims of the other plaintiffs. Four days later, on behalf of Suffolk County, we settled the claims against Stone & Webster. The settlement meant that the entire trial would be focused on LILCO and its racketeering acts that fraudulently convinced the PSC to let it pass on hundreds of millions of dollars to Suffolk County and the other LILCO ratepayers.

Judge Weinstein's decision to have Suffolk County go to trial against LILCO on its RICO charges without first certifying a trial on behalf of the entire class of ratepayers seemed to be following the same play book he had used before. In the case brought by Vietnam War veterans for damages they had suffered resulting from exposure to the defoliant Agent Orange, Judge Weinstein had directed that certain veterans try their case individually. Then, when the verdict came down in their favor, he approved certification for the entire class. This meant that every veteran who suffered damages from exposure to Agent Orange could receive compensation by filing a claim against a $180 million common fund created as part of the settlement.[22]

LILCO Takes Its Motion For a Delay of the Trial Up to the Circuit Court

Just as we were about to start jury selection, LILCO threw us a curve ball by filing a motion for a stay of the district court proceedings before Judge Weinstein until the PSC had an opportunity to decide whether

LILCO officials had lied to the commissioners. When Judge Weinstein immediately denied their motion, LILCO filed an emergency appeal to the Second Circuit Court of Appeals. On September 27, 1988, both sides appeared before a three-judge panel of the Second Circuit to argue the case. Located on the seventeenth floor of the Federal Building at Foley Square in lower Manhattan, the massive, wood-paneled courtroom of the Second Circuit quickly filled with dozens of lawyers, law clerks, and press representatives as word of the oral argument spread.

As soon as Michael Lesch of the Shea & Gould law firm stood up at the podium to argue LILCO's case, the judges let him know from their high bench overlooking the courtroom that he was not going to have an easy time of it. Arguing that the PSC should decide whether the commission had been lied to and whether such lies had led to higher rates, Lesch tried to persuade the judges that the PSC "has the principal expertise in the area."[23]

Lesch was immediately interrupted by Judge Robert J. Miner. "The district court can direct the PSC to hear this?" he asked with a skeptical tone. "Suppose the Public Service Commission does not want to hear the case? How do we get the [PSC] to take this," he asked.[24] Lesch replied that if the PSC refused to rule on those issues, "then the stay is lifted." The three judges still appeared to remain troubled.

"Why does someone have to have special expertise to determine if someone committed fraud?" Judge Miner inquired. Lesch replied that ratemaking involves complex financial calculations, adding that the case could adversely affect LILCO's financial rating. At this point, Judge James L. Oakes interjected, asking rhetorically if the court should "make a decision on the law based on what some rating agency thinks?" The tone of his voice indicated that he strongly disagreed with the idea that any decision by a Wall Street rating service should impact the decision as to whether LILCO should be required to go to trial or not.

Judge Frank X. Altimari, a second judge on the panel, made it clear that he shared the same opinion as to the merits of the appeal by stating that the delay if granted, would "go on and on" and the trial "would be suspended without end." Finally, Judge Oakes announced, "We've had it. We're going to deny [LILCO's] motion."

The Trial Finally Gets Underway

The LILCO-Suffolk trial on Suffolk's RICO claims finally got underway before Judge Weinstein and a jury on October 3, 1988. There were six jurors and six alternates drawn from Brooklyn, Queens, and Staten Island. Jurors from Nassau and Suffolk Counties were excluded since they were part of the LILCO service area and would, therefore, be LILCO ratepayers. Judge Weinstein rejected LILCO's insistence that all the jurors be college-educated or mathematically trained, accepting our argument that all that was required for service on this jury was reasonable intelligence and enough basic common sense to evaluate a fraud case such as this one. We ended up with jurors who had at least a high school diploma and several who had at least one or two years of college.

Before making my opening statement, I tried to convince myself to relax, not to worry, that this was just another trial. After all, it was just a civil case where the plaintiff's side had a lesser burden of proof than in a criminal case, where guilt has to be proven beyond a reasonable doubt.

But there was no denying that this was the most significant case of my career to date. In important prior cases, the only client I had was somewhat impersonal – either the U.S. government or the State of New York. Here, I was technically representing only one government entity, Suffolk County, but in a very real sense, I also represented the interests of the 500,000 residents and utility ratepayers of Suffolk County, including family members and friends who had been suffering from skyrocketing electric costs as a direct result of the Shoreham fiasco. I did not want to let them down. I knew that, while Suffolk County was only one of many ratepayers, this would be the decisive test case on the Shoreham issue for not only all of Suffolk County's residents but also the half-million ratepayers of neighboring Nassau County. In other words, a lot was on the line, both for LILCO and for Suffolk County. We had been preparing the case for over a year, and now we had to prove it.

Although understandably nervous, I felt we were as prepared for trial as we could be. The documentary evidence and witnesses we had lined up presented – in my view at least – an overwhelming case of fraud and misrepresentations by LILCO and its executives. But there is no such thing as "a sure thing" when it comes to a trial. There is always an element of chance and uncertainty surrounding a jury trial, and the outcome can never be predicted with any high degree of certainty. Sometimes the best witness comes across as far less persuasive than expected, either because of their inability to articulate well or because some personality quirk or manner of speech tends to cause the jury to discount all or part of the witnesses' testimony. Sometimes a lawyer who has won hundreds of cases and has a top-notch reputation ends up pursuing the wrong strategy. They might aggressively cross-examine a witness who would have been better left alone or concentrate on a small aspect of the case while losing sight of the overall picture.

Even though this case was pretty complex, having to do with the construction and financing of a multi-billion dollar nuclear power plant, I viewed my most important task to allay the juror's fears that this case might be too technical or complicated for them. I had to convince them that they did not need a degree in engineering or finance to reach a proper verdict in the case. In truth, the heart of the case was nothing more than a simple, straightforward matter of conspiracy and fraud. I had to make sure that the jurors understood that.

Both sides were allowed to make an Opening Statement to the jury, which was our chance to speak directly to the jury and to lay out our case as clearly and succinctly as possible. As the plaintiffs' attorney, I went first. "Now, this case is a relatively simple one," I told the jury. "It's about an electric company, LILCO, that did not tell the truth. It's about corporate officers and executives who schemed together to deceive and defraud ratepayers to get rate increases they did not deserve." I further told them: "This scheme was successful. It was successful to the tune of over three billion dollars. Every penny of those three billion dollars came from the pockets of Long Island ratepayers."

An opening statement is like a roadmap or a preview of the evidence to come. I told the jury how Suffolk County and the other ratepayers had been wronged, how LILCO, when faced with massive delays in the construction of Shoreham, had misrepresented to the state regulatory agency about the total cost and projected completion date of the project. As a result of these misrepresentations, LILCO had received considerable rate increases time and time again, eventually totaling $3 billion of the $8 billion in construction costs:

> "Now, the Shoreham nuclear power plant. . . was supposed to
> be in operation by 1973. It was supposed to cost, as originally

scheduled, $77 million. But the plant was not completed in 1973. It was not completed in 1974. In fact, it was not completed until approximately 1985, twelve years later. During that period of time, the cost of construction skyrocketed from the original $77 million to over eight billion dollars today."

I also had to get across to the jury the essence of the fraud that we were alleging in as simple terms as possible:

"Now, when someone tells you one thing and knows another, that person lies to you. When you rely on what that person tells you, you have been deceived, and if that person takes money from you as a result of that deception, you're entitled to that money back and, that – ladies and gentlemen – is what the evidence, in this case, will show. That's exactly what happened.

I continued:

"LILCO went to the Public Service Commission and time after time, saying, 'we need just a little more time. Just give us a little more money. The plant is almost done. Shoreham is almost completed.' But these executives knew something quite different."

After I had completed my opening statement, Michael Lesch, the lead defense lawyer for LILCO, had his chance to speak on behalf of the defendants. He blamed the delays in the construction of the plant on the weather, the need to comply with the stringent requirements issued by the NRC for nuclear plants, and Suffolk County's opposition to the licensing of the plant. He suggested that our entire RICO lawsuit was part of a vendetta staged by Suffolk County in its continuing effort to close the Shoreham plant. He argued that even if LILCO's officials had lied and misrepresented the facts to the PSC about the cost of the plant and the projected completion date, this was irrelevant since the PSC – in LILCO's view – would have given it the money anyway by letting them pass the costs onto the ratepayers.

After we finished our Opening Statement, it was time now for the most critical part of the trial to begin, when the plaintiff's side introduces its most important documents as exhibits and puts its witnesses on the stand. Both sides had already agreed to most of the exhibits to be introduced. With Judge Weinstein's permission, we gave each jury a binder with the plaintiff's exhibits in them so that each juror could follow along as the witnesses discussed each document. We also had portions of the papers blown up and mounted on charts that we showed to the jury as each witness was testifying. Technology had not yet developed to the point in the late 1980s when each juror could have a video monitor to view documents and photographs introduced as exhibits. However, we could still present the evidence in a format that generally kept the juror's interest and kept them engaged in the process.

As for our charts, my practice while a government prosecutor was only to use very simple charts - nothing fancy. I only used charts that were essentially large white sheets of cardboard with large black lettering. Companies such as LILCO with large trial budgets often have a team of lawyers and assistants in the courtroom, using multi-colored and coordinated charts of aqua greens, lavenders, and hot pinks. I did not object. As LILCO's lawyers tried to dazzle the jurors with expensive charts and graphs, I counted on the fact that the jurors would start seeing me and my client – Suffolk County – as the David pitted against the corporate Goliath.

As the trial progressed, the evidence showed that LILCO was misrepresenting its actual cost and time projections, and shoddy construction practices on the site raised severe safety issues. There were well-founded rumors among the workers at the site that if the Shoreham plant ever actually went into operation, they were planning to move themselves and their families away from Long Island. They feared that there would be a major nuclear incident at the plant. For example, in the fall of 1979, a quality control supervisor was shocked to see that a work crew was grinding down a safety system pipe to remove defects. He later reported that they had the pipe up on sawhorses, grinding away as if it were a regular mom-and-pop shop, not a nuclear power plant. The piping appeared to be filled with voids, or subsurface cavities, which could lead to the pipe's failure and a serious accident if the plant ever went operational. When the supervisor called a halt to the practice, more than 500 feet of pipe had already been welded into place. He recommended that the pipe be removed and returned to the manufacturer, but Stone & Webster decided to leave the defective pipe in place. They wanted to show some construction progress, even though they knew they would probably be told to rip out the piping after some future inspection.

The pattern of shoddy construction continued month after month, during the entire construction period, according to our witnesses. It was a perpetual work project no one wanted to see end. Thousands of workers, contractors, and supervisors working on the project relied on these well-paid jobs for years and were looking forward to having the project continue indefinitely.

Our evidence showed that even the basic design of the plant had been flawed. Although this was LILCO's first venture into nuclear engineering, LILCO decided to use a reactor size for Shoreham three times larger than any nuclear reactor previously constructed. Moreover, LILCO settled on a GE reactor type – the Mark II – that had never been built before. The Mark I reactor was designed with a water pool at the bottom and a volume of air around the reactor, which was supposed to relieve steam pressure in an accident. The Mark II design had a larger volume of air and water, which, in theory, permitted the builder to save costs by using poured concrete for the containment walls. In actuality, however, it was discovered that the forces on the water pool would be greater – not smaller – in the event of an accident, much like a large drum sends out more sound waves than a smaller one. This one design problem alone cost tens of millions of dollars to redesign and reinforce the containment and reactor walls, known as "retrofitting," and over one year of delay.

One of our key witnesses at trial was Rosemary Pooler, a PSC commissioner from 1981 to 1986, and before that, she had served as a city council member in Syracuse, New York. She had also been the executive director and chair of the New York State Consumer Protection Board. After the trial was long finished, she was appointed by President Bill Clinton as a United States Circuit Judge of the U.S. Court of Appeals for the Second Circuit.

After reviewing the evidence we had amassed, Commissioner Pooler became convinced that LILCO had hoodwinked the PSC into authorizing the pass-throughs of Shoreham's construction costs to the LILCO ratepayers. Before testifying at trial, Pooler had a powerful and effective interview with reporter Mike Taibbi of CBS. She explained how the PSC worked and how the entire regulatory system breaks down if a utility gives false data and information to it, as with LILCO. During this televised interview, Pooler stated that the PSC had "granted [LILCO] rate increases based on what we thought was the best available information at the time we were required to make the decision. . . .We relied on LILCO to tell us what they knew." She further explained that the PSC counted on LILCO officials to tell the truth. Mike Taibbi asked, "And, did they?" Pooler answered, "Well, it appears now that they did not." She further stated that she believed that she and the other PSC commissioners were lied to and that this was "an unforgivable sin in our system of government."

Ann Mead, a PSC commissioner during the 1977-1978 rate proceedings, also testified at trial. She strongly disagreed with LILCO President Uhl's testimony regarding the unimportance of Shoreham's completion date. Mead further testified that if the commission had known the actual target dates for Shoreham's completion, it "may well have canceled" the rate increases.[25] Mead further testified that the Commission did not have the information about a delay in the construction schedule when it granted LILCO a Shoreham-related rate increase of $130.2 million. She testified under oath that it was not until about 1980 that the Commission and its staff began to suspect that "because of all their [LILCO's] problems, they'd been withholding information" about Shoreham.

Karen Burstein, another former PSC commissioner who served as the Chairman of the New York State Consumer Protection Board, also testified that if LILCO was lying about Shoreham's construction schedule, the PSC would not have granted the rate hikes.[26] Burstein explained that the construction schedules were vital in determining rate increases and that "the Public Service Commission relies on the integrity of people coming before it." She expressed the opinion: "I don't think the truth was spoken by LILCO, and I think the people got cheated."[27]

The trial was not without its lighter moments. When LILCO's lead attorney, Mike Lesch, was cross-examining Gregory Palast, Suffolk County's lead investigator, Lesch kept hammering on what became known as the "Palast and the dog issue." Lesch tried to show that Palast could never admit a mistake. At a PSC proceeding in January 1981, Palast added numbers while on the stand and made an error in his calculations. When the error was brought to his attention, Palast said the problem resulted from unfamiliarity with his new calculator. "My other calculator," he explained, "was demolished by my Irish Setter." Lesch tried to turn this statement into something akin to the age-old excuse: "The dog ate my homework." During their back-and-forth, Palast continued to stick to his story that while his dog was not to be "blamed," the simple fact was that the dog had, in fact, chewed his calculator. When some of the jury members started to snicker, Judge Weinstein directed Lesch to "move on."

The Jury Takes a Field Trip

The daily routine of the two-month trial was somewhat broken up when Judge Weinstein decided that the six jurors and the remaining four alternates (two had already been excused) should tour the Shoreham facility. On Wednesday, November 2, 1988, the jurors were bused to the plant under the watchful eye of U.S. marshals.

I was concerned that LILCO officials would use the tour as a public relations gimmick to unfairly ingratiate themselves with the jury, and my fears proved to be well-grounded. Although Judge Weinstein had explicitly directed that the expert representatives from each side, who would act as "tour guides" for the jurors, should not be witnesses in the case, LILCO insisted on William Museler, one of their chief witnesses. LILCO claimed he was the only one available with sufficient knowledge about the plant.

Donning hard hats, the jurors, Judge Weinstein, and the lawyers from both sides made their way around the secondary containment building for nearly two hours, with the experts pointing out the appropriate points of interest. At one point where the group was virtually surrounded by twenty-two-inch diameter pipes looking much like metallic spaghetti, Museler stressed that the area "was actually constructed and ripped out twice" because of changes in federal rules.[28] The third time it was built was "finally the way you see it today," Museler said. His statements were dutifully taken down by the court reporter, Eileen Himmer, who took notes on her stenographic machine as the group wound its way through the labyrinth of pipes. For our side, Dale Bridenbaugh of MHB Associates was present. He pointed out to the jurors the massive emergency diesel engines that were the subject of much of the testimony during the trial.

At first, we wondered why Judge Weinstein was making a special point to the jury that the nameplates on the engines indicated that they were manufactured outside New York State. Then we remembered that one of the elements of the RICO statute we were required to prove was that the fraud affected interstate commerce. The purchase of equipment from another state was enough to prove this element.

Always ready with an observation that would put matters in perspective, Judge Weinstein remarked during the Shoreham tour that he was "in the Pacific at the dawn of the nuclear age." He was alluding to his wartime submarine service at the time of the atomic bombing of Hiroshima and Nagasaki, and "now he may be present at its end," referring to the problems of the nuclear power industry as exemplified by Shoreham.

LILCO's Shareholders Approve a Settlement With the State

On November 4, the same day that former LILCO president Wilfred Uhl began his trial testimony, LILCO shareholders voted overwhelmingly to approve a Shoreham settlement with New York State. The settlement would lead to the plant closing in return for ten years of rate increases.[29] However, for the deal to go into effect, approval was needed from the New York State Legislature before the Shoreham plant could be turned over to the New York Power Authority for $1, which would then close and decommission it.[30]

Stockholders, like ratepayers, paid a hefty price because of the delays in the completion and licensing of Shoreham. Common shareholders had foregone about $1 billion in dividends, and preferred shareholders had not received $350 million in dividend payments. Many LILCO shareholders had bought LILCO stock years before, thinking that it was a conservative investment they could rely on in their old age.[31] Shoreham changed all that. They had seen their dividends stop and their stock values plummet. A palpable air of resignation and inevitability about the demise of Shoreham and a state takeover of LILCO pervaded the shareholders' meeting. The greatest excitement came when the Nassau County Bomb Squad was called in to investigate a briefcase left in the window well of a building nearby where the shareholders' meeting was taking place.[32] Only the tattered remains of underwear and a newspaper were found when a remote-controlled robot blew it up.

Closing Arguments At Trial and the Jury Verdict

After both sides finished submitting their evidence, Michael Lesch, the lead attorney for LILCO, and I gave our closing arguments. I went first, basically expanding on earlier remarks in my Opening Statement. With the aid of charts and blow-ups of the evidence, I showed that we had proved our case that LILCO had intentionally misrepresented the actual status of the construction at the plant to get the PSC to pass on billions of dollars in construction costs to the ratepayers. I needed to be both brief and thorough, which was not an easy task given the vast extent of the trial testimony and documentary evidence submitted. My central theme was that LILCO had done "whatever was necessary" to accomplish its goal of getting $3 billion in construction costs passed onto the ratepayers. To achieve this, LILCO had engaged in a decade-long pattern of outright lies and misrepresentations. I argued that there had been a "conspiracy at the highest levels of LILCO management to deceive the PSC by giving them outdated and stale schedules" regarding the completion of the Shoreham plant. "There was a method to their madness," I suggested to the jurors. "The older the schedule, the more outdated the figures, the more likely LILCO would walk away with its special rate increases."

I suggested to the jury that LILCO had engaged in two types of lies. There were "pure and simple" lies, and "lies of silence." Silence meant LILCO had an obligation to tell the truth, but opted not to say a word. "They just took the money and ran," I said.

As for LILCO's defense, which was mainly based on its attempt to shift the blame to Stone & Webster, I compared LILCO to a well-known New York baseball team – the Yankees – that had recently been down on its luck. "It's like George Steinbrenner firing Billy Martin because the Yankees are losing ball games," I argued. After I had completed my portion of the summation, my partner Bernard (Bernie) Persky gave a short but thorough summary of the diesel generator portion of our case. Then Greg O'Neill gave a highly effective refutation of LILCO's defense case.

Mike Lesch's Closing Statement on behalf of the LILCO defendants went on for over six hours. While he did a good job summarizing LILCO's defenses, I wondered whether he was testing the jury's patience by going over every minute detail of the voluminous evidence. He argued that "this is a political case" as "the latest chapter in Suffolk County's continuing battle to prevent Shoreham from opening."[33]

I could have objected when Lesch reached the six-hour point in his summation, and Judge Weinstein would have undoubtedly quickly shut him down. But I knew that Lesch had not yet gotten to making a point that I thought was LILCO's Achilles heel: its intense obsession with

Greg Palast. In his Opening Statement, Lesch had already suggested to the jury that Palast was at the center of a conspiracy by Suffolk County to destroy LILCO, and Lesch's intense cross-examination of Palast unsuccessfully, in my opinion, tried to prove that point. At the end of his summation to the jury, Lesch did not disappoint; he finally got around to Palast in his closing salvo.

"Suffolk County's entire case ultimately rests on the shoulders of Mr. Palast," Lesch told the jury. "He's the guy who sold the case to Suffolk County, and he's the guy who's trying to sell it to you." Lesch then launched into a deeply personal attack on Palast for several more minutes. As we expected and, indeed, hoped, he became quite emotional, calling Palast both a liar and a cheat, and characterizing Suffolk's case as "an evil case brought by evil men."

And Lesch could not resist the temptation to return to the question of Palast's dog, saying, "He'll blame anyone, even his dog." Lesch vehemently exhorted the jury: "You, ladies and gentlemen, have the power to force Palast to recognize that he has made some serious mistakes in this case. You can show him by your verdict that you see through his deceit and trickery, that you recognize that he's dead wrong." By so personalizing LILCO's defense arguments, I hoped that the jurors would see what I saw, which is that LILCO's defense team's extreme focus on Palast was nothing more than a transparent attempt to deflect attention from its own culpability.

After 42-days of trial and two days of summations, Judge Weinstein "charged" the jurors on December 1, 1988, by instructing them on the law that governed their deliberations. After a relatively short 16 ½-hours of deliberations over two days, the jury returned a verdict on December 5, 1988, finding that LILCO and its former president, Wilfred Uhl, had committed fraud in three PSC proceedings.[34] In rendering its verdict, the jury had to answer 72 written "special interrogatories." The jury assessed Suffolk County's damages against LILCO and Uhl at $7,647,243 (approximately $ 22.9 million after trebling under the RICO statute). When extrapolated to encompass the fraudulent overcharges on all of LILCO's ratepayers, this jury verdict was estimated to be $4.3 billion, which was more than the entire company was worth.

The jury verdict sent shock waves through the Wall Street financial markets. The New York Post headline summed up the consensus on the impact of the jury verdict: *"Huge Fraud Verdict May K.O. LILCO."*[35] New York State and LILCO had already been struggling to reach a settlement throughout the months that the trial was ongoing, and during the week before the verdict, state legislators had failed to approve a proposed settlement.[36] But the jury verdict may have been the final nail in the coffin. Upon hearing the news of the verdict, one investment banker was quoted as having reacted in shock. "Oh, my God," he groaned. "This [jury verdict] throws the whole deal into a cocked hat."[37]

The Bench Trial

During the jury trial, Judge Weinstein had *sua sponte* (on its own volition) severed one of LILCO's defenses for a "bench" trial (a non-jury trial before the judge). LILCO contended that Suffolk County had caused or contributed substantially to its damages. It claimed the County was the party responsible for delaying the operation of Shoreham. Judge Weinstein characterized this contention as an "equitable defense," which would be a matter for the judge to decide, not the jury.

The bench trial on this equitable defense was held before Judge Weinstein in early February 1989. In response to LILCO's argument that Suffolk County could not assert that LILCO had unduly delayed the project and had "unclean hands," we argued on the County's behalf that it had a constitutional right under the First Amendment to petition the government for a redress of grievances regarding the project. We asserted that this right could not be abridged with an "unclean hands" equitable defense.

We also argued that the County had a good-faith basis for raising safety concerns. For example, on August 13, 1983, the crankshaft of one of Shoreham's emergency diesel generators broke during a test after LILCO had ignored repeated warnings from George Henry, a quality control inspector, about the unusual degree of vibrations experienced by the diesel generator crankshaft. Henry testified that he had told the test engineer to stop the test when he saw the engine was experiencing dramatic load swings. He warned him that continuing the test could badly damage the engine and lead to its total failure, which is precisely what happened. When the test engineer refused to stop the test, the vibrations started shaking the entire diesel generator room until the engine finally shut down. Fortunately, this accident occurred during a test of the emergency electrical system rather than in a real emergency, where a loss of power could have resulted in a core meltdown.

To add insult to injury, LILCO decided to shoot the messenger when Henry tried to file his report on why the diesel generator crankshaft had severed. He was summarily fired for not going along with the cover-up of the accident. He was escorted off the site by a Shoreham security guard. LILCO then opposed Henry's application for unemployment insurance, claiming that there were discrepancies in his attendance records.

Judge Weinstein Sets Aside the Jury Verdict

On February 11, 1989, after a four-day bench trial, Judge Weinstein dismissed LILCO's "unclean hands" defense because the First Amendment protected Suffolk County's conduct.[38] Even though the first few parts of the Judge's decision he was reading out loud in his courtroom favored Suffolk County, I couldn't shake the increased sense of foreboding that seized my entire body. Sure enough, my warning instincts proved correct as Judge Weinstein lowered the boom on us. He acknowledged that, before trial, he had expressed the view that the federal RICO statute took precedence over state rate-regulatory policy. However, Judge Weinstein shocked us by stating that he had changed his mind after a lengthy two-month trial. He suddenly announced that he was granting LILCO's motion for judgment n.o.v. (notwithstanding the jury verdict) as a matter of statutory construction of the RICO Act.[39] In concluding "that RICO does not apply to this case,"[40] the district court relied on the doctrine of "clear statement." In other words, a court must determine whether there is a "clear statement that Congress intended to exercise its power in full" and that the RICO statute could be applied to the regulatory rate-making procedures set up by a state.[41]

In holding that Congress could not possibly have meant that the RICO statute should apply to the heavily regulated utility industry, Judge Weinstein was aware that Congress included no such express limitations in the statute when it was enacted. Nevertheless, Judge Weinstein, one of the most liberal and brilliant judges on the federal bench, concluded (somewhat ironically, I thought), that principles of state's rights were in the "atmosphere" when Congress enacted RICO and must have been taken into account:

[N]o one who understands state government and our federal political system can doubt that the states are still powerful sovereignties respected as such by all three branches of the national government. This knowledge permeates the very bones of our political system.[42]

Judge Weinstein concluded his opinion with a plea that it "was not too late to settle these swirling controversies [and that] there is no time better than now for resolution of the entire controversy."[43] The Judge was making it clear that his motivation for dismissing Suffolk County's RICO claims was that he wanted to put a process into motion that would lead to a "global settlement" of disputes between New York State, Suffolk County, and LILCO.

What may have led Judge Weinstein to throw a bucket of ice cold water on Suffolk County's RICO verdict were reliable reports that LILCO was considering seeking for Chapter 11 bankruptcy protection. If the company filed Chapter 11, it would have protected LILCO against the claims of most of its creditors, including Suffolk County and the ratepayer class, until it had an opportunity to work out a plan to repay its debts.[44] Texaco, Inc. had recently taken this option after being hit with a colossal verdict returned by a jury in Texas state court in a lawsuit brought by Pennzoil, another oil company.

Some analysts speculated that a "mega settlement" was the only real solution following the jury verdict. Such a settlement would assure Suffolk County and its residents that the Shoreham plant would be closed for good and that a reasonable damages award would be paid to the ratepayers in the form of reduced rates.[45] One plan that the New York State legislature was considering (and which was ultimately successful) was a takeover of LILCO by the state-owned Long Island Power Authority (LIPA), thus turning the utility into a public agency.[46]

Most recognized civil RICO experts were alarmed by Judge Weinstein's narrowing of the statute's application by essentially barring its use against state-regulated utilities. Michel Waldman, the legislative director of Public Citizen's Congress Watch, commented that the decision was troubling to the extent it implied that civil RICO could not be used against a state-regulated industry.[47] Citing the Supreme Court's decision in the *Sedima* case, which found that the civil RICO statute could be used against white-collar crime, as well as against traditional organized crime, he added: "It would be ominous for consumers and law-enforcement if this decision signals a trend towards sharp restriction on the use of civil RICO by victims."[48] Professor G. Robert Blakey of Notre Dame was blunter in his characterization of Judge Weinstein's dismissal of the RICO case against LILCO, describing it as "bizarre," "untenable," and, in certain respects, "specifically rejected by the Supreme Court."[49]

Blakey, however, conceded that Weinstein's ruling on primary jurisdiction and abstention presented "close questions."[50] Under principles of primary jurisdiction, federal courts may defer certain matters to administrative agencies with special expertise in an area. Under the *Burford* abstention doctrine, originating with the Supreme Court's decision in *Burford v. Sun Oil Co.*, 319 U.S. 315 (1943), federal courts can decline to hear cases that would force them to interfere with a complex state regulatory scheme. Weinstein had reasoned that the federal jury had usurped the duties of the state PSC, which should have been permitted to determine what rates should have been imposed on the ratepayers absent the fraud."[51]

The Shoreham Settlement

On February 13, 1989, two days after dismissing Suffolk's RICO claim, Judge Weinstein certified a mandatory class of LILCO ratepayers.[52] He also ruled that Suffolk County would be permitted to opt-out of the class. He found that the original individual plaintiffs and three additional ones were adequate representatives of the class. These five class representatives became quickly dubbed by the press as "the Ratepayer Five" since they comprised a broad cross-section of anti-Shoreham activists.[53] Peter Maniscalco, one of the most outspoken of the class representatives, declared: "We are going to pursue economic justice for all ratepayers, and if LILCO goes bankrupt in the process, so be it."[54] Christopher George, another class representative, echoed the same sentiment: "Our agenda is recovering cash damages, not closing Shoreham," he said. "Of course, we all want that, too."[55]

Judge Weinstein designated Judith P. Vladeck, Esq. - a well-regarded New York class action attorney - as counsel for the ratepayer class ("class counsel") and granted motions to intervene by Nassau County and a group of "Business Ratepayers." One of these business ratepayers was represented by Irving Like, a prominent Long Island lawyer who was one of my longstanding legal mentors, regularly referring to me as "the kid" even after I was well into my forties. Since Irving was at least twenty years my senior, he became a father figure to me after my father – also a lawyer – passed away prematurely as a delayed effect of injuries sustained in the U.S. Navy during World War II. Irving Like was also a LIPA director who had been a Shoreham opponent since the late 1960s, favoring a LILCO bankruptcy as a prelude to the appointment of LIPA as its bankruptcy trustee.

We started drafting our appeal papers from Judge Weinstein's decision dismissing Suffolk County's RICO verdict for filing in the Second Circuit Court of Appeals. At the same time, Judge Weinstein ordered settlement discussions to occur and strongly recommended that the mediator presiding over these discussions should be Kenneth R. Feinberg, an intensely energetic attorney with a great deal of experience as a mediator. Unlike arbitration, where the arbitrator's decision is binding on the parties, a mediator only can suggest a nonbinding resolution of the dispute, which the parties may accept, modify, or reject.

Feinberg had become closely identified with Judge Weinstein since he was appointed as a Special Master in the massive Agent Orange litigation dealing with the damage claims by 250,000 Vietnam veterans. Ken Feinberg's participation in settlement of the complex issues after Suffolk County's jury verdict was extremely assertive, involving considerable well-intentioned cajoling, jawboning, and arm twisting in an attempt to get the disparate parties to agree to a settlement.

Despite his hyper-assertive style, Ken and I hit it off from the start. The negotiations moved along quickly now that Suffolk County was recognized as a legitimate and essential party to any negotiated settlement involving LILCO and New York State. The County was finally getting the respect that had eluded it during the many years it had fought against the Shoreham plant, virtually alone. As Representative George Hochbrueckner succinctly put it, "Suffolk County is now a player. [The County] can sit at the table between LILCO and the state."[56] After some negotiations, we eventually got LILCO to agree to a settlement rebate of $390 million for all Long Island ratepayers, on a class-wide basis.

New York Governor Mario Cuomo also began to take an active role in settling the litigation. He advised Suffolk County officials to seek an immediate agreement from LILCO not to operate the plant while un-resolved issues were pending before Judge Weinstein. County Executive Patrick Halpin encouraged the governor's participation, suggesting that the state should play a role in any settlement negotiated before Judge Weinstein.[57]

On February 15, 1989, Judge Weinstein announced that the LILCO defendants had reached a tentative settlement agreement with the class representatives.[58] The settlement provided for, among other things, pay-ment of $390 million to the class in the form of rate reductions over ten years; the creation of a Citizens Advisory Panel to aid in improv-ing LILCO service; payment of up to $10 million in attorneys' fees for plaintiffs; and the release of "all causes of action arising from the RICO complaint...."[59]

On February 27, 1989, LILCO's counsel and class counsel (Judith Vladeck) - who I had initially contacted and persuaded to step into the case as class counsel - executed a Stipulation of Partial Settlement. The agreement announced by the court on February 15 set forth the settle-ment terms between the parties with more specificity.[60] Unsurprisingly, the civil RICO settlement figure of $390 million (plus a $10 million fund for legal fees) was precisely the number PSC felt that LILCO could absorb over ten years without jeopardizing the financial health of the company. Suffolk County, of course, would have liked for the reduction in rate in-creases to be more significant. Still, Ken Feinberg and Judge Weinstein were adamant that the settlement was sufficient and, even if on the low side, all that LILCO could sustain.

The Fairness Hearings

The next step in the class action settlement process was for Judge Weinstein to hold Fairness Hearings on the proposed class-wide settlement agree-ment, which he did on March 1, 3, 8, and 9, 1989. Notice was given to the public, with almost one million customers sent direct mail invita-tions to the Fairness Hearings. Advertisements were taken out in every daily and weekly newspaper, as well as on T.V. and radio. Like a town hall meeting, a fairness hearing on a controversial proposed settlement like Shoreham gave citizens one of the few opportunities to participate directly in their democracy by going into federal courthouses and sharing their opinions with a judge.

The first Fairness Hearing on the settlement was held in the ceremonial courtroom of the Brooklyn federal courthouse on March 1, 1989. There were members of the public as well as federal, state, and local officials and a multitude of lawyers present, representing the United States, New York City, Nassau County, the State Attorney General, the Long Island Association, and various businesses and corporations. One of them was Grumman Corp., the aircraft company that was Long Island's largest employer at the time.

When I entered the courtroom, I was reminded of the old aphorism: "Success has many fathers, but defeat is an orphan." It had been a long, lonely road up until the time of trial, with no help forthcoming from either the federal government or Nassau County, where one-half of LILCO's ratepayers resided, or from any of the other parties who decided to make an appearance on the eve of settlement. It was generally recognized that the settlement discussions for the ratepayer classes would have never gotten off the ground were it not for our successful jury verdict and the threat of its reinstatement on appeal.

The Fairness Hearing held on March 3, 1989, at the federal courthouse in Hauppauge, Long Island, was a much more rancorous affair than the first one held in Brooklyn since there were many more individual rate-payers who showed up to have their voices heard. The auditorium for a hearing held in Suffolk County was so crowded that an adjacent room had to be opened. The extra space was outfitted with a loudspeaker and video monitor so that all could see and hear the speakers as they formed a long line to say their piece about the settlement.

At the outset, Judge Weinstein got a taste of Long Islanders' healthy distrust of lawyers. "Now, I understand that some of the citizens who are here were under the impression that they had to come," he said. "You do not have to come," he added. "You can go home if you like . . .and the lawyer will take care of your rights." At that point, a voice from the gathered crowd packed into the room shouted out: "That's why we're here!"[61]

Many of the community groups and ratepayer organizations saw the settlement as a "sell-out." Political cartoons circulated depicting Judge Weinstein, Ken Feinberg, and Governor Mario Cuomo as lizards entering into a backroom deal to bail out LILCO. Peter Quinn, a community activist and one of the original individual plaintiffs in the RICO case, graphically characterized Judge Weinstein's dismissal of Suffolk County's RICO case. In Quinn's view, the dismissal was "just two more links in a brokered deal process in which Wall Street investment firms, a consortium of 42 banks [and] a corrupt corporation named LILCO" worked together to accommodate the status quo, not the public interest.[62] His remarks and detailed critique of Judge Weinstein's post-verdict ruling were punctuated with robust applause from the assembled crowd.

Despite the palpable public anger filling the courtroom that day, the March 3rd Fairness Hearing had one moment of relief as named plaintiff Peter Maniscalco described how he had been living in his car adjacent to the Shoreham plant for over a month "on my own particular spiritual quest, and I am dressed to harmonize with mother nature as opposed to a court of law."[63] Maniscalco further explained that he was holding in his hand an Indian prayer stick that had been given to him outside the Shoreham plant by an 83-year-old American Indian, Grandfather Bill, and that this was "one of the most personally rewarding experiences of my life."[64] To everyone's surprise, Maniscalco concluded his rather unorthodox presentation by actually giving the settlement his qualified approval: "As long as the Shoreham nuclear monster dies as part of this process, I am privileged to support this settlement," he said, adding: "I will finally get to symbolically plunge the sword of life into the dark heart of the Shoreham nuclear dragon monster."[65]

Judge Weinstein ultimately approved the class settlement agreement on March 22, 1989, no doubt relying heavily on the fact that settlement amount and payment schedule was the outside limit that the financially teetering LILCO could pay without declaring bankruptcy.[66] In his written decision approving the settlement, Judge Weinstein said that one thing was clear to him, which is that "the exhausting, debilitating and costly years of hostility, misunderstanding and poor judgments needs to be put behind the parties," he said, adding: "There are no absolutes, no clearly right or wrong way to end the dispute. All that is crystal clear and indisputable is that the controversy must be ended as soon as possible."[67] Judge Weinstein expressed the view that a LILCO bankruptcy was not a good solution and that this was the same opinion as that of the PSC staff, which had observed that "the chaos and uncertainty resulting from a bankruptcy . . . compels rejection of bankruptcy as a viable alternative."[68]

Judge Weinstein also acknowledged the judicial limitations on finding a comprehensive solution to a complex issue such as Shoreham. "To understand this case is to appreciate that money alone and economic theory of litigation do not fully explain the dynamics of mass tort litigation."[69]

Finally, Judge Weinstein definitively declared what almost everyone now knew: "Shoreham is dead. Those who refuse to acknowledge the obvious only make it more difficult to bury the controversy and get on with life."[70] Paraphrasing Shakespeare's words mouthed by Hamlet, Judge Weinstein wrote: "Imperious Shoreham, dead and turned to clay, Might stop a hole to keep the wind away."[71]

Judge Weinstein's approval of the settlement led to the establishment of the Long Island Power Authority (LIPA) by New York State and the shutdown of the Shoreham plant. Most considered that a good thing since Shoreham was generally viewed an accident waiting to happen.

In his settlement approval, Judge Weinstein also awarded attorneys' fees and expenses to Judith Vladeck's law firm as class counsel. Attorneys' fees were also awarded to counsel for three intervenors who had opposed the settlement, and to Jim Harmon, counsel for the United States and the whistleblowers Gordon Dick and John Daly in the related *qui tam* action. Ken Feinberg, the court-appointed mediator, was also awarded fees.[72]

Judge Weinstein, however, declined to award any attorneys' fees to my law firm or our client, Suffolk County, even though we were the ones who had, in essence, slain the LILCO dragon after a lengthy and arduous jury trial. The failure to award fees seemed – at least to Suffolk County and to us - to be patently unfair. Judge Weinstein had dismissed our civil RICO case after trial. But, the evidence we presented at trial and the jury verdict we won had laid the foundation for the global settlement between New York State and LILCO relating to the Shoreham plant.

The Second Circuit Court of Appeals Partially Reverses Judge Weinstein's Dismissal of Suffolk County's RICO Claims

Soon after we appealed Judge Weinstein's post-trial dismissal of our civil RICO claims against LILCO to the Second Circuit Court of Appeals, we were joined in this effort by Professor G. Robert Blakey of Notre Dame Law School. Blakey filed an amicus curiae ("friend of the court") brief on behalf of the Trial Lawyers for Public Justice, a public interest organization based in Washington, D.C. The National Institute of Municipal Law Officers also weighed in on our side of the appeal.

The Second Circuit Court of Appeals issued a landmark decision, reversing Judge Weinstein's decision by agreeing with our position that the civil RICO statute did apply to all entities, including public utilities such as LILCO.[73] The Second Circuit further found that the federal courts had no obligation to abstain from adjudicating RICO claims involving the state rate-making process. The court pointed out that the New York State Attorney General and the PSC had expressed that Suffolk County's RICO case did not infringe on their state prerogatives. Further, Suffolk County's prodigious efforts to ferret out the true scope of LILCO's fraudulent conspiracy to deceive the PSC and the public was a beneficial public service.

While refusing to accept Judge Weinstein's narrow interpretation of the scope of the RICO statute, the Circuit Court did affirm Judge Weinstein's approval of the $400 million ($390 million to a settlement fund and $10 million to an attorneys' fee fund). In affirming the settlement agreement, the Second Circuit rejected objections filed by Nassau County and specific individual and business ratepayers to the size of the settlement fund. The Second Circuit recognized that, under the legal doctrine of collateral estoppel, the LILCO ratepayers could have recovered a judgment of $4.32 billion if Suffolk County's verdict were reinstated. But the appeal's court concluded that it was not a "clear error" for the district court to have accepted the opinion of the PSC that the settlement amount was the most extensive sum that could be paid without having an adverse impact through bankruptcy.[74]

On the subject of legal fees, the Second Circuit reversed Judge Weinstein's decision to deny Suffolk County an award of any legal fees out of the $10 million fund that had been set aside as part of the settlement. The court accepted our argument that, although Suffolk County was not part of the class of LILCO ratepayers that agreed to the settlement, the County was entitled to an award of legal fees under the "equitable fund doctrine." This long-established doctrine is designed "to permit 'fair and just allowances for expenses and counsel fees to [those] parties promoting the litigation.'"[75] The theory is that an attorney whose actions have conferred a benefit upon a given group or class of litigants may file a claim for reasonable compensation for his efforts.

The Second Circuit was complimentary about the quality of the legal services that I and the rest of Suffolk County's legal team – including Gregory O'Neill, Bernard Persky, James Johnson, Lawrence Kolker, Tom Holman and Suffolk County Attorney E. Thomas Boyle - had rendered. They noted the extraordinary results that we achieved. The Court stated:

> It is clear that the efforts of Suffolk's attorneys substantially benefitted the class. Suffolk's attorneys conducted, to the benefit of the class, virtually all of the pre-trial discovery and motion practice, including motions for class certification. Its counsel were the only plaintiff attorneys who conducted the two-month trial, which resulted in a jury verdict that, through the use of collateral estoppel, could have entitled the class to damages against LILCO of approximately $ 4.3 billion – an amount sufficient to bankrupt LILCO, . . . if the verdict were reinstated on appeal. LILCO has admitted that its decision to enter into a settlement agreement was motivated partly by its fear that the jury verdict might be reinstated and collateral estoppel applied. Additionally, after the trial, Suffolk actively participated in the class settlement negotiations. Moreover, the district court repeatedly commended the quality of Suffolk's legal representation, e.g., "counsel [has] done a superb job [and] tried this case as well as I have ever seen any case tried"; "Suffolk's choice of counsel was superb"; "plaintiff's attorneys . . . are doing a very fine job and whatever [they] are being paid [they] are worth every penny." Indeed, the district judge apparently would have awarded Suffolk extensive attorneys' fees had Suffolk not opted out of the class.[76]

The Shoreham Case Legacy

Suffolk County's jury verdict in the Shoreham case added considerable fuel to the fire on the debate raging at this time over whether the civil RICO statute should be "reformed" or not. Consumer advocates such as Michael Waldman, legislative director of Public Citizen's Congress Watch, founded by Ralph Nader, lauded Suffolk's RICO verdict as a perfect example of why the civil RICO statute should not be weakened.[77]

Similarly, G. Robert Blakey, the Notre Dame law professor I had testified with before Congress, said that the verdict showed that RICO was the only way a large group of people with small claims could go against a big institution such as LILCO that had wronged them.[78] "The allegation is that these people lied, that they stole the money from the ratepayers. If they had stolen the money by breaking into each home one by one, we would have called it a burglary," Blakey explained. "Simply because these people stole so much from so many, should they go unpunished?" he rhetorically added.[79]

On the other side of the fence, the anti-RICO forces predictably viewed the RICO verdict as a calamity that virtually threatened the foundations of Western civilization as we know it. The specter of a Long Island darkened as a result of a LILCO bankruptcy was raised, even though most analysts agreed the court-appointed bankruptcy trustee could run the company at least as well as current management. "While the people of Long Island may want to punish LILCO, I'm not sure they want to put LILCO out of business and start buying a lot of candles," commented Marvin Pickholz, a Washington lawyer specializing in defending civil RICO lawsuits.[80]

On balance, Suffolk County's RICO victory in the Shoreham case reinvigorated the statute's use to prosecute major white-collar fraud cases civilly. The Shoreham plant was finally decommissioned in 1994, becoming yet another multi-billion dollar carcass of unfinished or unusable nuclear power stations dotting the American landscape. While it had proved to be a significant financial disaster for Long Island, it could have been much worse if it had opened and an accident occurred, as many suspected it would.

With the Shoreham case finally behind me, I moved on to handle several other high-profile human rights and environmental law cases. But the Shoreham case remains one of the most significant events in my legal career. It was precisely the kind of complex public interest litigation I had set out to become involved in after I left the corporate litigation practice of law at Rosenman & Colin to join the New York State Special Prosecutor's office to investigate nursing home crimes and Medicaid fraud.

The Shoreham case also solidified my professional relationships with other idealistic attorneys who were applying their legal skills to slaying the Shoreham dragon and saving the people of Long Island (at least from our perspective). After the Shoreham case marathon, I continued my longstanding professional relationship with Irving Like, who practiced law well into his 90s and joined forces with me to battle another Long Island utility, Keyspan, for groundwater pollution and property damage that impacted thousands of Long Island and Staten Island homeowners. Shoreham was also my introduction to Kenneth Feinberg, a great problem solver in challenging cases. Ken Feinberg later acted as the mediator in the French Bank Holocaust Restitution cases, in which I also played a major role, and in the 9/11 Claims Restitution Cases where I represented many of the families of victims of the World Trade Center collapse. I also had the honor and challenge of appearing before Judge Weinstein again, most notably in the Holocaust restitution cases.

As the years have sped by, Shoreham continued to play a central part of my life. I wrote my first book about it, and every summer, while sailing with my family on Long Island Sound, I can see the eerie, ghostlike structure sitting like some ancient ruin on the north shore of Long Island. The staggering extent of the colossally poor judgment, greed and corruption that led to this disaster never ceases to amaze me. It is truly a monument to man's folly.

After Shoreham, it turns out that I wasn't done with RICO and nuclear power. Some 25 years later, while my family and I were living on our sailboat in Charleston, South Carolina, I became involved in a second RICO case involving another utility company with a troubled nuclear power plant. Only this time it was located in South Carolina.

The South Carolina Nuclear Power Cases

The major publicly regulated electric gas utility companies in South Carolina and the surrounding region are SCANA Corporation and South Carolina Electric & Gas Company (SCE&G), its subsidiary. In April 2007, SCANA and SCE&G publicly announced their plans to break into the nuclear power plant business with the construction of two 1,117-megawatt nuclear reactors at the Virgil C. Summer Nuclear Power Station, located near Jenkinsville, South Carolina, approximately 20 miles northwest of South Carolina's capitol in Columbia. But since SCE&G is regulated by the South Carolina Public Service Commission ("SCPSC"), which is designed to protect the public from predatory and monopolistic behavior by the utilities regulated by it, SCANA and SCE&G first had to get approval from this state regulator to pass on the construction costs for the project before any such nuclear power plant was completed. They decided that some new legislation was needed to grease the wheels for such expedited pass-along approval.

In February 2007, several months before they announced their nuclear power ambitions, SCANA and SCE&G embarked on an intensive lobbying campaign with members of the South Carolina House and Senate,[81] resulting in the Legislature's passage of the Base Load Review Act of 2007 ("BLRA") with little public scrutiny or media attention. Ostensibly, the BLRA was designed to avoid a feared electricity shortage and to incentivize privately-owned utilities to create more nuclear power capacity in South Carolina. Because the costs of nuclear construction were so high, the reasoning went, utilities should be allowed to build nuclear capacity on a "pay as you go" model, and to charge rate-paying customers up front for the costs. In reality, however, the BLRA gave a blank check to the utility companies to rack up inflated expenses and cost overruns, and to pay themselves exorbitant bonuses.

Immediately upon its passage, SCANA took advantage of the BLRA by embarking on an expansive reactor construction project at the V.C. Summer Site, with the plan to bill rate-paying customers up front for the costs. Even the most knowledgeable observers in South Carolina were taken by surprise. Bob Guild, an environmental lawyer who chaired the S.C. Sierra Club in 2007, referred to it as a "stealth project," saying that he "knew nothing about it," even though he had been involved in utility regulation since the late '70s and early '80s.[82]

Even though the BLRA left the door wide open for these utilities to pass on the construction costs for their nuclear power construction programs to the South Carolina ratepayers, it still left these utility companies and their executives partially on the hook in the event that it was ever determined that there were "imprudent costs" incurred. Thus, SCANA's management and Board were on notice from the outset that their ability to recover costs from South Carolina ratepayers was contingent upon a later public review as to whether such costs were prudent.

SCANA Announces Two New Nuclear Power Plants

By April 2007—when it appeared that the BLRA would surely become law—SCANA started publicly touting a massive planned nuclear expansion at its V.C. Summer Generating Station. In the Company's First Quarter conference call on April 27, 2007, a SCANA executive stated that "we currently expect to file a joint application with the Nuclear Regulatory Commission later this year, for a combined construction and operating license which will cover two units ..." SCANA further stated that they expected to recover capital costs for the project under the BLRA.

In March 2008, SCE&G filed an application with the NRC for a license to build the two reactors. Kevin Marsh, the Chief Executive Officer and Chairman of the Board of SCANA at the time, promised the NRC that "a dedicated group of SCE&G personnel . . . will monitor each aspect of the construction process on a day-to-day basis. . . ."[83]

In May 2008, SCE&G and the South Carolina Public Service Authority (also known as "Santee Cooper") falsely represented that, as of March 31, 2012, the Company and its contractors remain on schedule. Similarly, on September 28, 2012, based upon the false and misleading statements made in SCANA's May 27, 2012 application for the approval of revised rates, the SCPSC issued another order granting its request to increase utility rates for South Carolina ratepayers.[84] SCANA also falsely informed SCPSC that there would only be some minor changes in its cost projections for the project.[85] On September 27, 2013, based upon these false and misleading statements, the SCPSC granted another rate increase.

This same misleading pattern of false statements to the state regulators and the grant of requested rate increases based upon the mounting costs of the nuclear project continued throughout 2014, 2015, and 2016. Approximately 18% of each SCANA customer's power bill related to costs associated with this nuclear reactor project, and SCANA customers paid a total of $1.4 billion towards the Project.

As my wife, Susan, and I started spending more and more time in Charleston, a city that is hard not to love, we kept running into an increasing number of SCE&G customers who were mad as hell at SCANA and SCE&G for announcing that they were abandoning this power plant project after having already spent billions of their customer dollars to partially built it. We had several friends and acquaintances in South

Carolina who were more than willing to step forward to represent the entire class of ratepayers in a federal civil RICO case that was being discussed among several prominent South Carolina law firms, as well as with me and some of my fellow attorneys based in New York, particularly Tom Holman, who graduated from Fordham Law School with me in 1972 and had worked on the *Shoreham* case.

Since there was already a case filed in South Carolina state court, known as the *Lightsey* case,[86] our thinking was that we should bring a civil RICO case in federal court in South Carolina, since the facts as set forth in the *Lightsey* complaint and legal papers filed in that case strongly suggested that these utility companies and their executives had engaged in a massive fraud over a period of many years, involving misrepresentations to the South Carolina PSC as to the costs of the project and estimated time table, and that they had reaped the benefit of this massive fraud by receiving billions of dollars thorough increased rates charged to their customers.

Tom Holman and I expanded our New York-based legal team to include Meaghan Glibowski, a bright young lawyer who proved to be instrumental in getting this South Carolina civil RICO case off the ground. However, since neither Tom, Meaghan nor I were admitted to the practice of law in South Carolina, it was first necessary that we affiliate with a first-rate South Carolina law firm to work with us on the federal civil RICO case. We were convinced that a civil RICO case had legal merit and would be strategically an important "second front" in the South Carolina ratepayers legal battle to win back some of the monies wrongfully taken from them by SCANA and SCE&G through rate increases to cover the construction costs of this massive boondoggle.

The South Carolina lawyers that we were fortunate enough to team up with were Daniel A. Speights and A. Gibson Solomons, III, the two partners in the law firm of Speights & Solomons, LLC, located in Hampton, South Carolina. I gave Dan and Gibson a phone call, briefly discussed my idea of bringing a civil RICO case in South Carolina federal court, and then made plans to meet with them in Charleston for lunch. My wife, youngest son and I were already down in Charleston harbor on our sailboat over the Christmas break, so it was convenient for all of us to meet in Charleston and to see if we could all work together on this legal venture.

As it turned out, we all hit it off well, and on January 31, 2018, we filed our civil RICO complaint on behalf of Timothy Glibowski and all other SCE&G ratepayers who had been charged for the nuclear power construction costs incurred by SCANA and SCE&G.[87] The case was assigned to Senior U.S. District Court Judge Terry L. Wooten, who had been nominated to his position as a federal judge by President George W. Bush and assumed his position in November 2001. He became Chief Judge of the U.S. District Court of South Carolina on January 16, 2013.

Shortly after filing our federal civil RICO complaint, we joined forces with the plaintiffs' attorneys in another civil RICO case also pending before Judge Wooten, entitled *Christine Delmanter et al v. State of South Carolina et al.*[88] The primary counsel on this other federal RICO case were two excellent Columbia, South Carolina attorneys: Kenneth M. Suggs of Janet, Jenner & Suggs, and Brian C. Gambrell.

On April 23, 2018, we filed an Amended Complaint in South Carolina federal court, naming both Timothy Glibowski and Christine Delmater as lead plaintiffs in the RICO action, along with other named plaintiffs who were added to represent an wide range of South Carolina ratepayers as representatives of the entire class of SCE&G customers.[89] The Amended Complaint also added an additional South Carolina utility company and its officers: the quasi-public South Carolina Power Authority (also known as Santee Cooper), which had been originally formed during the 1930s New Deal period to provide electric power and water to rural South Carolina. At the time, the Santee Cooper Project was the largest land-clearing project in U.S. history, with over 12,500 workers clearing over 177,000 acres of swamp and forestland. They constructed over 42 miles of dams and dikes, including a 26-mile, 78-foot tall earthen dike.

However, Santee Cooper made the fateful mistake of jumping on the nuclear power bandwagon being driven primarily by SCANA and SCE&G, and soon Santee Cooper's ratepayers were also seeing larger utility bill inflated by some of the construction costs for this recklessly conceived project. Santee Cooper's decision to join in the Consortium financing these two new power plants was largely engineered by Lonnie Carter, which was then the chief executive officer of Santee Cooper. We alleged in the Amended Complaint – with evidence to back it up – that Carter committed Santee Cooper to the project, at least in part, for his personal gain, and that Carter succeeded in enriching himself at the expense of Santee Cooper's customers through substantial bonuses supposedly related to his work on the nuclear reactor project.

In addition to the South Carolina lawyers with whom we had filed our original federal civil RICO complaint in the South Carolina federal court - Speights & Solomons, LLC, Ken Sugg's law firm and Brian Gambrell – our federal case legal team was now joined by some of the leading attorneys in the *Lightsey* state court litigation against SCANA and SCE&G. These included Pete Strom, the former U.S. Attorney for the District of South Carolina, who was joined by some extremely able associates: Mario A. Pacella, Jessica L. Flickling, and Bakari T. Sellers. Sellers had already distinguished himself as a member of the South Carolina state legislature from 2006 to 2014 after becoming the youngest African-American elected official in the country at the age of 22. He was also a prominent political commentator for CNN and vice chairman of the South Carolina Democratic Party. In addition, we were also able to recruit for our federal RICO team Terry Richardson and other outstanding attorneys associated with the law firm of Richardson, Patrick, Westbrook & Brickman, L.L.C., and Patrick A. Thronson.

As expected, SCANA, SCE&G, Santee Cooper, and the individual defendant executives of those companies filed motions to dismiss our Amended Complaint, basically arguing that the civil RICO statute did not properly apply in this case, and that this was more properly a matter to be handled by the state utility regulator, SCPSC, not by a federal court, under what was known as the "primary jurisdiction" doctrine.

In response to these motions to dismiss, we filed extensive legal briefs, arguing that our Amended Complaint met all of the necessary elements for civil RICO, and that a major fraud such as this committed by utility companies and their officers over a long and continuous time period for the purpose of getting construction costs of a nuclear power plant project passed onto their ratepaying customers was precisely what the Second Court of Appeals had approved in the Shoreham Nuclear Power Plant case, and was equally applicable here. We explained that, in the 1985 case of *Sedima, S.P.R.L. v. Imrex Co.*,[90] the Supreme Court stated that there are only four elements necessary for a proper civil RICO complaint: (1) conduct (2) of an enterprise (3) through a pattern (4) of racketeering activity.

We also argued that the "Nuclear Power Plant Enterprise" that we pleaded in the Amended Complaint fell squarely within the definition of "an enterprise" set forth in Section 1964(4) of the RICO statute, which included "any individual, partnership, corporation, association, or other legal entity, and any union or group of individuals associated in fact although not a legal entity." A RICO enterprise also had to be "an ongoing organization, formal or informal, in which the various associates function as a continuing unit."[91] We argued that SCANA, SCE&G, Santee Cooper, Westinghouse and the other companies and individuals who participated in this massive nuclear power construction project, which was often referred to over the years as a "Consortium," was a classic business-related enterprise falling within the scope of the RICO statute.

The defendants argued in their motions to dismiss that, even if we had properly alleged that they were a RICO Enterprise, the Amended Complaint was still defective in that the injury alleged – namely, the increase in the utility bills to the customers - was not proximately caused by defendants' alleged racketeering activity, which was a requirement of the statute. While the Supreme Court had made it clear that "proximate cause" for RICO purposes required "some direct relation between the injury asserted and the injurious conduct alleged,"[92] and that the injury suffered must be "actual or imminent,"[93] we had properly established that the ultimate objective of the defendants' racketeering scheme had always been "to obtain billions of dollars in proceeds and profits therefrom" to which they were not legitimately entitled, and that these monies would be coming (and did come) directly from the plaintiff ratepayers, not the Public Service Commission. In other words, we argued that it was the plaintiffs and their utility charges that were always the object of the scheme,[94] and that they were the ones who were directly injured as a result of the defendants' deceptive scheme. We further pointed out that the Amended Complaint alleged that defendants' fraudulent scheme was directly designed to extort money from the plaintiff-ratepayers by "instill[ing] the fear of economic and personal harm, *inter alia*, the cessation of electricity services to the Class. . .."

SCANA, SCE&G also argued that their mailing of the bills to their customers was just an "innocent" use of the mails, and not fraudulent, but we countered with federal case law establishing that mailings may be an essential part of the scheme, even though they may not contain express misrepresentations and fraudulent statements.[95] We also pointed out that the failure to disclose material information can be as much a part of a scheme to defraud as an affirmative misrepresentation.[96] Since the defendants certainly did not disclose to their ratepayers the fact that they were engaged in a fraudulent scheme to intentionally mislead both them and the South Carolina PSC as the cost and time estimates for the project, the mailing that they sent to their ratepayers were deceptive by omission.

Defendants also claimed that plaintiffs had failed to allege a pattern of racketeering activity that posed a threat of continued criminal activity, since it had already been announced that the project had been abandoned. In response, we argued that defendants were misstating the requirements under civil RICO for a "pattern of racketeering activity," which is the requirement – set forth by the Supreme Court in *H.J. Inc. v. Nw. Bell Tel. Co*[97] - that the alleged predicate acts "are related, and that they *amount to* or pose a threat of continued criminal activity." However, as we pointed out, the Amended Complaint clearly alleged that the pattern of racketeering activity engaged in by defendants spanned a period of years from 2009 to the present, which was the time period that defendants were sending fraudulently inflated bills to the ratepayers. We thus argued that this amounted to "continued criminal activity" within the meaning of the civil RICO statute, even if there were no threat that such racketeering activity were to continue into the future now that we had exposed defendants' fraudulent scheme.

Defendants further alleged in their motion to dismiss that plaintiffs had failed to properly allege a RICO Enterprise separate and apart from the alleged pattern of racketeering activity. We countered by pointing out that the Amended Complaint properly alleged that "the Nuclear Reactor Project" was a classic RICO "association-in-fact enterprise" included both the RICO Defendants (SCANA, SCE&G and the individual defendants), as well as other parties that were not named as RICO defendants - Westinghouse, Stone & Webster and other companies and contractors involved in the Nuclear Reactor Project. We further pointed out that the mere fact there were sometimes disagreements between members of the Enterprise did not negate the existence of the Enterprise, any more than a family quarrel will negate the existence of a family.

While we were still litigating the motions to dismiss in federal court before Judge Wooten, on November 24, 2018, SCANA and SCE&G agreed to a $2.1 billion settlement of the state court case in the *Lightsey* case,[98] with most of the settlement monies going to its 730,000 South

Carolina customers for overcharges relating to its failed nuclear plant construction project. This was the largest settlement of its kind in South Carolina history. In this class action case brought in South Carolina state court, plaintiffs Richard Lightsey, LeBrian Cleckley, and Phillip Cooper had brought the case as representatives of the entire class of South Carolina ratepayers and customers. South Carolina Circuit Judge John Hayes approved the settlement, which depended on the South Carolina Public Service's approval of Virginia-based Dominion Energy's offer to buy SCANA and to lower the average SCE&G customer's power bill by up to $22 per month. The settlement also included $180 million in cash refunds for SCE&G's current and former customers, to be paid out in portions based upon how much each customer paid in higher rates for the project The typical SCE&G residential customer's electric bill rose by about $27 a month after the nine rate hikes imposed on customers to finance the project.

A portion of that $180 million pot was set aside for legal fees to be awarded to the various law firms that had worked on the case, which was later determined to be a total of $51 million in attorneys' fees and costs.[99] One of the lead attorneys on the case, Pete Strom, expressed the view that the settlement was as far as the plaintiffs' attorneys could push SCANA and still leave SCANA sufficiently intact so that it was still a desirable acquisition target for a takeover by Dominion. As Strom explained, "We have some bad actors who did some bad stuff at SCANA. As a result of that, hundreds of millions of dollars are lost. . . . We've gotten as much money as we possibly can out of this and still make it somewhat attractive for Dominion to take it over."[100] Strom also noted that the investigation into potential criminal wrongdoing by SCANA executives was still on-going. "At the end of the day, the real justice is going to come for those who did anything criminally wrong," Strom said. "I would be surprised if there were no indictments."

At a court hearing leading up to the approval of the settlement, Ed Westbrook, another prominent South Carolina class action attorney who had also founded the Charleston School of Law, declared in open court: "For the first time in this whole debacle, the class of customers would have the right to be heard," adding: "Here, customers are going to have the right to speak up. They're going to have the right to comment on the settlement."

One of the most creative aspects of the settlement was that it required SCANA to turn over to its customers the $115 million in "golden parachutes" that had been set aside for the outgoing SCANA executives. It also forced the sale of a number of non-essential SCANA properties that could give SCE&G customers another $70 million or more in refunds or rate credits.

The settlement won the backing of South Carolina Attorney General Alan Wilson, who had issued a non-binding opinion that the 2007 law that enabled the V.C. Summer nuclear project and its nine rate hikes was unconstitutional. Wilson thanked Dominion Energy "for its willingness to provide the financial resources necessary to make this restitution."

Current and former SCE&G customers also benefitted from the sale of non-essential SCANA properties, including the Ramsey Grove Plantation in Georgetown, where SCANA executives duck hunted; the original SCE&G headquarters on Meeting Street in Charleston; and several properties near SCANA's Cayce, South Carolina headquarters. "We wanted to take away the golden parachutes and the toys for anybody still left there," Strom said.

* * *

Both the Shoreham Nuclear Power case in New York and the South Carolina Nuclear Power cases demonstrated that the civil RICO statute and ratepayer class action lawsuits provide ratepayers and their lawyers with powerful weapons to recover substantial monies from public utilities and their executives who fraudulently pass along to ratepayers the costs of multi-billion dollar nuclear power plants that are either unnecessary, dangerous, or both.

Chapter 4

The Exxon Valdez Oil Spill Case

On the Rocks

On March 23, 1989, it was a quiet and windless night as the Exxon Valdez left the Port of Valdez and headed across Prince William Sound in Alaska on the first leg of its journey to the refinery in Long Beach, California. Captain Joseph Hazelwood and his crew had made this run so many times that one would have expected they could do it in their sleep. After all, Prince William Sound is no small pond. It is about the size of Rhode Island, and the shipping channels are well-marked.

Indeed, Captain Hazelwood may well have been asleep that night after consuming enough alcohol at several local Valdez watering holes to render any ordinary man comatose. His driver's license had been revoked in his home state of New York for drinking while under the influence (DUI). He had dropped out of the Alcoholics Anonymous 12-step program where he had failed to learn one of AA's most fundamental lessons: that denial is not a river in Egypt.

Nevertheless, despite the overwhelming evidence that Hazelwood had fallen off the wagon and was drinking heavily again, Exxon assigned him to skipper one of the largest supertankers afloat. The Exxon Valdez was more than three football fields in length – over 900 feet– and carried more than 3 million gallons of Alaskan crude oil. Under Coast Guard regulations, Captain Hazelwood was required to be on the ship's bridge until it had traversed Prince William Sound entirely or had another qualified officer take the helm. He turned control of the vessel over to the third mate, Jeffrey Cousins, who was neither sufficiently experienced nor qualified to pilot the ship in restricted waters. As he left the bridge, with the supertanker aiming for Bligh Reef, Captain Hazelwood's last words to Cousins instructed him to turn the ship when it "got abeam of Busby Light." Cousins missed the turn, and the rest is history.

Bligh Reef captured another trophy, living up to the bad-luck reputation of its ill-fated namesake, Captain William Bligh of the HMS Bounty. Bligh had been an officer on the HMS Resolute when it explored the Alaskan coast under the leadership of Captain Amos Cook, one of the great navigators of history. Bligh Reef, no more than a small grouping of barren rocks, seems an odd and obscure namesake for an up-and-coming officer like Bligh. But by the morning of March 24, 1989, as news of the disaster electrified the world, Bligh Reef was no longer obscure. It was now world-famous.

The whole story of why the Exxon Valdez landed upon the rocks may never fully be known, despite an intensive investigation by numerous state and federal agencies, as well as by a small army of plaintiffs' attorneys, of which I was but one. Shortly after the news hit the wire services and TV screens, one rumor and plausible conspiracy theory was that Exxon had intentionally grounded the vessel to drive up the price of crude oil on the West Coast. It was difficult to accept that a supertanker could hit a rock in Prince Williams Sound on a clear and calm night when any 12-year-old with basic video game skills would have been able to steer clear of the disaster with little difficulty. In fact, the price of crude oil did rise sharply for a brief time upon fears that the supply lines for the West Coast refineries might be interrupted. It turned out, as with most major disaster cases - whether it be the Chernobyl meltdown or the Exxon Valdez oil spill - a series of seemingly small mistakes cascaded into a catastrophic event.

First of all, Exxon had fair warning that Joe Hazelwood was a chronic alcoholic and should have been at a desk job onshore where they could keep a close eye on him. The captain of a ship answers to no one – with the possible exception of God – once the boat leaves the shore. Aboard a ship, it is impossible to monitor whether a known alcoholic has started drinking again or not. It was widely known throughout the Exxon empire that Jack Daniels was Joe Hazelwood's best friend, and it would have posed no serious problem for Hazelwood to smuggle a bottle or two of his "best friend" aboard, to help him through the long, dull days and nights while at sea.

While he was still on the bridge, Captain Hazelwood probably did make one prudent move. He ordered that the vessel steer east of the shipping lanes, avoiding a heavy concentration of ice that had built up in the area. Hazelwood's major mistake (other than being drunk) was to leave the bridge and go below deck only two minutes before the ship's rudder had to be turned to avoid Bligh Reef. Turning a huge oil tanker has been compared to turning a car on ice. You can turn the wheel, but the momentum of the car (or tanker) tends to keep it going in the same direction until you gain some traction. Hazelwood also compounded this error in judgment by putting the vessel on autopilot, which automatically speeds the ship up, making a tricky turn even trickier.

Without Hazelwood on the bridge, Third Mate Cousins and helmsman Robert Kagan thought they had conducted the maneuver ordered by Hazelwood. Tragically, they had not. By the time they realized their mistake, it was too late. Upon impact, the reef tore a massive hole in the ship's hull like a can opener opening a can of sardines. Although experts for years had recommended that oil tankers have two hulls instead of one to increase the margin of safety, this recommendation was not ordered to be mandatory by the Coast Guard until *after* the Exxon Valdez ran aground, spilling 11 million gallons of oil.

Exxon was part of the Alyeska consortium of oil companies that built the Alyeska pipeline from the North Slope down to Valdez on the Kenai Peninsula. To gain the necessary political agreements to build the pipeline and the Valdez Terminal, Alyeska had to persuade the native Alaskan groups to give up their ancestral and aboriginal claims to the land on which the pipeline and its terminal were to be built. The oil companies understandably didn't want to spend billions of dollars on the pipeline unless they had clear title to the land on which the oil facilities would be constructed.

Congress responded to these concerns by enacting legislation granting the Alaskan natives clear title to millions of acres of Alaska wilderness, in return for their agreement to give up their claims to the right of way for the pipeline and the land on which the Valdez terminal would be built. This federal legislation, known as the Alaska Native Claims Settlement Act, popularly known by its acronym ANCSA, also established Regional native corporations throughout Alaska, which had their own by-laws and Boards of Directors like any other corporation. However, before a settlement could be finalized in 1969, various concerns of the native groups had to be satisfied. These concerns included guarantees that the native landholdings would be protected from oil spills along the pipeline route and throughout the Prince Williams Sound and Lower Kenai Peninsula areas.

The maneuverings lasted for a couple of years until the Native Alaskan groups finally agreed to take title to defined properties in the names of the various Alaska Native Corporations, plus some cash. In the Prince William Sound area, the native Alaskan regional corporation was named the Chugach Alaska Corporation, taking its name from the Chugach natives who had settled the area hundreds – if not thousands - of years ago. The native Alaskans may trace their roots back to 11,000 B.C., when the first homo sapiens crossed the Bering Strait's ice bridge from Siberia. After Russian traders brought the Russian Orthodox Church to Alaska and intermarried with the native population, most native groups took Russian surnames. The Chugach region encompassed various village corporations – Chenega, Port Graham, English Bay, and Eyak - where the Chugach peoples lived a subsistence way of life, as they had for hundreds (if not thousands) of years. They were primarily hunter/gatherers who lived off the land and the water for their basic communal needs, with very little need for money. The hunting of seals and the netting of the great runs of Alaskan salmon each summer season was an essential part of this subsistence culture when the sun would be shining for about 23 hours a day. Some of the villages were "dry," or alcohol-free, since alcohol was one of the curses Westerners (and Russians) had inflicted on the Alaskan natives, as elsewhere in North America.

In the late 1960s, the Chugach leaders were concerned that an oil spill from the proposed pipeline terminal at Valdez could devastate the sensitive fishing and shellfish-producing areas of Prince William Sound and surrounding inlets. Since they were highly accomplished fishermen and knew the surrounding waters better than anyone else, they insisted that they receive the oil spill response contract to be assured of a quick response in the event of an oil spill. Before agreeing to the ANCSA legislation, they received the solemn promise from the Alyeska oil company consortium that the Chugach peoples would be the spill response sentinels of the Sound. It took the oil companies only about 2 1/2 years to break this promise, eliminating the Chugach spill response contract as a cost-savings measure and transferring responsibility to Alyeska workers who primarily worked behind desks and knew little or nothing about

Prince William Sound. In many cases, the new so-called "spill response" team members did not even know how to handle the boats and equipment that were supposed to be used to contain and clean up oil in the event of a spill.

On the night of the Exxon Valdez oil spill, much of the spill response equipment was buried under several feet of snow and ice, and one of the largest spill response boats was unseaworthy since it had a hole in it that had not been repaired for several months. In the critical hours after Captain Hazelwood reported that the Exxon Valdez had run aground, the spilled oil remained near the ship and spread very slowly since there was only a light breeze for the first 24 hours after the spill. In fact, I reached the site before most of the spill response team, and I had to travel all the way from New York.

A few hours after the first press reports about the oil spill, I received a phone call from a local Anchorage law firm, Birch Horton Bittner and Cherot. The firm, which represented Chugach Alaska Corporation, asked me to come up to Alaska as soon as possible to help out on certain legal aspects of the case. I had recently been up in Anchorage for depositions relating to the *Shoreham* case, and the law firm I was working with at the time – Hill, Betts, and Nash—was well known for handling maritime disaster cases. I had been an avid sailor my entire life, so I was already familiar with most Coast Guard regulations and navigation issues. That day, I caught a plane from New York to Seattle and then changed planes to Anchorage, where I transferred to a small plane that flew over the Exxon Valdez.

I was shocked to see that, more than 24 hours after the grounding, there was virtually no spill response equipment in the area, and only a few floating containment booms had been laid out around the vessel. The sea was calm as glass, and it was evident that if enough spill response equipment had been brought in, much of the crude oil could have been contained by booms and then cleaned up. The oil was still lying primarily on the water's surface since there was not enough turbulence to mix it with the saltwater. But this window of opportunity did not last long. On the second day after the disaster, the wind picked up. It blew the oil slick in a northwesterly direction, directly toward the village of Chenega and other points along the Chugach shoreline. A small armada of fishing boats from the City of Cordova and elsewhere tried gallantly to stem the inevitable tide of oil flowing across Prince William Sound. But they could mop up very little of the 11 million gallons with the few absorbent pads they could find.

Soon the sea of oil began silently rolling up onto the beaches with each incoming tide. Large tarballs of oil mixed with seawater had formed, and one of the saddest sights I have ever seen in my life were seals, sea lions, and all species of local and migratory birds covered in oil. In Chenega, I saw several giant bald eagles dying on the beaches after eating oil-contaminated fish. Nothing could be done to save them. Much of the news coverage showed workers trying to scrub oil off the birds and other wildlife, but most of these efforts, although well intended, were fruitless.

Exxon Shipping Company tried to contain the growing public relations disaster by taking responsibility for the oil spill and, over the next several months, spending over $2 billion in efforts to remove the oil from the water and shoreline. Much of these efforts were counterproductive, as small armies of untrained cleanup workers hired by Exxon on an emergency basis descended on remote and, in many cases, pristine and untouched areas of Prince William Sound and the Lower Kenai Peninsula. Much of the Chugach peoples' cultural history consisted of archaeological sites, referred to as "special places," spread along the coastline for hundreds of miles. These pre-historical and historical sites (depending on whether the native peoples first used them before or after the first contact with Russian fur traders) included campsites, caves, and sites of former villages. Before the oil spill, the sites had been protected by the simple fact that the native Alaskans had kept the location of these unique sites confidential, passing on their locations from one generation to another but not sharing this information with outsiders. With the onslaught of the oil spill and the arrival of cleanup workers walking remote beaches, picking up and trying to clean anything that had oil on it, many of these significant sites were disturbed. Artifacts were either moved inadvertently or, in some cases, stolen and sold on the black market. Since the significance of an archaeological site depends mainly on the specific location of one artifact in relation to another, the movement of an artifact without first recording its presence in relation to other artifacts can destroy the context of an archaeological site.

In one notorious incident, some oil spill workers found the skeleton of a Native American in a cave, removed the human remains, and put them on display in Cordova. Only after the outraged native leaders protested were the remains returned to the sacred cave burial site, but this did not mean that this important site was now safe. On the contrary, now that there was widespread public knowledge of the sites in the oil spill area, the risk of these archaeological sites being plundered was increased exponentially. The oil itself did direct damage to the archaeological sites since once an artifact becomes oiled, it is more complex, or in some cases impossible, to date the artifact using Carbon-14 dating techniques. Carbon-14 has a half-life of about 5,000 years, which means that as the amount of Carbon-14 in an artifact decreases, it is known to be more ancient, and the date of its origin can be set relatively accurately. However, once an artifact is covered in oil, this dating technology is thrown off.

In short, the archaeological, cultural heritage of the native Alaskans was placed in grave danger due to the oil spill. One of the difficult tasks we had to deal with was quantifying those damages in dollars and formulating a reasonable plan to prevent further damages. This was not an easy process. What price can you place on the loss of a culture? How do you put a price on the loss of something essentially priceless, or at least virtually incalculable in traditional Western economic theory? These were some of the questions the lawyers and economics experts for the native corporations had to deal with.

The secrecy surrounding the precise locations of archaeological sites had been compromised due to the oil spill and the cleanup efforts. But it was not feasible to protect the archaeological sites with armed guards, given the vast coastline area to be protected, the remoteness of the area, and the bitter cold and darkness during the winter months. Some other approach was necessary. So, to calculate cultural damages, we had experts estimate the cost of having teams of trained archaeologists and knowledgeable native representatives conduct an intensive archaeological exploration and record at least the major known sites. At least then there would be a more complete archaeological, cultural record of the Chugach peoples. We also estimated the cost of establishing a native Alaskan cultural museum, where artifacts could be displayed and incorporated into various educational, cultural programs.

The problem of valuing the native Alaskan lands that had been damaged by oil was equally challenging. The lands that the native Alaskan corporations had selected were generally not chosen for their potential for being commercially developed into malls or for any other kind of economic or development value. For the most part, the pristine wilderness areas were selected so that the native Alaskan peoples could continue to live their subsistence way of life as hunters, gatherers, and fishermen, just as their fathers and ancestors had done for many generations before them. Some of the native villages were so remote that there were no roads to them, and the only way to reach them from Anchorage was by small airplanes equipped with pontoons for water landings, since there were no landing strips in some of the villages. To reach these villages by plane, you had to fly through some narrow mountain passes, and on a clear day, you could see the wreckage of various aircraft that never made it. But flying was necessary in many areas, so I had no choice but to put my faith in the experienced Alaska bush pilots who regularly flew to these remote villages.

Generally, in economic theory, the value of a property is determined by its economic or developmental value. This is calculated by looking at the sale or exchange price of similar properties. This valuation process is reasonably straightforward when you are valuing a residential home. All you have to do is find a few recent "comparables" of houses of about the same size and amenities as the house being valued. But how do you value wilderness properties? There is not a big market for wilderness properties. Most large tracts of wilderness lands are owned by the government and held as national or state parks, or by environmental organizations such as the Nature Conservancy, which purchases property to keep it out of the hands of developers.

To be sure, there have been various sale exchanges of property between various governmental entities since some states have transferred certain lands to the National Park Service, and some valuation must take place when these transfers are made. However, the criticism of using these kinds of exchanges as "comparables" is that some appraisers, and most certainly the appraisers who worked for Exxon, argued that the valuations set for such public exchanges were unreliable since they often were not wholly arms-length purchases. There may have been political and other non-economic considerations that came into play in valuing such properties.

These problems in valuing the wilderness properties that were damaged by the oil spill were compounded by the simple fact that the native people generally never intended to put their ancestral lands up for sale. The idea was to hold these native lands in perpetuity. As a result, Exxon's lawyers could – and did – argue that if there was no intent to sell the property, then the fact there was some oil on the property for a limited period did not reduce its value.

Another problem with valuing the native Alaskan wilderness property was that it was difficult to determine whether the damage to the property was temporary or permanent from a valuation point of view. In other words, how long was the oil going to remain on the beaches? On behalf of the native corporations, we retained several scientific experts and consulting groups to investigate and calculate the quantities of oil on the beaches. Still, each of them was reluctant to make any estimates or predictions on how long it would be before each shoreline segment would return to its pre-spill condition. The biologists were willing to survey the various living species and tell us how many mammal and fish species were impacted each season following the oil spill. The shoreline ecologists could tell us what different kinds of shorelines there were and map the location of the oil, but no one seemed to want to predict how long the oil would remain. The major problem was that the long-term impact was likely to vary depending on the type of shoreline. In the "high energy" beaches and unprotected segments of the coastline, where the waves tended to pound the shoreline directly, the blanket of oil on the beaches would likely be broken up over a relatively short period, such as a few years. However, in "low energy" areas, such as the most sensitive creeks and wetlands, the oil tended to form an asphalt-type surface resembling a poorly maintained road. Since the high wave action never reaches these places, the oil residue could remain for many years or decades.

The shoreline specialists working with us, such as Jim Bush of the ICF consulting group, pointed out that the more common and larger the stones on the beaches, the more porous it was. The oil would tend to percolate through the rocks and managed to dissipate faster than on finer, sandy beaches. Any "predictive model" would have to consider that the oil trapped in the sediment near the shoreline would tend to be released during winter storms. Each new winter storm managed to create a "new" oil spill on the beaches each Spring until, after a certain number of years, most of the oil had been released, and only trace amounts remained.

But we could not afford to wait a decade or two to determine precisely how much oil remained on the beaches. I insisted that our team of consulting scientists and land value experts design a predictive model that would enable us to calculate the total monetary value of the damages to the land over time. Only then could we move the case to trial as quickly as possible.

Bill Mundy of Mundy & Associates - based in Seattle, Washington - was perhaps one of the most renowned land valuation experts of wilderness properties. Bill and I coordinated closely with our various scientific experts to consider all the critical factors in designing our predictive model. Dr. Hayden Green, a Professor of Real Estate at the University of Anchorage, was also an invaluable resource in developing a strategy for valuing damaged native properties.

Bill Mundy and I also shared a mutual passion for long-distance biking, and some of our most productive discussions took place out of the office, during bike rides to various destinations in the greater Anchorage area. I had competed in a few triathlons, which included long-distance biking, swimming, and running, but I was no match for Bill, who set a fast pace and had to slow down for me every few miles to catch up. The scenery was, of course, spectacular, whatever direction you cared to take out of Anchorage. There were a series of bike trails rivaling the most beautiful and extensive as any I had seen in the Lower 48 states. Also, even after putting in 12 to 16 hour days, 6 or 7 days per week, I and some other members of our team who loved the outdoors would use the evening sunlight to climb to the top of Flattop Mountain outside Anchorage, where there was a clear view for hundreds of miles.

After weeks of research and debate among team members, I suggested developing a graph with the Axis representing shoreline types, from sandy to rocky beaches. The other variables on the graph represented the degree of oiling on each beach segment (light, medium, or heavy) and the energy category of the shoreline segment (light, medium, or heavy wave action). Then we had scientists and native representatives survey the portion of the coastline owned by the native corporations and categorize each shoreline segment for these three factors. One team spent several weeks on a small boat traveling along the remote coast and recording their findings. Then we could identify the high-energy pebble beaches that were lightly oiled, which would recover the fastest. In contrast, low-energy wetland shoreline segments that were most heavily oiled would take the longest to recover to their pre-spill condition. In this way, we estimated the time– from one to 25 years – that it would take each shoreline segment to recover.

Once we had calculated how long the oil would remain on each beach segment, the next step was to put a value on the lost use of the lands to calculate damages. The one approach that we found most useful employed aspects of the "contingent valuation" theory that certain economists, such as Bill Mundy, had developed over the years. There is not a significant rental market for wilderness properties, but one thing was clear: Exxon had "trespassed" and dumped its oil on the native Alaskan wilderness properties without permission. So, the contingent valuation theory presented was: what would the native Alaskans want to be paid if Exxon had approached them in advance and offered to pay them for using their shoreline as an oil dump? Private companies pay municipalities substantial fees for permission to dump toxic waste. So, it seemed logical to charge Exxon after-the-fact the "rental" value of each segment of property used by Exxon to "store" its oil for a period of one to 25 years, depending on the shore type, degree of oiling, and other factors.

Another way to look at it was to take a survey. Ordinary Americans were asked what they would be willing to pay to ensure that this pristine, wilderness property remained in its unblemished and unpolluted condition. Surprisingly, many Americans surveyed were willing to put a relatively high value on preserving these properties.

Exxon, of course, had experts who took a more traditional approach, which places a greater value on "improved" property, *i.e.*, previously undeveloped property that is paved over and turned into a shopping mall and parking lot. Their basic premise was that there was a lot of undeveloped land in Prince William Sound that was not of much use to anyone. No one wanted to buy or rent it anyway because it was so remote, so – according to Exxon's experts - a little bit of oil on it didn't make much difference, at least in economic terms.

It was much easier to get a handle on the damages to the commercial fishing industry in the area. The State completely shut down the issuing of licenses for salmon fishing following the oil spill. It established a "zero tolerance" policy, preventing the catching or selling of any Alaskan salmon that the oil could have tainted. Late-night T.V. talk show hosts had already started joking that Alaskan salmon would soon be available in "leaded" or "unleaded" varieties. The fishing industry and government regulators were concerned that if any tainted salmon reached the supermarkets in the lower 48 states, the impact on the billion-dollar Alaskan seafood industry would be even worse than it already was following the Exxon Valdez disaster.

It was also relatively easy to determine the losses to a fishing boat's business each season because the fishing boat owners presumably had a record of their income and profits in prior years, sometimes exceeding $1 million per year. As long as the owner was prevented from fishing, these losses would be 100%, which added up to tens (if not hundreds) of millions of dollars when multiplied by the entire fishing fleet. The commercial fishing vessel owners could also rent or lease their vessels to the Exxon cleanup effort, which was throwing as much money as possible at the problem to counteract the public relations beating they were taking. The press started referring to some boat owners as "spillionaires" since they were both claiming damages to their businesses on the one hand, while profiting from the cleanup effort at the same time.

Exxon tried to settle many of the fishermen's claims and others as part of a claims process, separate from the litigation. Over $300 million in settlements were paid out to claimants as part of this process, and in many cases, Exxon made these payments without requiring the claimant to release their claims entirely. This meant that some fishermen could receive a partial payment on their claims and continue participating in the lawsuit against Exxon.

As part of the formal litigation process, the private, non-governmental claimants' cases - primarily fishermen, native corporations, and other property owners - were consolidated in federal court before Judge H. Russel Holland. However, the native corporations and some non-native municipalities succeeded in keeping their claims in Alaska state court. The hope was that the state law of negligence and strict liability would be more favorable than federal maritime law applied to the cases in the U.S. District Court.

But, for the same reason that we wanted to keep our cases in state court, Exxon's lawyers wanted to keep all the cases in federal court. Exxon's lawyers filed "removal" legal papers on several occasions in federal court, automatically removing the native corporations' cases from state to federal court. To get our cases back to state court, we were forced to file "remand" motions with Judge Holland in federal court. We attempted to persuade Judge Holland that the native corporations' claims were primarily "garden variety" common law negligence and nuisance claims that are most appropriately tried in the state courts.

While these motions were being briefed and decided in federal court, nothing could move forward in state court until Judge Holland ruled in our favor and sent us back to state court. Although we won each one of these legal battles with Exxon, we were forced to waste a lot of time, money, and energy in the process, which is precisely what Exxon's lawyers wanted.

The State of Alaska and the United States governments brought their federal actions against Exxon for the injury to the environment, which resulted in a consent decree being signed by those parties on October 8, 1991, requiring Exxon to pay at least $900 million to restore the damaged natural resources. Both Exxon and the governmental plaintiffs held that this settlement resolved all natural resource damage claims, including those of the native Alaskan corporations. In response, we successfully argued that the state and federal governments could not possibly settle the native corporations' private claims for environmental damages. Simply stated, the native corporations were not parties to the Exxon-government settlement agreement, so it could not be legally binding on them. Consequently, we argued these native corporations and other private landowners had the right to bring negligence and nuisance damage claims against Exxon for damages to the natural resources on their lands. This was their fundamental legal right under long-established English and American common law.

As luck would have it, I was scheduled to take the deposition of some executives from Exxon and Exxon Shipping at about the same time that the state and federal plaintiffs were finalizing their settlement with Exxon. When I arrived for the depositions at Exxon headquarters in Irving, Texas, I was greeted by several security guards, who had been assigned to keep an eye on the plaintiff lawyers such as me as we walked from the front gate to a vast conference room. I couldn't imagine why Exxon security was apparently on "red alert" when plaintiff lawyers were in the building. It was an eerie sensation. I guess they figured that a plaintiff lawyer was capable of almost anything and that, to be on the safe side, we should be treated in much the same way as they would a group of visiting environmental terrorists. It was rather flattering to be given so much attention by the highest executives of one of the world's largest corporations, with worldwide operations and net profits each year larger than the GNP of all but 20 countries on the planet.

At the deposition of Lawrence Rawls, the President of Exxon Corp., and Ray Alexander, then the President of Exxon Shipping, Exxon admitted the government lawyers had led them to believe that the $2 billion settlement would cover all natural resource damage claims. They believed that the settlement included all of the claims made by the native Alaskan corporations. Armed with this knowledge, we were in a much better position to challenge the settlement as an infringement on the legal claims of the native corporations.

I also took the opportunity to question Exxon officials regarding Exxon's position that Exxon Shipping Company was completely independent of Exxon and that Exxon Corp., the parent company, should not be held liable for the negligent acts of its subsidiaries. This notion was a significant issue since, if we succeeded in "piercing the corporate veil" between Exxon and Exxon Shipping, Exxon would be directly on the hook for any judgment we obtained. The only significant assets owned by Exxon Shipping were the Exxon Valdez ship itself and the other supertankers in the Exxon fleet, but this was just a drop in the bucket compared to Exxon's overall assets and net profits, which were more than $5 billion per year at that time. As it turned out, based upon our review of Exxon's documents and the depositions of Exxon executives, it was Exxon Corp, not Exxon Shipping, that was calling the critical shots and making the important financial decisions for Exxon Shipping. Consequently, we were able to persuasively argue that the vast resources of Exxon Corp could be reached if a jury verdict exceeded the financial resources of Exxon Shipping.

When Exxon executives learned that Exxon was on the line for the consequences of the Exxon Valdez disaster, a shiver must have run up their collective spines. Following the Exxon Valdez oil spill, Exxon not only changed the name of the damaged Exxon Valdez ship after it was repaired and put back into service, but it also broke up the Exxon Shipping Company and created separate companies as owners of record for each of Exxon's tankers. Thus, in the event of another major oil spill, Exxon anticipated that the only company that could be held liable for any negligence would be the relatively small company owning the particular oil tanker in question.

This practice was a typical tactic for companies seeking to limit their liability. Instead of investing heavily in increased safety measures, they concentrate much of their creative energies hiding assets behind a labyrinth of corporate structures, many of them offshore companies beyond the reach of the U.S. courts. Different countries and even states in the U.S. compete to attract corporate revenues from corporate fees by providing the least amount of oversight and regulations. Much of the world's merchant marine fleets fly "flags of convenience," such as the flags of Liberia or Panama. They fly these flags not because they have any relationship with those countries, but because the regulations demanded by these countries range from minimal to none. Similarly, various states compete to be the state of incorporation for major corporations, not by advertising themselves as the strictest regulators with hefty corporate taxes, but by requiring the least. Thus, there is a "race to the bottom," with companies seeking to incorporate and register assets in states and countries "friendly to business" and with the loosest regulations.

Certain companies such as Haliburton have taken the process one step further by setting up subsidiaries in Bermuda and elsewhere as a corporate tax avoidance strategy while, at the same time, aggressively bidding on U.S. government contracts. Even Stanley Tools, one of the icons of American industry, succumbed to the offshore fever by announcing its plan to give up its Connecticut corporate roots in favor of some Caribbean island.

Faced with the government/Exxon's settlement purporting to extinguish many of the native corporations' claims, we quickly filed a declaratory judgment action seeking a court ruling on the issue. We did so in the United States District Court for the District of Columbia, in Washington, D.C., where the case was assigned to Judge Stanley Sporkin. He had previously been a very high-profile commissioner of the U.S. Securities Exchange Commission (SEC). We argued that when Congress enacted the Clean Water Act, giving the executive branch the power to sue for damages to natural resources caused by a company, Congress did not intend to take away any common law rights of private landowners. Judge Sorkin agreed with us and set aside the settlement agreement between Exxon, the state, and the federal governments. Shortly after that, the agreement was rewritten to make explicitly clear that the legal rights of the native corporations would in no way be adversely affected by the settlement.

The lawyers for the U.S. Department of Justice were quite put out by the ruling and what they considered our meddling with their agreement, but with Judge Sporkin's ruling, we were finally able to ensure that our clients' rights were not going to be lost in the shuffle. The plaintiffs who were sports fishermen, however, were less fortunate. The federal Ninth Circuit Court of Appeals held that only the U.S. government and the State of Alaska, as public trustees, could recover under the Clean Water Act and its related federal statute, CERCLA. Private sports fishermen's claims for lost recreational use were barred.

We coordinated our legal work with many native corporation leaders and with the local Anchorage-based law firms that represented the various villages and regional native Alaskan corporations. One of these leaders was George Gordy, an athletic and dynamic leader. During fishing season, he flew small planes as a fish spotter. He would radio into the fishing fleet when he spotted one of the substantial salmon schools swimming through Prince William Sound on their return trip to spawn in one of the many rivers and streams that fed into the Sound. George was a great fisherman in his own right. However, his enthusiasm for fishing dampened when his son went overboard while fishing and died of exposure in the icy cold waters fed by the Columbia glacier. Surviving in the Alaskan waters can be difficult after only a few minutes. Several small plane pilots, known as bush pilots, confided in me that if they ran out of fuel flying over water in Alaska, they would roll the planes to hit the water upside down and avoid a more painful but sure death going into the water upright. After hearing this story more than once, I always made sure the pilot double-checked the fuel gauges before takeoff, and I checked a few times to make sure the top on the fuel tank was secure before takeoff. If you lose fuel in a car by forgetting to put the top back on, you can just pull over at the next service station or call AAA for roadside assistance. You don't have that same option when you are on a small plane in the Alaska wilderness.

My favorite Alaska plane was a T. Havilland, built in Canada and equally reliable on either wheel or pontoon landings (although you have to make sure that the wheel was retracted before landing with pontoons, or you can flip the plane over). I made dozens of trips to remote native Alaskan villages this way without mishap.

Although the native corporations successfully kept archaeological damages in the case, since it was an aspect of the property values, the Alaskan native class comprised of individual native Alaskans (as opposed to their corporations) did not fare so well. The Ninth Circuit Court of Appeals held that the Alaska native class had failed to prove any "special injury" to their communal life, so they were barred from recovering any communal damages.

One of the significant problems we faced in Alaska state court before Judge Brian C. Shortell was that, at the time of the oil spill, several native corporations had selected certain federal lands to transfer title to native corporations under ANCSA. However, the title to these lands had still not been conveyed. The question then was: who had the cause of action for damages to these lands - the federal government or the native corporations? This problem was solved by lobbying Congress, with the federal government's agreement, to pass a statute conveying to the native corporations these critical causes of action for property "already selected but not yet conveyed." Judge Shortell, however, found that the law alone was not sufficient to establish damages since the native corporations were not using the property at the time of the spill, since the federal government still owned these parcels.

While the state and federal cases slowly moved along, the native corporations filed claims with the Trans-Alaska Pipeline Liability Fund ("TAPLF"). This was an administrative fund secured by Congress to be established by the oil companies who co-ventured the Alaska pipeline, whereby up to $100 million in claims could be paid from a single spill. Judge John Givens, a retired judge of the Third Circuit Court of Appeals, presided over a series of hearings held at his law firm's offices in Newark, New Jersey. Several of the native leaders traveled down from Alaska to prepare for the hearings with me at our World Trade Center offices and then took the PATH train to Newark to talk about Alaska Native Corporation losses, which had taken place thousands of miles away. There was something a bit surrealistic about the experience. Still, Judge Givens awarded us much of what we asked for, and well over half of the payments made from the Alyeska fund went to the native corporations.

Back in Anchorage, Judge Russell Holland ruled in federal court there that a commercial fishing class, a native class, and a landowners' class would be certified for purposes of determining punitive damages.

Judge Holland also certified a mandatory punitive damages class, meaning that no other case in any other court could award punitive damages. Over several months, the case was further streamlined by, among other things, an agreement among the parties, known as a "stipulation," that Exxon's negligence had caused the oil spill. Exxon wisely stipulated to this because the evidence of negligence was overwhelming. Strong evidence had been developed that Exxon management knew that Hazelwood, an admitted alcoholic who had been through various treatment programs, had fallen off the wagon and was drinking again. This fact, along with evidence that there were no mechanical malfunctions in the ship, led inexorably to the conclusion that Exxon was liable for serious lapses of judgment and probable violations of Coast Guard rules and regulations. These human errors by Exxon officers and employees constituted negligence, at the very least, and we argued that Exxon was also responsible for gross negligence that could trigger an award of punitive damages. Therefore, the question before the federal jury was whether Exxon's conduct was sufficiently reckless and indifferent to the consequences of the negligence, such that punitive damages should be imposed and, if so, what was the appropriate amount of those punitive damages.

Since there were simultaneous proceedings in federal and state courts, the plaintiffs' lawyers formed separate federal and state trial teams. The claims of the Native Alaskan corporations represented by my law firm and others were primarily brought in state court. But, I also worked on the federal trial team, where I was assigned to work with plaintiffs' witnesses and experts. I focused on Captain Hazelwood's prodigious alcohol consumption and Exxon's prior knowledge of his alcoholism. We took numerous depositions of Exxon officials as well as a memorable deposition of Captain Joe himself, who had a tough time trying to defend himself against the indefensible. By the time the case reached trial in federal court, there was a mountain of evidence showing that he was a ticking timebomb. A catastrophic accident was waiting to happen on his watch. Exxon did little or nothing to monitor his sobriety or keep him in an office where he could do no harm.

The lead attorney on the plaintiff's federal legal team was Brian O'Neill, a partner in the Minneapolis-based law firm of Faegre and Benson. Brian was an experienced trial lawyer with a straightforward military-style demeanor. He had grown up on army bases around the world since his father had been an officer in the U.S. Army. Brian himself attended West Point and served as a field artillery officer before attending law school at the University of Michigan.

The other law firms who participated in the federal court case on behalf of the many classes of plaintiffs read like a Who's Who of prominent plaintiffs' law firms from around the country, including prominent attorneys from Berger & Montague, Hagens Berman, Lieff Cabraser, Milberg Weiss, and Cohen Milstein. Some of the maritime lawyers associated with the law firm where I was a partner at the time – Hill, Betts & Nash – played a prominent role in the navigation and maritime aspects of the case. Our part included the rebuttal of the issues raised by Exxon about possible equipment failures being the cause of the accident, rather than gross negligence by Hazelwood and Exxon itself.

The plaintiffs' teams also included a wide array of the best and the brightest Alaska and Seattle-based lawyers and law firms. When I first arrived in Anchorage, I primarily worked out of the law offices of Birch Horton Bittner & Cherot since they represented Chugach Alaska Corporation ("CAC"). This regional native Alaskan corporation owned much of the land surrounding Prince Williams Sound that had been oiled and damaged due to the oil spill. I worked closely with Tim Petumenos, who was a partner at that firm. Later on, when more of my legal work related to the claims of the native Alaskan village corporations, I spent most of my time working with Sam Fortier out of the offices of Fortier & Mikko, the law firm representing several of the village corporations, including Chenega, Port Graham, and English Bay.

There were three phases to the federal court trial. In the first phase, the jury found that Hazelwood and Exxon had been reckless for purposes of establishing punitive damage liability. In the second phase, the jury determined the amount of compensatory damages attributable to the spill. The jury awarded $287 million in compensatory damages, which after deduction for released claims, settlements, and payments by the Trans-Alaska Pipeline Liability Fund, left net compensatory damages of approximately $19.5 million. The third stage of the trial, which established the amount of punitive damages, resulted in a $5 billion punitive damages verdict against Exxon, the most significant punitive damage award in American history. However, Exxon's stock price went up a little bit after the news of the verdict since the plaintiffs had asked the jury for $15 billion.

The trial was not without its difficult moments. One part of the federal case that I worked on involved the handling of our alcohol experts. This part of the case became one of the most problematic – and potentially fatal – parts of the case. A sample of Hazelwood's blood was not taken until several hours after the ship had run aground, which was at least a couple of hours before that when he had taken his last drink. The test results for his blood alcohol level had to be extrapolated backward to determine his BAL (blood alcohol level) when the ship landed on the rocks. But first, the state trooper who took the test had to get the blood samples to a qualified lab, and the chain of custody had to be sufficiently maintained so that it could be shown that the blood sample tested was, in fact, Hazelwood's blood. After spending several years as a federal prosecutor working with this kind of chain of custody issues with the FBI, DEA, and other agencies, I was appalled when I found out how Hazelwood's blood samples had been handled. First of all, there was not a federally approved laboratory in Alaska that was satisfactory to the Coast Guard. As a result, Hazelwood's blood samples spent at least one night outside on the window ledge, where the young Coast guardsman who had custody of it had placed them. Then the sample spent some additional time in a refrigerator at a Coast Guard station that virtually everyone at that station could have accessed. This type of haphazard handling of evidence was not something I was used to. Plus, the sample had been shipped by Federal Express to Seattle for delivery to the lab. Without the lab results, it would have been virtually impossible to prove by objective test results that Hazelwood was positively physically impaired by alcohol at the time of the incident.

Exxon and Hazelwood moved to exclude evidence of a .061% blood alcohol level in samples taken 11 hours after the Exxon Valdez ran aground. Plaintiffs' experts testified that his blood alcohol level must have been much higher 11 hours earlier since alcohol metabolizes at the rate of about 1 ounce (a shot glass) per hour. Judge Holland found that there had been "remarkable mishandling" of the blood samples but denied the motion in limine to exclude this evidence. He held that the chain of custody regarding the sealed tubes with Hazelwood's name and Social Security number on them was good enough. He felt reasonable jurors could conclude that even though there was a discrepancy in the lab notes as to the color of the stoppers on the tubes containing Hazelwood's blood samples, any changes in the blood samples due to improper storage would have been noted by the laboratory technicians. A physician's disability report on Hazelwood that had been submitted to Exxon, and a 1995 report diagnosing Hazelwood as having "alcohol abuse episodes" was also held admissible in evidence, even though they had been marked as "confidential."

Exxon's argument at trial and on appeal was that no punitive damages could or should be awarded. They claimed with all the criminal and civil sanctions imposed on the company, as well as the other $2.1 billion spent on cleanup expenses, it was already thoroughly punished and deterred from engaging in similar conduct in the future. In their view, a punitive damages award could serve no public purpose. Exxon had already been fined and sanctioned for environmental crimes to the tune of $125 million. In response, plaintiffs argued that prior criminal sanctions do not bar punitive damages.

After a jury trial in September 1994, the jury ordered Exxon to pay about $287 million in compensatory damages to commercial salmon and herring fishermen, plus $5 billion in punitive damages for behavior that led to the 1989 oil spill. One factor that the jury had to consider was whether Exxon was responsible for the negligent acts of Hazelwood. Under the law, a corporation may be held liable for its managerial employees acting within the scope of their employment. This is the legal principle of "vicarious liability." The $5 billion punitive damage verdict was about one year's net profits for the entire worldwide operation of Exxon.

Exxon immediately obtained a $4.8 billion credit line from J.P. Morgan & Co to avoid putting that much money in reserve to secure most of the verdict award if the verdict was affirmed on appeal. At the same time, Exxon appealed the jury verdict to the Ninth Circuit Court of Appeals, which remanded the case and ordered District Court Judge Russel Holland to reduce the $5 billion in punitive damages.[1]

On December 6, 2002, Judge Holland announced that he had reduced the damages to $4 billion, which he concluded was justified by the facts of the case and was not grossly excessive. Exxon filed a second appeal to the Ninth Circuit, claiming that this $4 billion in punitive damages was still far too much.

Between the time of that verdict and Exxon's second appeal, the United States Supreme Court had issued an opinion in *BMW of North America Inc. v. Gore*, 517 U.S. 559 (S. Ct. 1996), where the jury had awarded the plaintiff $4,000 in compensatory damages and $4 million in punitive damages. The plaintiff in that case claimed that BMW had failed to tell him that his car had been repainted after being damaged in transit. In the *BMW* case, the Supreme Court held that the $4 million punitive damage award violated the due process claims of the Constitution, reasoning that BMW was not fairly put on notice that such a severe award would be imposed. One of the factors the Court was concerned about was the ratio of the punitive damages awarded to the compensatory damages verdict. Although it did not set an absolute standard for the outer limits for that ratio, it found that the ratio in the *BMW* case was too high.

The Ninth Circuit remanded the second appeal of the Exxon Valdez punitive damage verdict to Judge Holland, with instructions to review the punitive damages award in light of the Supreme Court decision in the *BMW* case.[2] In response, Judge Holland increased the punitive damages to $4.5 billion, plus interest.[3] However, after more appeals, in December 2006, the damages award was cut to $2.5 billion. The Ninth Circuit Court of Appeals cited recent Supreme Court rulings relative to limits on punitive damages.[4] One of the cases relied upon by the Ninth Circuit in the Exxon Valdez litigation was *Hopkins v. Dow Corning*. In this case, the court affirmed a $6.5 million punitive damages award because Dow Corning had exposed thousands of women to painful and debilitating disease, gained financially from its conduct, and knew of the possible defects in its product but concealed the information for years. The Ninth Circuit held there was no clear line for the ratio, but noted that the ratio in the Exxon Valdez case between the $287 in compensatory damages to the $5 billion punitive damage verdict was high: about 17 to one. This ratio was greater than the four-to-one ratio that the Supreme Court had called "close to the line." Ultimately, the Ninth Circuit concluded that the punitive damage award was too high and should be reduced to $2.5 billion.

The U.S. Supreme Court granted certiorari, agreeing to review the Ninth Circuit decision. On February 27, 2008, the Supreme Court heard oral arguments. In a decision issued June 25, 2008, the Court vacated the $2.5 billion award, remanding the case back to the lower court, finding that the damages were excessive with respect to maritime common law.[5]

The punitive damages were further reduced to $507.5 million, which was the total compensatory damages awarded.[6] The Court's ruling was that maritime punitive damages should not exceed the compensatory damages, finding that there should be no more than a 1:1 ratio between compensatory and punitive damages.

Although the punitive damage award reduction was hugely disappointing to the plaintiffs, including the native Alaskan communities we represented, they were generally successful – following the Exxon Valdez oil spill - in rebuilding the economic, social, and cultural base of their villages and communities. The oil spill disaster also spurred Congress to pass the Oil Pollution Act of 1990 (OPA). This Act included a clause prohibiting any vessel that, after March 22, 1989, has caused an oil spill of more than 1 million U.S. gallons (3,800 m3) in any marine area from operating in Prince William Sound. This effectively barred the Exxon Valdez from ever entering Prince William Sound again. The OPA also set a schedule for the gradual phase-in of a double hull design, providing an additional layer of protection. While a double hull would likely not have prevented the *Exxon Valdez* disaster, a Coast Guard study estimated that it would have cut the amount of oil spilled by 60 percent.[7]

* * *

While the Exxon Valdez case was one of the most significant and richly rewarding experiences of my legal career, it also took a considerable personal toll on other East Coast plaintiffs' lawyers and me. We were required to spend long periods working in Alaska, away from our families and the rest of our legal practices. Every two or three weeks, I flew back to New York to spend at least a couple of days with my family and try to catch up with other ongoing cases at my law firm. I would fly out of Anchorage late in the day, change planes in Seattle or Salt Lake City, and then fly all night to New York, where I would often go directly to the office to work for a few hours before going home and crashing. However, my long absences from New York eventually took such a toll on my marriage that my first wife, Gail, and I divorced. However, before going our separate ways, Gail flew to Anchorage with our eldest son, Brendan, a teenager at the time. We toured Prince William Sound on a fishing charter boat for several days, where we did some salmon fishing and otherwise spent some quality time together. It was idyllic but short-lived. Brendan proved to be much more successful than I at catching salmon, which we packed up and shipped back to New York on ice. For the next few months, we dined on Alaskan salmon whenever I was back in New York, with Brendan proudly commenting each time that if it were not for him, we would have run through our salmon supply weeks earlier.

Chapter 5

The Bhopal Gas Disaster Case

One of the worst industrial catastrophes in history occurred in Bhopal, India, on December 2 - 3, 1984, when a Union Carbide of India chemical plant released large amounts of poisonous and toxic gases. More than 3,000 people in the surrounding area were killed over the next few days. Over time, more than 200,000 were injured, many of them permanently. The chemical being manufactured at the plant - methyl isocyanate – is primarily used for agricultural purposes. However, methyl isocyanate is one of the most dangerous chemicals manufactured for commercial purposes in its gaseous form. Within hours of the gas leak, thousands of Bhopal residents were sickened by the gas.

The Bhopal tragedy - which was later the subject of the best-selling book, *Five Past Midnight in Bhopal: The Epic Story of the World's Deadliest Industrial Disaster*, by Dominique Lapierre and Javier Mor - was a widely-followed wake-up call around the globe. It was perhaps the most egregious example to date of what can happen when corporate irresponsibility and greed leads to the construction of a highly-dangerous industrial facility in a developing country, without any state-of-the-art safety equipment. Bhopal was a significant inflection point in the growing awareness of the massive environmental damage and human devastation that can occur when mega-corporations build toxic chemical facilities in developing countries. These countries do not have the bargaining power or expertise to demand that such plants be equipped with the same level of safety equipment as equivalent plants in the U.S. or Europe. Like the Exxon Valdez oil spill, Bhopal provided a jolt of energy during the 1980s for the growing international environmental movement.

Today, the increasingly urgent topic of Climate Change and the international efforts to protect the planet from environmental degradation make front-page news. But in 1984, when the Bhopal disaster occurred,

Victims of Bhopal disaster march in September 2006 demanding the extradition of American Warren Anderson from the United States. Wikimedia Commons BHOPAL (231583728) CC.

environmental protection was not a high priority until the sheer scope of what happened in Bhopal shook the public from its stupor.

My involvement in the case brought in the U.S. against Union Carbide is still one of the most challenging and frustrating of my career. I was introduced to the subject by Raj Sharma, a young lawyer straight out of law school. He started working with me at the plaintiffs' law firm of Goodkind Labaton in New York City. I was impressed with Raj's knowledge of environmental law and his passion for seeking justice for the people of Bhopal, who had been so severely injured and financially damaged as a result of the explosion and its aftermath.

Raj came from a well-to-do Indian-American family based in Houston, Texas. In many ways, despite being raised in America, he was a traditional young Indian man who had an arranged marriage in India. We became very close professionally and personally. Eventually, our environmental and human rights law practice at the Goodkind Labaton firm broke off. We formed our law firm under the name of McCallion & Associates LLP.

Together we investigated, researched, and filed a complaint against Union Carbide and its CEO Warren Anderson in November 1999 in the U.S. District Court for the Southern District of New York. The case, which was captioned *Bano v. Union Carbide Corp. et al.,*[1] alleged that Union Carbide and its former CEO violated international human rights, environmental, and international criminal law.

As we explained in the complaint in November 1999, and elaborated on in the amended complaint we filed in early 2000, the Bhopal plant, which was built and owned by Union Carbide, was fatally flawed from the beginning. Union Carbide, which had its headquarters in Danbury, Connecticut, was led from the beginning of the Bhopal project by CEO Anderson. He was personally involved with many safety and quality control decisions. Generally speaking, Union Carbide managers, including Anderson, opted for economic and financial short-cuts in the design and construction of the plant, which included cost-cutting in the creation of the safety mechanisms.

Union Carbide formed a wholly-owned subsidiary, Union Carbide India Limited (UCIL), in order to distance the parent company to the maximum extent possible. Hoping to limit the potential legal liability of the parent company, it was UCIL that obtained the necessary permits and dealt with the Indian government officials. However, Union Carbide and

Warren Anderson made direct promises to the Indian Government that the plant would be a financial bonanza for the Bhopal community and the entire country in general, and that Indian nationals would be getting most of the well-paying jobs.

The Indian Government considered the production of pesticides to be a massive bonus for the country since large quantities of pesticides were being used to enhance Indian farming production, so it was expected that the plant would reduce the need for the importation of expensive chemical pesticides from abroad. The remainder of the chemicals produced by the plant would be available for export.

The main chemical used in the production process was methyl isocyanate (MIC), which, when mishandled and especially when mixed with water, releases a fast-acting, highly toxic gas. MIC was the most dangerous of chemicals used in the production process, but it was not the only highly toxic chemical being used. In addition, the production process required hydrogen cyanide, monomethyl amine, carbon monoxide, and other chemicals released from the plant during the fatal explosion.

Anderson and Union Carbide executives had assured the Indian Government that state-of-the-art safety systems would be installed, similar to those used in their Institute, West Virginia plant. They lied. The Institute plant was virtually identical to the Bhopal Plant, except that it had state-of-the-art safety systems that Bhopal - as a cost-savings measure – lacked.

UCIL built the plant on land in the outskirts of Bhopal city that was largely vacant. However, as soon as the UCIL plant was built, it became surrounded by slum neighborhoods of huts and poor sanitation. With the increased proximity to so many people, Union Carbide and UCIL should have belatedly added safety systems that were omitted in the first place, but they did not. Their attitude continued to be that Union Carbide was doing India and the Bhopal region a big favor. As far as Union Carbide and Anderson were concerned, the risk of a chemical accident was just one of the risks that the people of Bhopal had to take to reap the financial benefits that came along with it. After all, they were giving them jobs; that was enough. The company couldn't afford safety as well. As a result, on December 3, 1984, at 12:05 AM, when the gas started leaking, no alarm or warning system was triggered since none of the available safety technologies or state-of-the-art systems were in place.

Shortly after the disaster, victims and their relatives began to seek monetary compensation from Union Carbide in U.S. courts. There were press reports of American lawyers descending on the stricken Bhopal community with printed retainer agreement in hand. Our law firm was not one of them. Other larger plaintiffs' law firms eventually lost interest as the prospect of a quick settlement faded away. Our law firm and environmental organizations, such as EarthRights International, took over the legal "heavy lifting" necessary to persuade the U.S. federal judges that they had jurisdiction over the matter.

On the theory that it was more likely that the families of victims would do better in U.S. courts in valuing their wrongful death claims than in Indian courts, cases began to be quickly filed in U.S. courts. On February 6, 1985, the judicial panel for multidistrict litigation consolidated 145 purported class actions filed throughout this country in the U.S. District Court for the Southern District of New York. Judge John Keenan was assigned to the cases.

Alarmed that American lawyers were gaining control over the Bhopal litigation, on March 9, 1985, India adopted the Bhopal Gas Leak Disaster Act, popularly known as the Bhopal Act. This legislation gave the Indian Government the exclusive authority to represent victims of the Bhopal Disaster in the U.S. and other foreign courts. The Supreme Court of India later upheld the Act against various legal challenges.

In April 1985, the Indian Government filed a complaint in the United States District Court for the Southern District of New York on behalf of all the disaster victims. The following month, in May 1986, Judge Keenan granted Union Carbide's motion to dismiss the cases before him on the ground of *forum non conveniens* over the objections of the Indian Government and the individual plaintiffs.[2] Judge Keenan's decision concluded that, even though Union Carbide was headquartered in the U.S., the Indian courts had a greater interest or connection with the subject matter of the litigation than the U.S. courts since all the victims were located there. However, Judge Keenan conditioned his dismissal on, among other things, Union Carbide's consent to the jurisdiction of the Indian courts. The Second Circuit Court of Appeals affirmed Judge Keenan's decision.[3]

Having been dismissed from the U.S. courts, the Indian Government filed suit against Union Carbide in Bhopal District Court. In November

1987, the India Central Bureau of Investigation (CBI) brought criminal charges against UCIL and Warren Anderson, Union Carbide's CEO. Anderson had traveled to India soon after the disaster, where he was arrested as soon as he stepped off the plane. The U.S. government intervened, and he was released after he signed a bail bond promising to return for the criminal prosecution. Anderson then jumped bail and became one of the most notorious international scofflaws, despite his status as the CEO of one of America's largest Fortune 500 companies. Attempts were made through Interpol and the U.S. Department of Justice to serve Anderson with a warrant, but he just ignored them.

In February 1989, the Supreme Court of India approved a settlement under which Union Carbide agreed to pay $470 million to the Indian Government "in full settlement of all claims, rights, and liabilities related to and ensuing out of the Bhopal gas disaster."[4] However, the Supreme Court of India later modified their settlement order to clarify that the Settlement did not cover the criminal prosecution of Union Carbide and Anderson. When the criminal prosecution went forward in the Bhopal District Court, neither Anderson nor Union Carbide appeared for their arraignment. Consequently, in 1992, the Bhopal District Court declared them "absconders," which made them perhaps the best-known – and most notorious - international fugitives.

Two new civil class action complaints were filed in Texas state courts, challenging the validity of the 1989 settlement ordered by the Indian Supreme Court. Union Carbide removed the actions to federal court, and these two cases were assigned to Judge Keenan, who dismissed them on forum non-convenience grounds.[5] The Second Circuit affirmed, but on the basis that the plaintiffs lacked standing in light of the Bhopal Act's delegation to the Indian Government of the exclusive right to represent the victims.[6]

This was when Raj Sharma and I came into the picture. Even before we joined forces, Raj worked with the five victims' organizations in Bhopal and EarthRights International, a public interest group based in Washington, D.C. The Bhopal victims' organizations were asking whether another case could be brought in the U.S. courts since the $470 million settlement was proving to be woefully inadequate to meet the needs of the Bhopal victims and their families. This was especially true since much of the settlement monies were not being released by the Indian Government.

The claims process there had turned into a bureaucratic nightmare. In addition, the criminal actions in India could only be effectively enforced against UCIL's Indian managers, who shared some of the responsibility for the disaster. Meanwhile, Warren Anderson and Union Carbide had gotten off scot-free by failing to return to India to stand trial.

Raj and I thought we had a reasonable chance to get some relief for the victims in U.S. courts, despite the Bhopal Act. On November 15, 1999, we brought another complaint against Union Carbide and Warren Anderson, arguing that the Bhopal Act and Settlement was not definitive and that the victims still had standing in the U.S. under some new legal theories. Our arguments centered on the Alien Torts Statute, 28 U.S.C. § 1350, which we claimed gave the victims the right to sue for human rights violations by Union Carbide. We also argued that the fugitive disentitlement doctrine should be applied, based on the fact that, as fugitives, Anderson and Union Carbide should not be allowed to defend themselves in U.S. courts.

Then, on January 4, 2000, we filed an amended complaint which added causes of action for the ongoing contamination of the area around the Bhopal plant. The contamination in Bhopal because of the Union Carbide plant continued well into the 21st century, with the groundwater around the plant still compromised. We argued that this cause of action was independent of the explosion since Union Carbide had systematically been polluting the area around the plant since it had first become operational.

The first of the major hurdles we had to overcome was that the Bhopal Act and Settlement purported to put the jurisdiction and representation of the victims squarely and solely in the hands of the Indian courts. In its motion for summary judgment, Union Carbide argued that it had already paid the $475 million under the Settlement, and it was not their fault that the Indian Government was not dispensing the funds expeditiously. Further, they argued that the criminal charges were not a reason to ignore the Settlement terms. They claimed that the explosion had been an act of sabotage by Indian employees, who had been tried and found guilty. Of course, they made these claims from the safety of the United States, not in an Indian Court, where they would have risked the wrath of the families of the victims and the entire Indian nation.

Another major problem we faced was that we could not find Warren Anderson. We attempted to subpoena him to get his testimony under oath, but he had retired 12 years earlier and was nowhere to be found. We knew he had homes in Florida and Connecticut, but he never seemed to be there. We had hired a private investigator to find the former CEO, and our efforts began to receive press attention, renewing public interest in Anderson's fugitive status and notoriety. But, like Interpol and the Indian Government, we were never able to track down Anderson and serve him with legal process. By this time, Dow Chemical had announced the purchase of Union Carbide while claiming at the same time that Dow would not take responsibility for any of Union Carbide's remaining liability, if any, for the Bhopal disaster. We were also up against Judge Keenan, who by that time must have been sick and tired of hearing about Bhopal. He had consistently ruled in favor of the company and the Indian Settlement, but the hopes of the victims' organizations for some modicum of justice in U.S. courts never seemed to be extinguished, despite his best efforts.

We tried to distinguish our new claims for environmental damages from the personal injury claims of the victims that the prior Settlement had covered. We argued that – independent of the explosion itself and the damage caused by that explosion – there was longstanding and on-going chemical contamination of the land around the Bhopal plant. The contamination continued to harm the residents there. We further argued that Union Carbide was liable under common law for its failure to clean up the environmental contamination, and these damages were not considered or included within the four corners of the Settlement.

Despite our best efforts to convince the court that it had jurisdiction over the matter, Judge Keenan granted summary judgment to Union Carbide and Warren Anderson. We promptly appealed to the Court of Appeals for the Second Circuit. While upholding a portion of Judge Keenan's decision, the Second Circuit vacated and remanded his dismissal of the several common-law claims we had raised in the complaint, seeking relief for environmental contamination at the Bhopal plant allegedly unrelated to the 1984 gas leak.[7] The Appeals Court found that Judge Keenan had improperly dismissed the plaintiffs' entire complaint without directly addressing the environmental claims.[8]

Not surprisingly, when Judge Keenan considered our environmental claims on remand from the Second Circuit, he summarily dismissed them. After twenty years of dealing with Bhopal disaster cases, he had apparently decided that the matter could not be reopened. He continued to feel that the wrongs done to the people of Bhopal by an American company simply had no business being heard in a U.S. court. There was simply nothing that we could say or do that would convince him otherwise.

The Bhopal case helped me to understand the limits of litigation. You can't always win, although the struggle for justice is a worthwhile and noble cause, as long as there is a sound legal basis for each filed and litigated case. In the case of Bano v Union Carbide et al., we strongly felt that our cause was just and that we had tried the matter thoroughly and professionally, regardless of the outcome. A major U.S. corporation had victimized the people of Bhopal. The company had been attracted by the prospect of cheap labor and high-profit margins, with an inept government failing, for the most part, to oversee their operations properly.

Under the leadership of Warren Anderson, Union Carbide had taken full advantage of the situation and the vulnerabilities offered by locating such a potentially dangerous plant in Bhopal. They had the audacity to build two identical plants, one in the U.S. and one in India. The only difference was that the one in West Virginia was relatively safe, while the one in Bhopal was a ticking time bomb. Both Union Carbide and Anderson had been found guilty in the Indian courts of criminal manslaughter. But since they had fled India and were tried in absentia, they were never held accountable for their actions.

Alas, not every wrong in this world – no matter how grievous – has a legal remedy. But that fact should not stop us from seeking justice in an imperfect world.

Chapter 6

The Holocaust Cases

More than 50 years after World War II, the U.S. federal courts became the focus of efforts to recover Holocaust-era assets and redress for Nazi atrocities. In the mid to late 1990s, lawsuits started being filed in U.S. courts by attorneys representing Holocaust survivors, their heirs, and the families of those who did not survive Hitler's genocidal campaign against them.

The Swiss Bank Cases

The first three Holocaust-related cases were filed in New York in 1996. Three federal class-action lawsuits were filed in the U.S. District Court for the Eastern District of New York against the three largest Swiss banks on behalf of Holocaust survivors and their heirs. In 1997, these cases were consolidated before District Judge Edward R. Korman, a former U.S. Attorney who I had worked for. The cases were re-named as "In re Holocaust Victim Assets Litigation."[1] In these cases, plaintiffs sought the return of monies that Jews and other persecuted minorities in Europe had deposited in Switzerland for safekeeping before or during World War II. After the war, the banks refused to return the money, sometimes turning away family members trying to recover lost assets. The banks also lost track of a large number of accounts.

An investigation of the Swiss Banks established that tens of thousands of Holocaust victims deposited money in Swiss banks as the Nazis extended their grip in Europe, expecting to retrieve it later. Surrounded by Germany, Nazi-occupied France, and Nazi-allied Italy, Switzerland took in nearly 30,000 Jews. But it turned away an equal number, many of them to certain death.

After the end of the war, Swiss bank officials stonewalled survivors and their heirs, claiming they could not find accounts or demanding that death certificates be produced, which they knew were not available. The

Swiss banks well knew that Auschwitz and other Nazi concentration camps did not issue death certificates.

In addition to the U.S. court litigation, the Swiss banks and the Swiss Government tried to "handle" their Holocaust issues by establishing The Volcker Commission in 1996. Participants in the Commission were the Swiss Bankers Association, the World Jewish Congress, and other Jewish organizations who undertook an independent audit of Swiss banks to identify accounts that might have belonged to victims of Nazi persecution. As a result, they discovered nearly 54,000 accounts linked to victims of the persecution. The lawsuits also sought profits from assets looted by the Nazis, including gold and proceeds from slave labor that the Nazis "laundered" through several Swiss banks to raise Swiss francs to support the German war effort.

The Swiss banks – notably the Union Bank of Switzerland (UBS) and Credit Suisse - initially refused to cooperate with the U.S. litigation or make settlement offers. Instead, they filed motions to dismiss on various grounds, ranging from lack of jurisdiction to statute of limitations. The defendant banks argued in their motions that the actions should be dismissed because plaintiffs failed to state claims under Swiss and international law, failed to join indispensable parties, lacked personal and subject matter jurisdiction, and lacked standing. Defendants also argued that Judge Korman should abstain from adjudicating plaintiffs' claims in favor of ongoing non-judicial initiatives to redress plaintiffs' claims. They argued that Switzerland, not the United States, was the proper forum for the plaintiffs to pursue the relief they believed they were entitled to.

Judge Korman heard lengthy argument on defendants' motions on July 31, 1997. During this oral argument, Korman voiced serious concerns about the viability of some of the causes of action and identified several additional legal issues that the parties subsequently addressed in post-hearing memoranda of law. While the motions to dismiss were pending, the parties negotiated a Settlement Agreement, which made it unnecessary for Judge Korman to decide the motions.

Although I participated in some of the discussions between New York City/State representatives and Swiss representatives in New York City that laid the groundwork for settlement, I was not one of the attorneys of record for the plaintiffs in the Swiss Bank case. The lawyers for the plaintiffs who played critical roles in the case were Professor Burt Neuborne

Marseille, Gare d'Arenc, Deportation von Juden
Bundesarchiv, Bild 101I-027-1477-12 / photographer: Vennemann, Wolfgang

of New York University Law School, Melvyn H. Weiss, and Michael D. Hausfeld. I had previously worked with Mel Weiss and Mike Hausfeld in Alaska on the Exxon Valdez case, so I kept in close touch with them and other plaintiff lawyers as the settlement discussions progressed. The negotiations to settle the Swiss Bank case were facilitated by the Deputy Secretary of Treasury, Stuart Eizenstat, who also helped settle several other Holocaust-related cases.

During the protracted settlement discussions with the Swiss Banks, economic and financial pressure was brought to bear on the Swiss Government and the Banks by New York City and New York State. Other state and local governments throughout the United States also announced that their large pension funds would be withdrawn from Swiss-related investments if the Banks did not negotiate a settlement in good faith.

The Swiss Bank case was the first major Holocaust settlement when, on August 12, 1998, a landmark settlement worth $1.25 billion was reached with Swiss banks in New York City.[2] In response to the Swiss Banks' agreement to pay Holocaust survivors, New York City and New York State agreed to cancel proposed sanctions against them, including a boycott on investments by the mammoth New York City and State Pension Funds in Swiss companies. The sanctions, scheduled to start September 1, 1998, were announced in July after negotiations between the banks and the Holocaust survivors had broken down.

According to the settlement, the $1.25 billion fund was to be paid out over four years. Claimants could file claims establishing that they or their family members had dormant account claims against either one or both of the Swiss commercial banks, UBS AG and Credit Suisse, or against the Swiss National Bank, other Swiss banks, the Swiss Government, or Swiss industry.[3]

As a condition of settlement, the plaintiffs were required to publicly call for all elected officials to drop their threat of sanctions against Swiss financial interests.

In a written decision issued on August 2, 2000,[4] Judge Korman granted preliminary class approval and class certification. He also allowed for the implementation of the second step in the settlement evaluation process, which involved the dissemination of notice of the proposed settlement and class certification to the settlement classes. Since there was no list of all the members of the settlement classes, Judge Korman directed that potential class members be notified of the settlement through "worldwide publication, public relations (*i.e.,* earned media), Internet, and grassroots community outreach."[5]

The third and final step in the class action evaluation process in the Swiss Bank case – and every other class action case - was a final approval hearing, or "fairness hearing."[6] In the fairness hearing held by Judge Korman in the United States District Court for the Eastern District of New York on November 29, 1999, settlement class members attended and were invited to comment on the settlement. Judge Korman also presided (by electronic hookup) over a supplemental fairness hearing held in Israel on December 14, 1999.

Austrian and German Bank Case

Austrian and German banks also had Holocaust-related claims filed against them. A series of individual and class actions charged the banks with profiting from the looting of Jewish-owned assets and participating in and profiting from the use of slave labor during the war. These lawsuits were consolidated in the U.S. District Court for the Southern District of New York on February 19, 1999, under the name "In re Austrian and German Bank Holocaust Litigation."[7]

Austrian Bank Settlement

In December 1998, Judge Kram appointed former Senator Alphonse D'Amato of New York as Special Master to assist in settlement negotiations.[8] In March 1999, the plaintiffs and the Austrian banks reached an agreement on settlement terms. This agreement required the Austrian banks to pay $40 million to the putative plaintiffs' settlement class to pay claims, administrative expenses, and fees. It also established a historical commission that would report on the Nazi-era activities of the Austrian banks.[9] It provided that the Austrian banks would assign to the settlement class all claims that the Austrian banks might have against German banks that had controlled the Austrian banks and allegedly looted their assets.

In June 1999, Judge Kram granted preliminary certification of the settlement class. At a hearing to determine whether the proposed settlement was fair, reasonable, and adequate, Robert "Bob" Swift, co-lead counsel for the plaintiffs, described the settlement as "a door-opening settlement" that would hopefully encourage other defendants to resolve the Holocaust claims against them. The ongoing negotiations were conducted by Deputy Treasury Secretary Eizenstadt and Count Otto Lambsdorff of Germany.

On August 5, 1999, Judge Kram appointed famed Nazi hunter, Simon Wiesenthal, age 90, to head a special committee to distribute the $40 million in settlement proceeds of Holocaust-era claims against two Austrian banks. According to the settlement, whatever was left of the $40 million after original owners of stolen assets or their heirs were re-paid would be distributed to Holocaust survivors and families of victims of the Nazi regime.

However, on March 7, 2001, Judge Kram refused to dismiss the class-action lawsuit against the German and Austrian Banks, concluding that it would be unjust to dismiss the case since the German Foundation established to handle the settlement distributions had not yet been funded. The lawyers for both sides asked Judge Kram to reconsider, and to ap-prove the settlement since, without dismissal of the case approved by the judge, more than one million individuals who had been slave laborers during World War II could not be paid from the compensation fund. In response, the judge said she would not dismiss the lawsuit without assur-ance that the Foundation had been properly funded and that the claims of people who could not yet appear before the Court would be handled fairly. "Many of the absent plaintiffs in this case," Judge Kram noted, "have waited decades to receive compensation for their property claims, and it would be unjust to divert their claims to a forum whose funding remains in question." Finally, when the funding of the settlement in the case was in place, Judge Kram approved the settlement.

The German Settlement

In the fall of 1998, the German Government asked then Under Secretary of State for Economic Affairs (later Deputy Treasury Secretary) Stuart Eizenstat to facilitate a comprehensive resolution of the many class ac-tions then pending in federal and state courts in the United States against various German companies and banks for wrongs committed during the Nazi era.[10] A series of negotiations took place in Washington, D.C., and then in Berlin, where I and other lawyers for the plaintiffs in the various pending class actions met with representatives of the German Government and six other governments, including the Government of Israel.

My role in these negotiations was to represent slave and forced laborers from Russia and other eastern European countries who had been forced by the Nazi occupying forces to work without compensation in German factories and farms. The use of this slave and forced labor freed up the German workforce for military service. The German companies that used the slave and forced laborers transported into Germany included Siemens, Daimler-Benz (now Daimler Chrysler), Audi, Leica, and Volkswagen. An estimated 12 million people were put to work against their will to help in the Nazi war effort. Slave laborers were often worked to death, whereas forced laborers were compelled to work without compensation, but were not part of the Nazis' genocide program. An estimated 240,000 survivors of Nazi slave labor operations and a far larger number of forced laborers, primarily people from the former Soviet Union and Eastern Europe, were put to work in support of the Nazi war machine.

These cases settled in December 1999, when the companies and the German Government agreed to distribute a multibillion-dollar fund to the slave and forced labor camp survivors. The German Government and industry agreed to each contribute about $2.6 billion to compensate those forced to support the German war effort, with the total settlement amounting to $5.2 billion. In exchange for creating the settlement fund, the German companies received legal protection from lawsuits in the United States–backed up by a promise from the U.S. government to ask the U.S. courts where any cases were filed to formally refer those pending cases to the Foundation.

The Joint Settlement Statement contemplated the establishment of a German foundation to be known as "Remembrance, Responsibility and the Future." It included a recognition by the parties that the Foundation would be the exclusive remedy and forum for resolving all claims against German companies arising from the "National Socialist era and World War II." Slave and forced laborers still alive at the time of the settlement could apply to receive a lump sum payment of between $2500 and $7500 from the Foundation. In all, over 140,000 survivors from more than 25 countries received payments.

The German settlement was also a treaty between the Governments of the United States and the Federal Republic of Germany. It provided that, in any case brought in a court in the United States against German entities for Nazi-era acts, the U.S. Government would file a "Statement of Interest." This statement would inform the court that dismissing the case with prejudice would serve vital United States foreign policy interests.

The Insurance Company Cases

Another type of Holocaust litigation involved claims against European insurance companies. These insurers collected sizable premiums for life insurance policies and annuities from Jews before the Holocaust, but refused to pay out on the policies. Many of these insurance firms had disclaimed legal liability, arguing they no longer had obligations on the policies because Communist governments took over their Eastern European offices after the war. They claimed that the Soviet satellite governments assumed all of their assets and liabilities, and that they should therefore be let off the hook. The insurers also avoided paying out on the policies by demanding that claimants produce death certificates, which of course did not exist.

In November 1999, a confidential settlement was reached in *Stern v. Generali*,[11] which was the first lawsuit ever filed by an individual family against a European insurer over unpaid Holocaust insurance claims. The case was brought against an Italian insurance company–Assicurazioni Generali - by the family of Mor Stern, a Holocaust victim whose life insurance policies were purchased at the company's Prague office before he was killed in a gas chamber at Auschwitz. After trying to collect on Stern's policies for more than 50 years, the family sued Generali in 1998 for $135 million, alleging breach of contract and bad faith.

This lawsuit became a test case for victims and their heirs when Generali appealed a ruling granting California courts jurisdiction to resolve Holocaust claims. A state appellate court affirmed, and the California Supreme Court refused to review the case, allowing Californians to pursue their claims under the state's Holocaust Victims Insurance Act. Enacted in 1998, the law allowed bad faith claims to be brought in state courts if the plaintiffs could prove that the insurance company conducted business or litigation in California. It also extended the statute of limitations for these claims until 2010. Generali had claimed that the law was unconstitutional and that the lawsuits should fall under the jurisdiction of the countries where the policies were purchased.

California also enacted other legislation designed to crack down on insurance companies that had refused to pay out on policies bought before World War II. The Holocaust Registry Law, for example, required European insurance firms to publish a list of unpaid Holocaust-era insurance policies, and banned companies from doing business in California if they did not comply.

The French Holocaust Cases

France had been humiliated at the start of World War II when Paris fell to the Nazis on June 14, 1940, only one month after German forces invaded France. Eight days later, France signed an armistice with the Germans, and a French puppet state was set up with its capitol at Vichy, in southern France. General Charles de Gaulle and the Free French kept fighting as part of the Allied Forces, and a Resistance movement sprang up in occupied France to resist Nazi and Vichy rule. However, French historians largely ignored the extent that French antisemitism led many French officials and citizens to collaborate with the Nazis in the persecution of Jewish citizens. Indeed, a collaborationist French government helped deport 75,721 Jewish refugees and French citizens to Nazi death camps. Antisemitism in France started long before World War II. By the start of the 20th Century, antisemitism was being encouraged by the anti-republican movement Action Francaise, which had a strong following in the Catholic Church, the army, the civil service, and the judiciary. Many of them believed that Jews could never be truly integrated into a Christian country and were potential traitors.

Antisemitism in France intensified in 1936 when the Socialist Popular Front government was led by a Jewish prime minister, Léon Blum.[12] His appointment added to the fears of those convinced that France was on the verge of a Bolshevik revolution. The lightning defeat of the French army by the Germans in June 1940 brought down the democratic Third Republic, and many French were looking for a scapegoat to blame. French Jews were a convenient target.

In May 1941, anti-Semitic legislation led to the mass arrest of Jews in Paris by French police. More than 3,747 men were interned, and after two more roundups interned additional French Jews, the first deportation train provided by the French state railway left for Germany under French guard on March 12, 1942. In all, 13,151 Jews were interned, including many women and children, with the largest "Roundup," known as "La Grande Rafle" ("the big roundup"), taking place on July 16 and 17, 1942. This event is also referred to as the "Vel' d'Hiv' Roundup," since most of the detainees were temporarily confined at the Vélodrome d'Hiver ("Winter Velodrome") in Paris before being transported in railway cattle cars to Auschwitz and other concentration camps. Between June 22, 1942 and July 31, 1944, an internment camp was also set up in the northern Paris suburb of Drancy, where 67,400 French, Polish, and German Jews, including 600 children, were held and then deported from the camp in 64 rail transports. Only 1,542 prisoners remained alive at the center when the German authorities in Drancy fled from the advancing Allied forces.

A puppet collaborationist French state was established in the center and south of France, headed by 84-year-old Marshal Philippe Pétain, who had earned a distinguished military record in World War One. He set up his capital at Vichy, a spa in the Auvergne in central France. The Germans had divided France into occupied and non-occupied zones, leaving Pétain's administration in charge of about two-fifths of the country, including the cities of Lyon and Marseille.

Although not required by the Germans, the Vichy regime promulgated a Jewish Statute in October 1940. By then, about 150,000 Jews had entered into "Free France" by crossing the Demarcation Line, thinking they would be protected by the Vichy government south of Paris. What they found was something tragicly different. These displaced Jews were subjected to even greater discrimination than that practiced by the German occupation forces in the north. The zeal with which the Vichy regime in southern France hunted down foreign Jewish refugees in August 1942 resulted in the seizure and transport of about 11,000 Jews to the Drancy camp, which became the main transit center for shipment to the Auschwitz death camp. During 1942, 41,951 Jews were transported to Germany, although the deportations came to a temporary halt when some religious leaders warned Vichy that it was being too heavy-handed. After that, arrests were carried out more discreetly. In 1943 and 1944, the regime deported 31,899 people, with the last train leaving in August 1944, as Allied troops entered Paris. Out of the total of 75,721 deportees, fewer than 2,000 survived. The number of dead would have been far higher if the Italian fascist leader, Benito Mussolini, had not ordered Italian troops in France to defy German-French plans for mass roundups in Italian-occupied south-eastern France.[13]

The Vichy regime promulgated a series of anti-Jewish laws designed to strip them of their money and possessions, which made it more difficult – or impossible - for them to avoid being rounded up and deported to the death camps. The first anti-Jewish law was issued on October 3, 1940, called the *Statut des Juifs* (Statute on Jews) to deal with the Jewish "problem" in areas under Vichy control. According to a document finally made public in 2010, Pétain himself insisted that the laws be even more stringent than initially drafted.[14] The Jewish Statute embraced the definition of a Jew established in the Nuremberg Laws,[15] depriving the Jews of their civil rights and firing many of them from their jobs. The Statute forbade Jews from working in certain professions (teachers, journalists, lawyers, etc.). A related Law of October 4, 1940, required the incarceration of all foreign Jews in internment camps in southern France, such as the one at Gurs, in the southwestern Basque region of France. In addition, Jewish businesses were 'aryanised' by Vichy's Commission for Jewish Affairs, and their property was confiscated.

A General Commissariat for Jewish Affairs was created by the Vichy State in March 1941, with responsibility for supervising the seizure of Jewish assets and organizing anti-Jewish propaganda.[16] The Second Statute on Jews of June 2, 1941, called for the systematic registration of Jews throughout Vichy, France, and in Vichy-North Africa. Because the yellow Star-of-David badge was not made compulsory in the unoccupied zone, these records provided the basis for future roundups and deportations.

For several decades after World War II, there was relatively little research or study of the Holocaust in France. However, evidence of the suppression and mass deportations from the Jewish and Roma (Gypsy) communities between 1940 and 1944 eventually emerged. The French government was understandably reluctant to publicize the extensive French role in the persecution of French and foreign Jews during World War II. As a result, it kept many of the relevant documents hidden in French archives. These documents were not made available to the general public, or even to qualified historical and legal researchers. However, access to these documents increased over time, as persistent researchers such as Professor Richard H. Weisberg of Cardozo Law School in New York City were finally granted access to critical French archival material.

The post-war movement to expose the French complicity with the persecution and mass murder of Jews in France gained momentum when Serge Klarsfeld, a Jewish lawyer whose Romanian father died in Germany, succeeded in tracking down the German chief of the Secret Service in Lyon, Klaus Barbie, who was hiding in Bolivia. Barbie was subsequently sentenced to a life sentence in jail in 1987. His case led to a renewed interest in uncovering the full extent of Vichy's complicity in the French Holocaust. Klarsfeld's efforts, however, were partially frustrated by the Socialist president of France at this time, Francois Mitterrand, who had been an official at Vichy and was decorated by Pétain. Mitterrand had a great personal interest in not having the spotlight of public scrutiny focused on this chapter of French history.

It was not until 1992 that one of Barbie's French aides, Paul Touvier, was jailed for life for his crimes. Responding to Mitterrand's warnings that trials would cause civil unrest, French courts blocked other prosecutions, including that of the Vichy police chief René Bousquet, who had organized the Paris and Vichy zone mass arrests. A lone gunman later assassinated Bousquet in June 1993.

It was not until Mitterrand retired in 1995 that France began to face its responsibility for the persecution of Jews during World War II. When the new right-wing president, Jacques Chirac, came to power, he immediately condemned Vichy as a criminal regime. Two years later, the Catholic Church publicly apologized, asking for forgiveness for its failure to protect the Jews.

Another significant step forward for justice and remembrance of this period was the trial in 1997 of 89-year-old Maurice Papon for his role in the deportation of Jews from Bordeaux. After the war, he served as a French cabinet minister and waged a 16-year losing legal battle to avoid trial. He was released from jail because of poor health, but his ten-year prison sentence was at least some official acknowledgment of French complicity in the Holocaust. The Papon trial also led the French Government to open up previously hidden archives, which revealed a treasure trove of documents showing the complicity of the French banks in the persecution of Jews during the Vichy period.

In 1997, my law firm was contacted by several survivors of the French Holocaust. They wanted to know whether we could bring a class action suit similar to the one recently brought against the Swiss Banks. At about the same time, fate serendipitously brought Professor Richard Weisberg and me together, since my son, Brendan, was attending the same high school in Manhattan as Weisberg's son, Sam. When Brendan mentioned that one of his high school friend's father was studying the French Holocaust and the French legal system during World War II, I immediately reached out to set up a meeting with Professor Weisberg.

After a cordial meeting, Richard Weisberg and I agreed to work together on the investigation of the claims, and we soon determined that, after the end of the war, the French Banks had generally failed to turn over any of the assets of the Jewish bank accounts that had been frozen during World War II. Our research also led us to conclude that the U.S. courts had jurisdiction over these claims and that the cases could be pursued here.

In addition to the collaboration by the French banks with the Vichy government, we uncovered documents from the U.S. National Archives showing that Barclays Bank senior officials based in France "volunteered" information about its Jewish employees to the Nazis. The bank also helped to arrange financing for projects to sustain Hitler's war machine.[17]

Further investigation also revealed that Barclays also received a large cash deposit from the Drancy transit camp. The money was plundered from the Jewish prisoners bound for Auschwitz, and never returned. After the war, U.S. Treasury investigators who traveled to Paris unearthed evidence of the collaboration between this British bank's French officials and the German authorities. While it was known that Barclays' French branches had seized assets from their Jewish customers on behalf of the Nazis, it had not been previously disclosed that Barclays also served as the favored banker of the Nazis for the deposit of stolen Jewish assets from detention and concentration camp victims. Indeed, investigators for the Matteoli Commission first discovered that the cashier from the Drancy transit camp, Maurice Keiffer, deposited 290,000 francs at Barclays' Paris office in July 1944, taken from Jewish prisoners on their way to Auschwitz.[18] Other documents that were uncovered established that Barclays was also willing to lend the German Administrator of France all of the capital requested, even it was intended to finance the production of products for the German war effort.[19]

Adding insult to injury, the manager who ran Barclays' French operations during the occupation, Marcel Cheradame, was retained by the bank after liberation and continued to run the Barclays French branch until his retirement in the 1960s. Barclays management saw no ethical problem keeping Cheradame, even though the U.S. Treasury investigators' report described Cheradame as "very amenable to the wishes of the German administrator, Hans Joachim Caesar."[20] Another Barclays Bank official in France volunteered to the German Administrator of France information about the Bank's Jewish employees, obviously intending to ingratiate the bank further with the Nazi authorities. The U.S. Treasury investigators concluded: "This is one instance of the bank's unsolicited efforts to fall in line with German views."

To its credit, unlike the other French banks who had also seized the assets of their Jewish customers during the war, Barclays did not deny its part in this dark period of history. It willingly started collecting evidence from its archives. Barclays soon discovered that, of 16,000 accounts, it had approximately 335 depositors in 1941 who were probably Jewish, and whose accounts had been frozen. Faced with a lawsuit by us in the U.S. courts, Barclays agreed in December 1998 to create a £2 million fund (about $2,606,400 in U.S. Dollar) for the repayment of assets that were held in its French subsidiary during the Second World War and not recovered by the rightful owners afterward.

We brought two parallel and related cases in the U.S. District Court for the Eastern District of New York. The first one that we filed, entitled *Bodner et al. v. Banque Paribas*,[21] was brought on behalf of U.S. citizens who themselves had been victims of the French Holocaust but had survived and emigrated to the U.S. The plaintiffs in this case also included U.S. citizens who were the families of French Holocaust victims who had had their bank accounts "frozen" and then seized as part of the anti-Jewish banking laws in effect during that period.

Fernande Bodner, the lead plaintiff in the first French Holocaust case, was a U.S. citizen who lived in Brooklyn, where she had a small tailor shop. She was born in France in 1928. Her father, Chaim (Charles) Bodner, was deported to the Drancy prison camp in 1944. Before that, he had been a furrier who worked out of his home. His apartment, which contained his furrier machinery and equipment, silver, china, paintings, and jewelry, was sealed by the Vichy government, and the French authorities confiscated all of their possessions. The Bodners also had various bank accounts. Mrs. Bodner specifically recalled her father telling her of an account in her name. When her father was deported, she was forced to wear a yellow star and was placed in a Vichy Home for French Jewish children. Upon arriving home one day, she saw the French authorities loading children into trucks. Bodner escaped, went underground, survived the war, and emigrated to New York.

Although Bodner was the sole surviving heir of her father, she was unable to access the bank accounts and other property that belonged to him. All of the family business and personal assets were seized by Vichy authorities and then turned over to one or more banks that were cooperating with this anti-Semitic campaign. These banks also blocked Jewish bank accounts. The seizure of the Bodners' assets was part of the Vichy government's policy of 'aryanizing' the personal, real, and business property of Jews.

In addition to Bodner, other named plaintiffs identified in the complaint cited the blocking of their bank accounts as the chief reason their parents and family members could not finance their escape from the Nazi persecution, including letters from banks denying them their funds. As a result, many of the plaintiffs' families were deported to concentration camps, where they later died.

The companion case that we brought was *Benisti et al v. Banque Paribas*,[22] filed on December 23, 1998.[23] This case was brought on behalf of all those non-U.S. citizens ("aliens") who were survivors of the French Holocaust or who had family members who were victims. The *Benisti* case was brought under the Alien Tort Statute,[24] one of the first statutes passed by Congress as part of the First Judiciary Act of 1789. The Statute gives aliens the right to sue in U.S. federal courts for torts committed in violation of international law. At the time, Congress was most concerned about the international crime of piracy, since the Barbary pirates were wreaking havoc on commercial shipping in the Mediterranean Sea at the time. However, over time, a consensus developed following World War II that the universally recognized "big three" violations of international law were: war crime, crimes against humanity, and genocide.

Ann Marie Benisti, the named plaintiff in the French Holocaust case brought on behalf of non-U.S. citizens, lived in Paris during the war with her father, Charles Benisiti, an insurance salesman. Mr. Benisti had two bank accounts, one of which was at a branch of Credit Lyonnaise in Paris, where he had approximately 2 million francs. He was captured by the Germans and sent to a prisoner of war camp in Germany. However, he escaped and returned to Paris, where he hid for the remainder of the war. After the war, he went to withdraw funds from his Credit Lyonnaise account, but was told there was no money there. He was never given any explanation as to where the money had gone.

Other plaintiffs who lived in France, Israel, Canada, and other countries (other than the U.S.) had similar family experiences. Their families' bank accounts were blocked and frozen during World War II, with no restitution or explanation for the missing banking assets after the war.

The defendant banks were all worldwide banks that controlled the overwhelming majority of the banking market in France. Credit Lyonnais, Societe Generale, Credit Commercial de France, Credit Agricole Indosuez, and Banque Francaise du Commerce Exterior (later known as Natexis) acquired many of the smaller and regional French banks operated before and during World War II. These smaller banks were where many French Jewish families maintained their bank accounts and safe deposit boxes.

Two non-French banks – Chase Manhattan Bank and J.P. Morgan (who later merged to become J.P. Morgan Chase) – were also named defendants. These two banks, along with Barclays Bank, had decided to keep their French branches open even during the German occupation, and froze the bank accounts of their Jewish customers just as their French bank counterparts did. J.P. Morgan operated in France at the time as Morgan et Cie. The suit charged that the Paris branch of Chase, with full knowledge of its New York home office, collaborated with the German authorities and displayed excessive zeal in its enforcement of anti-Jewish laws, including blocking and freezing the accounts of depositors.[25]

As counsel for the plaintiffs, we located substantial evidence that these defendant banks actively participated and profited from the plunder of the Jewish bank accounts by the Vichy authorities. These actions deprived plaintiffs of their means to finance their escape from detention, deportation, and death. The banks' participation in the systematic discrimination of Jews - by seizing Jewish banking assets and other property

- constituted complicity and conspiracy with the Nazi and Vichy regimes in their genocidal policies. The banks were thus guilty of aiding and abetting these violations of international law during the war. In addition, we had a solid factual basis for alleging that, after the war, these defendant banks unjustly refused to return the looted assets, enriched themselves with the derivative profits, and concealed information, value, and profits of the stolen assets from the plaintiffs.

One "smoking gun" document that we found was a French Banking Association Circular written and distributed among the defendant banks at the time. It outlined their plan to seize plaintiffs' assets and to carry out the blocking and confiscation of Jewish accounts and safety deposit boxes in advance of any official compulsion to do so. We also established that the banks were asking depositors to fill out detailed genealogical questionnaires before allowing them, if non-Jewish, to withdraw or transfer funds. If they were Jewish or even part-Jewish, they could not withdraw funds from their accounts or transfer funds.

The banks also acted in concert with the Nazis and Vichy authorities in many other ways to profit from the confiscated assets. Then, after the war, they misrepresented to plaintiffs and the general public the critical role they played during the Vichy period, as well as their secret and continued retention of wrongly taken Jewish assets and their failure to provide an accounting and restitution to plaintiffs.

These two parallel actions – *Bodner* and *Benisti* - sought money damages and an accounting. They also sought to recover the cash, records, art, jewelry, bank deposits, financial instruments, securities, and other business, personal and real property wrongfully taken and withheld from them and their families by the defendant banks, with the collaboration of the Vichy government. Plaintiffs also sought recovery of the looted assets, full disclosure, accounting, disgorgement, restitution, compensatory, and punitive damages for the unlawful seizure and retention of the assets and defendants' unjust enrichment since the end of World War II. On behalf of the plaintiffs, we also claimed that these banks had a special duty and fiduciary responsibility to hold and maintain plaintiffs' assets with the utmost care for the account holders and their families and successors in interest. We alleged in the complaints that defendants breached their fiduciary and special duties to plaintiffs by seizing the assets and failing to conduct a full accounting after the war.

To adequately plead a violation of international law, we cited the Nuremberg Charter, Article 6(b), the Nuremberg Principles, the Hague Convention of 1907, the Genocide Convention (Article III(e)), the United Nations Charter, and the Universal Declaration of Human Rights, all of which condemned genocide and crimes against humanity as international law violations. We also claimed that the taking of property without compensation violated a 1959 treaty between the United States and France, which requires that the property of nationals of either contracting party cannot be confiscated without a public purpose and just compensation. On behalf of the U.S. plaintiffs, we claimed that they were covered by this U.S.-French treaty since they had emigrated from France and became citizens of the United States after World War II.

The Matteoli and Drai Commissions

To head off the U.S. litigation, the French Government formed an independent commission in 1997, comprised of historians, diplomats, lawyers, and magistrates. They were directed to "study the conditions in which goods may have been illicitly acquired ... and to publish proposals" regarding redress of Holocaust-era atrocities in France. This research body was called the "Matteoli Commission," named after its chairman, Jean Matteoli, a French politician and former member of the French Resistance during World War II. This self-styled "study mission" submitted its first progress report to the French Prime Minister on December 31, 1997. In that document, the Commission discussed its mandate, its inability to provide relief or redress to injured parties under its charter, and its largely information-gathering role.[26] The second progress report was released in February of 1999. The Commission published its final report and an English summary on April 17, 2000.

The French Bank defendants predictably claimed that the work of the Matteoli Commission eliminated the need for our litigation in U.S. courts, even though the Commission did not set up any program or mechanism to compensate plaintiffs and other victims of the French Holocaust. Also, as we pointed out to Judge Sterling Johnson, the federal judge assigned to these cases, the amount of money calculated by the Matteoli Commission that needed to be restituted to the rightful owners was about five billion francs short of what we conservatively calculated the unreturned Jewish assets to be. According to our analysis, the Commission estimated that the amount of assets blocked initially to be more than three times the amount distributed in restitution, which accounted for the missing five billion francs.

In addition to the Matteoli Commission, the French Government created the Drai Commission, which was charged with the responsibility for examining individual applications and working to compensate the victims of spoilation resulting from Holocaust-era anti-Semitic legislation.[27] It soon became clear, however, that the Drai Commission's compensation plan was a poor substitute for what we anticipated the U.S. litigation efforts could achieve.

The Breakthrough Settlements with Chase and J.P. Morgan Banks

While the French banks basically tried their best to "stonewall" us throughout the litigation, Chase Manhattan Bank and J.P. Morgan took a much more cooperative and conciliatory approach. This led to early settlements with both these banking defendants. Indeed, on February 23, 2000, Chase publicly admitted that, during the early years of World War II, one of its predecessor banks helped the German government exchange marks that may have come from the forced sale of assets by Jewish refugees.[28] Chase Chairman William B. Harrison announced in a written statement: "We are sad to learn and deeply troubled about the involvement of one of our predecessor banks in a program that benefited Germany during that period," he said. "We have a responsibility to make this information public and wish to express our sincere apologies to the Jewish community and the American public."[29]

Chase said research concerning the Paris-based accounts found that from August 1936 through June 1941, Chase National Bank participated in a German government program that enabled Germany to exchange German marks for U.S. dollars. Germany needed U.S. dollars, since some nations weren't accepting German currency in exchange for goods and services. In response, Germany created "blocked" marks that could be used in Germany but not for international trade. The program allowed German-Americans who may have been interested in returning to Germany to exchange dollars for marks at favorable rates, which in turn provided the German Government with U.S. dollars. "Historical records suggest that some of the 'blocked' German marks used in the program may have come from the forced sale of assets by Jewish refugees leaving Germany," a Chase spokesperson said.

The Motions to Dismiss

Shortly after we filed our two complaints in the *Bodner* and *Benisti* cases, the French Banks hit us with a formidable motion to dismiss, claiming that: (1) plaintiffs lacked "standing" to pursue their claims; (2) there was no federal question subject matter jurisdiction over either action, and that there is no diversity jurisdiction over the *Bodner* case; (3) the Court should defer to proceedings in France and decline jurisdiction under principles of international comity, the Act of State Doctrine, and the doctrine of *forum non conveniens;* (4) plaintiffs had failed to state a claim under either French or New York law, for the violation of any international law or breach of any treaty, and that these were time-barred; and (5) plaintiffs had failed to join indispensable parties, *i.e.*, all of the other banks that operated in France during World War II.

On the issue of "standing," the defendants argued that since plaintiffs did not have specific banking records showing the amount of money on deposit at the banks during World War II, we could not trace the banking assets allegedly taken to any particular transaction or transaction. Defendants also challenged the legal "standing" of family members in the bank accounts of their deceased relatives.

We threw ourselves into the legal and factual research necessary to respond to this motion to dismiss, since everything was on the line. Every other Holocaust-related case against European banks had either been dismissed, or, as in the motions to dismiss in the Swiss Bank Case, were never decided since a settlement was worked out between the parties before the judge had to decide the motions.

In response, we argued that the plaintiffs had the standing to sue each defendant bank, even those with whom they had no specific records of transactions. We reasoned that we had alleged facts sufficient to show a conspiracy that included even those banks where we did not have evidence of specific transactions with the plaintiffs. We also claimed the plaintiffs who were suing on behalf of the estates of family member who had held

French bank accounts had standing to sue for restitution of assets that had vested in them as a matter of law when their family members had died.

We also had to address the issue of whether we had included all necessary parties or whether there were "missing" defendant banks that had to be brought before the court before the case could proceed. The defendants argued that the two largest holders of deposits before and during the war had not been named in the complaints. These were two nationalized institutions: the Caisse d'Epargne (a national savings institution) and the French Post Office. Defendants also claimed that plaintiffs failed to name in their complaint hundreds of banks and financial institutions that did business during the war and which were still in existence.

On behalf of the plaintiffs, we countered that the defendant banks were the largest commercial institutions that participated in the looting practices during World War II. Together, they controlled 60-80% of the French banking market. We also pointed out that the French banks named in the two complaints were among the largest French commercial institutions doing business in the United States.

Judge Johnson ultimately accepted our argument that all plaintiffs were required to do was to accurately show general factual allegations laying out a good faith basis for how one or more of the defendants injured plaintiffs. The court also agreed with us that, under conspiracy law, each plaintiff did not need to allege facts against all defendants, and each defendant's relationship with each plaintiff did not have to be explicitly identified. Under conspiracy law, plaintiffs still have standing to sue members of the conspiracy with whom they did not have specific contact as long as there is some evidence that all the defendants subscribed to the overall goals of the conspiracy and committed at least one "overt act" in furtherance thereof.[30] Defendants may, therefore, be responsible for a co-conspirator's conduct in furtherance of the alleged conspiracy even if they have not dealt directly with plaintiffs.[31] The "silent partner" banks may thus be liable for their acts in furtherance of the conspiracy.[32]

Most importantly, in denying the motion to dismiss, Judge Johnson found that the defendants' actions deprived the French Jewish community members the means to finance their escape. In other words, the banks facilitated the Nazi genocide.

The Court further found that the non-U.S. plaintiffs under *Benisti* properly pleaded a claim under the Alien Tort Statute. Judge Johnson found that the genocide conspiracy theory that we asserted fell within contemporary norms of international law, in that the defendant banks were alleged to have aided and abetted the Vichy government and the Nazis in their plan to eradicate the Jewish community in France.

Judge Johnson's decision further found that there was no obligation for U.S. courts to defer to political or administrative proceedings in France under the doctrine of international comity or the so-called Act of State Doctrine. The judge pointed out that there were no judicial proceedings in France to redress victims and their families. The remedy of a class action complaint was not available under French law. Indeed, the court recognized that the class action device is a relatively unique procedural tool in American courts and is a highly efficient and effective means for providing judicial relief to a large group of claimants.

In denying the defendants' motion to dismiss, Judge Johnson further observed that "no [U.S.] court has ever deferred to an informal, historical commission." He specifically noted that the Matteoli Commission had concluded its work, published its final report, and dissolved the Committee. In addition, there was no pending litigation in France, and the court noted that the French Government did not have any specific law or policy which could either supplant or fully redress plaintiffs' claims.

Another key finding in the District Court's decision was that the Act of State Doctrine did not apply, since continued prosecution of this case neither violated France's sovereign interests nor interfered with laws or policies of the French Government. Judge Johnson noted that plaintiffs did not challenge current French law; rather, they were merely seeking to remedy the private defendant banks' failure to return the looted assets as mandated by postwar French law.

Judge Johnson's decision also rejected defendants' argument that the Court should dismiss the cases on the grounds of *forum non-conveniens*, which means that they claimed the U.S. courts were an "inconvenient forum." However, as the Court noted, there is a presumption in favor of the plaintiffs' choice of forum. The mere fact that there were relevant documents and witnesses located in France did not make it unduly "inconvenient" for the French banks to litigate in the U.S. courts. The French Banks were in a much better financial position to hire U.S. counsel and to have witnesses travel to a U.S. court to testify, instead of having the U.S. plaintiffs travel to France. The Court thus found that the French

Banks failed to show, as required to succeed in a motion to dismiss on the grounds of forum non-convenience, that (1) an adequate alternative forum was available to the plaintiffs in France; and (2) private and public interest favored trial in the foreign forum.[33] The Court added that, ordinarily, the presumption in favor of the plaintiffs' choice of jurisdiction will control the decision of where a case will be tried,[34] and that "unless the balance is strongly in favor of the defendant, the plaintiffs' forum choice should rarely be disturbed."[35]

In other words, this landmark decision virtually sounded the death knell for the "inconvenient forum" defense.

Judge Johnson concluded his written decision by finding that plaintiffs' claims were not time-barred, since there was equitable basis for plaintiffs' ability to prosecute these claims under what is known as the "equitable tolling doctrine." This doctrine holds that a defendant – such as the French Banks in this case - should be equitably estopped from raising a statute of limitations defense where plaintiffs had been kept in ignorance of vital information necessary to pursue their claims. In this case, the Court found that equitable tolling applied since plaintiffs reasonably alleged that the defendants had fraudulently concealed facts that would have alerted them to their claim.[36] The ruling eloquently noted that "there is certainly a strong undercurrent to the issues at bar suggesting a deceptive and unscrupulous deprivation of both assets and of information substantiating plaintiffs' and their ancestors' rights to these assets."[37] In other words, there was no reason to deny plaintiffs a forum for addressing their claims due to the deceitful practices of the defendants, who had kept them from knowing or proving the extent of these claims.

Despite a positive ruling from Judge Johnson in these French Bank cases, the defendant banks still resisted responding to our discovery requests. Our written demands called for them to turn over copies of account statements, all banking documents, and other relevant information about Jewish bank accounts they had seized during World War II. The banks argued that most of these documents were confidential, and they had an obligation to protect bank client account information. They also claimed a significant risk of prosecution by French authorities under various criminal statutes, known as "blocking statutes." These statutes prevented the banks from disclosing information in response to a foreign subpoena or document discovery demand related to foreign litigation, including U.S.

district court cases. They therefore sought a protective order from U.S. Magistrate Judge Marilyn Go of the U.S. District Court in the Eastern District of New York.

Magistrate Judge Go denied the application by the French Banks for a protective order, finding that there was no significant risk of the banks being criminally prosecuted for turning over records under France's Blocking Statute, based on what had transpired in similar cases.[38] The Court held that the American interests in discovery in this lawsuit outweighed the French interest in confidentiality.

The French Bank Settlement

Finally, realizing that there was no way to escape the federal litigation we had started, the French banks, at the urging of the French Government, entered into settlement discussions with us. In the process, we received substantial support from the U.S. State Department and Deputy Secretary of the U.S. Treasury Department Stuart Eizenstat. He and other U.S. governmental representatives participated with us in negotiation sessions both in Paris and in Washington, D.C.

During the first few days of negotiations in Paris, the French representatives took a tough line. Every time I proposed something, they responded in French with precisely the same words, loosely translated: "The proposition proposed by Mr. McCallion is totally unacceptable to the government of France." Unlike American negotiation techniques that I was familiar with, there were no incremental steps as both sides edged towards each other and ultimately, if successful, with a settlement somewhere in the middle. No, that was not the French style, which, at least for the first few days of negotiations, was to categorically reject every proposal made by our side.

However, these first few days of negotiations were not wasted. The French Government owned several excellent five-star restaurants in Paris. Each evening, the French delegation invited the American negotiators to exquisite French cuisine in one of the government restaurants. One restaurant was located inside the Gare du Nord (the north railway station) in Paris. We enjoyed excellent dining and had a wide-ranging discussion on almost every possible subject except, of course, for the cases themselves that we were in Paris to try to settle.

I was hoping that the French Government officials and bank negotiators were planning to use the informal dinner setting to hint where they were willing to go with a settlement. This did not happen, however, until after the four-course meal and several bottles of vintage French wine had been consumed, and everyone was feeling relatively mellow. Then, over coffee, one of the French representatives casually floated out a proposal that had never been tried before in any Holocaust settlement, at least as far as I was aware. He suggested we give some thought to creating two settlement funds. One fund would be for claimants with documented banking claims. The other fund would be for claimants who had a good faith basis for believing that their parents or other family members had accounts in a French bank, which was not accessed or recovered after the war.

This end-of-dinner proposal ended up being the basis for a comprehensive "global" settlement. After days of negotiations where the French negotiators were downright stubborn and intractable, they did a 180-degree about-face. They were now ready to seriously propose a settlement structure that, at first impression, seemed to make sense. There are two basic approaches to Holocaust settlements: one method gives all the claimants the same, or approximately the same, award, no matter whether their claim is strong or weak. The advantage of this is that the pay-outs from a settlement fund can be made relatively quickly, and there is a sense that rough justice is being served by giving all members of the class of claimants the same amount of money. The downside of such an approach is that some families had very modest bank accounts or only had a vague recollection of having a bank account. Conversely, other claimants knew precisely where their family's bank account was located and might even have some records indicating that the amounts in the bank account or safe deposit box at the specific bank were substantial. In these cases, limiting the family that had detailed records to the same amount of an award as that received by a family with no records had an aura of unfairness about it. However, distributing settlement proceeds to only those who can "prove" their claim with documentation is also fundamentally unfair.

The answer to this problem that both sides agreed upon was to set up two funds: "Fund A," which initially would be established with a $22.5 million transfer from the French Banks and the French Government, would distribute equal payments (originally a $3000 payment) to each claimant that submitted a "good faith" affidavit that one or more of their family members had a bank account in one of the defendant French banks, or a bank that was later acquired by one of the defendant banks. A second fund (Fund B) would be funded with an initial 50 million dollars. A commission would be established to process and consider claims of banking and other property losses (such as the appropriation of houses and apartments) during the Nazi or Vichy occupation of France, based on documentation or other evidence that could be collected. Once the $50 million was depleted, the banks would replenish the fund until all awards had been made.

The Commission established under the settlement agreement was named the "Commission for the Compensation of Victims of Spoliation Resulting from Anti-Semitic Legislation in Force During the Occupation" (also known by its French acronym C.I.V.S.). Its mandate was to investigate and compensate victims (or their heirs or successors) of anti-Semitic persecution in France. The Commission had access to historical information from French public archives and banks, including lists of over 56,000 wartime account holders whose accounts were blocked under anti-Semitic German or Vichy laws. The Commission examined claims relating to any property frozen, blocked, looted, or "Aryanized" in France. After such investigation by the C.I.V.S. staff and investigators, victims or their families whose assets were confiscated by the French or German Occupying governments were compensated by a committee set up within the French Prime Minister's Office.

Under the settlement agreement, the French Government was also required to establish a "Foundation for Memory of the Shoah." The Foundation's initial funding was approximately U.S. $375,000,000, including roughly $100,000,000 transferred by the banks. The Foundation was tasked with distributing funds to organizations inside and outside France, including those that aid elderly or needy Holocaust survivors and their families.

On January 18, 2001, the United States and France governments signed the Executive Agreement, settling the litigation and the French Holocaust claims. The ceremony took place on the historic seventh floor of the U.S. State Department in the Harry S. Truman Building in Washington, D.C., where many treaties have been negotiated and signed over the past decades.

Presiding over the signing ceremony was outgoing Secretary of State of the Clinton Administration, Madeline Albright. Like the other

Holocaust-related settlements entered into during the administration of then-President Bill Clinton, this settlement was personally significant for Secretary Albright. She had been born in 1937 in the Smíchov district of Prague, Czechoslovakia. She and her family fled after the Nazi invasion of that country, ending up in London. Eventually, in 1948, the family immigrated to the United States. Albright did not realize until many years later that her parents had converted from Judaism to Catholicism in 1941 to escape the antisemitism in Europe. Raised as a Catholic, she converted to the Episcopal faith when she married. She did not learn the truth about her Jewish roots until she was middle-aged. As she explained to us in a short speech, the Holocaust litigation gave her much on which to reflect.

In classic Washington, backroom fashion, we worked around the clock to negotiate the remaining terms and put the final touches on the agreement. We had set January 18, 2001 as the deadline for finalizing the agreement because, quite frankly, we were unsure that the incoming administration of President-elect George W. Bush would be as supportive of this and other Holocaust-related settlements as had the Clinton Administration. Also, even though Bush had been a classmate of mine at Yale College, I had been an active supporter of President Clinton and, in the campaign to succeed him, had been a vocal supporter of Clinton's Vice President, Al Gore. I had represented the White House and the Vice President's Office at various environmental conferences held at The Hague and elsewhere in Europe during the Clinton Administration. It was also widely known that I had participated in the Rome Conference of June and July 1998 that established the International Criminal Court. I had persuaded Vice President Gore and others in the U.S. delegation at the Rome Conference that, in addition to genocide, crimes against humanity, and war crimes, the I.C.C. should have jurisdiction over environmental crimes impacting the world environment. Although my proposal was included in the first draft of the treaty, it never made it into any of the other drafts or the final one. It was just too "radical" a concept at the time to think that the massive environmental destruction of the planet's vital resources by certain multi-national companies could be considered to be as serious as a war crime or other widely recognized violation of customary international law.

In any event, President-elect Bush knew that I was a staunch Democrat who had opposed his bid for the Presidency and that I was highly critical of the U.S. Supreme Court's decision to overturn the will of the majority of the electorate in its *Bush v. Gore* decision[39] of December 12, 2000, effectively handing the White House to Bush.

However, my fears about Bush's commitment to human rights turned out to be unfounded. I had clearly sold my old classmate short. My concerns as to whether President Bush would be a champion for human rights were allayed when Bush asked Stuart Eizenstat to continue to play an active role as an American diplomat brokering various Holocaust-related cases. To President Bush's credit, the U.S. State Department under his administration continued to give human rights and Holocaust-related issues a high priority

After the signing ceremony of the settlement with the French Government and the French banks on January 18, 2001, my wife Susan and I stayed in Washington for the inauguration of George W. Bush as president. After all, it is not every day that you can say that a college classmate is being sworn in as president. As Bush settled into office, I started to warm to his administration and his generally sensible policy initiatives, especially in the environmental and human rights areas I was most concerned about. When Bush agreed to open the White House to our class reunion, I actually looked forward to the event, which including a private tour of the Oval Office and other historically significant portions of the building. Since our reunion was taking place in early April 2003 on the same day that Coalition Forces led by the U.S. Army 3rd Infantry Division were entering Baghdad, I took the opportunity to congratulate President Bush on the quick military success of the Iraq invasion, but expressed my serious doubts as to whether the occupation of that country would be as successful. I specifically asked him if he had a plan in place for the occupation and an "exit strategy." He assured me and others gathered around him that his administration had a plan in place and that there was "nothing to worry about." As it turned out, unfortunately, there was no such plan. The subsequent clumsy efforts at improvisation, including the disbanding the Iraqi armed forces, proved to be disastrous. Many of our potential allies within Iraq quickly became our sworn enemies, as the U.S. became the laughingstock of the world with its illusory search for the WMDs that Vice President Dick Chaney and others had convinced Bush were there.

* * *

While what we referred to as the French Bank Case was a fascinating study in international and U.S. law, the people behind the case, the claimants, reminded us why the effort was so important. My law firm was fortunate that my wife, Susan, was available to work with the claimants. As she did later in the 9/11 cases, Susan spent hours on the phone and in person with Holocaust survivors and heirs. Her empathy was tireless, and I could hear her reassuring clients who were waiting for their compensation or needed help with the paperwork.

I doubt Susan would ever admit she had favorites, but one of the claimants, Vera Reichman, would be high on the list. Vera filed her claim with Fund B since she had a great deal of specific information about where the family had lived, her father's business name, and the bank where her father maintained his account. After she submitted her claim, some government researchers in Paris were able to investigate her claim further. They discovered that Vera's father had had other accounts and assets that she had not known about. This was good news, but it delayed her getting her check since the young French researchers didn't want to overlook anything. Once a month or so, Vera would call Susan and ask when she would get her money. One time she called and asked if Susan thought it would be okay to buy a new suitcase. Each time, Susan would reassure Vera and convince her that the time it was taking was a good thing. Finally, Vera got her money and called Susan tearfully, thanking her for her efforts. Susan would share with me all the beautiful memories Vera would tell her. Vera's father was a photographer, and he would take Vera with him when he went to the bank. She was only about six years old at the time, but that memory was not only a treasured remembrance; it also gave her and us some valuable clues about the location of the bank account.

Vera was one of many, of course, for whom the settlement was bittersweet. No amount of money could wipe away the pain of losing, in many cases, their entire families during this horrible period of European history. At least France and its banks belatedly recognized their collaboration with the Nazis and Vichy authorities during the occupation period.

Michel Japkowicz, a 65-year-old Paris pharmacist who lost his father and 15-year-old brother to the Holocaust and who was one of our named plaintiffs in the Benisti litigation, commented: "The deal was 55 years late. But it's moral satisfaction. For so long, we've had the impression that France was saying, 'we're not guilty - it's the others.' Now they're finally making amends."

Chapter 7

The September 11th and Flight 587 Cases

Wrongful Death

Although death is inevitable, it all too often comes prematurely due to negligence, recklessness, or medical malpractice. When someone dies before their time in a way that appears to have been preventable, the law allows the survivors to file what is known as a "wrongful death" action. Cases like these are filed all over the country regularly, such as when a doctor fails to diagnose a disease that a person could have survived. Similarly, when a plane crashes, or a drunk driver kills someone, survivors may bring state or federal court actions to recover money damages for the loss of life.

The very notion of "wrongful" death implies that the legal system allows survivors to file a complaint as almost a preventive measure. Many of these cases are settled out of court. Even so, a wrongful death action can provide compensation for the family of the victim. It also provides a mechanism for financially punishing the responsible party to such an extent that they and others similarly situated will never again engage in the same negligent conduct. Suppose an airline fails to train their pilots or maintain their planes adequately, and one of their airplanes crashes due to such negligence. In that case, the legal system allows families to bring an action to "punish" the companies involved so that they will get it right in the future. There will hopefully be no future loss of life based on the same mistake. The same applies to doctors who commit professional negligence, automotive companies who manufacture defective cars with exploding gas tanks, and any other virtually infinite range of human interactions where negligence can result in the tragic loss of life.

Unfortunately, the pursuit of justice on behalf of those who died due to negligence is rarely neat or easy. Death, money, and the judicial system are a challenging combination. Often when people are most hurt, troubled, and suffering, they find themselves forced into a judicial system that renders judgment on a cold, economic basis. For all too many, a lawsuit for wrongful death will mean the victim's family members will become victims themselves. They will be in the peculiar situation of having to defend their loved one's life from accusations that they were largely responsible for their demise or that their life was not worth that much anyway.

How does the legal system go about calculating the value of the deceased person's life? This is a complex and often painful process. On a philosophical level, every human life is invaluable. Still, in the sometimes harsh light of the law, the economic value of a person's life becomes an analysis of how much money they made in the past and how much they would have earned during their working lives if they had not died as a result of someone else's negligence. Putting a dollar value on the loss of a loved one is always a painful process because it invariably underestimates or trivializes the importance of the loss to the family members and friends who have suffered the loss. Just when family members are feeling the most emotional and psychic pain from their loss, they are thrust into a legal system that tells them that, for the most part, all they can recover is the lost income or other services that they suffered. Ironically and, in many cases, tragically, the surviving family members also become victims. They will be forced to defend the value of their loved one's life under grueling cross-examination by skeptical and sarcastic defense lawyers who, with rare exception, either explicitly or by implication, try to suggest to a judge and jury the person's life wasn't worth much. Often family members will turn on each other, with some wanting to take the first lowball settlement thrown out by the defendants and the others insisting that the case be tried to its conclusion. Families often become angry and frustrated with a legal system that, even at its best, is slow and confusing, more often than not dissolving into a marathon of interminable motions and delay tactics designed to grind down the family and their lawyer. Even when the family and their lawyer hang in there until trial, the amount awarded by juries usually does not - despite popular misconceptions to the contrary - reflect even remotely what the family feels the actual value of the loss was to them. For most families, no amount of money can stop the pain or make up for the big hole in their lives. All it can do is pay for some of the bills with, hopefully, enough left over to pay for their kid's college tuition.

View of Ground Zero from the northwest after the 9-11 terrorist attacks. In the left foreground are the ruins of the North Tower, and in the center, those of the South Tower. More than a million tons of rubble remained at the World Trade Center. Sept. 17, 2001, New York City. Everett collection Historical / Alamy Stock Photo F2AX1M.

Although I had handled some wrongful death cases before in my career, I was thrown headlong into this arena with the twin tragedies of 9/11 and – two months later – the crash of American Airlines Flight 587 in Belle Harbor Queens, on November 12, 2001. In the two years that I worked through these cases on behalf of the families who lost loved ones, I suffered along with them, as did other staff members of my law firm who worked on these cases on nearly a full-time basis. We shared their loss and frustration, and we even went so far as to ask some of the teenage children who had lost one or both parents to work in our offices after school to make sure that they were off the streets and got their homework done. We helped them navigate through the rocky shoals of a legal system that, at best, dispenses only imperfect justice.

The 9/11 Terrorist Attack Cases

The basic facts relating to the 9/11 terrorist attacks are well known to everyone on the planet. There were four coordinated terrorist attacks on September 11, 2001, by the Islamic terrorist group al-Qaeda. Two of the four hijacked commercial planes were intentionally crashed into the two World Trade Center towers; a third plane hit the Pentagon outside Washington, D.C. The fourth hijacked plane crashed in a field outside Shanksville, Pennsylvania. The attacks killed 2,996 people, injured 6000 others, and caused at least $10 billion in infrastructure and property damage. There were additional 9/11-related casualties from cancer and respiratory diseases in the months and years after these tragic events.

Shortly after 9/11, the American Trial Lawyers Association, which later changed its name to "The American Association for Justice" when the term "trial lawyer" (like "liberal") fell out of favor, began enlisting attorneys to represent the families of the thousands of victims who perished that day. Like many other plaintiff lawyers, I agreed to represent several families on a pro bono basis, thereby waiving my right to any legal fees, which would have amounted to one-third of any settlement or award. I agreed to participate in this program and to recruit other lawyers to join with some trepidation because my experience with pro bono legal programs was not always favorable. I was concerned that many lawyers, full of enthusiasm, often signed up for pro bono programs but failed to follow through in the actual representation of the clients as a case wore on. Like most people, lawyers become distracted by the mundane pressures of life, such as making a living, raising a family, and attending to the demands of fee-paying and contingency fee-based clients. Many large corporate law firms give lip service to support their associates' pro bono work (attorneys who are not partners in a law firm). Still, when the young associates find out that the hours they spend on "non-billable" cases are not considered when it comes time to distribute year-end bonuses or when they are "up" for partnership consideration, the pro bono cases often languish. From my own brief experience as a young lawyer with a large New York law firm, I remember asking the senior partner if I could work on a pro bono case on my own time. He was silent for a moment and then responded, "What do you mean by your own time?" The message was clear – when I wasn't eating or sleeping, I should be working on firm matters. After all, I was one of the highest-paid first-year associates in New York, making a whopping starting salary of $16,500. The amount seemed like a small fortune in the mid-1970s and was more than enough to quickly pay off the student loans and credit card debt I had accumulated in college and law school.

Immediately following the September 11 disaster, Congress realized that the financial collapse of American and United Airlines – the two airlines involved in the catastrophe - was likely if they had to bear the total liability for security lapses that permitted the terrorists to board the planes with concealed weapons. Congress quickly enacted the Air Stabilization Act, which set up a September 11 Victims Compensation Fund ("VCF") funded by the U.S. Treasury and presided over by Ken Feinberg as Special Master. Feinberg was given complete and final authority to review claims and make awards, with no right of appeal by claimants who opted to apply to the VCF rather than pursue negligence cases against the airlines, the Port Authority, and other owners of the World Trade Center properties.

Since I had gotten to know and respect Ken Feinberg during our settlement negotiations in the Shoreham Nuclear Power Case, I welcomed the opportunity to represent the victims' families in this streamlined claims process. Also, Ken Feinberg himself must have felt comfortable having me represent many families since, as time went on, he called me on occasion to ask me to represent "just one more family." Although I was concerned that my work on the 911 cases left me little or no time to work on other matters, I found it impossible to say "no." I knew he was under tremendous pressure to design and implement a claims process that both provided a high degree of fairness and justice, no matter what the family's socioeconomic station in life, while, at the same time, bringing the process to an expeditious conclusion.

The claims process got off to a bumpy start, with many families and lawyers skeptical of the entire VCF process and reluctant to waive their legal right to file a lawsuit. Some of the families also seemed to be put off by Ken Feinberg, who appeared at numerous public forums to answer questions about the program. Some people believed he was a bit lofty and overbearing, probably due partly to his Boston accent and wry sense of humor. At one forum, it was reported that, in response to questioning, Feinberg responded that, as far as the VCF was concerned, "I am God." This hyperbole did not sit well with the primarily New York area audience, which tends to have a healthy skepticism of authority and all those who presume to exert it.

As deadline after deadline came for the filing of claims, only to have it extended due to the low percentage of filings, Ken Feinberg enlisted other prominent New York attorneys and my support to advise victims' families as to their legal rights. We helped them weigh the option of either filing an administrative claim with the VCF versus pursuing their case in court. Soon, we were representing many more families than we had initially planned on. Still, it was impossible to say "no," especially to families in the Indian-American community who already knew us from the Bhopal Gas Disaster case or were referred to us by word-of-mouth by other families we had already agreed to represent. Also, we started getting phone calls from families that were nominally represented by other attorneys who had lost interest in filing and processing claims on their behalf. Adding to the pressure on us were periodic calls from Ken Feinberg's office, asking us if we would please take up just one more case. Much to our chagrin, we began to find out that many lawyers had entered into contingency fee agreements with families, albeit often at a reduced fee percentage of 5 or 10 percent, even though we continued to represent the victims' families on a purely pro bono basis.

Edward and Juanita Lee

Our first client, Edward Lee, gave us hope that we could do the job within our limited resources. Mr. Lee was a prime example of the thousands of simple people whose lives were forever altered by that terrible event of 9/11. He was a quiet, dignified man who had worked for many years as a brakeman for the New York City Metropolitan Transit System, or MTA. He worked hard and lived quietly in Queens with his wife, Juanita, and he was particularly close to her daughter, Nicole, from a previous marriage. Nichole was grown now, and Juanita and Edward lived a comfortable life. She had just gotten a job as a receptionist with Cantor Fitzgerald when United Flight 11 went into Tower One of the World Trade Center. As we worked through the paperwork (this being a government operation, there is always paperwork), we learned that Juanita had survived the attack and been told to go up to the roof, only to find that the roof was locked. She perished after starting down the stairs again.

Even though we suspected that Mr. Lee might have a potential lawsuit against Juanita's employers for providing inadequate emergency training and, even worse, leading her to believe the roof was a safe exit, Mr. Lee would have none of it. He wanted to file his papers with the VCF, receive whatever it was felt was due to him and his stepdaughter, and quietly honor his wife. He did just that. This soft-spoken man would diligently do whatever needed to be done, including retrieving the necessary papers from the surrogate's court, filling out the essential releases, and bringing them all to our offices in a timely fashion. One afternoon as we were going over the inventory of lost items as part of the claim process, he provided us with some receipts for Juanita's clothing at the time of her death. He remembered everything about that last morning, including what his wife was wearing when she left home for the last time. "Juanita had a taste for good things," he laughed, and, sure enough, the items were all high-end jewelry and clothing. Of course, with Mr. Lee and all our other 9/11 clients, there were pictures for us to view and send to the Fund. The VCF staff dutifully reviewed all the evidence, including the smiling photos of the victims. However, I suspect that this review of the victims' photos was motivated more by the compassionate nature of the VCF staff than the photos' relevance to the calculation of an award for economic losses.

Those family members left behind on 9/11 had a genuine need to tell their lawyers and the faceless people at the VCF about their loved ones. This need was heart-wrenching, and the Fund's request for pictures and other narratives about the victims provided a way for the families to complete their healing process.

Mr. Lee was our first VCF client to complete the process and to receive a check. After we closed the file, he came by one last time to present us with a small mounted statue of the twin towers engraved, "With Thanks."

Everyone handles loss and grief differently, and while Mr. Lee seemed to have made peace with what had happened and was anxious to settle things, many others were not. To these survivors, filing with the Fund meant letting go and giving up hope that their loved one's remains would be found or that they would miraculously come walking through the door one day. It took most families a long time to get to that point, where they could let go and find some closure. For one of our clients, it took until the very last minute, literally. The Fund recognized this problem and had extended the deadlines several times, but eventually, even the VCF had to have a "last call." As the final deadline approached, my wife Susan came to the rescue again. As she had during the Holocaust cases, she spent many hours getting the final paperwork to Washington, D.C. for a few of our procrastinating clients.

Meena and Prem Jerath

One client was proving particularly elusive. On the night of 9/10, Meena Jerath and her husband, Prem, had lingered over dinner, talking about the future. Their son Neel was at Boston University doing well, and it was time to think about the next phase of their lives together. Both of the Jeraths were accountants. Meena had her own accounting firm, and she was looking forward to Prem joining her full time after he retired from his job with New York State. Like many Indian couples of a certain age group, theirs had been an arranged marriage that had worked out exceptionally well. Mutually devoted to each other, on the morning of 9/11, Meena had brought a cup of coffee out to Prem and noticed he had a button missing on the sleeve of his blazer. Her last thought as she said goodbye was, "what kind of wife am I to let my husband go to the office with a button missing." Within hours Prem would be gone, and

Meena, an otherwise self-sufficient woman, would retreat, overwhelmed by her loss. Neel would begin failing in school, and numerous investments would be left unattended in a stack of unopened mail, causing significant financial loss.

Prem Jerath worked as an engineer at the Port Authority since 1985, working on many of the most significant transportation projects in the New York-New Jersey area over the next 16 years. At the time of his death on September 11, he was working on the design of the monorail that would connect Kennedy Airport to downtown Manhattan. His base annual salary was $86,788 at the time of his death. In addition to working at the Port Authority, Mr. Jerath also provided bookkeeping and computer services to his wife's accounting business, looking forward to retirement so they could work side by side.

The Jerath's son, Neel, eventually transferred to Rutgers University in New Jersey, where he continued to do poorly. No amount of money could assure that the bouts of depression suffered by Mrs. Jerath and her son over Mr. Jerath's loss would ever subside. Ironically, it seemed it was often the most closely-knit families that were the ones who had the most significant difficulty getting over the loss of one of their family members.

Meena Jerath came to us through a lovely woman who ran a social services organization for south Asian women in Brooklyn. One afternoon, she had stopped by the office to ask if we would help some of the Indian women left behind in the 9/11 disaster. She had become concerned that many women were not coping well with their loss, and she was afraid that they would not take advantage of the VCF process. We received referrals from four surviving families, all different, who touched us in indescribable ways.

Meena was one of those four, but unlike the others who had provided us with the necessary paperwork, Meena was proving difficult, not because she was unpleasant, but because she was resisting moving on. Susan kept calling her to get her in with the necessary missing documents, and she kept promising to come in to meet with us, only to cancel at the last minute. Finally, on the last day at 5:30, with a half-hour to go, Meena arrived with the promised paperwork, and we made the deadline.

One of the most challenging but necessary tasks we faced was calculating a dollar value for the loss of each life. We had to develop an economic theory to capture financial losses, such as lost earnings over the person's anticipated work-life and non-economic values the decedent's family suffered. The costs included the loss of advice, counsel, guidance, instruction, and training services sustained by the surviving family. There was also the loss of companionship, or "accompaniment services" suffered by the surviving family.

Rajesh Mipuri

Rajesh Mirpuri was a 30-year-old Indian-American single male who was a rising star as Vice President of Sales for Data Synapse, Inc., a technology company located in the World Trade Center. Rajesh was born in Hong Kong in 1970 and lived with his parents in New Jersey. He had graduated with a Bachelor of Science degree from New York University. During 2001, it was anticipated that Rajesh was on target to receive a bonus of between 50% to 100% of his base salary of $150,000 per year because he had closed the largest software contract in 2001 for Data Synapse with a major global bank. The CEO of Rajesh's former employer, Askari, Inc., estimated that, based upon Rajesh's skills and potential he had shown in the rapidly expanding software industry, Rajesh's earning would be over $500,000 within a relatively short period if he had survived. Based on a life expectancy for a U.S. male of 76.4 years and work-life expectancy of an additional 29.36 years for a 30-year-old, and assuming that his 2001 income was $300,000, with a conservative wage growth rate of 3% per year, Rajesh's wage losses over an average work-life came to $8,968,413. This was the easy part of our damage calculations.

To evaluate the non-economic damages suffered by Rajesh and his family, which consisted of damages other than his lost income, we enlisted the assistance of Stan W. Smith, Ph.D., an economic and financial consultant based in Chicago. Stan had worked for the Federal Reserve, Board of Governors, in Washington, D.C., and received a Ph.D. from the University of Chicago. The Nobel Laureate, Gary S. Becker, had been his thesis advisor. Over the years, Dr. Smith had created an economic model for quantifying the lost value of the enjoyment of life, often referred to as "hedonic damages" or "hedonic value."

Rajesh's lost income was used to support his parents and pay for the mortgage on their house. Rajesh also helped his parents with their financial matters and provided them with advice and guidance on many issues. Even assuming that Rajesh only offered 30 minutes per day helping has parents around the house and providing them with advice, and based upon the U.S. Bureau of Labor Statistics wage scale for educational, vocational, and school counselors of $17.21 per hour in 2001, Rajesh's parents together lost approximately $200,000 in such services. In addition, Rajesh's parents lost the value of his company and companionship, referred to as "accompaniment services." This loss was virtually impossible to discuss with Rajesh's parents, who were devastated by his loss and whose entire lives were centered on their only child. But we felt we had to calculate this incalculable loss, so we assumed only one hour per day for lost accompaniment services since Rajesh worked full time. We then consulted the U.S. Bureau of Labor Statistics, Occupational Labor Statistics, which showed an hourly wage rate of $12.02 per hour for licensed practical and licensed vocational nurses and home health aides in 2001. Calculating this loss over Rajesh's parents' expected lifespan, we came up with an additional $286,000 in losses.

We came to know Rajesh's parents well during the time we represented them before the VCF. Mr. Mipuri would arrive at our offices after six, so he could park on West 40th Street in Manhattan, where our offices were located. Then he would come up to the 13th floor and tell beautiful stories about his son. He was having a tough time accepting what had happened, and he kept wanting to revisit the settlement from the VCF. It was as if he was thinking that if he took the considerable amount that had been calculated as an award, there would be nothing left in his life to do. Once the job of negotiating on behalf of his son before the VCF was over, Rajesh would be gone for good. One evening, he talked about all the dreams he and his wife had for Rajesh and how their world had been knocked off its axis. "Who will take care of Mother now?" he would lament. "Rajesh was supposed to be there for his mother when I was gone." His voice cracked, and we all felt his enormous pain.

On September 10, 2003, two years after the 9/11 disaster, the parents of Rajesh Mipuri were finally able to move a bit closer to acceptance of the loss of their son by planting a tree in his memory at Johnson Field in Ft. Lee, New Jersey. Mr. and Mrs. Mipuri were overwhelmed with emotion as dozens of Rajesh's co-workers and friends turned out for the ceremony in his honor. They then went to a special memorial service at their temple. They were amazed that 1400 people attended, many of whom had personal stories about acts of kindness and generosity by Rajesh that they weren't even aware of during his lifetime.

In a typical court case, insurance proceeds, Social Security death benefits, and other so-called "collateral source" payments would not be offset or deducted for a damage calculation. However, in establishing the VCF, Congress had decided that it would be unfair to U.S. taxpayers if life insurance and accidental death insurance proceeds were not deducted from any damage calculations. In this case, Rajesh's parents were not only beneficiaries of two insurance policies, but they also received Social Security benefits and New York State Workers' Compensation Benefits as a result of their son's death.

The staff of the VCF and Ken Feinberg always carefully considered our calculations, and we always had the opportunity to introduce the testimony of the victim's family members and employers at a formal hearing. However, the VCF staff rarely accepted our damage calculations in their entirety. They were especially wary of awarding significant hedonic damages, and while they considered "enjoyment of life" damages, they rarely, if ever, fully accepted Stan Smith's damage calculations. These were the losses in the pure enjoyment of life, totally separate and apart from lost economic values. Assuming, for example, that the purely "hedonic" value of one's life is $130,000 per year, an injury – such as a car accident – that leaves one partially disabled and confined to a wheelchair for a year could be considered to diminish the value of one's life by 50%, or $65,000 per year. Of course, there is a 100% loss of the enjoyment of one's life in a death case.

Once the VCF calculated a "Presumed Award," we had an opportunity to dispute their calculations. We could also ask for a personal conference with Ken Feinberg himself, which we did several times. VCF regulations did not require him to grant such requests, but perhaps because of our prior professional dealing together, he never turned us down. He seemed to enjoy reminiscing about the previous cases we had worked on together. We always traded a few legal "war stories" whenever we had a chance to get together.

Yubelly Santos

Inevitably, however, our cordial relationship with the VCF staff and Ken Feinberg became strained on a few occasions when fundamental disagreements arose as to what the final awards should be. In one such case, we represented Yubelly Santos, a young mother of two who had recently immigrated to the New York area from Colombia. Yubelly was widowed on September 11 and counted on us to win an award that would help her raise and support her two boys through at least high school, and hopefully, college. The VCF's records showed that a Presumed Award Amount letter was sent out by regular mail on April 25, 2003, but inexplicably it was never received by Mrs. Santos or our office until June 27, 2003. If it had been faxed to us or sent by registered mail, there would have at least been some confirmation, but the VCF apparently decided to rely exclusively on the U.S. Postal Service. Since Ms. Santos' time to request a review of the Presumed Award or a hearing had passed, I personally appealed to Ken Feinberg for his review of the matter, especially since the VCF had failed to comply with their own rules and regulations by allocating part of the award to the decedent's father, without any evidence that the father was a legal dependent at the time of the decedent's death.

Ken Feinberg agreed to meet with us regarding this problem. We discussed the question of the amount misallocated to the father. We were able to show he had not been listed as a dependent on the deceased's tax return in 2000. Thankfully the money was restored to the wife's settlement package. However, we still believed the overall amount was not sufficient, but Ken Feinberg disagreed. Then my wife Susan, sitting in on the meeting, raised a concern that may have gone overlooked. In 2001 Yubelly's boys were relatively young. Both were under ten, and while the award seemed generous in 2001, Susan said it wasn't enough to get them through college. What had been overlooked was that Yubelly wanted to raise them in the United States. She did not want to return to Colombia. To raise them in America was her husband's dream, and she wanted to honor it. But raising them here would cost more money, so the award had to be increased.

Susan's argument carried the day, and the final amount was increased. Of course, no amount of money would be enough to fill the void in this family's life or any other for that matter. Still, at least Yubelly Santos could now afford to buy a home for herself and her two sons, raise them in the U.S. and have some degree of financial security.

The Flight 587 Air Disaster Case

The American Airlines Flight 587 crash in Belle Harbor, New York, occurred on November 12, 2001, two months and one day after 9/11. It was initially thought to be another terrorist attack on New York. It was a regularly scheduled flight from New York's JFK Airport to Santo Domingo, the capital of the Dominican Republic. The Airbus A 330 crashed shortly after takeoff into the Belle Harbor/Rockaway neighborhood of Queens, one of the five boroughs of New York City. All 260 people aboard the plane were killed, along with five people on the ground. It was the second-deadliest aviation disaster involving an Airbus 300,[1] and the third-deadliest aviation disaster on U.S. soil.[2]

The National Transportation Safety Board (NTSB) ruled out terrorism as a cause based on its investigation. Instead, the Board found that the crash was due to the first officer's overuse of rudder controls in response to wake turbulence from a Japan Airlines (JAL) flight that took off minutes before it. According to the NTSB report, the Flight 587 pilots received a warning from the control tower that they might encounter wake turbulence from the JAL airline that took off immediately before it. The American Airlines pilots did not adequately heed that warning. When the plane encountered turbulence, First Officer Sten Molin attempted to stabilize the aircraft through the aggressive use of the rudder controls, causing the vertical stabilizer to snap off and fall into Jamaica Bay.

"Hang onto it, hang onto it," Capt. Edward States could be heard imploring Molin on the voice recorder tape. "Let's go for power, please," Molin said.

A second later came a loud bang, which investigators believe was the tail breaking off. Then came the roar of air rushing against the aircraft and alarms sounding in the cockpit. "What the hell are we into (inaudible)?" Molin said. "We're stuck in it." States' last recorded words came five seconds later: "Get out of it! Get out of it!"

The aircraft pitched downwards after the stabilizer separated from the aircraft, which went into a flat spin as the pilots struggled to control the plane. The plane also lost its two engines, which separated from the aircraft before impact.

American Airlines blamed Airbus for the crash, alleging that the rudder control system was defective. Most aircraft require increased pressure on the rudder pedals to achieve the same rudder control at high speeds.

However, the Airbus A 300 did not operate based on this "fly-by-wire" flight control system; rather, it used conventional mechanical flight controls. The NTSB report supported this critique to some extent, finding that the A300 rudder control system was vulnerable to unnecessarily excessive rudder inputs. The Airline Pilots Association also submitted a statement to the NTSB, arguing that the unusual sensitivity of the rudder mechanism amounted to a design flaw that Airbus should have communicated to American Airlines. In addition, an earlier 1997 report identified ten incidents in which A300 tail fins had been stressed beyond their design limitations.

Unsurprisingly, Airbus blamed the crash on American Airlines' pilot training, arguing that the A.A. pilots were not trained to take into account that the A300 systems were not designed to withstand an abrupt shift in rudder from one direction to another. The NTSB provided some support for this position, pointing out that American Airlines' Advanced Aircraft Maneuvering Program (AAMP) tended to exaggerate the effects of wake turbulence on large aircraft. Therefore, A.A. pilots were being trained to react more aggressively than was necessary. The over-use of flight simulators in training was also a concern.

The Flight 587 Air Disaster had a devastating effect on the families of those who died, and the entire New York Dominican community in general. In 2001, American Airlines had a virtual monopoly on the New York/Santo Domingo routes, with 51 weekly direct flights between JFK and the Dominican Republic. 90% of the passengers on the flight the day of the accident were of Dominican descent. Every Dominican in New York has either taken the flight or knew someone who had. David Rivas, the owner of a New York City travel agency, was quoted as saying: "For the Dominican to go to Santo Domingo during Christmas and summer is like the Muslims going to Mecca."[3]

A memorial was constructed in Rockaway Park in memory of the 265 victims, which was dedicated on November 12, 2006, the fifth anniversary of the accident. A ceremony commemorating the disaster is held annually at the memorial, featuring a reading of the victims' names. We attended every one of them for the first few years. The memorial wall, inscribed with the victims' names, was designed by Dominican artist Freddy Rodríguez and Situ Studio. It has windows and a doorway looking toward the nearby Atlantic Ocean and angled toward the Dominican

Republic. Atop the memorial is a quotation, in both Spanish and English, from Dominican poet Pedro Mir, reading "*Después no quiero más que paz*" (Translation: "Afterwards I want nothing more than peace.").[4]

My law firm represented several Dominican families living in the New York area who had lost their loved ones on Flight 587. We were introduced to two families by Willy Quinones, a burly, gregarious New Yorker of Puerto Rican descent who had worked with us for many years and who we considered family. One of the passengers was Johnny Flores, who had been Willy's close friend. Johnny perished with his wife and son, Isaiah, who was under two. Isaiah was sitting on Johnny's lap when the plane went down. The couple left behind two daughters from prior marriages and Johnny's mother.

One of the first things we had to do was advise the families that their ability to recover compensation for their loss might be limited by an international agreement to which the United States was a party. Formally known as the "Convention for the Unification of Certain Rules for International Carriage by Air," The Montreal Convention is a multilateral treaty adopted in 1999 by over 100 countries who are signatories to the 1944 Convention on International Civil Aviation ("ICAO"). It amended essential provisions of the 1929 Warsaw Convention provisions concerning compensation for the victims of air disasters. First of all, it increased the minimum guaranteed payment for each victim from $75,000 to $170,000, whereby the air carrier was required to pay that amount for each victim regardless of fault. Even more importantly, the Montreal Convention eliminated the previous requirement of proving willful neglect by the air carrier to obtain more than the minimum amount of damages. This meaningful change was significant because it shifted the plaintiff victims' burden to the air carriers, who now had to prove that the loss was not the result of their negligence – a virtually impossible task.

One significant challenge faced in the Flight 587 litigation, as with almost every other air disaster case, was determining the value of the loss of each life and the appropriate level of the damages to be awarded to the victim's families. As in the calculations for the victims of 9/11, this system produces settlement offers by airlines that varied widely from passenger to passenger on the same plane. Again, questions about the passengers' nationality, income levels, and expected future earnings played a significant role in arriving at a final settlement amount. But in the case of Flight 587, these numbers were tough to accept.

Most of our clients had lost family members who were low-wage earners. A few were home healthcare workers making $11.00 per hour. Daisy Montalvo and her daughter, a student, fell into this category. Daisy left behind two sons and her ex-husband, their father, with whom she had recently reconciled. Many passengers held green cards but were still citizens of the Dominican Republic. Although the settlements in the Flight 587 case were strictly confidential, it is widely known that many of the payments were quite low based on the calculations used to determine the amounts. In addition, the unavoidable fact that people's lives and relationships can get quite messy added another layer of complication. We soon discovered husbands who had not finalized divorces and relatives claiming false family connections. In one case, two women claimed to be the mother of one of the victims.

Although all cases for victims' families represented by McCallion & Associates LLP were filed in the United States District Court for the Southern District of New York, other law firms filed their complaints in federal courts in other states, including Texas, or in various states courts. American Airlines promptly "removed" all state court cases to federal court, claiming that the federal courts had primary jurisdiction over them since the Montreal Convention controlled the cases.[5]

Since the facts and the law relating to each of these cases were substantially the same, all of the cases were considered by The United States Judicial Panel on Multidistrict Litigation ("the MDL Panel"). The MDL Panel is a unique body within the United States federal court system which manages multidistrict litigation. It was established by Congress in 1968 by Pub.L. 90–296 and has the authority to determine whether civil actions pending in two or more federal judicial districts should be transferred to a single federal district court for pretrial proceedings.[6] If such cases are determined to involve one or more common questions of fact and are transferred, the Panel will then select the district court and assign a judge or judges to preside over the litigation. The purpose of the transfer or "centralization" process is to conserve the resources of the parties and their counsel and the judiciary, thus avoiding duplication of discovery and preventing inconsistent pretrial rulings.[7] The Chief Justice of the United States, currently John Roberts, appoints the panel members composed of seven United States federal judges serving on either district courts or courts of appeals.

On April 24, 2002, the Judicial Panel transferred all Flight 587 lawsuits to the Southern District of New York, under 28 United States Code §1407. The transferred cases were assigned to Judge Robert W. Sweet for consolidated pretrial proceedings with the 72 related actions already before him, including our cases. A Plaintiffs' Executive Committee ("PEC") then was appointed to coordinate the work of plaintiffs' counsel. Plaintiffs in the underlying litigation, including the plaintiffs that we represented, sought monetary relief under various theories, including wrongful death, products liability, and breach of warranty.

In each case, the first steps involved protracted discovery proceedings with the exchange of voluminous documentation, interrogatories, and depositions. The depositions of surviving family members could be quite painful, and many were not prepared for the hostile questioning by the attorneys for American Airlines. The families had lost so much, and their settlements would be low because of earnings, but that wasn't good enough. In one instance involving the Flores family, the mother of Johnny's oldest daughter was grilled on her teenage daughter's behavior and moral character. Then she was interrogated about how close the father and daughter were.

After all the discovery procedures, and despite the unpleasantness, each family entered into confidential settlement agreements with American Airlines to avoid the uncertainties and delays that a complex trial would necessarily entail. But as with the 9/11 cases, the amount was never going to be enough or to matter. I apologized to Daisy Montalvo's recently reconciled first husband that the amount we could get for his sons was much less than we had hoped. He made a point of saying it was ok, and it didn't matter. He told me that "all was lost when the plane went down."

One of our clients, a Dominican who moved to Canada from the D.R., had married a woman lost in the crash. She lived with her children in the Bronx, but her husband was moving to the U.S. Her daughter went to Surrogate Court to try to have the new husband cut out of any award, arguing that the marriage was an immigration scam. This question was significant because if we failed to prove that our plaintiff was legally married to the decedent, he would receive nothing from a settlement or award.

This dispute triggered an extended Surrogate Court trial to resolve the issue. Witness after witness (all related to each other) swore the marriage was not legitimate. Our poor client only had himself to speak on the validity of the wedding. As the proceedings were winding down, he was cross-examined by the attorneys for the children, who kept pressing him on things he didn't know about his new wife or events he couldn't remember. In an outburst that summoned up what many may feel in situations like this, he said he hadn't kept a receipt from McDonald's because, at the time, it didn't occur to him that he would later need it as evidence in a lawsuit. Unfortunately, he lost and returned to Montreal with only the memory of what he had hoped would be a new life with the woman he loved.

The Settlements

When a tentative settlement recommendation was made in each case by a settlement committee comprised of lawyers from both the plaintiffs and the defendants, the matter would have to go before Judge Sweet for final approval. These settlement hearings were the last chance to argue for a larger settlement for our clients, based on factors we felt were not correctly treated.

One major issue we brought to Judge Sweet's attention was the amount awarded for Isaiah and other children who died on Flight 587. The judge and various committees determined that for children under the age of two, there would be a fixed award of $500,000. The argument was that the only loss that these young children experienced was for their own pain and suffering. There were no lost wages or other economic losses since a child that young had no track record even to begin to estimate what potential earnings might be in the future. Flight 587 was in the air for approximately two minutes; it only took a minute or so for the plane to fall from the sky.

Another part of the reasoning for the relatively low award for the infant victims was that the child's pain and suffering would be mitigated by being in the loving arms of a parent or caretaker. Susan, however, found this formula to be highly upsetting since she had been the one on our legal team who had been working most closely with the families. Also, being a mother herself, she instinctively knew it was not an accurate portrayal of a child at least 15 months or older. She did copious research on the issue and found a similar problem arose on another flight taking off from Lima, Peru. In that case, the pilot could land the plane, but not before about a minute of in-flight terror. What happened aboard that flight was recorded in hearings afterward. From reading those transcripts, we could reconstruct a pretty good idea of what the passengers on 587 were experiencing. The next step was to determine if the "loving arms" theory was valid. Again, our research showed that a child sitting in the loving arms of a parent - as Isaiah was on Johnny Flores's lap - would have still experienced pain and suffering. He would have felt his own father's terror.

Armed with this research, we made the argument during our hearing with Judge Sweet that the amount awarded to Isaiah's family and other similar cases should be increased. The judge was highly complimentary of our analysis but ultimately decided to make only a minor adjustment to the recommended settlement amount. This highlighted one of the drawbacks of MDL proceedings, which is that a few settlement committee members can make decisions that are difficult to get reversed by the trial judge or an appeals court.

* * *

The Flight 587 air disaster and the World Trade Center's attack exposed some troubling aspects of our justice system. Affluent and well-educated families usually have little difficulty getting satisfactory results when there has been a wrongful death. They often have wills and attorneys that can support the survivors' efforts to distribute their estates according to the decedent's wishes. On the other hand, people who do not have those resources and support systems often find themselves adrift and can end up being victimized. For example, in one case we handled, Johnny Flores' stepdaughter - who lost her mother in the crash of 587- was a minor. The settlement money for her had to be held by the public administrator until she was 18, and then she received all of it without any real support system as to what to prudently do with the money. It wasn't long before the money disappeared into the hands of non-family members.

As another example, the surviving two children of Daisy Montalvo were entitled to checks for $100,000 each from American Airlines. This money was made available to the next of kin of all passengers as emergency funds. Both boys, who desperately needed the money, couldn't get it because they didn't have birth certificates correctly translated and filed with the clerk of the Surrogate's Court in Brooklyn. It took weeks to get the necessary papers from the Dominican Republic. Even though the sense of loss and grief was roughly the same for all the victims' families in a fundamental human sense, there were delays in compensating the children and other family members who were the most vulnerable and in need of emergency relief. Our representation served to level the playing field to a significant extent, but not entirely in some cases.

These time-consuming and emotionally exhausting cases also took a toll on our entire legal staff and me. Many of the families that we represented became a genuine part of our law firm's extended family. We found ourselves dealing with family and personal issues that went far beyond the standard lines of attorney-client relationships. For example, we received a distressing phone call late one evening from a teenage girl who was one of the family members we represented. She had been living with an uncle who had made some inappropriate sexual advances, and she had fled the apartment. We helped her find alternative accommodations and carefully monitored the situation to ensure she continued attending school and received the therapy she needed.

Perhaps, as lawyers, we should not have extended ourselves so far for the victims' families. But we were human beings first and lawyers second. So we could not avoid comforting the afflicted when they needed it, while, at the same time, afflicting the comfortable whose negligence caused these disasters. To help these wonderful people was – in a very real sense – a large part of our reward.

Chapter 8

The Ginsburg Case

Fatal Attraction: the Legal Campaign to Prevent Suicides from Iconic Bridges and Buildings

They say the greatest tragedy is for a parent to outlive a child. Perhaps it is even more painful if the child commits suicide. Suicides among teenagers are particularly troubling because so many of the suicides are preventable. According to the National Institute of Mental Health, between 500,000 and one million teens and young adults attempt suicide every year. Most do so as part of a temporary impulse. The same research shows that if the impulse to commit suicide is thwarted by intervention or an inability to find a way to attempt suicide, the urge passes, and the teen lives and rarely tries it again.

Suicides on college campuses are an ongoing concern to administrations everywhere. Given the propensity of teens and young adults (18-24) to be more susceptible to a suicidal impulse, many colleges and universities have established programs to decrease the number of attempted suicides on their campuses. Usually, these programs have several components, including counseling services, peer-to-peer support, faculty training, and general increased awareness. But often overlooked among these preventative measures is the necessity of conducting an audit of each campus to determine whether students have ready access to the means to commit suicide. This is just plain common sense. Colleges know that the age group that is the bulk of the population on campus has a higher risk of attempted suicides than the entire population, and often has fleeting or brief bouts of depression. This means that the safeguarding and "suicide proofing" of the most obvious means to commit suicide – such as high iconic bridges – should become an urgent priority.

Some college campuses have the unfortunate reputation of providing students with far too easy access to high buildings or bridges used for suicide attempts. Cornell University in Ithaca, New York, is perhaps the most notorious of these college campuses. Located on the shores of Lake Cayuga and crisscrossed by a series of deep ravines and gorges, the Cornell campus has several bridges spanning those deep gorges that students and residents have regularly used over several decades to leap to their deaths.

In the case of *Ginsburg v. City of Ithaca and Cornell University*,[1] in the United States District Court for the Northern District of New York, Cornell ignored the ongoing danger of their bridges for decades, despite a long history of students tragically jumping to their deaths. The failure of the University to protect its students left the college with a reputation as "Suicide U," and a growing number of grieving families were left to wonder why the college had ignored the threat.

In July 2013, I received a phone call from Howard Ginsburg, a distraught real estate attorney in Boca Raton, Florida. He told me that one of his two children, Bradley Ginsburg, an 18-year freshman at Cornell, had jumped to his death from one of the bridges crossing the deep gorges cutting through the campus. The specific bridge from which he had jumped – the Thurston Avenue Bridge – connected Cornell's North Campus, where Bradley and other Cornell freshmen lived, to the main academic campus. Bradley had crossed the bridge daily before leaping to his death on February 17, 2010.

Bradley's suicide came as a complete shock to all who knew him. He came from a stable and happy family, with two devoted parents and a younger sister with whom he had a good relationship. He was an honors student at the Boca Ratan High School and was an A student in his first year at Cornell. He participated in extracurricular activities, was well-liked by his classmates, worked diligently in the dining halls at Cornell, and was a pledge at one of the most popular fraternities on campus. Bradley had never suffered from depression or other psychological disorders.

By all indications, Bradley's suicide was an impulsive act that was tragically successful due to the ease with which he could jump the low railing on the Thurston Avenue Bridge and leap to his death in the gorge far below. After his death, a police analysis of Bradley's computer revealed that he had, in the few days before his death, researched topics involving depression and suicide, and he listened to some depressing songs just before leaving the dorm. Bradley's roommates were unaware that he was dwelling on these dark subjects before his death. Outwardly, he appeared

Officer overlooking the Thurston Avenue Bridge.
Lucas Policastro, MD

to be as happy and well-adjusted as ever. Before his death, Bradley left a suicide note on his computer, apologizing for what he was about to do. He then left his dorm room, walked the short distance to the Thurston Avenue Bridge, and jumped to his death.

Bradley was far from the first to do so. There had been jumpers from the Cornell bridges for decades. Bradley's father was himself a Cornell alum, and when Howard was a student at the University, the fact that bridges were used for suicides was well known to the student body even then. After Bradley's death, Howard, like many grieving parents before him, sought an explanation from the Cornell administration. He wanted to know why, despite several decades of suicide by jumping from the bridges, Cornell had not insisted that safer railings or other suicide-prevention barriers be installed on all the gorge bridges. Not surprisingly, Howard never got any reasonable explanation from Cornell. What he got was the old fashion run-around. Cornell's first excuse was to claim that since the Thurston Avenue Bridge was owned by the City of Ithaca, not by Cornell, the University couldn't be responsible and had no authority to fix anything on the bridge. While Mr. Ginsburg wasn't a legal scholar or an authority on the shared responsibility of municipal facilities in a private setting, he knew intuitively that Cornell's answer didn't make sense. Here was a world-class Ivy League college, which was of significant importance to the City of Ithaca's economy, and they couldn't do anything except watch? Year after year, students jumped to their deaths off a bridge owned by Ithaca but connecting two parts of the college campus. The bridge was an intrinsic part of the college infrastructure. Mr. Ginsberg rightly figured there had to be some connection or collaboration between the City and the college. That relationship affected what Cornell could or should do to stop the ongoing threat to its students.

It was only logical that Cornell bore some responsibility for the bridge's safety. After all, the City didn't even have access to the bridge without passing over private Cornell property. Even more apparent was the ongoing importance of the college to the City. It was - and still is - a major employer. Every year thousands of students arrive in Ithaca and, along with fellow students at Ithaca College, support the local business and provide prestige to the community.

Contrary to Cornell's position that the bridge was only the City's responsibility and that the University didn't have any legal connection with the City, Howard Ginsburg proved that the City and the University had an interwoven web of relationships. Both of these entities had been involved in the discussions regarding bridge safety in connection with plans to renovate and expand the bridge. Through the course of the litigation brought by Mr. Ginsburg, hundreds of pages of documents would show just how false the University's public position on its responsibility was and how negligent and irresponsible the University had been, costing the lives of numerous students and citizens of Ithaca.

Before I became involved in the case, Mr. Ginsberg worked with a local lawyer, Leland T. Williams, who learned that the bridge had been redesigned and rebuilt only a few years earlier, during 2006 and 2007. He also discovered that Cornell had played a significant role in that redesign and reconstruction project. During this process, Cornell gave some lip service to the idea that the railings on the bridge should be designed to prevent suicides. Still, it decided that the concern for the "aesthetics" of the bridge was more critical than suicide prevention. This irresponsibility might have been understandable if no one had ever committed suicide from the bridges at Cornell. It might have made sense if there was no information about 18-24 years old being more susceptible to suicide, or that between 1990 and 2010, 27 people - including 15 Cornell students -had jumped from one of these gorge bridges. Finally, scientific, well-respected psychological research concerning suicides among college students was plentiful and consistent. Regardless of all this evidence, the new railings were, inexplicably, just as easy to vault as the old ones.

In response to continuing questions from Bradley's parents, Cornell took the position that Bradley's suicide, however tragic, was not reasonably foreseeable. Cornell thus argued that it had no liability or responsibility for his death. Cornell reasoned that since Bradley had exhibited no signs or symptoms of depression or other psychological distress, Cornell had no duty to provide psychological counseling to him or any other form of support. What Cornell failed to acknowledge was that as a psychologist affiliated with Cornell explained, "The people who are at the greatest risk are the ones who are best at hiding what's wrong with themselves."[2]

In seeking to avoid any responsibility for Bradley's death, as well as that of other students who had ended their lives in the same way, Cornell also relied on the argument that "if someone wants to kill themselves, they will find a way to do it." This age-old (but false) argument for leaving high bridges as they are, without any suicide barriers, rests on the notion that anyone contemplating suicide will find another place or way to kill themselves. In Bradley's case, Cornell argued that since Bradley was so hard-working and goal-oriented, he would have found some way to kill himself even if he was prevented from doing so on one of the gorge bridges.

However, this argument – that it is virtually inevitable that someone contemplating suicide will find a way to do so- was utterly unsupported by studies on the subject or psychological literature. The overwhelming evidence was that most individuals who would jump from iconic sites are ambivalent, act impulsively, choose a specific area, and if thwarted from an attempt at that site at a particular time, will rarely seek out an alternative means to kill themselves. For example, after 480 suicide deaths on the Bloor Street Viaduct in Toronto, the erection of suicide barriers led to no significant increase in suicides on other bridges in the area.[3]

Cornell itself had its homegrown evidence of the folly of this argument. In October of 1991, a student jumped from the Thurston Avenue Bridge and survived. According to Rob Fishman, a Cornell alum writing for the Huffington Post, this student was the only one to survive such a jump. Once recovered, he returned to campus and graduated from Cornell. Therefore, the strong inference was that the desire to kill oneself is, for the most part, temporary, and that when suicide becomes more difficult, people tend to get help rather than switching to another method. Finding help is what happened in England when the formula for gas ovens changed and carbon monoxide levels were reduced.[4] The suicide rate was drastically reduced in the U.K, and that country continues to have a suicide rate about one-half that of the U.S.[5]

The survival rate is much higher for the small percentage of people deterred by suicide prevention barriers on elevated bridges and then try to end their lives by some other means. Jumping from a high structure is fatal 98 percent of the time, making it a much more effective and lethal form of suicide than anything else available to most people, even those with guns. By comparison, poison is only 15 percent effective; drug overdose, 12 percent; wrist cutting, 5 percent. Undoubtedly, jumping from such a high bridge is truly, as the adage puts it, a "highly effective and permanent solution to a temporary problem."

Even Cornell itself had to admit finally that suicide-prevention barriers on bridges saved lives. As a group of experts later commissioned to study the subject stated in a report issued after the death of Bradley and two other students within a short period, "the decision to attempt suicide may be a transient response to a particular set of emotional circumstances that resolve with time."[6]

Eventually, it became clear to Bradley's parents that the only thing Cornell or the City of Ithaca had to do to save Bradley's life was install effective safety measures on the gorge bridges. The fix was simple: higher and suicide-proof railings, or nets underneath the bridges, or both. Had preventative measures been installed at an earlier point in time, such as when the bridge had been redesigned and reconstructed, Bradley would have likely not been able to succeed in his impulsive rush to end his life. However, these last lines of defense against suicide were not there. Cornell and the City had done nothing to minimize or eliminate the risk of people intentionally jumping from one of the gorge bridges, despite the certain knowledge that, sooner or later, someone else would jump to their death.

Finally, after growing increasingly frustrated with Cornell's response, on November 21, 2011, Howard Ginsburg, as the Administrator of Bradley's Estate, filed a lawsuit against both Cornell and the City of Ithaca in the United States District Court for the Northern District of New York. The lawsuit charged Cornell and the City with negligence and other causes of action relating to the lack of effective suicide prevention measures on the Thurston Avenue Bridge.[7]

This Complaint was quickly followed up with an Amended Complaint, filed on December 8, 2011. This Amended Complaint included fourteen causes of action, essentially alleging that both Cornell and the City were negligent in failing to design and install adequate railings and other safety and suicide prevention measures during the reconstruction of the Thurston Avenue Bridge. The Amended Complaint further alleged that given the long and tragic history of suicide by jumping from the bridges (popularly referred to by generations of Cornell students as "gorging out"), it was reasonably foreseeable that college students and City residents would do the same in the future. According to our reasoning, Cornell and Ithaca knew or should have known the bridges were a real risk to the students and residents of Ithaca. It was grossly negligent for them to do nothing to correct this ongoing danger.

Cornell and the City filed motions to dismiss the Amended Complaint in January 2012, and Ginsburg cross-moved to supplement the pleadings.

On March 15, 2012, the federal district court judge, David N. Hurd, denied both motions to dismiss.[8] The district court also rejected the defendant's motion for reconsideration or reargument. Among other things, Judge Hurd rejected the defendants' argument that Bradley's suicide was "unforeseeable," finding that "it was foreseeable that *someone* may commit suicide by jumping off the Thurston Avenue Bridge." Judge Hurd further found that "as owner and controller of the Thurston Avenue Bridge, defendants had a duty to maintain that property in a reasonably safe condition to prevent foreseeable suicides."[9]

Finally, in the Conclusion section of his Decision, Judge Hurd found:

> Plaintiff has sufficiently alleged that Ithaca and Cornell owned and controlled the Thurston Avenue Bridge and thus had a duty to maintain that property in a reasonably safe condition to prevent foreseeable suicides. Plaintiff has also adequately alleged that Ithaca and Cornell failed to fulfill that duty when they did not implement appropriate suicide prevention measures on the bridge despite having an opportunity to do so when the bridge was redesigned and reconstructed in 2006-2007.

Judge Hurd thus agreed with the plaintiff's position that there was overwhelming evidence in the record that Cornell had sufficient "control" over Thurston Avenue Bridge. He found that Cornell's collaboration with Ithaca over the 2006/2007 redesign and reconstruction established a duty on Cornell's part to repair and prevent a known hazard. The hazard was the ease with which a person could jump from the Bridge. The defendants could be held accountable for damages resulting from their failure to remedy this known hazard.

Once I agreed to act as counsel for Bradley's Estate and had thoroughly reviewed what had transpired in the legal proceedings to date, I started doing some additional research on the correlation between college-age students and suicide. The statistics were shocking. For decades, every university, including Cornell, knew or should have known that the risk of student suicides is always a clear and present danger. A survey of 26,000 students at 70 colleges and universities found that over fifty percent of college students had suicidal "ideations;" 18% of college students had seriously contemplated suicide, and 8% had made an attempt.[10] Ten to 15 percent of college students regularly consider suicide, and one to two percent attempt it.[11] These statistics meant that at Cornell, with approximately 20,000 plus students, between 2000 to 3000 students were contemplating suicide at any given point in time. Cornell, in particular, has been acutely aware of the issue of student suicides since the number of student suicides by jumping from campus bridges was much higher than the national average. According to Cornell's own Timothy C. Marchell, Ph.D., while only 2% of student suicide deaths were caused by jumping nationwide, approximately 50% of Cornell's student suicide deaths were by jumping from bridges.[12]

Although it was impossible to anticipate that Bradley would be the next Cornell student to fall victim to the lure of the iconic bridges and gorges, it was virtually inevitable – as Judge Hurd found – that someone else would attempt to jump from one of the bridges. The only question was "when."

History of Suicides from Bridges At Cornell

The history of suicides at Cornell left little question that successive Cornell administrations were painfully aware of the dangers posed by the gorge bridges. Since the first bridge opened over the gorges in 1897, the specter of suicide haunted Ithaca's gorges.[13] From 1970 to 1973, there were eight suicides in Ithaca, seven associated with Cornell, and four were at the gorges. Cornell considered installing suicide prevention railings and other "safety mechanisms" on the bridges but ultimately decided not to include these expenses in the university budget. Instead, the decision was made to do nothing.

* * *

In March 1976, a young Cornell student, Judy Kram, committed suicide by jumping from one of the gorge bridges. On May 25, 1977, Judy's father appeared before the Ithaca Board of Public Works members to plead that they consider erecting suicide barriers on the City's several bridges.[14] Mr. Kram also wrote Cornell's president, requesting that safety structures be installed on the bridges. President Corson responded by stating that Cornell continued to prefer bridge designs that were "functional and aesthetically pleasing."

Undaunted, Mr. Kram then took his case to the Cornell Board of Trustees, sending each Trustee an article about the recent cluster of suicides (at least 5) during 1977 and 1978. Cornell's response was to start keeping a file on Mr. Kram, noting "that he has become highly overzealous on the issue."

In October 1976, Cornell's vice president wrote a memo to President Corson, entitled, "Suspension Bridge -Aesthetics vs. Suicide Deterrent." The memo noted the importance of aesthetics, concluding: "We do not program our design efforts for suicide prevention." In 1978, Cornell's vice-president reminded grieving parents of a suicide victim that "since 1970, there has [only] been, on average, one suicide a year at Cornell." He seemed to suggest one suicide per year was an acceptable attrition rate. He went on to lament the fact that "the suicide myth seems to have taken on a reality of its own . . .."

It is not surprising that over the years, Cornell earned the nickname, "Suicide U," and Ithaca was often referred to as "the suicide capital."[15] The attraction of gorges and bridges continued to have a macabre hold on the imaginations of both Cornell students and graduates. One Cornell graduate returned ten years after his graduation to jump to his death into the gorge.

In the fall of 1977, however, Cornell was finally forced to take some limited safety measures following a series of three suicides by jumping into the gorge in rapid succession from the university-owned Suspension Bridge. Cornell declared a "mental state of emergency" and installed "suicide bars" (but no netting) on the Suspension Bridge. Unfortunately, neither Cornell nor the City of Ithaca took steps to place any "means restrictions" on any of the other gorge bridges, which would have made it more difficult for students to end their life by jumping from one of the bridges.

Two years later, on April 13, 1979, the body of a missing Cornell student was recovered from Fall Creek, which runs through one of the gorges. The boy's father issued an "open letter" to Cornell's president, noting that his son, like Bradley Ginsburg thirty-one years later, had no history of emotional problems. He had graduated from high school with the highest awards and honors, came from a relatively happy and stable family, and entered Cornell with otherwise excellent credentials.

In May 1979, Cornell approved plans to add a 6 ½ foot metal bar railing to the Collegetown Bridge. Still, when opposition emerged, including complaints that the Suspension Bridge's "suicide bars" created a "prison-like atmosphere," the plan was shelved.

In short, even though Cornell and the City of Ithaca were repeatedly placed on notice by parents, community members, and experts as to the need for urgent action to prevent suicides from bridges, they did nothing regarding the Thurston Avenue Bridge or any other gorge bridges.

Between 1990 and 2010, 29 people attempted suicide by jumping off gorge bridges.[16] Twenty-six were successful. During this 1990-2010 period, the tragic history of suicides continued to prompt repeated calls for suicide prevention measures to be installed on all bridges in the area. In November 1994, for example, Ithaca Police Officer Dan Slattery proposed to the City that "netlike chain-link safety barriers [be installed] about 15 feet under the five bridges on campus . . .."[17] However, Cornell's response to two student deaths in November 1994 was to deny that there was any "problem." David I. Stewart, Cornell's Director of Community Relations, blamed the bad press on "mythology," stating: "There is a myth surrounding the number of suicides here. There is not a larger than average number of suicides on the Cornell campus."[18]

Finally, after the death of Bradley and two other students in February and March 2010, one of Cornell's leading psychiatrists acknowledged that the gorge bridges were "iconic hot spots," drawing people to them in moments of despair, and that "means restrictions" at such spots saved lives.[19]

Bridge Safety Versus Aesthetics

Cornell was not the only school facing the suicide by jumping problem. In 2003, New York University experienced two suicides inside the Bobst Library. The students jumped from the open-air crosswalks inside the library. N.Y.U.'s response was immediate; it constructed plexiglass barriers on all stairways and crosswalks on all levels. In 2009, a third student managed to scale the plexiglass and jump to his death. This time the University went even further, constructing a floor-to-ceiling metal barrier on each level. Unlike Cornell, N.Y.U. felt three suicides over three years was too many.

Another New York City college had a similar rash of suicides and, like N.Y.U. (and unlike Cornell), responded quickly with preventative measures. Two suicides by jumping out of windows of a student dorm on 18th Street in Manhattan led to the immediate placement of bars on the windows. A May 2014 suicide at the college building at 17 Lexington Avenue in Manhattan was met with similar action, including forming a psychiatric "Suicide Squad" to help curtail suicide attempts.

Everyone knows that suicide attempts from high bridges or buildings are almost always lethal. As the eminent suicide expert, Dr. James Motto, eloquently put it, the jumping from an iconic hot spot, such as the Ithaca Gorge Bridges or San Francisco's Golden Gate Bridge, "is seen as sure, quick, clean and available, which is the most potent factor. . . It's like having a loaded gun on the table."[20]

Nor is there any serious question that safety barriers on bridges and buildings are effective in preventing suicides. In 2001, the U.S. Dept. of Health and Social Services developed a "National Strategy for Suicide Prevention," emphasizing the crucial importance of "means restrictions" for preventing suicide. The National Suicide Prevention Lifeline Position Paper dated June 16, 2008, definitively stated: "The use of bridge barriers is the most effective means of bridge suicide prevention."[21]

Iconic "hot spots" worldwide - like the Memorial Bridge in Augusta, Maine, the Eiffel Tower in Paris, the Empire State Building in New York, and the Bloor Street Viaduct in Toronto - were all solid magnets for suicide seekers. Once suicide barriers were erected on all of them, the suicide rate dropped to nearly zero.

The puzzling question then is: If there have been so many suicide attempts from iconic high bridges or buildings, and they almost always result in death, why is it that effective suicide prevention barriers had not been installed at Cornell? As I continued my research on this subject, it became apparent that many people – including influential college professors and administrators – felt that installing effective physical barriers would detract from the aesthetic beauty of the iconic bridges that attract potential suicide victims. Most colleges and universities' art and architecture departments often have substantial influence over the design or modification of campus bridges or tall buildings. At the same time, the corresponding lobby for suicide prevention through physical barriers is virtually non-existent. Colleges like Cornell are willing to spend millions of dollars on first-class mental health counseling programs, but virtually nothing on "means restrictions." Unfortunately, not all students, such as Bradley, seek help and do not show any outward signs of distress. As a result, the availability of mental health counseling is not, by itself, enough to prevent campus suicides.

To prevent suicides by jumping, there must be a recognition that there may be minimal adverse effects on aesthetics to increase safety on bridges. This trade-off is both a moral and a legal imperative, which many institutions and governmental entities have been slow to accept. As Dr. Motto emphasized: "If people started hanging themselves from the tree in my front yard, I'd have a moral obligation to prevent that from happening. I'd take the limb off, put a fence around it. It's not about whether the suicide statistics would change, or the cost, or whether the tree would be as beautiful. . .A barrier would say, 'Society is speaking, and we care about your life.'" [22]

In other words, no one knows who will pick the gun up and shoot, but logic and reason tell us with a high degree of certainty that over some time, someone will. Put another way, while it is impossible to identify all those persons suffering from severe mental health issues that will impulsively jump, it is virtually certain that someone will try to commit suicide and succeed without adequate means restrictions. The inescapable conclusion that our research showed, and which the Ginsburg court ultimately accepted, was that cities and universities with iconic suicide bridges on or near them were playing "Russian Roulette" with young people's lives by not implementing effective suicide-prevention measures on those bridges.

Thus, long before Bradley jumped to his death from the Thurston Avenue Bridge, experts already had a widespread consensus that barriers were the most effective means of preventing bridge suicides. Cornell, in particular, knew about the importance of bridge barriers in preventing suicides. Nevertheless, as of February 2010, when Bradley jumped to his death, neither Cornell nor the City of Ithaca had taken any practical steps to design suicide-prevention barriers on the gorge bridges. There were no specialized high railings or netting that had proven effective at other "suicide bridges."

Another notable exception to the general worldwide focus on suicide prevention in designing and constructing suicide prevention barriers on iconic bridges and buildings was the Golden Gate Bridge in San Francisco, where over 1600 persons jumped to their death since it opened on May 27, 1937.[23] A record 46 people plunged to their deaths from the bridge in 2014 alone.

The railing on the Golden Gate Bridge, like that on the Thurston Avenue Bridge in Ithaca and most of the other gorge bridges, was only four feet high and a short walk from a parking lot. The original plans in 1937 called for railings of 5 ½ feet, but for reasons that remain obscure, the height was reduced to four feet. Over the years, there were seven unsuccessful campaigns to persuade or pressure the Golden Gate Bridge, Highway, and Transportation District to erect practical suicide barriers. The failure to install such effective suicide prevention barriers was particularly frustrating to mental health professionals. A study published in 1978 entitled "Where Are They Now?" was published by Richard H. Seiden, a former professor at the University of California, Berkeley, School of Public Health. Professor Seiden's article showed that of 515 people who had been restrained from attempting suicide by jumping off the Golden Gate Bridge from 1937 to 1971, over 90% were still alive in 1978 (the year he conducted his study) or had died of natural causes.[24] In other words, if prevented from committing suicide, there was less than a one in ten chance that the person would try again.

In March 2005, the Golden Gate Bridge District directors voted to authorize a $2 million feasibility study but then delayed the funding for the study. It was not until 2014 that the directors reversed their longstanding policy and voted for using toll money to supplement state and federal funds to implement suicide barriers on the bridge.[25] The plan called for a $66 million stainless-steel net system 20 feet below the sidewalk.[26] One of the reasons the Golden Gate Bridge directors changed their views on the subject was that psychiatric experts and mental health professionals introduced mounting evidence that the suicidal impulse was typically fleeting, especially in young people.[27] The average age of the jumpers also dropped alarmingly; while previously the largest group of Golden Gate Bridge suicides were between 35 and 45, suicides by 20 and 30-year-olds became more common.[28] Some psychologists explained that the brains of teenagers and young adults were still developing, so they are subject to the transitory urge to commit suicide more than fully mature adults. Another factor in play in the change of heart by the 19-member bridge board was that, while it was once an exclusively male institution, seven board members were now women.[29] Senator Barbara Boxer, who had served on the board, was instrumental in getting a clause inserted in the 2012 federal transportation bill authorizing funds for the "installation of safety barriers and nets on bridges."[30]

The 2006/2007 Reconstruction of the Thurston Avenue Bridge

When Cornell and the City of Ithaca undertook to redesign and reconstruct the Thurston Avenue Bridge during 2006 and 2007, they gave "lip service" to the goal of suicide prevention. However, they ended up subordinating that goal to the competing and partially inconsistent goal of maintaining an "aesthetically pleasing" bridge design. In the June 6, 2002 Minutes of Project Meeting No. 2, passing reference was made to the "Use [of] railings with all vertical elements to minimize 'climbers.'" However, Cornell and the City left little question as to their main priority: "aesthetically pleasing bridge railings would be preferred." The July 9, 2002 "Cornell Information Meeting Minutes" noted that the only two priorities for the railing design were (1) meeting New York State Dept. of Transportation ("NYSDOT") crash test criteria, and (2) aesthetics. The reasoning was that the "railing design is a high priority due to the aesthetic nature of the area and the function of the bridge as a gateway into the Cornell campus." "Suicide prevention" was barely mentioned in the planning documents.

Indeed, when the new railings on the Thurston Avenue Bridge were finally built, they were *lower* than the original ones. Although the specifications called for an increase in the railing height from 3' 5" to 4'7," this intended increase was illusory. The reason for this was that, before reconstruction, there was no concrete parapet wall (sometimes referred to as a "concrete footing") between the surface of the Bridge and the bottom of the railings. However, a "concrete footing" installed during the reconstruction was 18" high at the bottom of the railing. A person could easily stand on this parapet wall, making it easier to climb over the railing. Before the new construction, the distance from the top of the parapet wall to the top of the railing was 3'7." The new railing was, in reality, only 3'1" high, making the new railing four inches lower than the older 3'5" railing it replaced. In other words, the concrete footing ultimately defeated the purpose of raising the railing.

The railing was also designed with an inward curvature. If a person wanted to jump over the new bridge railing, they would stand on the concrete footing and hoist themselves up over the railing, with the curvature of the barrier making it more manageable. Thus, the curved railings had absolutely nothing to do with enhanced pedestrian safety or suicide prevention. Neither Cornell nor the City took the trouble to conduct a study to test this novel theory, i.e., that curved railings improve bridge safety.

Even before the reconstruction of the Bridge was completed, documents obtained from Cornell during the "discovery" process, where each side produces relevant documents requested by the other side, revealed that Cornell knew the railing design it adopted was inadequate to deter climbers. In an email exchange, dated February 22 and 23, 2006, between Frank Perry, Cornell Project Manager, and Curtis Ostrander, Cornell Police Chief, Mr. Perry wrote: "I do not see anything to keep people from crawling over the railing. . ..The railing is curved to the inside as shown in the presentation, but only 1.4 meters or 4'7" high." Police Chief Ostrander agreed: "Obviously, I'm not happy with the low height of the railing . . ." Their concerns, however, were buried.

Cornell Denies Responsibility For the Reconstruction of the Thurston Avenue Bridge

During the ensuing federal litigation by Bradley Ginsburg's Estate against both Cornell and the City of Ithaca,[31] Cornell denied any involvement in the 2006/2007 reconstruction of the Thurston Avenue Bridge, arguing that the City held title to the Bridge and was, therefore, entirely responsible for its redesign and reconstruction. However, one of the documents that we obtained during the discovery process in the case was a May 2002 study commissioned by Cornell and conducted by the consulting firm of Sasaki Associates Inc. This study noted that while the City owned the Bridge, Cornell owned the property on both sides needed to redesign and reconstruct the access roads leading to the Bridge.[32] Indeed, Cornell had considerable leverage over the design of the reconstruction project because the City required an Easement and Right of Way ("R.O.W.") from Cornell before it could finalize the design of the bridge project and get approval from the NYSDOT. Cornell finally agreed to "donate" this easement and R.O.W. to Ithaca for no compensation, only after receiving the City's tacit agreement to incorporate Cornell's recommendations into the final plan.

Also, the City and Cornell and some other interested parties entered into a formal "Partnership Agreement" during February-March 2006 for the Bridge reconstruction project. The design of the bridge railings fell within the area of Cornell's responsibility. Cornell's Sasaki Report showed that considerable time, money, and effort was spent studying various means to protect the safety of pedestrians and bicycles. However, Cornell conducted absolutely no studies on the design of bridge railings to prevent any further suicides from the Bridge. Not one dime was spent studying the means restrictions on iconic bridges around the globe to determine the most effective suicide barriers. Was a railing height of 1.4 meters (4 ½ feet) high enough to deter climbers and prevent suicides? Was a curved railing a help or a hindrance to a person attempting suicide by jumping from the Bridge? If curved railings were a suicide deterrent, why weren't they used on other iconic bridges that attracted suicide seekers? Neither Cornell nor the City of Ithaca deemed it essential to answer these questions, with tragic results.

Moreover, Cornell had no "suicide prevention" consultant to eliminate the risk of future suicides during the Bridge reconstruction. No one from Cornell or the City ever sounded the alarm (or questioned) whether the addition of an 18" footing at the base of the railing created a hazard by making it easier for someone to jump the railing.

Ithaca's Mayor Declares a "Public Health Emergency"

After the six suicides of Cornell students during the 2009/2010 academic year, with three of those deaths (including Bradley Ginsburg's) taking place at the Gorge bridges within a few weeks of each other, Ithaca's Mayor declared a public health emergency on March 26, 2010. This declaration permitted Cornell to erect and pay for temporary chain link fences on all three City-owned bridges crossing the gorges, including Thurston Avenue Bridge.

During the next two years, from mid-2010 through 2012, the threat and then the reality of the *Ginsburg* case in Federal Court, as well as the overwhelming public outcry to finally put an end to suicides from the gorge bridges, shocked Cornell and the City of Ithaca into taking effective action. On August 4, 2010, the City Common Council, at Cornell's request, issued a Resolution extending the public health emergency and allowing Cornell to erect and pay for the replacement of the temporary chain link fences with black-coated, "suicide-proof" rectilinear fences on all three City-owned bridges.

Cornell also took the lead in redesigning other suicide prevention measures, such as security surveillance cameras. It also paid for installing nets underneath the Bridge to catch any jumper who might succeed in scaling the railings. An agreement dated December 21, 2011 between Cornell and the City gave Cornell primary control over the design of other safety components on the Bridge to prevent additional suicides. Cornell hired the consulting engineers/designers who designed these additional means restriction measures, and on April 13, 2011, Cornell published its "Bridge Means Restriction Study" on the internet.

In short, when Cornell finally decided that the time had come to install effective "means restrictions" on the gorge bridges, it knew precisely how to take control and accomplish that goal, regardless of whether they were technically "City-owned" or not.

The Summary Judgment Motions

After voluminous document discovery and depositions of at least one dozen witnesses from Cornell and the City of Ithaca, as well as various consultants, experts, and Mr. and Mrs. Ginsburg themselves, both Cornell and the City filed motions for summary judgment. The defendants claimed that the Court should not permit the case to move forward to a jury trial and that by law, they had no legal responsibility for Bradley's death.

Just as it had done in its previously unsuccessful motion to dismiss, Cornell argued in its summary judgment motion that Bradley's suicide was not "foreseeable." But Judge Hurd had already rejected this argument when Cornell raised it in its motion to dismiss, noting in his opinion that it was reasonably foreseeable that *someone* would jump from the Bridge.

Undaunted by Judge Hurd's prior decision, Cornell submitted an expert report from Paul Barreira, M.D., a psychiatrist. He speculated that since Bradley had left a suicide note dated June 6, 2009, eight months before his death, he "must" have been contemplating suicide. Dr. Barreira concluded that Bradley's decision to kill himself was carefully planned, not a fleeting impulse. He also argued that Bradley was a "hard worker," if his "goal" were to commit suicide, he would have found a way to accomplish his goal, regardless of whether or not it was easy to jump from the Thurston Avenue Bridge.

However, a closer analysis of Bradley's suicide note revealed that the date of "6/6/09" for his suicide note must have been a mistake since Bradley did not even own the laptop computer on June 6, 2009. The laptop was purchased two months later, in August 2009. Moreover, although Bradley was not a student yet at Cornell on June 6, 2009, his suicide note referenced the AEPi fraternity at Cornell. The inescapable conclusion was that the note must have been created after Bradley arrived at Cornell in the late summer of 2009, most likely in the few days before his death on February 17, 2010, when he was doing extensive research on topics involving depression and suicide.

Cornell argued that because Bradley was a hard worker and very goal-oriented, he would have found an alternative means to kill himself if he had been prevented from jumping off the Bridge. However, this argument ignored all of the scholarly research showing that the overwhelming majority of people who try to commit suicide and survive do not try it again. Instead, these suicide attempt survivors generally obtain help from mental health professionals and then live normal and productive lives.[33] Therefore, the more reasonable explanation was not that Bradley would have persisted in his "mission" to kill himself but that if the Bridge had effective suicide prevention measures in place, Bradley's suicidal impulses would have been thwarted. Then it was likely that he would have sought psychiatric counseling to manage his first serious encounter with self-destructive impulses.

In denying Cornell's motion for summary judgment,[34] the district court appears to have favored the opinion of the plaintiff's expert, Dr. Michael Bernstein, which was that Bradley was having a transitory bout with depression. Bernstein believed Bradly's suicide was an impulsive act and that if effective means restrictions were in place on the Bridge, it is likely that his death would have been prevented. It was also pointed out that all factors indicated that Bradley was looking towards the future until just before his death. He had recently applied for and was accepted for a camp counselor's job that coming summer. He had asked his mother to send him his passport for a fraternity trip to Montreal the following week, and he had just changed some of the courses he was taking that

Spring semester. In short, there was absolutely nothing about Bradley's life indicating he was depressed or contemplating ending it.

Dr. Bernstein further noted in his expert report that numerous studies had shown that adolescents and young adults are more prone to impulsive behavior. A study found that 10% to 15% of college students were contemplating suicide at any given time. This meant that at Cornell, with approximately 20,000 students, between 2000-3000 were thinking of suicide every day. In any event, Judge Hurd ruled that Bradley's state of mind was mainly irrelevant to the issue of Cornell's duties and responsibilities.

In his March 24, 2014 decision denying both Cornell's and the City's motions for summary judgment, Judge Hurd declined to dismiss the plaintiff's negligence claims against Cornell based upon a "premises liability" theory for wrongful death and personal injuries.[35] The Court found that "an issue of material fact remains for a jury as to whether Cornell exercised sufficient control over the design, construction, and maintenance of the Thurston Avenue Bridge to justify holding it liable, with Ithaca, for injuries caused by alleged hazards on the bridge." Judge Hurd reached this decision based on a finding that "Cornell provided invaluable assistance and input during the design phase of the bridge reconstruction project." He noted "Cornell also retained Sasaki [Associates] to study pedestrian, vehicular, and bicycle traffic and other campus safety matters as part of the bridge's redesign." The Court found, in its written decision and order, that "a rational juror could view this . . . as evidence of Cornell's understanding that [the Thurston Avenue renovation project] was a joint endeavor with Ithaca."[36] Further, Judge Hurd noted that "Cornell employees participated directly in numerous meetings with representatives for Ithaca . . . .." The district court relied on the fact that after the third suicide in March 2010, "Cornell paid for, installed and maintained temporary fencing and permanent netting." Finally, Judge Hurd found that "whether Thurston Avenue Bridge was reasonably safe in light of the allegedly foreseeable risk of future suicide attempts is a factual issue to be determined by a jury."[37]

Judge Hurd thus agreed with our argument that there was overwhelming evidence that Cornell had sufficient "control" over the Thurston Avenue Bridge and its 2006/2007 redesign and reconstruction. This "control" by Cornell over the Bridge established a duty on its part to repair and prevent a known hazard. The hazard was the ease with which a person could jump from the Bridge, and the Court held that Cornell could be held accountable for damages resulting from its failure to remedy this known hazard. The responsibility was especially true since Cornell had detailed knowledge of the long tragic history of suicides from the Thurston Avenue Bridge and other bridges. It was common knowledge on campus that "gorging out" was a relatively painless way to end one's life. In other words, Cornell's liability arose from its "failure to exercise reasonable care to prevent or minimize foreseeable future danger."[38] Cornell also assumed joint responsibility with the City to improve safety on the Thurston Avenue Bridge and represented that one of the primary objectives was to design bridge railings to prevent suicides. Having assumed responsibility for bridge safety, we successfully argued that Cornell was liable for having failed to design bridge "means restrictions" that achieved those objectives.

The Settlement

Judge Hurd scheduled jury selection for September 29, 2014, with the trial to commence on October 1, 2014. On the eve of trial, Cornell offered to settle the matter in consideration of establishing a full perpetual scholarship in Bradley's name. The University initially placed a value on the scholarship (in writing) of $1.5 to $1.6 million, which was based on the estimated amount of an endowment that would be required for a private donor to establish a scholarship.

Plaintiff's calculations placed a value of a full perpetual scholarship at a slightly higher number, i.e., $1.8 million. These calculations were based upon the then-current Cornell cost of tuition, room and board, and other miscellaneous college expenses, which was $60,000 per year. Therefore, the value of the scholarship to the Estate would be - at a minimum - 30 years, times $60,000 per year, or $1.8 million.

In addition to Cornell's settlement offer of a scholarship in Bradley's name, Howard Ginsburg also received a settlement offer from the City of Ithaca. On September 10, 2014, shortly before a scheduled settlement conference with the district court, Mr. Ginsburg accepted Cornell's offer of a full perpetual scholarship in Bradley's name. He also accepted the City's settlement offer, thus terminating the case without a trial.

Although I had been looking forward to the trial, and we had been preparing feverously for it for more than two months, a plaintiff such as Howard Ginsberg can never be faulted for settling a case on the eve of trial. No matter how modest the settlement, it has the salutary effect of bringing closure to the grieving parents. They could at least be reassured that Bradley's memory would be honored with a continuing Cornell scholarship in his name and a memorial plaque on campus.

Judge Hurd's two decisions – rejecting Cornell's and Ithaca's motions to dismiss and summary judgment motions – stand as landmark decisions regarding the responsibilities of a college or municipality to take reasonable and prudent safety measures when designing high bridges and other infrastructure projects.

However, the families of suicide victims in other college cases were not so successful, as demonstrated by the 2018 case against the Massachusetts Institute of Technology.

The M.I.T. Case

On May 7, 2018, the Supreme Judicial Court – Massachusetts' highest Court – ruled that M.I.T. could not be held responsible for the 2009 suicide of one of its students.[39] In its 44-page decision, the Court said that while M.I.T. had no duty to prevent the suicide of the student in question, there could be limited circumstances in which universities could bear some responsibility for protecting their students. These circumstances could include when a student expressly states plans to commit suicide. But overall, the Court found that universities "are not responsible for monitoring and controlling all aspects of their student's lives," and there is "universal recognition" that the age of "in loco parentis," in which universities stand in place of parents, is long over.

In the M.I.T. case, the student, Han Nguyen, was 25 and a Ph.D. candidate at M.I.T.'s Sloan School of Management when he jumped to his death from a campus building. In court papers, his family's lawyers said that they believed that M.I.T., two of its professors, and a dean of student life were legally bound to care for Mr. Nguyen and prevent suicide. They even suggested that one of the professors, Birger Wernerfelt, had caused it, noting that Mr. Nguyen had leaped to his death just moments after the professor had harshly criticized him. Lawyers for the family also said that M.I.T.'s student support services were inadequate. Some campuses — notably, the University of Illinois — had long ago put in place programs that reduced the rate of suicides. However, the rate at M.I.T. remained disturbingly high. In response, the University argued that Mr. Nguyen had been dealing with mental health issues long before coming to there, including two previous suicide attempts. Also, while at M.I.T., he received care from nine different mental health professionals, none of whom deemed him at "imminent risk" of killing himself.

* * *

The M.I.T. case represents the prevailing view of U.S. courts, which is that universities and colleges are not generally responsible for the death of one of their students by suicide. The *Ginsburg* case, however, stands for the proposition that a university has a responsibility to take reasonably prudent steps to protect its students. These steps include installing appropriate suicide-prevention barriers on bridges and other structures that are known to attract troubled students seeking to end their lives.

The suicide deaths of Bradley Ginsburg and two other Cornell students during the span of only a few weeks – followed by the federal court litigation brough on behalf of his estate - finally shook Cornell University and the City of Ithaca out of their decades-long refusal to recognize the need for the installation of effective suicide-prevention measures on the other bridges spanning the gorges. With the City's consent, Cornell quickly erected some temporary chain link fences on Thurston Avenue Bridge, which were later replaced with sufficiently high and specially designed railings intended to prevent potential jumpers. These specialized railings were backed up by the installation of netting below the Bridge and security cameras.

The results were dramatically positive: There were no reported suicide deaths by jumping from any gorge bridges for at least several years following the installation of safety measures. There was also no evidence that a student who was thwarted in their intent to jump from a gorge bridge committed suicide by alternative means.

One "takeaway" from the *Ginsburg* case is that litigation and heightened public awareness are often effective means to force universities and municipalities to acknowledge the importance of physical suicide prevention barriers on major bridges and buildings. Universities and cities have a legal obligation to take reasonable safety measures to protect students in particular, and all citizens in general, who may be attracted to iconic bridges and buildings. These bridges and buildings are known magnets for those seeking to end their lives by jumping to their deaths. Colleges and universities that ignore this obligation do so at substantial risk since the grieving families of suicide victims have shown an increased willingness to utilize the judicial system to hold them accountable.

Chapter 9

The Parajito Homesteaders and Concepcion Cases

The Legal Struggle for Civil and Human Rights in the U.S.

Lawyers have always played critical roles in America's struggle for human and civil rights. The most significant civil rights movement in the United States was the long struggle by African Americans and their allies to end institutionalized racial discrimination, disenfranchisement, and racial segregation. This civil rights movement is still ongoing, rekindled with the brutal police killings of George Floyd, Tawana Brawley, and others over a short period in the summer of 2020, leading to protest marches across the U.S. and demands for the end of institutional racism.

The civil rights movement originated in the late 1860s, following the end of the Civil War. With the defeat of the southern states and the end of slavery, amendments to the U.S. Constitution granted freedom and citizenship rights to all African Americans. For a short time, African American men voted and held political office. This progress, however, was short-lived. Through Jim Crow laws, African Americans were subjected to discrimination and sustained violence by white supremacists in the South. Over the following century, African Americans and their allies made sustained efforts to re-secure and expand their legal and civil rights, with limited success.

Then, in the spring of 1951, black students in Virginia protested their unequal status in the state's segregated educational system. Students at Moton High School protested the overcrowded conditions and failing facilities.[1] Some local leaders of the NAACP tried to persuade the students to back down, but the students did not budge. Inspired by these courageous young people, the NAACP filed five cases challenging the school systems, known collectively as *Brown v. Board of Education of Topeka*.[2] Under the leadership of Walter Reuther, the United Auto Workers donated $75,000 to help pay for the NAACP's efforts in the U.S. Supreme Court.[3]

However, before they could convince the Supreme Court that the "separate but equal" policy was inherently discriminatory and in violation of the Equal Protection and Due Process Clauses of the U.S. Constitution, the NAACP lawyers had to gather plausible evidence to support their arguments. They did so by documenting the detrimental impacts of school segregation policies and the positive effects of interracial contacts in a school environment. They argued that school interracial contacts in educational settings enhance all people's development and training to enrich society and that segregation inhibits that process.[4]

While *Brown v. Board of Education* was pending before the Supreme Court, the federal government filed a "friend of the court" brief. The brief urged the justices to consider segregation's adverse impact on the country's image while the Cold War was still raging. In the words of then-Secretary of State Dean Acheson, "the United States is under constant attack in the foreign press, over the foreign radio, and in such international bodies as the United Nations because of various practices of discrimination in this country."[5]

On May 17, 1954, the Supreme Court's *Brown v. Board of Education* unanimous decision (9–0) overruled the Court's prior 1896 decision in *Plessy v. Ferguson*, which held that segregated public facilities were legal for blacks and whites. In *Brown*, the Supreme Court held that "separate educational facilities are inherently unequal" and therefore violated the Equal Protection Clause of the Fourteenth Amendment of the U.S. Constitution.[6] *Brown* held that the state laws establishing racial segregation in public schools were unconstitutional, even if the segregated schools were otherwise equal in quality. However, the decision did not spell out any sort of method for ending racial segregation in schools, and the Court's second decision in *Brown II* only ordered states to desegregate "with all deliberate speed."

In addition to *Brown*, the Warren Court made a series of other landmark rulings against racist discrimination, including *Heart of Atlanta Motel, Inc. v. United States*,[7] and *Loving v. Virginia*,[8] which banned segregation in public accommodations and struck down all state laws prohibiting interracial marriage.

The civil rights movement picked up steam in the early 1960s. Martin Luther King, Jr., Whitney Young, James Farmer, and a host of other civil rights leaders won the backing of President Lyndon Johnson for passage of several significant pieces of federal legislation that overturned discriminatory laws and practices. These civil rights laws also authorized oversight and enforcement by the federal government. The Civil Rights Act of 1964,[9] which the Supreme Court upheld in a series of cases, was followed by The Voting Rights Act of 1965. This legislation, which the current Supreme Court has recently gutted, protected voting rights for minorities. The Act authorized federal oversight of registration and elections in areas where historically minority voters were under-represented. Finally, in 1968 The Fair Housing Act banned discrimination in the sale or rental of housing.

It is unlikely any federal court would have reversed almost a century of discriminatory laws if there had not been widespread non-violent demonstrations around the country supporting equal rights for African-Americans. Although the civil rights demonstrators almost universally adhered to non-violent means protected by the First Amendment of the U.S. Constitution, they were often met with hatred, violence, and bloodshed. The triple murders of civil rights workers James Chaney, Andrew Goodman, and Michael "Micky" Schwerner in Neshoba County, Mississippi, in June 1964 shocked the entire country. I was not an exception.

I had grown up in the small suburban town of Pelham, New York, where Micky Schwerner had graduated from Pelham Memorial High School. Although Schwerner was a few years older than me, we graduated from the same public high school, and my older brother, Douglas, shared many of the same friends and acquaintances as him. I remembered him from the various civil rights marches and demonstrations that I attended with my parents and brothers in the New York City area in 1964.

Schwerner and the two other murdered civil rights workers were associated with the Council of Federated Organizations (COFO) and its member organization, the Congress of Racial Equality (CORE). They worked with the Freedom Summer campaign to register African-Americans in Mississippi to vote. This registration effort was a part of a concerted effort to challenge the discriminatory "Jim Crow" laws in the South. For over 70 years, these laws had succeeded in disenfranchising potential Black voters with "poll taxes" and other hurdles that barred many

- primarily poor Black people - from participating in elections. The Civil Rights Law of 1964, which Congress passed after the murders of the three civil rights workers, was designed to bar such practices. However, the entrenched white ruling classes of most counties in the South still tried their best to use force and intimidation to bar Black residents from registering to vote and exercising their franchise rights.

During this period, thousands of young people – including myself - were becoming socially conscious of civil rights issues and the economic, housing, and other issues that affected disadvantaged Americans across all racial and ethnic lines. While still in college, I participated in numerous civil rights marches and rallies in New Haven, where the charismatic Yale Chaplain, William Sloane Coffin, emerged as one of the most articulate religious leaders for civil rights anti-war movements. After graduating college, I joined VISTA and spent a year working on a housing project in West Seattle and then working with farmworkers in Oregon and California as part of the effort by Caesar Chavez and the United Farm Workers Union. As discussed, I then went to Fordham Law School and ended up spending the better part of the next two decades as a state and federal prosecutor. After that, I went into private practice, and some of my most significant cases were in the civil rights and human rights fields. One such case was on behalf of the Parajito Homesteaders in New Mexico.

The Parajito Homesteaders Case

Just as the struggle for civil rights for African Americans in the U.S. has been long and arduous, Hispanic Americans faced seemingly overwhelming obstacles to their similar efforts. For decades, they had been trying to achieve full citizenship rights in the U.S. and compensation for land and other property taken from them in the American Southwest.

One of the most protracted legal battles by Hispanic settlers in what was later to become New Mexico was the struggle of the Parajito Homesteaders. They had their lands confiscated in the Los Alamos area in 1943 to support America's crash program to develop the atomic bomb before the Germans. The code name for the secret project was "The Manhattan Project." The isolated location for the project was a short distance northeast of Santa Fe, on a remote high desert plateau known as the Parajito Plateau. For several decades before 1943, Hispanic homesteaders migrated north from

Mexico and acquired ownership of small family farms and ranches on the Pajarito Plateau. Some homesteaders traced their roots back to the early Spanish settlers who had settled on the Plateau in the nineteenth century. One prominent homesteader family – the Romeros – built a cabin in Los Alamos shortly after New Mexico was admitted to the United States as the forty-seventh state in 1912. The original Romero homesteaders, Victor and Refugio Romero, built a one-room cabin at Los Alamos for their six children and worked their fifteen-acre farm. Like many other home-steaders, the Romeros were forced to sell their land for far less than its actual value to make way for the research labs of the Manhattan Project.

Prior to the Los Alamos National Laboratories construction, these Hispanic property owners were forcibly removed from their lands during the 1943 to 1944 period. Army personnel forced them off their land, sometimes with little or no notice, and many of the homesteaders were paid little or nothing for their lands in what amounted to an illegal taking without just compensation. The Anglo (non-Hispanic) owners of the Los Alamos Ranch School and the Anchor Ranch received much larger payment per acre than the homesteaders, who received less than an eighth of the total amount paid to the Anglo owners of the ranch properties. The Los Alamos Ranch School received $367,000 for its land —the bulk of $414,000 appropriated in the 1940s to buy property for the lab. The school received $225 per acre; the Hispanic Homesteaders, in contrast, only received a mere $7 to $15 per acre.

In 2004, the families of the Homesteaders commenced legal action in federal court in Albuquerque, seeking just compensation for the ex-propriation of their property and, in many cases, the forced labor they provided to build the Los Alamos facility. Although the Government, through the Department of Energy, claimed that there were hearings conducted on valuation issues, many homesteaders never received notice of these hearings. They were denied their due process rights under the U.S. Constitution, which prohibits taking private property without due process or just compensation. As a result, many Hispanic families received much less for their acreage than non-Hispanic landowners in the area, who tended to be better represented and connected than the homesteaders. For example, Peter Gomez of El Rancho, New Mexico, recounted how his grandfather, Elfego Gomez, farmed and raised cattle on the Plateau until the government took the land in the 1940s, paying him next to nothing for it. As Gomez recalled, "They were so brokenhearted that they never spoke about it after it happened," he said of his grandparents. The claims by the Homesteaders raised fundamental constitutional issues. The freedom of private persons from expropriation and "illegal takings" is one of the fundamental grievances that led the American colonies to rebel against British rule. While the U.S. government can appropriate property for legitimate governmental uses, compensation must be paid at market value. In the case of the Homesteaders, their lands were also the basis for their way of life. Lives were severely disrupted and, in some cases, destroyed when they were forced off their lands into towns and cities without the skills to survive.

Adding insult to injury, the Homesteaders were not only forced off their lands at gunpoint, but many of the non-disabled Hispanic males were forcibly pressed into service building the Los Alamos facilities. They were housed in detention centers, where their movements were restricted under high security. Some Homesteaders recalled that they were forced to move "black boxes" that, in retrospect, appear to have contained radioactive materials.

In the late 1990s, the original Homesteaders and their families formed the Homesteaders Association to recover compensation for the unlawful 1943 takings. The organization was motivated, in part, by highly publicized reports of compensation programs related to other World War II takings, including the compensation of Japanese-Americans who were forced into internment camps, the compensation program for landowners in Rocky Flats, and other locations. The Homesteaders were also well aware of the World War II Holocaust restitution cases that had successfully recouped tens of millions of dollars in lost property and slave labor claims.

In November 1999, two New Mexico attorneys, Gene Gallegos and Michael Gross helped incorporate the Pajarito Plateau Homesteaders, Inc., under the leadership of Joe Guttierez, the Association's president. Gallegos and Gross filed a complaint against the U.S. Government in New Mexico federal court and at the same time attempted to enlist the support of the New Mexico congressional delegation in the effort to win compensation for the Homesteaders. Gene Gallegos had been a classmate of Pete V. Domenici, New Mexico's senior United States Senator, at the University of New Mexico. The Department of Energy (D.O.E.) was in the process of divesting itself of surplus property in the Los Alamos area

LOS ALAMOS
PROJECT
MAIN GATE
PASSES MUST BE
PRESENTED TO
GUARDS

POST
No. 1

to allow for private residential and commercial development, and Senator Domenici was concerned that the Homesteaders litigation would complicate those plans by the D.O.E.

In early January 2000, Gallegos and Senator Dominic discussed the possibility of settling the Homesteaders' claims in the range of $5-10 million, but Joe Guttierez and other members of the Homesteaders' Board advised them that what they wanted was land, not money. However, when this alternative was presented to Senator Domenici, they were told that a land settlement was not a viable option. The possibility of a settlement further receded when Guttierez advised Gallegos that the Board was not interested in any settlement. All the Board wanted was to litigate. Gallegos disagreed with this strategy and became increasingly concerned that Guttierez, who had opposed any kind of settlement, was not an actual claimant himself and that his mother-in-law and father-in-law were the genuine claimants to lands expropriated in 1943. When Guttierez instructed Gallegos that there be no communication with anyone else in the Homesteader organization other than him, Gallegos and Gross concluded that they could no longer represent the group. They then filed a motion to withdraw as counsel for the Homesteaders Association in May of 2000.

After Guttierez and Gross withdrew as counsel for the Association, two Homesteaders – Jose Gonzales and Teresita Garcia Martinez - asked Gallegos and Gross to represent them individually. Gallegos and Gross agreed to do so. After filing a new action for these individual plaintiffs in August 2000, they sought to have them named as class representatives of the entire class of Homesteaders who had lost their property in 1943 had not been fully compensated. This class action was certified by the federal judge, and Gallegos and Gross were designated as class counsel.

Meanwhile, in October of 2000, the Homesteader Association retained new counsel, Cheryl Mackell, who was practicing law in Santa Fe, New Mexico at the time. They also retained the law firm that I headed up. The directions the Association Board gave us were challenging to follow. We were directed to aggressively pursue the litigation in federal court while trying, at the same time, to negotiate a settlement through Senator Dominici's office. However, we were also given explicit instructions *not* to coordinate with Gallegos and Gross. This created a monumental problem since Senators Domenici and Bingaman took the position that they were unwilling to introduce legislation to settle the litigation and plaintiffs' claims unless all of the plaintiffs and the Association agreed to work together to accomplish that goal.

We tried as best we could to move the settlement process forward. At the same time, following the clients' instructions, it became increasingly clear that it was impossible to proceed on parallel tracks without at least some communication between the Gallegos/Gross team and us. Cheryl Mackell, my wife Susan, and I had a meeting in Washington, D.C., with Pete Lyons and other staff members from the offices of Senators Dominici and Bingaman. In consultation with these two senators, we drafted our version of a settlement proposal calling for the appropriation of $10 million and land for a cultural center in Los Alamos that would honor and keep alive the Homesteader heritage. We also retained Dr. Stan V. Smith, an expert economist based in Chicago, who developed a land valuation appraisal of $60 million based on the loss of rental value that the Homesteaders had suffered since 1943. The prior assessment commissioned by Gallegos and Gross had only a $6.7 million loss valuation based upon lost sale value.

Senators Bingaman and Dominici did not fully accept Dr. Smith's appraisal values. Still, they eventually sponsored a bill calling for an appropriation of $10 million, which was incorporated as part of the Defenses Appropriation Bill. The final approved bill was similar to prior legislation that compensated landowners whose property was seized under the Government's eminent domain powers around the White Sands Missile Range in New Mexico.

It soon became increasingly clear to us that no settlement could occur as long as Joe Guttierez remained as President of the Association. His instructions that we could not communicate directly with members of the Association also presented us with an ethical problem. An attorney cannot agree to communicate with clients solely through "lay intermediaries," such as a Board of Directors or an Association's President, since we represented each of the Homesteaders individually. It seemed clear to us that only a "regime change" in the Association could break the impasse. Still, I felt that it would be unethical for us as counsel to attempt to oust Joe Guttierez as President of the Association. If any change occurred, it had to come from the members themselves. We decided that the only thing we could do was to move to withdraw as counsel, which we did in September of 2002. The Court granted our motion to withdraw on October 7, 2002.

At the beginning of March 2003, Guttierez wrote an unflattering article about Senators Domenici and Bingaman, and the Senators' staff predictably were extremely upset and perplexed. The staff members let it be known that the proposed bill was "no longer a viable option" in light of the article and disunity among the Homesteaders. After this, it is somewhat unclear whether Guttierez stepped down voluntarily or was pushed, but the result was the same. On March 18, 2003, the Association informed Senators Dominici and Bingaman that Guttierez had been removed as the board president. The Association and its members wished to move ahead with a settlement. The way was now clear for a legislative appropriation of $10 million, to be allocated by a Special Master appointed by United States District Court Judge Johnson.

In addition to the unlawful takings and land valuation claims, a related case was also brought based upon the allegations of forced labor, false imprisonment, and torture in connection with medical experimentation relating to the radioactive materials handled by the Homesteaders who worked on the Los Alamos facilities. These claims never got to a hearing stage since they were dismissed on statute of limitations grounds, given the lengthy hiatus between 1943 and October 2001, when the federal claims were filed. The elderly Homesteaders who had survived this ordeal told us that they had been too fearful of government retaliation to tell their story publicly before, but the court found that this fear was not enough to stay, or toll, the statute of limitations. The Tenth Circuit Court of Appeals affirmed the District Court's decision without ever reaching the merits of the claims.[10]

However, as is often the case, the mere fact that federal litigation is dismissed on technical statute of limitations grounds did not mean that it is a lost cause. The political dimension of the campaign for restitution bore fruit when, in November 2004, the U.S. Congress finally created a $10 million fund for awards to the descendants and heirs of those original Homesteaders. The Pajarito Plateau Homesteaders Compensation Fund was part of a massive spending package approved by Congress and sent to President George W. Bush for signature.

To establish and validate their claims to receive their portion of the money in the Compensation Fund, we helped many of the families gather and review old deeds, land records, and even wills to support their claims. We also helped draft affidavits to further document claims to the various tracts of land and kinship lines to the original Homesteaders.

* * *

The Pajarito Plateau Homeowners case was just one of many civil and human rights cases that I worked on over the years, but it left an indelible impact on how I handled these cases. I realized that historical compensation claims are generally much more than just court cases. To achieve a just result for plaintiffs who are the victims of past injustices, there must be a parallel political and public relations campaign to exert maximum pressure. Those in the entrenched power structure must be forced to realize that a past injustice that is ignored is like a wound that never heals. It can never be indefinitely ignored or swept under the rug. A successful human rights or public interest campaign is like a three-legged stool: the court case is just one of those legs. The other two legs – political pressure and an effective public relations/media campaign - are just as crucial to achieving the ultimate goal.

Concepcion v. New York City Department of Education

Following the 2020 killing of George Floyd by Minneapolis police officers, a national debate erupted about police brutality towards minorities in general and over whether there should be school-based policing on high school and college campuses across the country. The 2021 indictment of an armed school safety officer in Long Beach, California, added a particularly brutal new dimension to the debate over whether there should be cops on campus.[11] 51-year-old Eddie F. Gonzalez was arrested on October 27, 2021, and charged with murder in Manuela "Mona" Rodriguez shooting near Millikan High School a month earlier. Gonzalez was reportedly patrolling an area near the school when he observed a fight between Rodriguez, who was not a student, and a 15-year-old girl. On the job for less than a year, Gonzalez shot Rodriguez in the head as she rode in the passenger seat of a fleeing car. The incident was captured on video and went viral online. The shooting left Rodriguez, the mother of a 6-month-old boy, brain dead, dying shortly after the shooting.

* * *

Years earlier, the distraught mother of an African-American high school student at New York City's Curtis High School in Staten Island came to us to help pursue her claims for her son against the New York City Board of Education. Her claims were for civil rights violations against her son by school personnel, including school safety officers. On February 13, 2015, Raymond Concepcion, who was sixteen years old, had been scheduled to be with his class for a Black History Month event taking place in the auditorium. However, when Raymond got to the auditorium, a teacher told him and one of his classmates to leave because they supposedly did not belong there. Principal Auriela Curtis overheard what was going on and told Raymond to go to the Dean's office.

Raymond started to walk down the hall to the Dean's office, but the teacher watching the door to the auditorium called him back because he had verified that Raymond did belong in the auditorium with his class. However, Principal Curtis told him to go to the Dean's office anyway, and she directed Assistant Principal Joseph Burbano to take him there. Raymond walked with Burbano about halfway down the hallway to the Dean's office. Then they were approached by School Safety Officer Barrios and School Safety Agent Ruperto in response to a call over the radio to assist Mr. Burbano in getting Raymond to the Dean's office – even though he had been walking there voluntarily.

All of the school personnel involved in the incident were well aware that Raymond was, at that time, being treated for various psychological and emotional issues requiring special accommodations for him by the school. They had access to a Psycho-Educational Report prepared while he was still in middle school and that he had been undergoing therapy for panic attacks and anxiety since 2012.

At that point, Raymond became anxious from the response to A.P. Burbano's unnecessary radio call and concerned about what would happen to him. He stopped walking and asked to call and speak to his mother before going further. A.P. Burbano refused to let him do so until he was in the Dean's office, and then grabbed and pulled Raymond towards the office.

After Raymond pulled away from A.P. Burbano's grasp, Officer Barrios asked to speak to him privately and then led him into the stairwell and told him to sit on the stairs while he tried to convince him to go to the Dean's office. Over the next few minutes, Raymond and Officer Barrios calmly engaged in a conversation. Raymond, at times, was gesturing or "speaking with his hands" to emphasize his point. Soon, they were joined by A.P. Burbano, SA Ruperto, Dean McGee, Dean Rautenstrauch, one of the school gym teachers, and another male Dean or teacher, who all stood near and/or over Raymond, who was still seated on the steps speaking to Barrios.

A.P. Burbano then began to yell at Raymond, who remained outwardly calm. Burbano suddenly grabbed and tried to pull Raymond off the stairs, which prompted Officer Barrios and SA Ruperto to also forcefully grab and pull Raymond up to his feet. They then restrained him until Raymond "went limp." After finally letting go of him, Raymond calmly adjusted his pants which had fallen down a little bit while they were all grappling and wrestling to get him up. Ruperto began pushing him and holding him by the back of his arms to move him, with A.P. Burbano following immediately behind them.

Raymond had one hand in his pocket as he walked. He continued to plead for permission to speak to his mother. He was also gesturing and talking with his hands as he walked before abruptly stopping just short of the doorway to the Dean's office.

As A.P. Burbano approached Raymond and ordered him to proceed, SA Ruperto and Officer Barrios grabbed and restrained Raymond's arms above his head, turned him around towards the door in an attempt to handcuff him in the Dean's office. However, in the process of "taking him down," all three of them fell forward and down through the Dean's office doorway. As they were falling, A.P. Burbano and another Dean decided to jump on top of them, causing Raymond to land and hit the side of his head on the ground. A.P. Burbano and Raymond landed on the floor head-first, with SA Ruperto falling to the left and Officer Barrios falling to the right of Raymond, both still holding him as they all hit the floor.

While Raymond was on the ground with his face down, A.P. Burbano forcefully pressed his knee several times into the sides of Raymond's head. At the same time, SA Ruperto and Officer Barrios pulled Raymond's arms behind him and handcuffed him.

After he was handcuffed and brought to his feet, Raymond was taken to an area in the back of the Dean's office, where Mr. Burbano began screaming at him for several minutes before leaving. Raymond was dazed, had a terrible headache, and didn't have his coat or backpack with his antianxiety medicine and EpiPen for his epilepsy. He continued to plead for the opportunity to speak to his mother but was denied. About 45 minutes or an hour later, some police officers from the local precinct came and took him to the precinct in handcuffs. It was freezing outside, and he did not have his coat or medicine. One of the police officers told him that they were going to make an example out of him and that he was going to get sent to Rikers Island, the notoriously antiquated New York City prison island near LaGuardia Airport.

Raymond, who was having an anxiety attack the whole time, was put in a holding cell with an adult, and did not feel safe. Feeling increasingly dazed and confused, Raymond experienced a severe panic attack. Later that evening, Raymond started to feel extremely claustrophobic and began to have problems breathing.

Raymond was taken by ambulance in handcuffs and leg shackles to the hospital, but was still not allowed to call his mother until one of the E.M.T.s let him call her from his phone. Although Tina Concepcion came to the hospital to see him, they did not allow her to do so, and they also refused to give her any details, only saying that he was "still in custody." After a couple of hours, they took Raymond back to the precinct in a squad car and kept him in a holding cell until he was arraigned the next afternoon, after more than 24 hours in custody.

Because his heart was racing and his adrenaline pumping, Raymond experienced intermittent anxiety attacks from the time of his arrest through his arraignment and release to his mother's care over twenty-four hours later. Raymond did not realize that he had had a concussion until the night he was released from custody, when he experienced a throbbing headache and inability to maintain focus. When he tried to sleep, he began to feel increasingly confused, dizzy, and nauseous. His mother realized that something was wrong and took him back to the emergency room, where the police had taken him the night before.

At the hospital, Raymond was diagnosed with a concussion and other injuries to his neck, upper back, and arm. The doctor told him that nothing could be done regarding the concussion, except that Raymond should take it easy for a few weeks and take Tylenol or other pain medication that worked whenever he felt a headache coming on. He was also told that he should never play contact sports like football again because it would be even worse if he got another concussion. Later that evening,

Raymond's mother took him back to the emergency room of Richmond University Medical Center after he complained about headaches, and she found him to be sluggish and somewhat non-responsive to her questions.

For a substantial period after that, Raymond continued to have severe headaches, and his neck and back injuries continued to cause him to have spasms in his neck and upper back. Although he started attending a college in the fall of 2017 that was part of the State University of New York college system in upstate Broome County, the continued headaches, anxiety attacks, and depression prevented him from focusing on his studies. He was forced to return home after only one semester. He also had trouble sleeping because of nightmares that forced him to relive the terror he experienced when he was arrested.

A criminal complaint was filed, charging Raymond with misdemeanors of Obstruction of Governmental Administration ("O.G.A."), Resisting Arrest, Harassment, and a violation, Disorderly Conduct (Discon). These charges were eventually dismissed, but not before they caused him considerable additional psychological and emotional trauma.

A Suspension Hearing was held on March 6, 2015, where Dean McGhie falsely testified that Raymond elbowed SA Ruperto when they were across the hall from the Dean's office. A.P. Burbano also falsely testified at the Suspension Hearing that he called for assistance with Raymond because he thought he would try to run out of the building and wanted to prevent that.

Officer Barrios testified at the Suspension Hearing that Raymond initially refused to proceed because he was angry that A.P. Burbano had touched him. Barrios said that he and SA Ruperto were trying to "guide" him into the Dean's office and that he got slapped across his face, which broke his glasses and bruised his nose. However, none of this testimony was supported by the videos or the testimony of any other witness. Critically, however, Officer Barrios did concede that Raymond told him he didn't want to go into the Dean's office because he didn't feel it was safe for him to go inside.

On February 23, 2015, Raymond was suspended from Curtis Highs School. The suspension was based on the factually unsupported claim that he had assaulted Officer Barrios and Agent Ruperto. This claim was proven false by the videos, the officers' contemporaneous log notes, the arrest incident report, and the fact that Raymond was never charged or prosecuted for an assault. All of the defendants who had testified about the alleged assault recanted or denied any recollection of the incident in their depositions. On April 20, 2015, Raymond's suspension was reversed after it was determined at an impartial hearing that Raymond's behavior was a manifestation of Raymond's disability and that the School District was aware that Raymond had emotional difficulties. The Hearing Officer also found that the Committee on Special Education ("C.S.E.") did not conduct a Functional Behavioral Analysis ("F.B.A.") or develop a Behavioral Intervention Plan, include strategies and social/emotional goals on his Individualized Education Plan ("I.E.P.").

The Litigation

On May 31, 2016, our law firm filed an Amended Complaint on behalf of Tina and Raymond Concepcion in the U.S. District Court for the Eastern District of New York. The complaint alleged federal civil rights violations under Title 42, United States Code §1983 for false arrest and imprisonment, excessive force, violations of Due Process, and New York State common law claims for false arrest, false imprisonment, assault, battery, intentional and negligent infliction of emotional distress.[12]

The case's discovery phase, which was defended by attorneys working for the Corporation Counsel of the City of New York, involved extensive documentary discovery and depositions. It took many months to conclude, but there were some beneficial facts that we were able to elicit from the school personnel to support Raymond's claims. For example, SA Ruperto confirmed at his deposition that Raymond asked to speak to his mother before going into the Dean's office, and that Raymond expressed the belief that Burbano was going to assault him. In addition, A.P. Burbano testified that Raymond was never read his Miranda rights in the Dean's office. Nor did Burbano see Raymond strike Officer Barrios or SA Ruperto during the takedown and struggle. In addition, most of the extensive video surveillance evidence turned over to us supported Raymond's version of the events.

However, on May 6, 2019, U.S. District Judge Ann M. Donnelly, sitting in federal court in Brooklyn, granted the defendants' motion for summary judgment, finding that the school safety officers had probable cause to arrest Raymond.[13] The court – in our view erroneously – focused on his refusal to go to the Dean's office without first speaking to his mother by phone. The court also found that, although it was the school personnel who directed him to a nearby stairwell, he was appropriately arrested for "blocking traffic" in the stairwell and interfering with "the public order," because "the bell was about to ring for students to change classes. . .."[14] The court discounted Raymond's testimony to the effect that any motions he made outside the Dean's office were merely conversational hand gestures and could not be reasonably construed as threatening. Judge Donnelly found that, regardless of Raymond's intentions, "a reasonable officer or school employee" could view the plaintiff's actions as threatening. She, therefore, found that they had a reasonable basis to believe they had probable cause to arrest him for disorderly conduct.[15]

Because the district court found that the school safety officers had probable cause and "arguable" probable cause to arrest Raymond, they were entitled to "qualified immunity" from any false arrest claim.[16]

Judge Donnelly also dismissed our "Excessive Force" claims arising from the defendants' excessive force in arresting and handcuffing Raymond. The court noted that the Fourth Amendment prohibits unreasonable and excessive force during an arrest. It found that the force used during Raymond's arrest for disorderly conduct was not excessive and that while he was "seized," such seizure was justified and "reasonable in scope."

The district court further found that the defendants did not violate Raymond's "substantive due process" rights under the Fourteenth Amendment of the U.S. Constitution, which provides that no person "shall... deprive any person of life, liberty, or property, without due process of law." The court noted that there is a reasonably high bar to clear in finding a substantive due process violation, which requires a finding that "the government action was 'so egregious, so outrageous, that it may fairly be said to shock the contemporary conscience.'"[17] The court thus rejected our argument that the defendants violated Raymond's rights by physically assaulting him during his arrest; handcuffing his hand too tightly; failing to provide him with medical attention; refusing to let him call or see his mother; transporting him to the precinct without his coat in freezing weather and without his antianxiety medicine or his EpiPen; and putting him in a holding cell with a grown man, and transporting him in handcuffs and leg shackles to the hospital. The court explained away all of the facts and circumstances we presented by finding that "the defendants did not act maliciously, and they had a legitimate interest in disciplining Mr. Concepcion and in maintaining order at the school."[18]

The Second Circuit Court of Appeals Decision

On November 30, 2020, the Second Circuit Court of Appeals vacated the District Court's judgment granting the defendants' summary judgment motion and dismissing our case. The Second Circuit reversed the lower court's finding that the officers and school personnel involved could not reasonably be found to have used excessive force, noting that a reasonable factfinder could conclude that the officers' conduct was objectively unreasonable.[19] The court thus reinstated Raymond's Section 1983 claim for violation of his civil rights. The appellate court specifically noted that two S.S.A.s tackled Concepcion with such force that he suffered a concussion. At least four S.S.A.s and Assistant Principal Joseph Burbano pinned Concepcion to the ground by holding his legs and keeping a knee on his head.[20] The court found that the mere fact that Raymond had resisted arrest was not dispositive on the issue of whether excessive force was used. The appellate court further pointed out that there were two other factors that the lower court had not fully considered, which were: (1) the nature and severity of the crime leading to the arrest, and (2) whether the suspect poses an immediate threat to the safety of the officer or others.[21]

The Second Circuit Court of Appeals further found that a reasonable factfinder could easily find that Concepcion's crime was minor since obstruction of governmental administration is a misdemeanor offense. It also noted that the issue of whether Raymond posed a genuine threat to the officers' safety was not an issue that could be decided on summary judgment. In addition, the court found that the issue of whether the officers involved had immunity from liability for excessive force was also a factual issue that could not be resolved by way of a summary judgment motion.

* * *

Although we were fortunate enough to produce favorable results for many of our clients who brought federal civil rights cases against municipalities under Section 1983, most civil rights cases prove to be difficult uphill battles. This is due to the defense of "qualified immunity" that law enforcement officers may use to shield themselves from legal liability in some of the most egregious circumstances. For example, the Fifth Circuit Court of Appeals held that a prison guard who pepper-sprayed an inmate in a locked cell "for no reason" could not be held liable for his action since it did not violate any established law or precedent.[22] Thus, if the correctional officer had used a taser, or had hit the inmate, he would have been potentially liable for a civil rights violation since he was on sufficient notice that it is illegal to gratuitously taser or hit an inmate. However, incongruously, since no prior case had found that officers are prohibited from pepper-spraying an inmate, the guard got off scot-free.

In 1967, the Supreme Court established qualified immunity as a defense for public officials who were in danger of being held financially liable for violations of constitutional rights. In *Pearson v. Callahan*,[23] the Court ruled that qualified immunity was extended to any officials who have not violated a "clearly established" law, even in cases that deal with constitutional violations. This doctrine has been expanded by other federal courts to protect clearly unreasonable – and indeed outrageous – conduct due to "the vagueness of the doctrine's wording and the leniency it gives to the courts."[24] Many courts have made it a practice to dismiss any case on qualified immunity grounds that is not virtually identical to a prior case where a police officer or other public official has been held legally liable for their conduct.

Instead of pairing back the qualified immunity defense, the Supreme Court has expanded it, such as in an unsigned, unofficial decision in *Rivas-Villegas v. Cortesluna*.[25] In that decision, the Court implied that only the Supreme Court – not lower federal courts - can establish a clear "precedent" that can be used as a basis for a finding that the public official was not entitled to a qualified immunity defense.

Hope that the Supreme Court will see the light and reform the qualified immunity doctrine has largely been crushed. It is now clear that the current conservative-leaning Court is not going to take any such action. In the past fifteen years, 16 of the 18 cases that the Court has heard regarding alleged constitutional violations by government officials have ended with a finding that the public officials were entitled to qualified immunity.

The only way that this country's civil rights laws can be effectively enforced against public officials who engage in excessive force and other abuses is through Congressional action. Only through the passage of legislation that levels the playing field in court for victims of excessive force and other civil rights abuses will plaintiffs truly have a fair shake to recover monetary damages from public officers who abuse their public trust.

Chapter 10

The Robert Manning Case

The Legal Battles to Recover
for Catastrophic Injuries

Bob Manning experienced two major tragedies in his life. The first occurred on February 27, 1962, when he fell off a utility pole in upstate New York while working as a lineman for Niagara Mohawk Power Company. He was descending a utility pole near the Saint Lawrence Seaway on the U.S. Canadian border when a jolt of electricity sent him flying headfirst into the pavement. The fall rendered him a quadriplegic, leaving only limited use of his arms. He would never walk again.

The second major tragedy in Bob Manning's life was that, for 25 years, the workers' compensation insurance company for Niagara Mohawk employees refused to pay for the expenses relating to his care and treatment. Instead, the insurance company engaged in a bad faith scheme to shift the cost of those medical expenses to Medicare, a federally taxpayer-funded program. After Bob was injured in 1962, Niagara Mohawk and Utilities Mutual Insurance Company representatives, the workers' compensations company formed by Niagara Mohawk and other utility companies, visited Bob Manning while he was still at Mercy Hospital in Watertown, New York. They assured him that he "shouldn't worry" and that he would "always be taken care of." For a while, after Bob was discharged from the hospital, Utilities Mutual kept its promise by sending Bob weekly checks to cover the round-the-clock nursing care and specialized equipment he required to survive. But the checks stopped coming in 1968 when Niagara Mohawk and Utilities Mutual hit upon a technical excuse to suspend Bob's benefit payments.

In 1968, Bob Manning had recovered a judgment of $388,000 against New York Telephone Co., which owned the utility pole from which he had fallen. After that, Utilities Mutual used this award as a rationalization to stop making any further payments to him until it received a "full accounting" of the money he had received, including a detailed record of all checks and medical bills spent for Manning's medical expenses and supplies. Utilities Mutual took the position that it did not have to restart making payments to Bob until all the monies for the New York Telephone award had been expended and accounted for.

By 1973, Manning had exhausted the funds he had received from New York Telephone since he required full-time nursing care and other special services due to his almost total incapacity. He even needed a special hoist to lift him in and out of bed each day. At first, Perry Woods of Niagara Mohawk assured Bob Manning that his workers' compensation payments would be restarted, and his mounting medical bills would be paid, just as soon as the New York Telephone monies were used up. Bob Manning felt understandably secure that there would be no problem since Niagara Mohawk and Utilities Mutual shared the same headquarters in Syracuse, New York. If an official of Niagara Mohawk told him that its insurance carrier would make payments, he reasonably expected that payments would be made.

However, when the time came for Utilities Mutual to resume paying benefits, the company refused. They claimed there was no absolute proof that the New York Telephone monies had been fully depleted. As a result, Perry Woods of Niagara Mohawk informed Manning that they had not completed the "accounting" and did not have to resume making benefit payments until they finished an "accounting" of how the funds had been spent.

With no incentive to finish its "accounting," Utilities Mutual dragged its feet on completing the accounting for the next 24 years. At first, naively thinking that Utilities Mutual was acting in good faith, Bob and his wife kept supplying Utilities Mutual with detailed information about how the money had been used to pay his ongoing medical expenses. They even hired an accountant to help them show Niagara Mohawk and Utilities Mutual that all the funds had been expended and that Manning desperately needed to restore his benefits.

Not surprisingly, nothing seemed to satisfy Utilities Mutual. As long as the Company kept running the clock and leaving the "accounting" incomplete, it cynically figured that it would not have to resume its payments to Manning. As a result, starting in 1973, Bob and his wife could not pay his medical expenses. His health providers began submitting their unpaid bills to Medicare, a U.S. government program 100% financed with taxpayers' money.

Finally, out of complete frustration and desperation, Manning sued Utilities Mutual and Niagara Mohawk Power Company in 1979 before the New York State Workers Compensation Board and obtained several orders from the Board directing that benefits be paid to him. However, the defendants continued to litigate the case and appealed to the New York State appellate courts on three occasions. The defendant companies lost each appeal,[1] but they still refused to comply with these court orders to pay Manning the insurance benefits he was due.

Understandably frustrated, Bob couldn't understand why the companies would spend so much time and money on appeals rather than just complying with the court orders. He asked Paul Terzulli of Utilities Mutual whether or not it was a fraud to force Medicare to pay for these medical expenses. Terzulli replied, "What difference does it make to you who pays the bills so long as you get the care you need?" In other words, Utilities Mutual didn't want to acknowledge that it was defrauding the government and U.S. taxpayers by foisting off onto Medicare bills that it should have been paying itself.

Although Medicare was paying for some of his medical benefits, Medicare did not cover some essential medical supplies and expenses that Manning needed to maintain even a minimal quality of life. For example, a specialized table was required to rotate Manning, in order to prevent the development of bedsores. Utilities Mutual refused to pay for it, and so did Medicare. As a result, Manning developed blood clots and other complications in one of his legs, which led to the amputation of that leg just below the knee. Also, on one occasion, the ancient hydraulic lift Bob was using collapsed and broke his left leg, requiring emergency ambulance services to take him to the hospital.

Despite this ongoing nightmare, the insurance company remained unmoved, refusing to make further payments for necessary medical equipment or services. Their attitude was that if Bob couldn't use his leg anyway, the amputation didn't make much of a difference. The insurance company continued to routinely stamp the bills received from Bob Manning with their "Rejected" stamp, and the same invoice would then be sent to

Medicare. Medicare would then make "conditional payments" of part of the bill, which would be forwarded to Bob Manning to pay the balance.

Starting on May 5, 1997, a series of investigative articles by David Cay Johnson about the Manning case appeared in the New York Times. The case was described as "the longest-running workers' compensation dispute on record—the longest by a matter of decades."

In a follow-up article on May 6, 1997, entitled "Officials Vow to Intervene in Injury Case," New York Governor George E. Pataki said the fact that Niagara Mohawk and Utilities Mutual had not paid Manning's workers' compensation benefit all these years was "a disgrace." The article also quoted Governor Pataki saying that the arguments Niagara Mohawk Power Corporation and Utilities Mutual were making for not paying benefits were "ridiculous." This follow-up article also indicated that Attorney General Dennis Vacco had written to the lawyers for the two companies, demanding an explanation of why workers' compensation benefits were not being resumed. Under the glare of such adverse publicity, William E. Davis, Niagara Mohawk's Chairman and President, promised to ask Utilities Mutual to "reconsider its position."

Niagara Mohawk's position particularly vexed Governor Pataki that Bob Manning's wife—a registered nurse—should not be paid about $230 per week for the nursing services she provided. Pataki was quoted as saying, "If your spouse cooks for you, does normal activities, it is one thing, but to perform the services of a registered nurse, to me, is a different category." Pataki also said it was absurd for an insurance company to have taken such a position for 35 years.

Representatives of the insurance industry started expressing concern that the Manning case and its publicity might negatively affect the entire industry. Finally, in July 1997, just two months after Manning's case was profiled in The New York Times as the longest-running dispute before the Workers' Compensation Board ("WCB"), Utilities Mutual relented and agreed to pay Manning $1.9 million. This amounted to about $44,000 per year for his wife's services from 1968 to 1995. Under the settlement agreement, Manning released all claims within the exclusive jurisdiction of the WCB. However, Manning expressly reserved the right to litigate claims according to federal or state law that were *not* within the WCB's exclusive jurisdiction.

This was when I came into the picture.

From everything I had heard about Bob Manning, he seemed almost too good to be true. Here was a paraplegic, who had been forced to move to California from his home in New York to reduce his living expenses, and as if raising two children of his own wasn't enough of a challenge, he had adopted two more. Bob never ceased to amaze me with his optimism and complete commitment to doing the right thing for the next seven years. When I had bad news to report on the case, more often than not, it would be Bob cheering me up – urging me to "hang in there" because we would get them in the end.

The Mannings had been referred to me because they were looking for an attorney who was not afraid to take on the insurance companies. I had a reputation, deservedly or not, for successfully representing clients in complex and sometimes impossible cases, and usually after more cautious or business-minded attorneys had turned them down.

While most people would not have concerned themselves with the cost to the taxpayers of Utilities Mutual's failure to pay, the Mannings felt strongly that it had been wrong for the insurance company to dump Bob's medical expenses on Medicare. They asked if anything could be done to make Utilities Mutual reimburse Medicare for the charges improperly passed on to it.

Congress was also concerned that Medicare was being stuck with hundreds of millions of dollars in medical expenses that should have been paid through private insurance companies. In 1980, Congress passed the Medicare Secondary Payer (MSP) Statute, establishing that Medicare was only secondarily responsible for the medical bills of privately insured individuals.[2] The Act required any insurance company, which should have paid a claim but did not, to pay two times the amount that Medicare paid. The MSP Statute also contained a provision entitling attorneys to act as private attorneys general and to file lawsuits to recover these payments on behalf of the federal government and taxpayers, in return for a percentage award to the whistleblowers, such as Bob Manning, and their attorneys.

This kind of provision is uniquely an American phenomenon, which originated with the enactment of the False Claims Act in 1863. During the Civil War, many fraudulent claims were being made to the Federal Government for supplies being sent to the Union Army as part of the war effort. The False Claims Act gave the incentive (in addition to the obvious patriotic one) to give 10% of any overcharge or false claim recovered by the government to the whistleblower who first identified the fraud. This statute had the added advantage of increasing the number of private attorneys working on behalf of a very short-handed government.

It could be claimed the origins of the private attorneys general concept goes back even further, to the days of the privateer. Sir Walter Raleigh and others were given letters of marque by the British Crown, authorizing them to set forth on their sailing ships and capture and sink as many French and Spanish commercial trading vessels as possible in return for a percentage of the booty. This kind of legalized piracy proved to be highly successful. The privateers benefited by acting as agents of the Crown. The Crown benefited since it did not require any expense on its part, as it would if it had to expand its own Navy and pay for additional officers and sailors. Similarly, by enlisting private attorneys to bring civil fraud cases against insurance companies who failed to pay legitimate medical claims, the U.S. government was being spared the expense of hiring additional government attorneys and investigators, as well as the cost of prosecuting the cases in court.

On July 7, 1998, we filed one of the first complaints under the MSP Statute in the United States District Court for the Southern District of New York, in lower Manhattan, seeking recovery of two times the $876,321 in medical costs for Bob Manning passed on to Medicare since 1992. In addition, we added a second count charging Utilities Mutual and Niagara Mohawk with fraud for bad-faith refusal to pay for Bob's medical expenses promptly, resulting in physical injury, emotional distress, and inferior healthcare. We asked for an additional $10 million award under the state common law claim for the defendants' bad faith refusal to pay these claims.

Although there was no statute on the books of New York or most other states recognizing these types of claims, there was a whole body of case law built up over the years, and this judge-made law was generally referred to as the common law. Common law causes of action, such as negligence or nuisance, traced their origins to the Middle Ages. The English courts developed a body of case law independent of any formal Acts of Parliament. This English system of law, which was transplanted to the American colonies and all other British colonies, evolved quite differently from other European and "Napoleonic Code-based" countries, where the only laws recognized were in the literal text of the written statutes.

The second issue we had to deal with in the Court of Appeals was the statute of limitations under the MSP statute. As is the case with many laws enacted by Congress, there was no specific provision in the MSP statute setting forth the limitations or time that a person was permitted to file a complaint in court. Since the MSP statute was relatively new and there was virtually no case law on the subject, the Manning case was known as "a case of first impression," at least in the Second Circuit.

On September 30, 1999, District Judge Richard Casey dismissed our common law fraud claim for our alleged failure to plead "reliance" by Manning on material misrepresentations by the defendants.[3] However, the court denied the defendants' motion to dismiss the plaintiff's MSP claim, finding that the claim was timely under the applicable three-year statute of limitations. Both sides moved for reconsideration, and in its second decision, the district court ruled for the defendants on both issues, affirming the dismissal of the fraud claim and dismissing the plaintiff's MSP claim as time-barred.[4]

We immediately filed an appeal to the Second Circuit Court of Appeals and spent the next month or two organizing the voluminous record of the case and briefing the issues. Since we were the moving party on the appeal – known as the appellant – we got to go first with an opening brief about 40 pages long. The other side – Utilities Mutual – then filed an opposition brief, and we then responded to them in a short Reply Brief.

The oral argument on April 6, 2001 before three judges in the Court of Appeals was an exhilarating experience for me. After briefing the issue for months, both sides had only ten minutes to argue their case in the seventeenth-floor courtroom at 40 Foley Square in lower Manhattan. I had learned from experience that there was virtually no possibility that the three judges would sit back silently for ten minutes and listen to my oral presentation, no matter how well prepared and compelling it was. By the time the case gets to oral argument, both sides have a full opportunity to make their legal arguments on paper. Hence, the oral argument is usually a free-wheeling give and take between the judges and the attorneys. I found the only way to prepare for oral argument effectively was to be totally familiar with the facts and entire record of the case and the relevant case law.

On June 20, 2001, almost two years after the original decision by Judge Casey, and after the expenditure of much time, money, and effort appealing a complex case such as this, the Second Circuit Court of Appeals reversed and remanded the case back to the district court.[5] The Second Circuit decision permitted us to replead the claims to clarify that Manning did, in fact, rely to his detriment on fraudulent representations by the defendants.

The Second Circuit Court of Appeals also reversed the district court on the MSP statute of limitations issue. In a landmark decision, the court decided that, although Congress had not explicitly set forth any statute of limitations in the MSP statute itself, the most appropriate limits would be the six years prescribed under the False Claims Act. By so ruling, the Court of Appeals rejected the defendants' argument that the appropriate time limitations depended on the local analogous state statute. Instead, they found a strong public policy reason to have a uniform national standard for the MSP Statute, and that there was a strong federal interest in having a longer statute of limitations apply to MSP actions than those used in many state court fraud actions.[6] The court reasoned that a longer statute of limitations would act as a deterrent to those insurance companies and other primary payers who were tempted to allow Medicare to pay for costs that the insurers would otherwise cover.

The U.S. Supreme Court previously had made a similar decision concerning the federal civil racketeering (RICO) Statute. The court established a uniform national four-year standard, reasoning that since the civil RICO statute was similar to the federal antitrust statutes, the four-year limitations period for the antitrust law should be adopted for purposes of the civil RICO statute.[7]

Even after a successful trip to the Court of Appeals, we still seemed no closer to a trial on the case's merits. The defendants continued to use every procedural device available to either get the case dismissed or to put off the ultimate day of reckoning. It felt like they were using a "scorched earth" policy to wear us down to the point where either the plaintiff (Bob Manning) or his lawyer (me) died or gave up from exhaustion. Even after we submitted a Second Amended Complaint addressing the issues dealt with by the Court of Appeals, the defendants moved for summary judgment again. We countered by ourselves moving for summary judgment on the MSP claim, arguing that there was no serious question that the defendants had failed to pay for at least $873,000 in claims.

Unfortunately, the motions languished before Judge Richard C. Casey of the U.S. District Court for the Southern District of New York for about two years. During that time, Manning was close to death from infections and various medical complications on a few occasions. Still, we suspected that one of the things that kept him holding on was his desire to see his federal case through to a conclusion. I continually urged Bob to keep his spirits up and not to lose faith, reminding him that Judge Casey, as the first legally blind federal Judge, was himself disabled and should be expected to have some understanding and empathy for Bob's predicament.

Finally, our patience was partially rewarded when, on February 5, 2004, Judge Casey issued a decision granting Manning's motion for summary judgment for two times the approximately $873,000 in claims not paid by the defendants under the MSP Statute. However, Judge Casey dismissed Count Two of Manning's Second Amended Complaint, which sought damages under state common law for defendants' bad-faith refusal to pay. Although we had amended the complaint based upon the permission granted by the Court of Appeals, Judge Casey found that under New York State law, there was no independent tort, separate from Manning's contractual rights, to recover for bad-faith refusal to pay.

Of course, we did not agree with the portion of the decision dismissing our second cause of action and felt reasonably confident that if we appealed it to the Second Circuit Court of Appeals, Judge Casey would be reversed yet again. However, since the case had been pending for six years, we did not want to wait another year or more to find out. Furthermore, even if the decision were reversed, the case would just be remanded back to Judge Casey in the district court for further proceedings, which could well consume another few years.

In the end, Bob did not want to give the defendants the satisfaction of seeing their campaign of delay succeed by learning of his demise before the case was concluded. In a May 5, 1997 New York Times article, Bob had candidly told the reporter: "They want me to die." Eight years later, Bob still thought this was the defendants' goal. So, he authorized us to enter into settlement discussions that would give him a degree of vindication in federal court and hold the defendants accountable for their actions.

Sometimes the best time to settle a case is when your position is relatively strong, and you have just won an important decision. Most parties to a case (and many of their lawyers) only think about settling a case when things are going poorly for them. However, in my experience, this is usually not the best time to initiate settlement discussions for all the obvious reasons. When your stock is low, you have to sell at a low price; but when your stock is on the rise, you should consider selling it because, while it may go even higher, it can also go down. As the adage goes, you should "buy low and sell high." However, this is easier said than done. Timing is everything.

I discussed the possibility of a settlement with the lawyers for the defendants, and they welcomed the suggestion. The Judge had just ruled against their summary judgment motion on the MSP claim. Although our "bad faith" claim had been dismissed for a second time, there was always a degree of uncertainty as to what the Court of Appeals would do and whether it would reinstate the claim for a second time. In other words, the timing was ripe for both sides to explore the possibility of a settlement.

After several long negotiating sessions with the assistance of U.S. Magistrate Judge Henry Pitman, we finally reached a settlement between Bob Manning and Utilities Mutual, and separate negotiations with Niagara Mohawk also produced a settlement in early 2005. Finally, after 43 years from the date Bob Manning was paralyzed, and eight years after filing his federal MSP claim on behalf of Medicare, the litigation was over. Now 68 years old, Bob Manning could feel some degree of satisfaction and vindications that Niagara Mohawks and Utilities Mutual had finally been held accountable, although at a tremendous cost in time and money.

The ultimate irony of the *Manning* case was the federal government didn't even cash the rather large check we sent it from the settlement funds. Bob was beside himself when our repeated letters and phone calls to the government went unanswered, and the money sat in our escrow account month after month. Bob didn't necessarily expect a "thank you" letter from the government or even a medal recognizing his dedication to the public interest, but at least he thought they would cash the check we worked so hard to recover. Finally, after many months, I got a call from our bank saying that a large check made payable to the U.S. Treasury had come in and whether it was all right to honor the check even though the date was stale due to the passage of time. I, of course, said "yes," and so ended the *Manning* litigation saga, at least until Utilities Mutual failed to pay the next legitimate bill submitted to it.

Corporations all too often act with outrageous impunity, perhaps because they have neither a body to be jailed nor a soul to be damned. But sometimes, just sometimes, they are held accountable for their transgressions and made to feel some pain where it hurts them the most – financially.

Chapter 11

The William Jacobsen Case

Failure to Accommodate Disabled Employees in the Workplace

Bill Jacobsen's problems with his pulmonary system and ability to breathe started in 1979 when he first began working with the New York City Health and Hospitals Corporation (HHC). He joined HHC as an assistant health facilities planner, which required him to visit construction sites within HHC's hospital network about twice a week. On those visits, he met with project directors, inspected the structures of HHC buildings, and supervised the progress of HHC construction projects. For the rest of each week, Jacobsen worked at HHC's central office at 346 Broadway in Manhattan, completing reports on the site visits and performing any other necessary office work. In 1982, he was promoted to health facilities planner and assigned to HHC's Bellevue network. Although he was assigned to larger projects, his responsibilities remained the same, and he continued to make site visits only once or twice a week. In June 2005, Bill was first diagnosed with a pulmonary disease that made breathing difficult. His doctor suspected that the construction dust to which he was regularly exposed may have been a cause of his difficulties and warned him to try to avoid such exposures.

In August 2005, HHC reassigned Bill Jacobsen to its Queens hospital network. He oversaw projects at the Queens Hospital Center (QHC), where HHC conducted extensive renovations and asbestos abatement. As a result of this transfer, Bill was required to relocate his office to QHC and visit construction sites more frequently. He was no longer allowed to visit the central office in Manhattan regularly. Bill protested the reassignment, but his objections were overruled.

In September 2005, Jacobsen was diagnosed with pneumoconiosis, an occupational lung disease caused by repeated and prolonged inhalation of asbestos or other dust particles. In October 2005, he requested a three-month medical leave of absence, during which time he was scheduled to undergo an open lung biopsy to evaluate his condition further. In support of his application for medical leave, Jacobsen's physician, Gwen Skloot, M.D., certified to HHC that he "currently could not perform usual tasks" and "should not be exposed to inhaled dust." In December 2005, Dr. Skloot sent a letter to HHC informing the Corporation that, because Jacobsen "had been treated with systemic corticosteroids and had demonstrated clinical improvement," he was "ready to return to work." However, Dr. Skloot cautioned that he could "not be further exposed to any type of environmental dust" or "be present at any construction site." In a reply letter, HHC asked Dr. Skloot to identify the "exact date [Jacobsen] could return" to work and inquired as to whether he was "medically cleared to perform the essential functions of his duties fully." A list of his job duties attached to HHC's letter specified that he "spent approximately 75% of his working hours in the field monitoring several construction projects and attended construction management meetings on-site." The list stated that he "spent approximately 25% of his working hours in the office."

In January 2006, while waiting for Dr. Skloot to respond, HHC filed a Workers' Compensation Board report, which stated that Jacobsen had been exposed to asbestos dust at an HHC facility and that his supervisor had been aware of his injury since January 2005. Around the same time, Jacobsen's union representative wrote to HHC that the union was "requesting a reasonable accommodation" for Jacobsen that allowed him to return to work by assigning him to work in an office free of construction dust and asbestos.

In March 2006, Dr. Skloot replied to HHC's inquiry about Jacobsen's return date and ability to perform his essential job functions, stating:

> He is ready to return to work immediately (as of the date of this letter). He is medically cleared to work in the field so that he can attend project meetings. I have advised him that it is imperative that he not be exposed to any type of environmental dust, and he has assured me that his fieldwork will not include such exposure.

Jacobsen returned to QHC and performed regular site visits until May 2006. During this post-leave work period, Jacobsen told his supervisor, Vincent James, that he was having difficulty breathing. He asked James to provide him with protective respiratory equipment and reassign him to the central office in Manhattan. Bill also complained to Anita O'Brien, HHC's director of the QHC facility, that he was having trouble breathing. O'Brien provided Jacobsen only with a dust mask, but he did not use it at times because it impeded his communication ability. Jacobsen requested that O'Brien supply him with a respirator, by which he meant a device that was "fit tested by an industrial hygienist" and "specifically designed to filter the particulates one is exposed to" in asbestos abatement projects.

In May 2006, Jacobsen wrote to HHC requesting a transfer back to the central office, stating that he was "able to perform any and all functions, which had been assigned to him prior to his relocation to QHC." He attached to his request a letter from Stephen M. Levin, M.D., stating, "it is my strong recommendation that he be placed in a work setting free from exposure to airborne irritant or fibrogenic dusts, fumes and gases, if his current lung condition is not to be made worse by such exposure." Apparently, in response to this request, Vincent James sent a memorandum to HHC's Human Resources Department in which he observed:

> Jacobsen's job responsibilities require that he spend 80% of his working hours in the field and 20% of his working hours in central office. It was my understanding that he was cleared by H.R. to return to work at full capacity. Due to the high volume of work at Queens Hospital Center, it is imperative that we have a network manager cover the projects at that facility.

Jacobsen's union counsel then wrote to HHC, insisting "that HHC find an appropriate place in the agency for him to work where he is not regularly assigned to construction sites."

On June 5, 2006, Jacobsen filed a disability discrimination complaint against HHC with the New York State Division of Human Rights. Approximately two days later, HHC placed him on unpaid medical leave for six months, offering to return him to his position if his medical condition improved. HHC wrote to Jacobsen as follows:

> Given the nature of your duties as a Health Facilities Planner, there is no position in your title available in the Corporation that would not, of necessity, involve your working in conditions hazardous to your health. Therefore, we must conclude that at present you are not able to perform the essential functions of your job.

In an August 2006 letter to HHC, Dr. Skloot wrote that Jacobsen would never be medically cleared to fully perform the essential functions of his duties because "it was imperative to his health that he not be further exposed to any type of environmental dust." Dr. Skloot continued, "He recently attempted to return to the field and developed significant worsening of his respiratory status, requiring a course of systemic steroids," adding, "Therefore, the only work he is cleared to do is office work."

Without any discussion with Jacobsen as to the option of his continuing to perform his duties from an office setting, HHC summarily terminated Jacobsen in March 2007 at the end of his involuntary medical leave.

I first met Bill in March 2008. Looking back on that first meeting, little did I realize at the time that his case would be one of the most significant cases of my career. He was a mild-mannered and unassuming professional who lived alone in an apartment in Stuyvesant Village in lower Manhattan, cared for his mother, and enjoyed weekends on the Jersey Shore. By the time he came to us, he was very sick, and he knew it. He was also keenly aware that his job had made him ill and that his supervisors had not treated him fairly. Because of HHC's treatment of Bill, he would never be able to work again. We agreed to represent him on a contingent fee basis.

Shortly after that, we filed a complaint in New York State Supreme Court on Bill's behalf, alleging that HHC had unlawfully discriminated against him based on disability in violation of the State Human Rights Law (State HRL)[1] and City Human Rights Law (City HRL).[2] The Complaint further claimed that HHC had engaged in gross negligence by exposing him to environmental dust without protective respiratory equipment. We reasoned that HHC could have reassigned him to the central office and provided him with the protective and respiratory equipment necessary to protect him from further respiratory damage if and when it may have been necessary for him to visit a construction site.

HHC answered the Complaint, and then moved for summary judgment seeking to dismiss it. HHC contended that it had terminated the plaintiff due to his inability to conduct field visits, which they claimed was essential for the job requirements of a health facilities planner. Also, HHC argued that the relevant three-year statute of limitations barred Jacobsen's gross negligence claim. We strongly opposed HHC's motion, asserting that, had HHC granted him a reasonable accommodation when he first requested one, he would have been able to perform occasional field visits with proper respiratory equipment.

The New York State Supreme Court, the lowest court of general jurisdiction in the State, granted HHC's motion for summary judgment and dismissed the complaint.[3] In the court's view, no reasonable accommodation was available for the plaintiff because his medical evidence led "to the inevitable conclusion that the plaintiff could not, for medical reasons, spend any time at a construction site, and therefore, could never return to his old duties." Moreover, the court found that plaintiff made no allegation that "specific equipment could overcome the doctor's warning and prescription" to stay away from construction sites. The court further determined that Jacobsen's gross negligence cause of action was time-barred.

The Appeal to the Appellate Division, First Department

We immediately appealed this dismissal of the Complaint to the Appellate Division, First Department, which covers appeals from New York County (Manhattan), the Bronx, and neighboring counties. We were hopeful that this intermediate appeals court would agree with our position that Jacobsen had been denied his right to a reasonable accommodation for his disability. Unfortunately, with only one justice dissenting in part, the Appellate Division affirmed the Supreme Court's order. The Appellate Division ruled that Supreme Court had correctly dismissed the complaint, stating, "HHC established that plaintiff could not, even with a reasonable accommodation, perform the essential functions of his job." The court determined HHC had inquired of Dr. Skloot regarding the plaintiff's ability to work and had kept the plaintiff's job open during his medical leaves of absence. The court also concluded that HHC had engaged in a "good faith interactive process" when it determined that a reasonable accommodation for the plaintiff's disability was not available.[4] In so ruling, the court rejected the plaintiff's assertion that HHC could have reasonably accommodated his disability by giving him a respirator upon returning to QHC in March 2006. According to the court, the plaintiff focused on this potential accommodation "only on appeal." In any event, the court concluded, given that plaintiff had not consistently worn the dust mask he had received from HHC, the plaintiff could hardly complain about the inadequacy of the protection he had been given.[5]

Finally, the Appellate Division concluded that the plaintiff's gross negligence claim was correctly dismissed as time-barred because more than three years had passed since the plaintiff had allegedly been exposed to asbestos. In any event, the court found that the claim had been "barred by operation of Workers' Compensation Law."[6]

Fortunately for us, in a comprehensive dissenting opinion, Justice Sallie Manzanet–Daniels voted to modify the Supreme Court's order to reinstate plaintiff's disability discrimination claims.[7] In her view, triable issues of fact existed regarding whether the plaintiff would have been able to perform the essential functions of his position if he had been provided the appropriate respiratory equipment and whether HHC had "made a reasonable accommodation for plaintiff's disability."[8] In her dissenting opinion, Justice Manzanet-Daniels also argued that HHC could have reasonably accommodated the plaintiff's disability by providing proper respiratory equipment or reassigning him to the central office. She pointed out that he had worked there for 27 years while making only limited site visits.[9] Justice Manzanet–Daniels thus concluded that the dust mask provided by HHC was not a reasonable accommodation, explaining that "a specialized mask or respirator device designed to filter and protect against airborne dust from known toxins or potential carcinogens" was a statutorily reasonable accommodation. She agreed with us that "a dust mask, of the type to be found in any hardware store," did not meet that criterion.[10] The dissent further argued that the record was devoid of evidence that HHC had engaged in any good-faith interactive process designed to determine the existence of a reasonable accommodation.[11]

The Appeal to the New York State Court of Appeals

Although we were extremely disappointed that the majority of the Appellate Division justices did not agree with us, we were heartened that the court permitted us to appeal the decision to the New York State Court of Appeals, the highest court in the state. The Court of Appeals does not have to hear an appeal from the lower court if there is only one dissent. Since we only had one dissent, we were relieved that they agreed to take up the appeal and scheduled oral arguments, which is also not required.

After extensive briefing in the Court of Appeals, the Court heard oral argument at the courthouse in Albany. We doubted that Bill would be able to appear at the oral argument personally. Surprisingly, however, he showed up with a full oxygen tank in tow, which was by then a permanent and necessary part of his life. At this point, his lungs had almost wholly ceased functioning. He sat in the back of the courtroom and listened intensely to the oral argument. When it was over, he turned to my wife, who had come to hear the argument, and had worked closely with Bill. "That was as good as it gets. Ken did an impressive job, and you could see the Judges agreed with him." While I was flattered by Bill's compliment, I learned early in my career, you never know what a judge will do, and in the Court of Appeals, I had seven judges asking me questions. I did agree with Bill, though. I thought it went well. In particular, the late Associate Judge Sheila Abdus-Salaam seemed outraged at the HHC's treatment of Bill. She ultimately wrote the Court's Opinion.

On March 27, 2014, in the landmark decision of *Jacobsen v. New York City Health & Hospitals Corp*,[12] the Court of Appeals unanimously reaffirmed the legal requirement under the New York City Human Rights Law,[13] as well as under the New York State Human Rights Law,[14] that an employer must provide reasonable accommodations for their employees' disabilities. In her opinion, Judge Abdus-Salaam decisively held that the New York City Health and Hospitals Corp. – and any employer in New York State – has a duty to consider in good faith the reasonableness of a proposed accommodation for an employee's disability via a good-faith interactive process.

In resolving this issue, the Court denied summary judgment to the defendant under both the State Human Rights Law and the City Human Rights Law since the employer failed to demonstrate that it responded in good faith to a disabled employee's request for a particular accommodation. In so ruling, the Court of Appeals reversed the lower appellate court's decision, issued by the Appellate Division, First Department, which had upheld the trial court's grant of summary judgment, dismissing Bill Jacobsen's case.[15]

In its *Jacobsen* decision, the Court of Appeals clarified and strengthened the law protecting all people with disabilities in the State. The Court found that, under the State HRL, if a reasonable accommodation would permit the employee to perform the essential functions of the employee's position, the employee has a "disability" within the statute's meaning, and the employer must provide a reasonable accommodation for that disability. A "reasonable accommodation" for an employee's impairment is one that "permits an employee with a disability to perform in a reasonable manner activities involved in the job" and does not impose an "undue hardship" on the employer's business. Thus, the Court of Appeals noted that a proper State HRL claim must be supported by substantiated allegations that, "upon the provision of reasonable accommodations, the employee could perform the essential functions of his or her job." The individualized standard also naturally flows from the State HRL's original purpose "to assure that every individual within this state is afforded an equal opportunity to enjoy a full and productive life."[16]

The Court of Appeals interpreted the State HRL's definitions of "reasonable accommodation" and "disability" to require that, where the employee seeks a specific accommodation for their disability, the employer must give individualized consideration to that request. It may not arbitrarily reject the employee's proposal without further inquiry to protect "individuals who can perform a job, but who may use special equipment or some other special arrangements in performing the job."[17]

The Court further noted that the evidence we presented in opposition to the summary judgment motion indicated that a jury trial was warranted on the issue of HHC's ability to have reasonably accommodated Bill Jacobsen's impairment by reassigning him to its central office in Manhattan. Although HHC wrote to Bill's doctor claiming that 75% of his official job duties consisted of on-site construction supervision and 25% office work, Bill himself was adamant that, during the decades in which he worked at the central office in Manhattan and before his transfer to QHC, he did office work 80% of the time. Also, in May 2006, the plaintiff sent a letter to a senior official at HHC stating that, although the conditions at QHC were hazardous to his health, he was "requesting reasonable accommodation" in the form of a transfer to the central office, where he would be "able to perform any and all functions, which were assigned to [him] prior to [his] relocation to QHC." Plaintiff's union counsel sent a follow-up letter requesting that plaintiff be transferred to any location within HHC's overall organization that would allow the plaintiff to avoid working at construction sites.

In the face of evidence that Bill had worked at the central office for decades doing only limited on-site work and could continue working there despite his disability, the Court of Appeals found that HHC had not satisfied its burden. Under the law, HHC had to show that no reasonable accommodation existed under the City HRL, which it failed to do. The Court reasoned that the parties' conflicting evidence created a triable issue of fact that only a jury could decide.

Also, since Bill had requested a respirator to perform site visits, the Court found that the plaintiff had properly raised a material factual issue. The issue for the jury was: Did HHC have the ability to reasonably accommodate Bill's disability by providing him with a respirator or comparable protective gear? The Court thus accepted our argument that it was a matter of common sense that a respirator would have reduced Bill's exposure to dust, thus allowing him to continue working at construction sites. The Court further found that because HHC never contested the value of a respirator or argued that providing him with a respirator would have caused it "undue hardship," HHC was not entitled to summary judgment.

The Court of Appeals further rejected HHC's argument that Jacobsen's disability could not be accommodated since his condition had deteriorated when he was fired. He was so disabled that no accommodation would have allowed him to continue working. The Court explained that, under the State HRL and the City HRL, the relevant inquiry was whether the employee could perform the core functions of the employee's position with an accommodation.

Jacobsen's journey to a final vindication of his rights by the New York Court of Appeals was a long and torturous one. Still, neither Bill nor his attorneys ever considered giving up his fight for justice. HHC's callous indifference to his respiratory problems and failure to provide him with proper respiratory equipment was so horrendous that we believed the Court of Appeals would finally see it our way. Our persistence paid off, which is fortunate since the highest court in the state was our last chance for Bill to obtain at least some modicum of justice.

Shortly after the Court of Appeals handed down its landmark decision in favor of *Jacobsen*, HHC settled the case in a confidential settlement agreement. However, Bill was unable to enjoy any of the monetary benefits of the settlement since he died within weeks of the settlement. His lungs ultimately gave out, and his pulmonary oxygenation rate approached

0%. However, he died at least with the satisfaction of knowing that his long-term epic battle with HHC was finally won. HHC and other City agencies would no longer dare to send inspectors and other City personnel to hazardous construction sites without proper protective equipment.

Chapter 12

The Estate of Wallace and Estate of Djavaheri-Saatchi Cases

Wills, Trusts, and Estates Litigation

It has often been said that there are only two things that you can count on in life: death and taxes. However, whether you die having left a will can make a big difference. If you die without a will – called "dying intestate" – then your estate (whatever assets you have at the time of death) is distributed according to law, which is not necessarily how you would like it divided. While state statutes vary slightly as to how an estate will be divided absent a will, your estate will generally go first to your spouse (if you have one), then to your children (if you have any), and if you don't have either, to your closest relatives.

In most cases, the state statutes more or less track how people would have wanted their property to be divided anyway. Estate taxes can also be minimized through a well-drafted will. You can appoint an executor that you trust to handle your estate and wind up your financial affairs, such as paying outstanding bills, canceling your credit cards, and notifying the bank and other business establishments. You can appoint a bank or other financial institution to be your executor, and most of the time, they can be counted on to do an honest and professional job of it.

But sometimes, if you die without a will, the result may seem harsh and unfair. For example, in one case, the estate of a young man was awarded over $1 million for a wrongful death lawsuit involving an automobile accident. When the man died, his father inherited the entire estate. He had not been a part of the son's life and was estranged from the young man's mother shortly before his birth. His mother had passed away several years before the young man's fatal car accident. This result of not having a will left close relatives and older siblings entirely out of the picture, even those who had helped raise the young man.

A will is also likely to shorten the probate process, whereby a court will review and order how your estate should be distributed. If you have a will, the Surrogate's Court (or Probate court as it is called in some states) will be informed of your wishes regarding your estate, and if you were legally competent to sign the will, the court will make sure that your wishes are followed.

When there is a question of whether someone was competent when they signed their will, or whether they were subject to duress or undue influence by someone to sign a will, an estates and trusts litigator may be called upon to either challenge or defend the will in question. These cases are typically litigated in specialized state courts that deal exclusively with processing wills and trusts and resolving disputes involving deceased persons when necessary. In New York, each county has a Surrogate's Court. Sometimes, the estate in dispute is worth hundreds of thousands or even millions of dollars. Here are some examples of some of the more significant cases I have handled.

The Curious Case of Heinrich J. Ziegler (Estate of Howard C. Wallace)

Heinrich J. Ziegler was an Austrian citizen who became a permanent resident of the United States in May of 1974. He was highly educated, having received a Doctorate of Law from the University of Vienna, Austria, and a Master of Arts degree in International Relations from the University of Southern California. He also completed the coursework for a doctorate in Economics at the University of Vienna, but he did not complete his dissertation because he accepted a job offer from the International Bank for Reconstruction and Development, popularly referred to as the World Bank. Over several years, he worked for the World Bank in Washington, D.C., Paris, and Calcutta.

After working for the World Bank, Ziegler transferred to the United Nations. In January 1970, he began serving as the Deputy Resident Representative of the United Nations Development Program (UNDP) in Bogotá, Colombia. For some time, he was the acting chief of the UNDP office in Bogotá, where he was responsible for ensuring the proper functioning of all aspects of that office. As part of that responsibility, he took necessary steps to prevent corruption or illegal activities involving UNDP personnel, such as transporting illegal narcotics and other substances under U.N. diplomatic cover. This was an especially important task, given his posting in one of the globe's cocaine capitals. While laudable, his anti-corruption efforts in the Bogotá office had significant repercussions for Ziegler, including death threats by members of Colombian drug cartels who had been relying on the illegal transport of narcotics by U.N. diplomatic staff members. Ziegler returned to New York for his safety and eventually resigned from the U.N., since he did not want to be posted outside the U.S. again.

As for his living arrangements, Ziegler bounced between short-term rental apartments in Manhattan before eventually settling in as a permanent resident at the West Side YMCA on West 63rd Street in Manhattan. He selected this location as his primary residence not only because it was inexpensive and in a great location (near Lincoln Center and Central Park) but also because it allowed him to maintain a "low profile." He feared that the Colombian cartels were looking to retaliate against him for interfering with their lucrative transport of illegal drugs into the U.S. via U.N. diplomatic couriers. Ziegler was so worried that the Colombian narcos would retaliate or even kill him that he started using the pseudonym "Paul Traun" to remain incognito.

During 1975, Ziegler (using the name Paul Traun) met a man named Howard C. Wallace while working out at the YMCA gym. Wallace, an elderly and very private person from a wealthy family, lived on Manhattan's Upper East Side and swam almost every day at the YMCA. Once they met near the pool, they quickly realized they had many common interests, including an interest in foreign literature. Wallace had studied Philosophy and Religion at Columbia University, and both Wallace and Ziegler were fluent in several languages, including French. As their friendship developed, they often shared dinner at the Biarritz, a modest French restaurant in Manhattan, or at the Trustees' Dining room at the Metropolitan Museum on Fifth Avenue in Manhattan.

In late 2001, Mr. Wallace broke his left hip and underwent a series of operations. While recuperating, Wallace spent considerable time in Lenox Hill Hospital in Manhattan and in a rehabilitation home. Ziegler frequently visited Wallace while recovering, and their friendship grew even deeper. Based on what Wallace was telling him, he had no close family, few friends, or even acquaintances. It soon became apparent to Ziegler that Wallace needed increasing assistance in managing his apartment, including the essential daily chores of buying groceries, cooking, and meeting his other basic needs.

Over the next five years, Ziegler spent more and more time with Wallace, both in his apartment and outside, when Wallace could do so. Besides assisting him as a friend, Ziegler coordinated and supervised Wallace's various helpers, nurses, and medical staff daily. When possible, Ziegler took Wallace to Central Park or, later, to restaurants, although Wallace was now confined to his wheelchair. Ziegler even shopped for Wallace, prepared meals for him, and the two enjoyed many pleasant evenings together engaging in lively conversation.

Since they spent so much time together, Ziegler got to know Wallace quite well. Wallace told Ziegler what it was like growing up as the only child in a large estate in Westchester County, just north of New York City. Wallace had the good fortune to be born into a fabulously wealthy family – complete with a private school education and long vacations touring Europe – but there was also loneliness and isolation that made Wallace something of a recluse. Wallace was quite literally a "trust fund baby" since he was the beneficiary of a large trust created in 1923 by his mother, Charlotte C. Wallace. She asked her bank, the Central Union Trust Company of New York (the predecessor of JP Morgan Chase Bank), to set up a trust with millions of dollars in it for the benefit of her son, Howard.

Although it appeared for some time after his last operation that Wallace's condition was improving, it eventually became clear to Wallace and his doctors that the surgeries had been unsuccessful and that he would have to spend most of his time in a wheelchair. His doctors held open the option of an additional operation or operations, but Wallace declined to undergo any more elective surgeries. His severe arthritis continued to reduce any remaining mobility that he had. However, according to Ziegler, Wallace's mental acuity never failed him. At his deposition and in affidavits, Ziegler testified that Wallace continually demonstrated a quick wit and a sharp mind.

During Wallace's hospitalizations and rehabilitation in late 2001 and early 2002, Wallace's longstanding attorney – B. Harrison Frankel – had Wallace sign an all-inclusive Power of Attorney, giving Frankel the power to take whatever actions regarding Wallace's affairs that Frankel deemed necessary and appropriate. However, according to Ziegler, Wallace stated that he had not requested or desired that Frankel take control of his affairs, at least not indefinitely. To be sure, Frankel had arranged to pay the rent on Wallace's apartment and to take care of Wallace's other financial obligations while Wallace was in the hospital and undergoing rehabilitation. However, when Wallace returned to his apartment, he wanted to resume the routine handling of his own financial affairs, such as signing checks for charities and apartment rental.

Also, Wallace told Ziegler he was unhappy with how JPMorgan Chase had invested his assets and that he wanted to sell some of his investments and reinvest the proceeds to increase his earnings. However, a representative of JP Morgan Chase – Mr. Petrosky – informed Mr. Wallace in March 2002 that he (Wallace) had relinquished all his legal powers to Frankel on January 15, 2002. Consequently, the Bank would only be able to take instructions from Frankel. Understandably surprised and outraged, Wallace immediately contacted Mr. Frankel's office at the Kelley Drye law firm at 99 Park Avenue in Manhattan to discuss the matter. However, according to Ziegler, Wallace did not receive a response to his inquiries. Wallace then sent a letter to Frankel dated March 27, 2002, requesting the return of the written power of attorney that Frankel possessed.

Still, Frankel did not respond to Wallace's requests and inquiries. Wallace then asked Robert Abrams, a New York attorney, to assist him in recovering Frankel's written power of attorney, which was eventually accomplished after some difficulties and delays.

When his condition gradually deteriorated again, Wallace gave Ziegler two written "Durable Powers of Attorney" in April 2003. One of these, which was on a JPMorgan Private Bank form and set forth Wallace's specific bank account numbers, was delivered to Mr. Petrosky at JPMorgan Chase.

As a result of Wallace's prior dissatisfaction with Mr. Frankel, he decided to have a new will drafted up, substituting Ziegler for Frankel as the executor of his estate. Wallace also told Ziegler and others that he wanted to make a new will to provide bequeaths to several other people who had helped him over the past few years of his life, including some of the doormen in the building. However, Wallace made it clear to the lawyer who drafted this new will that he wanted the remainder of his estate going to Ziegler.

To move forward with his plans to sign a new will, Wallace asked Frankel's office to send him a copy of his 2001 Will, which was the one that was currently in force. Wallace then executed a new will on March 3, 2006, at his apartment, in the presence of three witnesses and Mr. Peter Chen, an attorney and tax specialist, who notarized Wallace's signature as well as those of the three witnesses.

During this time frame, Wallace consulted with John Walsh of Walsh & Walsh, an attorney and expert in estate planning. Walsh visited with Wallace in his apartment, where he was shown the March 3, 2006 Will that had recently been executed, and discussed with Wallace the proposed contents of a First Codicil to the Will, as well as other legal documents. Later in 2006, the First Codicil that attorney Walsh drafted was forwarded to attorney Abrams to handle the execution and signing by Wallace, since Walsh was not available.

Upon John Walsh's advice, Wallace also signed a Trust Agreement of Limited Partnership between Wallace and Ziegler, which was filed by the law firm of Walsh & Walsh. He forwarded the agreement to Mr. Petrosky of JPMorgan Chase with a cover letter signed by Wallace on May 12, 2006. Wallace also signed another letter on the same day (May 12, 2006), directing JPMorgan Chase to transfer $900,000 to Ziegler from one of Wallace's bank accounts. When the Bank later claimed that these documents had never been received, the papers were again sent to JPMorgan Chase. Nevertheless, the bank still refused to follow Wallace's instructions.

Instead, JPMorgan Chase sent some representatives from the "fraud investigation" department of the Bank to visit Wallace. These Bank representatives then accused Ziegler of acting improperly regarding Wallace's financial affairs. Mr. Wallace was furious at these unfounded accusations since he had explicitly authorized Ziegler to act on his behalf by giving him the written General Powers of Attorney in April 2003, on file with the Bank.

The Bank's accusations of "fraud" and "undue influence" regarding Ziegler were odd since Ziegler had only exercised his Powers of Attorney for Wallace in minimal ways, such as writing a few checks for expenses relating to Wallace's apartment and similar expenses. The Bank also had specific letters of instruction signed by Wallace and dated May 12, 2006, transferring one-half of the assets of the Limited Partnership to

Ziegler, which JP Morgan was refusing to honor. Although the amount of money that the Bank was claiming would be transferred to Ziegler was a considerable sum – $25 million – there did not appear to be any basis for the bank and Wallace's prior attorney (Frankel) to claim this was improper, since Wallace – at least in the view of Ziegler and various aides and workers who were in contact with Wallace on almost a daily basis – still seemed to be perfectly competent to make his own decisions regarding the disposition of his assets at that point in time.

Frankel or one of the JPMorgan Chase representatives next told Wallace that the matter had been referred to the New York County District Attorney's Office as a possible fraud. Wallace, therefore, asked attorney Robert Abrams to inquire of the D.A.'s Office regarding the status of the criminal investigation of these allegations. Abrams reported to Wallace and Ziegler that no charges were pending against Ziegler, but the D.A.'s Office neither confirmed nor denied whether there was an ongoing investigation.

To get to the bottom of things, Ziegler himself then decided to call the D.A.'s Office. He spoke by telephone to an investigator from that Office, who informed Ziegler that there was no ongoing investigation. The investigator explained that the D.A.'s Office had closed its file on the matter after attorney Abrams provided them with copies of the relevant documents establishing the authority given to Ziegler by Wallace.

On May 8, 2006, Wallace signed a First Codicil to his March 3, 2006 Will. Wallace signed this Codicil in the presence of two witnesses and attorney Abrams, who notarized Wallace's signature, as well as those of the two witnesses.

The following month, at the end of June 2006, Wallace was admitted to Lenox Hill Hospital. He was diagnosed with pneumonia by his attending physician, Dr. Joseph Mulvehill. Wallace's condition improved, and he returned home shortly after that. However, his condition quickly deteriorated again, and he died at home on July 14, 2006, at the age of 87.

The law firm of Tuan & Cho, which was holding Wallace's 2006 Will for safekeeping, filed the Will with the New York County Surrogate's Court at Ziegler's direction. The Manhattan law firm of Carter Ledyard and Milburn assisted Ziegler with filing an Amended Petition for Probate. However, Mr. Frankel and his law firm, Kelley Drye & Warren, beat

Ziegler to the punch when they swiftly filed a Petition for Temporary Letters Testamentary, based upon Wallace's prior 2001 Will.

This is where I entered the picture. I would like to think that clients ask me and my law firm to represent them based upon my stellar legal reputation (in my biased view anyway) in New York, throughout the U.S., and other parts of the world. However, while this is how I often get involved in most of my cases, I met Heinrich Ziegler under quite different circumstances. The truth is that Ziegler frequented a health food store on the street level of the building where my law firm was located (100 Park Avenue). Following Wallace's death, Ziegler asked the store manager whether he knew of a good lawyer to handle a wills and trust litigation matter. The manager recommended me, presumably based on the fact that I was a longstanding customer of his establishment. As a reasonably serious marathon runner and athlete for most of my life, I had always been an enthusiastic advocate of holistic health remedies (within reason) and vitamin supplements.

After being retained by Ziegler, my first task – as always – was to review and investigate the entire matter. This is generally referred to as "due diligence." The most important question, of course, was whether Mr. Wallace's Last Will and Testament, dated March 3, 2006, and the Will's First Codicil, dated May 8, 2006, were legally valid. If so, they would have superseded Wallace's prior 2001 Will, which would no longer have any force and effect. Since the 2006 Will and Codicil gave the lion's share of Wallace's more than $30 million estate to Ziegler, while the 2001 Will had only given him a small piece, the stakes were understandably very high for Ziegler.

One major factor that Ziegler had going in his favor was that he was unquestionably the one person who had been responsible for Wallace's care and well-being for many years. Hence, it was not unusual for Wallace to have wanted Ziegler to receive most of his estate. This was especially true since Wallace did not have any immediate family. He had never been married and had no children. To the extent Wallace had cousins or extended family, there was no evidence that he had been in touch with them for decades, or that any of his blood relatives had reached out to Wallace to inquire about his well-being.

In addition, Ziegler had continued to act as Wallace's best friend and closest survivor. After Mr. Wallace died, Ziegler made the funeral arrangements and paid Frank E. Campbell Funeral Home with a check from his account. Ziegler also paid Father Anthony Schueller of Eglise St. Jean Batiste Church for Wallace's memorial services. He paid Mrs. Joan Szony (the landlady for Mr. Wallace's apartment) the September and October rent on Mr. Wallace's apartment. He also dutifully paid Ziegler's utilities and insurance bills.

Of course, there are two sides to every story, especially when there is a dispute over the legitimacy or enforceability of a will. Since I represented Heinrich Ziegler (a/k/a Paul Traun), I wanted to present as strong a case as possible that Wallace was of "sound mind" when he executed the new will and codicil in 2006. We also had to prove that Wallace was not the subject of fraud by Ziegler or under any undue influence by him.

On the other side, the Objectants to the 2006 Will (giving most of Wallace's estate to Ziegler) naturally took a quite different view of the facts and circumstances surrounding Wallace's signing of the 2006 Will and Codicil. There were three sets of attorneys representing the Objectants, so from the start I knew that my hands would be full. Harvey E. Corn of the law firm of Greenfield Stein and Senor LLP – an experienced and well-respected attorney and law firm – played the lead role for the Objectants. They objected to the 2006 Will on almost every possible ground, including lack of proper execution (signing) of the Will; lack of "capacity" (mental competence) of Wallace; fraud; and undue influence by Ziegler.

Specifically, the Objectants and their lawyers pointed out in papers filed with the New York County Surrogate's Court that, when Wallace signed the 2006 Will, he was suffering from "arterial fibrillation, aspiration pneumonia, congestive heart failure, and debilitating and excruciating painful decubitus ulcers." Not a pretty picture at all. The Objectants further showed Wallace's medical professionals had described the pain from Wallace's ulcers as "intractable." He apparently could not be turned or moved by his 24/7 health aides without expressing intense pain. Based on Wallace's medical records, he was "unable to toilet himself, feed himself, bathe himself, medicate himself, turn himself or perform any functions of daily living on his own." Perhaps the most alarming factor regarding Wallace's state of mind was the list of opiate painkillers he was on in 2006: Vicodin, Roxanol, Tylenol with Codeine, Percocet, and morphine, which was injected both inter-muscularly and intravenously.

The Objectants to the 2006 Will noted Wallace had executed prior wills in 1993, 1994, 2000, and 2001, all of which had been drafted by his longtime attorney, Harrison Frankel of the Kelley Drye & Warren law firm. In some of these prior wills, Ziegler had only been identified by the name "Paul Traun," indicating that this was the only name by which Wallace knew him. The 2006 Will, by contrast, had been drafted by attorney Chen, a full-time accountant who "moonlighted" by doing some legal work for Ziegler, such as drafting Wallace's 2006 Will. Instead of giving his true residential address at the West Side YMCA, Ziegler had instructed Chen to list his address as that of Chen's office. Another alleged irregularity in the 2006 Will was that Chen did not have a lawyer's written retainer agreement with Wallace, a requirement to do legal work for a client in New York and most other states.

As for signing the Codicil to the 2006 Will, the Objectants elicited testimony that Wallace had to be awakened from a deep sleep to sign the Codicil. One witness testified that Wallace was so tired and weak that he could not even withstand the rigors of signing more than two documents at that time. The lawyer had to return on another occasion to have Wallace sign a third document. The Objectants' lawyers pointed out the witnesses to Wallace's signing of the 2006 Will and other documents were some of the health care workers assisting Wallace and that they had a limited command of English. They claimed the witnesses were not told what they were doing or why, and that they were paid for their "services" as witnesses.

Since the settlement discussions that Surrogate Judge Renee R. Roth encouraged did not go anywhere, I had to spend a considerable amount of time preparing for trial. This was a complex case with hundreds of documents and thousands of pages of depositions. I also had to prepare our witnesses, which included Ziegler, the attorneys involved, an expert witness on Wallace's mental capacity at the time of the signing of the 2006 Will, and a variety of health care workers, doormen, and others who had contact with Wallace around the relevant time period.

I also had to both bring and respond to a series of "in limine" motions, which are pretrial requests to the judge designed to limit the evidence that one side or the other can present at trial. Sometimes the argument is on the grounds of "relevance," such as when the evidence sought to be introduced at trial is too far afield from the central factual issues in dispute. At other times, the evidence may be tangentially relevant to the issues in the case, but is so prejudicial to one side that a court may decide that it should be excluded.

In this case, there was some evidence that Wallace had given Ziegler a substantial amount of cash and valuable artwork shortly before he signed the 2006 Will. The Objectants sought to introduce this evidence to show that Ziegler supposedly had a tremendous degree of "undue influence" over Wallace. The Objectants tried to show that the new Will was part of Ziegler's alleged "scheme to defraud" Wallace, first by taking as much cash and valuables from Wallace's apartment as possible and then having Wallace sign a new will and other documents giving Ziegler control of the entire estate.

But the court never had to decide these pre-trial motions. Before the trial began, a final round of settlement discussion was successful, giving Ziegler about one-half of Wallace's estate. Surrogate Renee R. Roth wrote that this settlement "represented a notable achievement [by Ziegler] given the serious problems burdening his case for probate [of the 2006 Will]."

The Estate Of Molhammad Reza Djavaheri -Saatchi Case

In the will dispute relating to the estate of a wealthy Iranian-American businessman, Mohammad Reza Djavaheri- Saatchi, I was in the reverse legal position than I was in the Estate of Wallace litigation. Instead of representing the designated major beneficiary of the last will and testament by the decedent, I was representing the decedent's son, Pasha Djavaheri-Saatchi, who had been basically cut out of the last disputed will. Our task was to try to set aside the will signed by his father, which gave virtually everything to his sister, while leaving him little or nothing of this substantial estate. Our legal theory was that Pasha's sister (Parisa) had exercised undue influence over the father by cajoling and forcing him to sign a will and related trust documents, even though the father's mental capacity was severely diminished when he signed those documents.

Mohammed Reza Djavaheri-Saatchi, known to his friends and family as "Reza," was born in 1936 in Iran. He came from a wealthy family, and Reza did very well in the jewelry business, real estate, and other ventures. Reza had two children: one son, Pasha, by his first marriage, which ended in divorce, and one daughter, Parisa, by his second marriage, which also ended in divorce. Pasha (our client) and Parisa were two years apart in age; Pasha was born in February 1980, and Parisa was born in September 1982.

After the Iranian revolution in 1979 and the fall of the Shah, Reza and his wife fled to the U.S. Although Pasha was primarily raised by his mother in Queens, New York, he maintained a close relationship with his father, who never lived very far away. The father and son were so close that when Pasha's mother tried to raise him under a different surname after their divorce, Reza brought a successful lawsuit against his ex-wife to force her to use the family name (Djavaheri-Saatchi) concerning Pasha.

In 2008, while Reza was still active and able to travel, he and Pasha went on an extended vacation in Thailand together, further cementing their close bond. However, Reza's mental status and memory had already seriously deteriorated by that point, which made it necessary for Pasha to monitor him constantly. That same year, Reza and Pasha drove to Florida together, but Pasha had to do all of the driving since Reza was in no condition to drive safely.

After that, from 2008 through 2010, when the disputed Will was signed, Reza's mental health and memory issues continued to worsen, requiring him to be constantly monitored by caregivers. Indeed, Parisa had closed-circuit cameras installed in Reza's residence to be continuously monitored.

During this period, while Reza's condition was rapidly deteriorating, there was evidence introduced to the effect that Parisa yelled at Reza on a virtually constant basis, insisting that he give her a Power of Attorney, which Reza initially refused to do. However, Parisa finally wore Reza down, and he relented. He signed a Power of Attorney ("POA") in Parisa's favor, giving her the authority to make most important decisions regarding his life and estate.

Armed with this POA, Parisa promptly sold Reza's house at 2 Centreview Drive in Oyster Bay, Long Island. She then pocketed the proceeds. Parisa also sold Reza's one-half interest in a catering hall and again took the profits.

Despite his advanced age and deteriorating condition, Reza had a young girlfriend during this time frame. Parisa considered her to be a threat to the financial control that she was asserting over her father. She expressed her concerns to Pasha that Reza's girlfriend might easily influence him to give her a large portion of his cash assets. These fears seemed to be confirmed when the girlfriend persuaded Reza to provide her with a check for about $50,000. Indeed, Parisa became so alarmed about this that she asked Pasha to join her in filing a complaint against the then-girlfriend with the Nassau County District Attorney's Office.

At no time before Reza's death did Parisa ever inform Pasha that she had arranged for Reza to sign a will and various trust documents, leaving his entire estate to Parisa. Pasha was under the impression that if Reza had any will, it provided for an equal distribution of his estate between his two children. Reza understood this to be the norm in the U.S., as opposed to Iran, where the son traditionally inherits two-thirds of the father's estate.

Reza died at age 79 on April 20, 2015, at St. Francis Hospital in Roslyn, New York, in Nassau County, New York. A copy of his death certificate identified Pasha as next of kin, with no mention of his daughter, Parisa. In addition to being listed as "next of kin" on the death certificate, Pasha was also listed as the Reza's "closest relative" in the Funeral Record of the Imam Al-Khoei Islamic Center, which conducted Reza's funeral service according to Islamic law. Pasha made most of the arrangements for his father's funeral services and burial since he, like his father, was a Muslim, while Parisa was Jewish, as was her mother.

Even while Pasha was making the funeral arrangements for their father, Parisa still did not tell Pasha that Reza had signed a will with an attorney that Parisa personally knew. She had driven their father over to the law office for him to sign it without telling Pasha.

After more than two weeks had elapsed since their father's death, Pasha – reasonably believing that their father had not left a will – filed a Petition seeking Letters of Temporary Administration to be given to him for his father's estate. This Petition was filed with the Surrogate's Court for Nassau County, located in Mineola, Long Island. Parisa and her attorneys quickly responded by filing objections to Pasha's Petition. She also filed a cross-petition seeking to be appointed as the Executor of Reza's estate. Parisa and her lawyers were forced to disclose that Reza signed a will before his death. They were now required to file it with the Surrogate's court and provide us with a copy. Until we received a copy of the 2010 Will in the mail, attached to Parisa's Petition, we were not even aware that Reza had recently signed a last will and testament.

As you have probably guessed by now, the central issue in this "will contest" was whether Reza was of sufficiently sound mind and had the requisite testamentary capacity to sign the will that was presented to him at Parisa's attorney's office. There was also the question of whether Parisa had exercised an undue influence over him and manipulated him into disinheriting her brother.

By the time Reza signed the will in question, there could be little dispute that he had had a long history of mental illness. His mental condition sharply deteriorated in the years immediately preceding the Will's signing. As far back as 2001, Reza had been hospitalized in Mercy Hospital in Syosset, Long Island, for approximately a 7 to 8-month period due to severe mental health problems. During this time frame, Reza gave Pasha a full durable General Power of Attorney, dated March 9, 2001, including a Special Provision granting Pasha the power to handle "all real estate management and real estate rental matters." Parisa admitted in a deposition taken in a case involving one of Reza's companies, the Djavaheri Realty Corp., that her father had dementia and Alzheimer's disease in February 2010. This was only a few months before the execution of the Will on July 9, 2010. Pat Caroleo, Reza's primary real estate manager, also expressed grave concerns around that time, as he was worried that Reza was subject to the undue influence of his girlfriend.

Parisa provided further evidence about their father's lack of competency at her deposition in the related real estate litigation case in 2010. She testified that he had been making "bad business decisions" for years and that he had made a particularly bad business decision selling a building he owned in Miami in 2008 for far less than she believed it was worth. Perhaps the most damning piece of evidence was that only three months before the date that Reza signed the Will in dispute, Parisa testified that she did not think that Reza was "in the right frame of mind" to sign a contract for real estate in Miami.

Parisa's testimony in the real estate dispute litigation created a problem for her in the Will contest since her objectives in the two different cases were completely opposite. This problem often arises when a person is involved in multiple cases simultaneously without considering the fact that the lawyers in one case can get access to the deposition transcripts in another case. This allows them to use a sworn witnesses' testimony in one case against them in another case.

In the real estate litigation involving Djavaheri Realty Corp., Parisa was seeking to have the Miami 2010 real estate contract invalidated, based upon her claim that Reza was mentally incapacitated when he signed the contract. What Parisa did not fully realize at the time of her sworn testimony in the real estate case was that by testifying under oath that Reza had dementia and Alzheimer's disease in 2010, she was making it impossible to not appear like she was contradicting herself by saying, at the same time, in the Will contest case that Reza was competent to dispose of his execute a last will and testament. We argued – I believe persuasively – that Parisa could not have it both ways: either Reza was competent to sign both the real estate contract and a will, or he was incompetent to do both.

Other than the Miami real estate transaction, Parisa also expressed the opinion in one of her depositions that there was further evidence that Reza could no longer be presumed competent to handle his business affairs in 2010. For example, Reza let his girlfriend have unrestricted access to his checkbook and ATM card in 2010, which she unscrupulously exploited to withdraw substantial amounts of cash.

Parisa dug an even deeper hole for herself regarding her father's competency around the time that he signed the Will. She testified at her deposition that Reza also signed papers she had prepared for him in 2010, giving her a 49% ownership interest in his real estate company. This decision to transfer nearly one-half of the company to her was made without discussing it with Pasha, even though she knew full well that Reza and Pasha had been close. It simply made no sense that Reza would cut him out of both the ownership of the real estate company and his Will. The only reasonable explanation was that Reza was manipulated by Parisa.

During the will contest in Nassau County Surrogate's Court, we also introduced evidence that a neurologist, Jyh-Haur Lu, M.D., had examined Reza on May 29, 2010. In his written report of the visit, Dr. Lu concluded that Reza suffered from "Dementia." Dr. Lu's report understatedly commented: "It is unclear to me if he has the ability to make sensible financial decisions." Needless to say, this medical evaluation called into serious question Reza's mental capacity at the time to execute any will and trust documents drafted for him.

Realizing that she had a problem, Parisa quickly sought a "second opinion" by arranging for another neurological examination of Reza to be conducted by Dr. David Podwall, which took place on June 7, 2010, only one month before the execution of the Will. However, this second medical examination also resulted in a diagnosis of "dementia" and "early stages of Alzheimer's disease" for Reza. This diagnosis was especially damning, since the medical diagnosis of dementia contains the following criteria: "[a]t a minimum, assistance should be required with complex instrumental activities of daily living, such as paying bills or managing medications."[1]

Thus, within one month of the execution of the Will in question, Reza was examined by two neurologists, both of whom determined that he had dementia and Alzheimer's disease, and both of whom suggested that he undergo further testing and therapy to deal with the issue. It does not appear that Parisa opted to have her father undergo any of the more intensive neurological testing and treatment recommended by either of these neurologists. Instead, she quickly arranged for the drafting attorney to get her father to sign the papers giving her his entire estate.

The law office that Parisa selected to draft her father's Will should have conducted at least minimal due diligence. However, the drafting attorney did nothing to investigate whether it was indeed Reza's intention to leave his entire estate to only one of his two children. There was no evidence that we could uncover indicating that Reza had ever been asked that question. The simple and obvious question that the drafts-person should have asked Reza was: "Since you have two children, do you want the two of them to share equally in your estate and if not, why not?" However, the draftsperson never asked his client this fundamental question. Instead, he entirely relied on the representations of an interested party – Parisa – that Reza did not want his son to be a direct beneficiary of his estate. Nor did the drafting lawyer advise Pasha that his father was about to execute a will that left him with nothing.

Even in the unlikely event that it was Reza's genuine intention to leave everything to Parisa, it was improper (in our view) for the lawyer to have relied entirely upon Parisa as an intermediary between Reza and the lawyer since she was an interested party. For example, when the drafting attorney wanted information regarding one of the buildings in which Reza had an interest, he asked Parisa, who provided the requested information. In fact, it does not appear that the attorney spoke directly to Reza at all, except for a few brief minutes when Reza signed the Will and other documents at the lawyer's office.

We also felt that it was highly unusual for Reza to have willingly named his ex-wife (Parisa's mother) as a co-trustee of the trusts established under the 2010 Will. Indeed, it was remarkable, given the fact that they had been engaged in longstanding and acrimonious litigation over the validity of a prenuptial agreement.[2] This also, in our view, strongly supported the inference that Reza was being subjected to undue influence by Parisa. This conclusion was further supported by the testimony of Reza's real estate manager, Pat Caroleo, who described how Reza reacted when Parisa called him on the phone: "Well . . . he'd make expressions of fear when she called. And then he would pick up, and it would be a little drama. But from facial expressions and body language, you could write a book." Caroleo further testified that he could recall no instance from 2009 through mid-2010 when Reza refused to follow – or did not follow – a direction from Parisa. In addition, Caroleo disclosed that, during the summer of 2010, at precisely the time when the Will was being drafted and then executed, Parisa moved Reza into her mother's home in Manhasset, Long Island, as part of her successful campaign to maintain total control over him.

When Caroleo visited Reza at Parisa's mother's house, and after having not seen Reza for two to three weeks, he was shocked to see that Reza's eyes were glazed. He was smiling for no apparent reason and was "not really communicating." Caroleo thought that Reza was being "overmedicated" at that time and was "you know, in happy land." He further testified that Parisa and her mother were making all the decisions for Reza at that point. According to Caroleo: "[Parisa] told me that she was seeking full custody of her dad and full control and that I was not to share that information with her half-brother, Pasha, at any time and then threatened me. . . . That she would sue me, make me penniless, and my life would end."

Parisa also asked Pat Caroleo to be present at the lawyer's office when Reza signed the Will in the summer of 2010. He described Reza's condition at the meeting as follows: "He was not . . . there in his right mind. He was – I believe [in] my opinion, medicated or overmedicated, and he was not really all there at all. Glaze in his eye, not communicating. Even with me, he wasn't communicating." Caroleo further recalled that "Reza was not talking one word," which was unusual since "he was a talker."

During the Will contest, we also felt that it was highly significant that, while Parisa was communicating with her brother Pasha throughout the summer of 2010 on other family matters, she never told him about her plans for their father to execute a will and trust agreement conveying all of their father's assets and estate to her. Nor did she tell Pasha that she was taking Reza to be evaluated by two neurologists to see whether he had dementia or Alzheimer's disease. This failure by Parisa to tell Pasha about these important matters in their father's life was, in our view, strong evidence of a guilty mind on Parisa's part. The clear inference to be drawn was that Parisa was concerned that if Pasha were alerted to her plans, he would "interfere" with them. Pasha would either speak directly to their father about dividing his estate equally between his two children or object to his signing of any will in light of the medical reports showing his deteriorating mental capacity.

In short, Reza always expressed his intention to divide his assets equally between his two children. He loved them equally. It did not seem rational that Reza would sign a will giving everything to only one child unless, of course, he was being unduly influenced. Reza often bragged about "his Pasha" owning a dental practice and being "a big doctor," so there did not appear to be any reason why he would want to cut him out of his estate.

As with the will contest relating to the Wallace Estate, the Reza Djavaheri-Saachi Will was settled through a confidential settlement agreement before going to trial. This was accomplished after the Nassau County Surrogate Judge Margaret C. Reilly issued a written decision on September 27, 2018, granting summary judgment to Parisa Djavaheri regarding some of our objections, but not others.[3] This mixed result set the stage for settlement discussions that proved to be ultimately successful.

* * *

Both the Wallace and Djavaheri cases prove the point that much time consuming and costly litigation can be avoided through the proper preparation and execution of a will or trust, that the drafting attorney has the primary responsibility to ensure that the testator is sufficiently competent to execute the legal instrument, and that the contents of the will or trust truly reflect the testator's wishes. Even young people who don't think a will is necessary owe it to those they love to execute one. When people are grieving the loss of a loved one, the time has already passed for a family to start thinking about how to divide up someone's estate. All too often, old family conflicts and grievances rear their ugly head, triggering an estate dispute making the loss all the more painful.

Chapter 13

Toxic Tort Litigation

Love Canal, The Agent Orange Product Liability Case, and the Dow Chemical "Dursban" Cases

Poison is the wind that blows
    from the north and south and east. . .

Radiation underground and in the sky,
    animals and birds who live nearby all die. . .

What about this overcrowded land

How much more abuse from man
    can she stand?

**From Marvin Gaye's 1971 hit song,
"Mercy Mercy Me (The Ecology)"**

Toxic tort litigation is one of the law's most challenging and complex areas. *A Civil Action,* the 1995 non-fiction book by Jonathan Harr about a water contamination case in Woburn, Massachusetts in the 1980s, accurately describes how difficult it is to successfully pursue a claim against a chemical polluter. Equally challenging is to hold polluters legally liable for the personal injuries of victims living in the vicinity of a toxic chemical spill. In particular, the book describes in excruciating detail just how difficult it is to establish "causation" for those personal injuries, which requires substantial medical and scientific evidence tracing the cause of the injuries back to the chemical exposure. This cautionary tale is required reading for any young lawyer who dares to wade into the field of toxic tort litigation.

Notwithstanding all of the hurdles presented by toxic tort cases, I leaped into these treacherous waters on several occasions and survived to tell the tale. In fact, I did quite well, all things considered.

Before getting into the details of the cases I was involved in on behalf of individuals and communities devastated by exposure to toxic chemicals, I would be remiss if I did not give a brief history of how the modern environmental movement came of age in the late 1960s and early 1970s. During that period, I graduated from college, attended law school, and spent a year on the West Coast as a community and union organizer. I worked for some community organizations closely affiliated with the United Farm Workers Union, led by the legendary organizers Cesar Chavez and Dolores Huerta. The U.F.W. and the community organizations I worked with were deeply concerned about the damage to human health and the environment caused by the overuse of pesticides by the large agri-business companies that were already dominating food production in the U.S.

The Modern Environmental Movement

Rachel Carson's *Silent Spring*, first published in 1962, is often cited as marking the beginning of the modern American environmental movement. *Silent Spring*, which spent thirty-one weeks on the *New York Times* best-seller list, graphically depicted the adverse ecological effects of DDT, a potent insecticide extensively used in American agriculture since World War II. In a larger sense, however, *Silent Spring* sounded the warning that humans were destroying their natural environment and that the hazards of unchecked and unregulated industrial growth posed an existential threat to both the planet and all the species inhabiting it, including our own.

As public awareness and membership in environmental groups skyrocketed, President Lyndon Johnson took an interest in environmental issues, signing into law almost 300 conservation measures between 1963 and 1968, along with $12 billion in authorized funds. The most important of these was the Wilderness Act of 1964, permanently protecting certain federal lands from commercial and economic development. Congress also enacted significant anti-pollution legislation, including the Clean Air Acts of 1963 and 1967, the Clean Water Act of 1960, and the Water Quality Act of 1965.[1]

DISASTER
AREA

CITY
FAILED
US
TAXATION
WITHOUT
REPRESENTATION
FED. GOVT. HELP

JOHN 3:16

A protest sign stands in front of an evacuated and boarded up house in the Love Canal neighborhood in Niagara Falls. The area was abandoned after it was learned that tons of toxic waste were dumped in the canal beside the houses.
Bettmann/Bettmann 514682140 via Getty Images

In 1970, President Richard Nixon added to the growing constellation of environmental laws by signing the National Environmental Policy Act (NEPA), which required an Environmental Impact Statement (EIS) for all "major federal actions significantly affecting the quality of the human environment."[2] During the 1970s alone, more than 12,000 such statements were prepared.

Also, during the 1970s, Congress passed important legislation to control pollution, including the Clean Air Act of 1970, the Pesticide Control Act of 1972, the Ocean Dumping Act of 1972, the Federal Water Pollution Control Act Amendments of 1972, the Clean Air Act of 1974, the Safe Drinking Water Act of 1974, and the Toxic Substance Control Act of 1976. Together, these laws established national environmental quality standards to be enforced by a federally dominated regulatory process, sometimes referred to as "command and control." The Clean Air Act, for instance, established national air quality standards for significant pollutants that were enforced by the Environmental Protection Agency (EPA).

Other significant environmental legislation enacted in the 1970s included the Endangered Species Act of 1973, the Federal Land Policy and Management Act of 1976, and the Comprehensive Environmental Response Compensation and Liability Act ("CERCLA"), also known as the Superfund Act, which was passed in 1980. Designed to help control toxic hazards, CERCLA established federal "superfund" money to clean up contaminated waste sites and spills.

The modern environmental movement evolved into a significant social, human rights, and political force on the first Earth Day on April 22, 1970. Millions of people around the country gathered for the event, including 100,000 people in New York City, to show their commitment to protecting the earth and its natural environment.[3] Organizers estimated that fifteen hundred colleges and ten thousand schools took part in Earth Day. *Time* magazine estimated that about twenty million Americans participated in the event in some fashion.

Like many others crowding Fifth Avenue in New York City that day, I resolved to use whatever skills and knowledge I was learning then in law school to do something significant to help protect the environment. It was clear to me and countless other young people that we had to take forceful action to stop industrial polluters from turning our environment into the global equivalent of a dumpster fire. Time was running out on our ability to reverse the seemingly inexorable march of "progress" towards the self-destruction of the only planet currently available to us.

Love Canal

While it was not the first story of its kind to receive comprehensive news coverage, no prior environmental disaster so caught the public's attention as did the 1978 saga of Love Canal. It was reported that dozens of families living near Love Canal in the LaSalle neighborhood of Niagara Falls, New York would have to be evacuated due to their exposure to chemical wastes dumped and buried in the Canal. The number of families that were eventually evacuated rose into the hundreds.

The digging of Love Canal had been the lifelong dream of entrepreneur William Love. In 1890, Love proposed that the Canal be dug to facilitate the generation and transmission of hydroelectric power from the Falls to the City's industries. Early 20th century photos show kids happily swimming in the water. However, after the Canal was abandoned, Hooker Chemical bought it and started burying barrels of chemicals there between 1942 and 1953. The land, complete with 21,000 tons of toxic waste, was then sold to the Niagara Falls School Board for $1.00. The transfer deed included a warning not to build the school on the sixteen-acre landfill. Although the school board complied with this warning by building the school slightly to the east, the school playground was placed squarely over the top of the toxic dumpsite.

Over the following decades, reports of strange chemical odors and oozing chemical pools became common. Still, it was not until 1977 that a huge blizzard triggered a massive release of chemicals from the Canal, bringing this toxic nightmare to the forefront of the national consciousness. Extensive news coverage led President Jimmy Carter to issue two disaster declarations. These actions led to the evacuation and buyout of more than 900 families as part of a $230 million cleanup.

After years of protracted litigation, 1,300 former residents of Love Canal agreed to a $20 million settlement of their claims against the City of Niagara Falls and Occidental Chemical Corporation, which had taken over Hooker in the late 1960s. However, the settlement with Occidental did not end the litigation. As of January 2021 – more than 40 years after the catastrophe began to unfold – many of the families that moved back remained part of a group of plaintiffs totaling more than a thousand people who filed 18 pending civil lawsuits.[4] Many of them have well-documented claims of leukemia and other illnesses linked to the dangerous chemicals buried at Love Canal, which they are convinced ruined their lives and destroyed their health.

THE AGENT ORANGE LITIGATION

Although I followed the Love Canal litigation from afar, I had more significant involvement in another major environmental tragedy caused by the exposure of U.S. military personnel to a toxic chemical in Vietnam. This case involved "Agent Orange," a herbicide and defoliant used extensively during the Vietnam War to clear large tracts of foliage that North Vietnamese troops and the Viet Cong used as cover.

One of my close legal colleagues and mentor, Irving Like of the law firm Reilly Like and Tenety, was representing veterans who had been exposed to Agent Orange while serving in Vietnam. I assisted Irving Like on this exceedingly complex case to the extent I could, given my numerous other litigation commitments at the time. It turned out that we were in for quite a bumpy ride, as the case took twists and turns too numerous to fully recount here.

The U.S. military widely used Agent Orange in Vietnam from 1961 to 1971. In addition to its devastatingly damaging environmental effects, traces of dioxin in the mixture caused significant health problems for tens of thousands of individuals exposed to it and for their offspring. While disputing the extent to which Agent Orange damaged the civilian population of Vietnam, the U.S. government documented numerous cases of leukemia, Hodgkin's lymphoma, and various kinds of cancer in exposed U.S. military veterans. An epidemiological study done by the Centers for Disease Control and Prevention ("CDC") showed a significant increase in the rate of congenital disabilities of the children of military personnel as a result of Agent Orange.[5]

In the late 1970s, U.S. Vietnam War veterans began filing class actions in various U.S. courts. The Judicial Panel combined these cases into a Multidistrict Litigation, designating the United States District Court for the Eastern District of New York as the Multidistrict Litigation ("MDL") court for all federal Agent Orange-related cases brought by military veterans.[6] After that, Judge George C. Pratt and, later, Judge Jack B. Weinstein presided over proceedings involving approximately 600 plaintiffs, hundreds of thousands of putative class members, several years of motion practice (including motions for class certification), and one appeal to the Second Circuit Court of Appeals.[7]

On May 7, 1984 – the eve of trial of those cases – the seven defendant chemical companies, led by Monsanto, reached a "final global settlement" with plaintiff class representatives and their lawyers. Defendants agreed to create a fund of $180 million to settle Agent Orange-related cases.[8] Monsanto agreed to pay slightly over 45% of the settlement sum. However, the plaintiffs in 287 cases opted out of the class and thereby the settlement. In addition, many other veterans who were victims of Agent Orange exposure were outraged the case had been settled instead of going to trial. They felt their lawyers had betrayed them.

"Fairness Hearings" were held in five major American cities, where veterans and their families had the opportunity to voice their approval – or condemnation – of the settlement. The voices of opposition to the settlement were far more numerous and vocal than those who indicated their support. Many objected to the settlement since the $180 million settlement figure was a mere drop in the bucket considering the enormous scale of the human suffering and illness experienced by veterans exposed to Agent Orange. To other opponents of the settlement, their opposition was a form of public protest at the national indifference to Vietnam veterans. They used this cause as an organizational rallying point for their fellow veterans.

Despite the widespread opposition to the settlement, Judge Weinstein nevertheless approved it as "fair and just."[9] He also granted the defendants' motion for summary judgment in the opt-out actions. He found that "no opt-out plaintiff could prove that Agent Orange caused a particular ailment. Nor could a plaintiff prove which defendant had manufactured the Agent Orange that allegedly caused their injury, and that the military contractor defense barred all the claims."[10]

Under the military contractor defense, the chemical companies argued that they were just the vendors of the product (Agent Orange) to the United States government, which used it in waging war against enemy forces in Vietnam. As the Second Circuit Court of Appeals noted in a later review of the case:

It would be anomalous for a company to be held liable by a state or federal court for selling a product ordered by the federal government, particularly when the company could not control the use of that product. Moreover, military activities involve high stakes, and common concepts of risk averseness are of no relevance. To expose private companies generally to lawsuits for injuries arising out of the deliberately risky activities of the military would greatly impair the procurement process and perhaps national security itself.[11]

The class certification and settlement inevitably caused the number of claimants and the variety of ailments attributed to Agent Orange to climb dramatically. Soon, upwards of 240,000 veterans were claiming a portion of the settlement pie, which meant that each claimant's share kept shrinking as the ranks of the claimants swelled.

In addition, growing discord and disunity among plaintiffs and their lawyers precipitated a sharp increase in the public controversy surrounding this case. The district court and the Second Circuit judges hearing the case received correspondence from many original plaintiffs, most of whom had joined the motions for class certification. This correspondence alleged that they were never advised that the use of the class action device might lead to being represented by counsel whom they did not select and who could settle the case without consulting them.[12]

Moreover, amid this litigation, the original class counsel – Yannacone & Associates – asked to be relieved for financial reasons. The head of the law firm, Victor Yannacone Jr., was recognized by many as the "grandfather of environmental litigation," having been credited with groundbreaking legal work in the 1960s relating to the destruction caused by DDT. However, in the Agent Orange litigation, his law firm was, quite simply, going broke due to the overwhelming burden of representing the colossal plaintiff class in the case.

With the departure of Victor Yannacone as lead class counsel, legal control of the class action passed to nine lawyers who comprised the Plaintiffs' Management Committee ("P.M.C.").[13] Six of the nine members of the P.M.C. agreed to advance money for expenses, which was urgently needed since the plaintiffs' case was near collapse for lack of financial resources. This money was furnished under an ingenious but ethically troublesome agreement providing that three times the amount advanced by each lawyer would be repaid from an eventual fee award. These payments to the lawyers bankrolling the litigation would take priority over payments for legal work performed by other plaintiffs' lawyers on the case. The Second Circuit expressed the view that the P.M.C.'s fee agreement "created a conflict of interest that generated impermissible incentives on the part of class counsel to settle."[14] Nevertheless, the Second Circuit affirmed the district court's settlement approval.

In retrospect, the Agent Orange litigation showed some of the strengths and weaknesses of class action environmental litigation relating to personal injury claims. The litigation proved to be highly controversial and divisive, and the settlement amount was woefully inadequate. However, given the causation and other factual and legal weaknesses of the case, the fact that the manufacturers of Agent Orange were finally forced to pay $180 million for the injured veterans was an extraordinary result under these unique, stressful, and complex circumstances.

Williams v. Dow Chemical Co. and Pelican Pest Control

Massapequa, Long Island in New York is one of those solidly suburban towns epitomizing the American dream. In the mid-1990s, it was a town where hard-working families could still find a reasonably priced home, despite the rapidly escalating New York real estate market. The neighborhoods were made up of young families, usually with a child or two, who had abandoned New York City to raise their children in a "proper" house with good schools, parks, and beaches. For most of these families, the most significant single investment they would ever make was in their homes, and a great deal of time was spent on weekends working around the house to improve that investment. Like so many generations of Americans, to own a home meant everything. Jack and Tina Williams felt no different.

A handsome, robust, and blonde-haired man, Jack Williams looked precisely what he was: a hard-working truck driver who cared deeply about his wife and two children and did everything to provide them with as good a life as possible. He had always wanted his own business, and he was naturally drawn to lawn care, as it offered him a chance to work outside with his hands. As a young man, he was smitten when he met

Tina – a pretty, petite brunette college student. Soon after they married, their lives together were made all the richer with the birth of their first daughter, Megan.

Jack had grown up on Long Island. His brothers and parents still lived there. He was naturally drawn back to this area, and Jack and Tina agreed to move to Long Island from the upstate New York area where they met. He hoped there would be other children in time and that he would be able to give them the kind of upbringing he and Tina had themselves enjoyed, with a solid and loving family nearby. His brother was a fireman with the New York City Fire Department, and Jack was close to him and his nieces and nephews. Jack didn't have a college education, but he did have a strong work ethic and an equally strong sense that a man's duty was to provide for his family.

In 1995, when Jack and Tina found the house at 129 Boston Lane, Massapequa, it was just what they had dreamed of. Sitting on half an acre a short block or so from a beautiful park, the house had plenty of space to grow their family and start their own lawn care business. The Williamses had found the place through luck and a family connection before it even went on the market. An older couple who had raised their children in the home were retiring to the south, and they knew Jack's mother. One phone call between friends and Jack and Tina had made an offer that was quickly accepted. The home was theirs.

As with most home sales, the bank that holds the mortgage requires an inspection, including an inspection for termites. Before the closing, Pelican Pest Control assessed the property and discovered termites, which they assured the owners could be safely treated with a popular insecticide, Dursban T.C.

In 1995, Dursban T.C. was the dominant chemical insecticide, following the withdrawal of Velsicol's Chlordane from the market. Tests by the EPA had shown that the chemicals in Chlordane were dangerous to human health. When the Williamses faced the problem of ridding their new home of termites, Dursban was assumed to be a safer option than Chlordane for the extermination of termites and other bugs. This comfort level with the pesticide was due in no small part to aggressive marketing by Dow Agrosciences, the manufacturer of Dursban, which began in the late 1980s to market their pesticide as "worry-free."

The Dow marketing campaign was a huge success, with professional pesticide applicators and homeowners buying Dursban products at their local hardware or gardening store. Dow, however, failed to mention that chlorpyriphos, the "active" ingredient in Dursban, was part of the organophosphate class of chemicals designed to attack and incapacitate the nervous system. German scientists developed chlorpyriphos during World War II as part of their chemical warfare program, and the Nazis used it in the concentration camp gas chambers as part of the "final solution" to annihilate the Jewish population of Europe. The chemical organophosphate proved to be highly effective as a cholinesterase inhibitor. The chemical prevented one nerve cell from communicating with adjacent cells, incapacitating and killing its victims. Although Dow, of course, only intended it to harm termites and other insects, it also led to "collateral damage" to people exposed to it.

Pelican Pest Control applied Dursban to the Williams home in February 1995, issuing them a guarantee that the house would remain termite-free. In April 1995, the Williamses – Tina, Jack, and Megan – moved into their new home.

Over the next several years, the Williamses added two new daughters to their family: Sara and Jaclyn. Meanwhile, Tina and Jack started their lawn care business and worked hard to improve their home. Everything was going reasonably well for the Williams family. Jack was making good money driving an oil delivery truck, and together they were making a go of their lawn care business – Clean & Green. They loved the house even though they had discovered extensive termite damage, much more than the home inspection had revealed. However, it never occurred to them to sell. Instead, they renovated. Then the termites came back.

Despite Pelican Pest Control's prior guarantee, swarmers (termites with wings) would appear every spring and fall. David Kane, the President of Pelican Pest Control, was called, and he confirmed that the house was again infested. The first time he was called, he decided to put off any further insecticide treatment since Tina was pregnant. They weren't particularly concerned about the use of Dursban since they were assured it was safe, but like many pregnant women, Tina decided to err on the side of caution and put off the necessary pesticide application until after Jaclyn was born.

By March of 1998, as the annual swarmers appeared at their house, the Williams family decided it was okay to go ahead with another application of Dursban, hopefully to end the termite invasion. David Kane again came to the house, found more evidence of the termites, and scheduled two of his employees to treat the Williams' home.

What happened next and who was legally responsible became the subject of over five years of litigation, a jury trial, and seemingly endless appeals. While it was difficult to legally link some of the family's injuries to the use of Dursban, the three Williams children became chronically ill, suffering symptoms from rapidly decaying teeth to learning disabilities. Ultimately, their Boston Lane house – which had been the source of so much pride for them – had to be torn down due to the toxic contamination. The Williams family dream had turned into a nightmare, leaving them homeless and destitute.

* * *

On March 11, 1998, two Pelican Pest Control applicators arrived at 129 Boston Lane. Jack was driving an oil delivery truck, and Tina was home with the children. It was recommended that the occupants leave home during the application. After letting the Pelican Pest employees into the house, Tina took the children and a babysitter down the road to a play park. By the time she returned, approximately twenty minutes later, the application had begun. Although unversed in pesticide application, Tina was surprised to find workers had dragged the pesticide-filled hose through the house's front door, snaking it through the living room and down the cellar stairs rather than around the outside of the house and into the basement through the outside stairs. Following the hose, she went down into the basement to discover the two workmen drilling holes in the concrete floor and filling them with pesticide. She was told this was "standard operating procedure." But Tina was uneasy with all the pesticide splashing back-up over the holes as they became filled. The man filling the holes did not appear to have any way of measuring the amount of the toxic liquid splashing everywhere. Turning to one of the workers, she mentioned that the smell was pretty intense, and she asked again whether it was safe to be in the house.

At first, the Pelican applicator assured her it was fine. But as the back splashing continued and the smell got stronger, Tina told the man that the basement was generally used as a giant playpen for her kids and that she was concerned that the smell was so strong. At that point, he turned to her and said: "You didn't hear this from me, I am supposed to tell you it is perfectly safe, but if I were you, I would stay somewhere else tonight." At this point, with the work almost done, Tina left to pick up the children.

Shortly after Tina left the house, the workers packed up and departed. Jack Williams then returned home from his job, entered the house, and was immediately shocked by the chemical smell. Going to the basement where the smell was coming from, he immediately noticed cement dust everywhere. Alarmed, he tried to clean up the dust, but his teeth quickly went numb, his nose started running, and his eyes began to burn. He fled the house, fearing he would pass out, running into Tina on the driveway. He started yelling, "don't go in there – something is wrong." The Williamses left immediately and took the children to Jack's parents' house.

Jack returned home to open windows and create enough ventilation to clear the air, but the family stayed away all weekend to be on the safe side. Jack returned a day earlier than the family to try again to rid the house of the chemical smell.

When Jack returned to the house, he tried everything to decontaminate the home, but the place made him feel sick. The floors in the basement were covered with fine white dust that seemed to be everywhere, and no amount of scented candles or open windows seemed to help. On Tuesday, when the rest of the family returned, and the place was still a mess, Tina and Jack called David Kane, telling him something was very wrong. Kane soon arrived there, and the Williams noticed the first thing he did – before coming into the house – was to poke around in the bushes. He appeared to be pushing dirt around on his hands and knees for reasons the Williams at the time could not understand. It didn't much matter to Tina and Jack, as all they wanted was to fix their home. However, guessing that something was wrong with the application, they took pictures of the outside and inside points of the pesticide application. At the time, they thought the photos might help fix the problem, but as it turned out, these were very helpful in the litigation since they graphically displayed how the pesticide had been negligently applied.

Once in the house, David Kane sensed right away something was wrong. Going to the basement, he grabbed a broom and started sweeping the dust around. Later it would be determined that the sweeping had the effect of causing recontamination of the air in the house, as the dust was saturated with pesticides. The act of sweeping caused the pesticide to become airborne again.

David Kane told the Williams to go to a hotel and "have a steak dinner" on him. He also told them to find out what it would cost to clean the rugs and send him the bill. He assured them he would take care of everything and not to worry.

Because the chemical smell was so strong and nothing seemed to make it disappear, Tina decided she needed more information. She was looking for reassurance that the chemical smells – while unpleasant – were not harmful. So she called the New York State Department of Environmental Conservation ("DEC") and explained what was going on. They told her they would call her right back, but they did not until much later in the day.

After David Kane's visit and while waiting for the return call from the DEC, Tina started dinner, and Jack went down to the basement to see if Kane had made any improvement. It was March 17, 1998, St. Patrick's Day, and the traditional corned beef had been put in the oven. Around 5:30 p.m., the DEC called back. Tina was on the phone in the kitchen discussing the situation with the DEC representative when Jack came running up the basement stairs screaming, "get out, get out now. Hang up the phone. We have to get out."

Jack had been holding his youngest daughter in the basement when he became overwhelmed with chemicals. Fortunately, he was able to make it upstairs with the baby and got everyone out of the house before he passed out. This was the last day anyone lived in the house at 129 Boston Lane, Massapequa.

For the next several years, Jack and Tina tried to solve the contamination problem in their home. They called an environmental specialist, had the place tested, got estimates for decontamination, and went through every cent they had. On numerous occasions, they tried to get David Kane to make good on his promise to pay for at least some of the damages to their home but never received any compensation from him (not even the steak dinner). In addition to losing their property, they were also rapidly losing their health. The children, who had a history of sinus problems while living in the house, exhibited even more pronounced respiratory issues and other disorders. Jack and Tina were also ailing. Jack, in particular, was suffering from memory loss and had difficulty dealing with petroleum smells. While making deliveries, he became wholly disoriented and decided he had better stop driving. The result was that Jack was unable to work just when his family needed his income the most. They say that most Americans are just a paycheck or two away from total devastation, and the Williams family was no exception.

Jack and Tina Williams also reached out to Dow Chemical for information about the Dursban product to see just how dangerous it was, if at all, to human health and whether Pelican Pest Control had misapplied it at the Williams' home. In response, Dow provided them with a pamphlet entitled "I Can Smell Dursban In My Home – Does That Mean It's Dangerous?" which stated, in part:

> An important fact to know is that odor is not necessarily a sign
> of excessive or harmful concentrations of products in the air.
> Most of the odor associated with Dursban insecticides is not
> caused by the active ingredient, chlorpyrifos.

However, what Dow failed to disclose in this pamphlet was that among the non-active or "inert" ingredients that caused the odor associated with Dursban were toxic volatile organic compounds ("VOCs"): xylene and trimethylbenzene. Constituting over half the ingredients in Dursban, these chemicals posed serious dangers to human health, including damage to the nervous system, brain damage, and even death in extreme cases. In our view, statements such as those contained in the pamphlet were reasonably understood by the Williamses (and could be understood by reasonable jurors) to mean that the inert ingredients were safe and posed no health risks and that these statements were blatant misrepresentations of the dangers posed by Dursban.[15]

* * *

It would take five years for Jack and Tina to finally get their chance to get some compensation from Pelican Pest Control and Dow Chemical. When the Williamses first came into our office, they were desperate. Tina had become an advocate of sorts against the use of pesticides. Jack's health had continued to decline because of the chemical exposure, and as a result, he had become profoundly depressed and angry. He could no longer support his family, and was now without a home and virtually destitute. The Williams family had already had two sets of lawyers represent them. When they came to our firm, they had just found out that they were about to lose their right to sue the pesticide manufacturer. To their shock, their prior lawyer had never filed a complaint for them, so the statute of limitations clock was still ticking away.

We did not have time to do as thorough a due diligence investigation of the Williams' case as we would have liked to, since we had to file a complaint right away to preserve their legal rights. Based upon what we quickly learned, it seemed like a compelling case to us, and the Williams family members were so sympathetic that it was virtually impossible to say "no" to them. Like many plaintiffs who came to us, they had not been well served by prior counsel, and we had a lot to do to make up for lost time. Our experience with environmental and toxic tort cases put us in a position to make the legal system work *for* them instead of *against* them, which is too often the case.

Within days, our conference room was stacked with boxes filled with everything that had anything to do with their case against Pelican Pest Control. Over the next three years, we would add many more boxes to their file, and we started another case for them against Dursban's manufacturer, Dow Chemical Co.

Our research showed that, back in 1995, the EPA fined Dow $876,000 for failing to report hundreds of possible adverse reactions to chlorpyrifos, the active ingredient in Dursban. In 1998, testing by the New York State Department of Health at a Dursban-user's home revealed that the so-called "inert" ingredients in Dursban contained VOCs known to be hazardous to human health.

In June 2000, rather than face an adversary proceeding by the EPA investigating the safety of Dursban, Dow agreed to the EPA ban of the product for residential use. In December 2003, Dow paid a $2 million fine to the State of New York, the largest fine ever paid by a pesticide manufacturer as of that date. The fine was paid to settle an action commenced by New York State Attorney General Elliot Spitzer involving claims that Dow had distributed false and misleading information about Dursban's safety to human health and the environment.

Despite this record of admissions regarding the dangers of Dursban, Dow continued to insist in the *Williams* case and numerous other cases across the country that their product was perfectly safe, and that the complaints of lost health and ruined lives attributed to Dursban were unfounded.

* * *

Over several years, we battled the pesticide applicator – Pelican Pest Control and its owner, David Kane – in New York State Supreme Court in Nassau County. Kane and his company were just the nominal defendants in this state court case. Their insurance company, which was on the financial hook for the Williams family's injury and property damage claims, hired the law firm that defended the action.

In this case, the defense attorney was a local member of the Nassau County Bar who understood clearly that he was paid by the hour and had every intention of running the clock to the maximum extent possible. He also was a good deal younger than me and certainly much cockier. He was very sure that he could beat us at trial and was not shy about telling anyone – including me – who cared to listen to his boasting.

The trial was conducted before Judge Daniel Palmieri in the Nassau County Courthouse in Mineola, Long Island. The courthouse was in desperate need of repairs. There were pigeons nesting in the rafters of the courtroom where the trial was held, which proved to be ironic. One of the non-toxic pest control companies mentioned during the trial – also owned by David Kane – was named "Bye, Bye Birdie," which used bird netting to provide what its' brochure described as "a discreet yet effective barrier against all types of birds." Nevertheless, given the ongoing fiscal crisis at the time, Nassau County did not have the financial capability to pay for the humane removal of the pigeons, so they continued to roost there throughout the trial, occasionally cooing no doubt in appreciation of the legal drama unfolding below them.

Both Jack and Tina Williams testified at trial. I did not spend much time with either of them preparing for their testimony. They knew the facts all too well since it had destroyed their home. The house had ultimately been bulldozed due to the extensive contamination.[16] My general practice is to not "rehearse" my direct examination with a witness too much since most people are not very good actors, and a jury can quickly sense when a witness has been rehearsed. Witnesses tend, in my experience, to testify in their way no matter how hard you try to change their style or focus their testimony. If you try to counsel them to stay away from a particular area during their testimony unless specifically asked about it in cross-examination, they almost inevitably volunteer that information at some point during their examination. The truth is not easy to avoid, except in the case of a few well-practiced sociopaths who have made a career of dissembling and often lose focus on the line between truth and fiction. They can effectively fabricate a fictional story on the stand, and if they were hooked up to a lie-detector polygraph machine, it would not detect a thing. However, it is virtually inevitable at trial for the overwhelming majority of us, where testimony is subject to rigorous cross-examination, that "the truth will out," even if we try to hide it. To paraphrase Henry Kissinger, "speaking the truth is not only the right thing to do, but it is easier to remember and verifiable."

I also made it a practice not to predict the outcome of any trial, even when repeatedly asked by an anxious client. Every lawyer knows that they cannot promise or even predict a favorable outcome to the litigation. A case is much like a horserace, and I tell my clients that even though your horse is favored by 10 to 1 odds and you expect it to come in first, things can happen during a race that can lead to an unexpected outcome. Your horse can come up lame or just have a bad day. The same goes for trials.

However, many lawyers make it a practice to "lower the expectations" of their clients. That way, if they win, they anticipate that the client will be surprisingly delighted and think the lawyer had pulled off some kind of legal miracle. But this strategy too has its limitations. I once represented a plaintiff whose husband had died of undiagnosed stomach cancer. We brought a case against the decedent's closest friend, a doctor who gave him free samples of antiacids and painkillers he had lying around in his office. The doctor never once thought to order diagnostic testing for his friend until it was too late. In preparation for the trial, one of my younger colleagues was prepping the wife for her testimony at trial when I was alarmed to hear a woman's wailing coming from the conference room. I ran in to find our client on the floor of the conference room, beating her fists against the floor and crying as loud as she could. I asked my colleague what had happened. He told me that he had been trying to "lower her expectations" by telling her that it was virtually impossible that we would win the medical malpractice trial that was scheduled to start the next day. I took my colleague aside and suggested that perhaps he had lowered her expectations a bit too much. As it turned out, on the following day, the defendant doctor burst into tears on the stand when I started to cross-examine him and tearfully apologized to his dead friend's wife in front of the jury. A quick settlement was reached during a brief recess.

In the case of Tina Williams, it was also not possible for me to go over the case with her too many times since she would break down in tears every time we spoke about it. I wanted her, of course, to be as truthful and authentic at trial as possible, so I stayed away from the most painful part of her testimony until she took the stand. At trial, the courtroom was utterly still during her testimony. You could hear the proverbial pin drop. Tina held back her tears long enough to look straight at the jurors and directly convey the agony she and her family went through. She talked about the dangers of exposure to her husband and her dear children. She even talked about their pet goldfish that died from chemical exposure and about their dog, who was never quite the same again. Jack – her truly loving husband – comforted her when she finally got off the stand. He then took the stand himself, testifying about the "brain fog" and depression he faced for years after the chemical exposure at their home.

By the end of the trial, the jury had heard enough. However, the young defense lawyer was not reading the jury correctly since he acted as if he were sure of a win. He started his closing arguments to the jury by comparing me to the lead character in the film *Chicago*. "Ladies and gentlemen, do you remember the film *Chicago?* Remember how Richard Gere (the star) kept talking about "razzle-dazzle?" Well, that is what the plaintiffs' lawyer has given you, razzle-dazzle but no real facts."

I kept my closing argument short by thanking my opponent for comparing me to Richard Gere, a far better-looking man, if not more talented. I got a laugh from the jury, and I sensed that our presentation had been effective. I did not want to belabor the issues, so I concluded with a summary of the basic facts and asked the jurors to do the right thing. I tried to get the case in the jurors' hands as quickly as possible.

The jury did not disappoint. After deliberating for perhaps half an hour, they submitted a question to Judge Palmieri, which was whether they had to consider the issue of compensatory damages to the Williams family before considering the imposition of punitive damages. Punitive damages are designed to punish companies for gross negligence and impose sufficient financial pain on them so that they –and all similar companies – will take adequate preventative measures to ensure that such a failure or mistake does not happen again. Judge Palmieri told them that they would first have to consider whether the plaintiffs were entitled to an award of compensatory damages.

After a 13-day trial in May and June 2003, the jury awarded John and Tina Williams $495,000 in compensatory damages for personal injuries and property damage and $300,000 in punitive damages. Although not a particularly large award for the Williams family, it was welcomed and desperately needed. When we spoke to the jurors in the hallway after they had been dismissed with the thanks of Judge Palmieri, they told us that they wanted to give the Williams family enough to compensate them for their loss, but not too much to make it look like they had received some windfall.

The reaction of the defense lawyer was to start swearing and muttering under his breath. As soon as John and Tina Williams were in the hallway on their way to the restrooms, he confronted them, threatening that they "would never see a dime" of the money because he was going to get the verdict reversed on appeal.

Unfortunately, he was half right. After the appeal worked its way through the Appellate Division, Second Department, located in downtown Brooklyn, the appellate court handed down its written opinion on October 4, 2004. On the bright side, the court upheld the award of compensatory damages, explaining that a jury verdict should not be set aside as against the weight of the evidence "unless 'the jury could not have reached the verdict on any fair interpretation of the evidence.'"[17] Applying this standard of review to this case, the Second Department found that "the jury could have concluded, based on a fair interpretation of the evidence, that the defendant was negligent and that its negligence was the proximate cause of the plaintiffs' injuries."[18]

However, as to its review of the jury verdict regarding punitive damages, the court dropped a bombshell on us, finding as follows:

> However, as to the plaintiffs' claims for punitive damages, the awards were not supported by sufficient evidence and therefore should have been set aside [citations omitted]. The plaintiffs failed to establish that the defendant's conduct was so gross, wanton, or willful, or of such high moral culpability, as to justify awards of punitive damages [citations omitted].[19]

We, of course, disagreed with the appellate court's dismissal of the punitive damages verdict, which the trial jury had obviously felt very strongly about. Nevertheless, the Williams family was anxious to get this matter behind them so that they could finally receive some compensation from the defendants' insurance company, which would go a long way to helping them rebuild their lives.

But the defense lawyer who had shouted at John and Tina Williams that they would never receive the award money continued his campaign to delay the insurance company's payments due to the plaintiffs. In a letter dated October 29, 2004, he claimed that Jack and Tina Williams had not been paid the amount awarded by the Appellate Division because there was a "charging lien" by the Williams family's former attorney against the judgment amount due to them. Although there is nothing in New York law to support the view that an attorney's lien is a basis for withholding the entire amount due under a judgment, defense counsel continued to use this as an excuse for the insurance company's non-payment. He even went so far as to personally attack me, claiming that I was to blame for the delay because I had taken a "Scrooge-like approach" in negotiating with the plaintiffs' former attorney. He added that my failure to resolve the issue with this attorney "will surely ruin Christmas for the Williams family."

The defense lawyer further promised to testify on behalf of the prior attorney if there was ever a court hearing regarding the prior lawyer's legal services. In a blatant attempt to continue depriving Mr. and Mrs. Williams of the judgment monies to which they were entitled, the defense attorney also threatened to deposit all of the award monies into court, snidely asserting: "Based upon my own past experience, getting money out of Court can be much more difficult than paying it into Court." He implied that, unless the Williams family agreed to pay their prior lawyer what they considered to be an excessive amount of money out of their judgment award, the Williams family would be unlikely to see any of the funds for the foreseeable future.

Unfortunately for the defense lawyer, the issue was quickly resolved in the Williams family's favor. They finally got the money to which they were more than entitled.

* * *

While pursuing the *Williams* case in New York state court against Pelican Pest Control, we filed a federal class action on behalf of the Williams family and other similarly situated families against Dow Chemical in the U.S. District Court for the Southern District of New York.[20] The class action complaint, filed on May 5, 2001, alleged that Dow had fraudulently obtained approval from the EPA for the use and sale of Dursban. In all, seven individual plaintiffs were suing on behalf of themselves, their children, and two nationwide classes. The first class consisted of all children under eighteen who were "exposed to Dursban products and who had symptoms consistent with chemical poisoning." The second class consisted of all persons who "have suffered an injury to their employment, business and/or property" from exposure to Dursban.

On August 27, 2001, on behalf of the plaintiffs, we filed an Amended Class Action Complaint, adding as a defendant Dow AgroSciences, L.L.C. ("Dow AgroSciences"), the Dow subsidiary that manufactures Dursban. We also added claims for conspiracy and racketeering in violation of the Racketeer Influencing Corrupt Organizations Act ("RICO").[21]

On November 8, 2001, Dow and Dow AgroSciences filed a motion for judgment on the pleadings according to Rule 12(c) of the Federal Rules of Civil Procedure ("F.R.Civ.P.") and a motion for summary judgment under Rule 56. We then sought (and were granted) leave to submit a Second Amended Complaint rather than respond to the motion. The Second Amended Complaint added nine new causes of action, including claims of false advertising under the Lanham Act, intentional and negligent misrepresentation under state law, and breach of express warranty under state law.[22]

In our Second Amended Complaint, plaintiffs explained that Dursban was a pesticide developed and patented by Dow in 1965. Between 1965 and 2000, Dursban became one of the most widely used pesticides in the United States, used in products ranging from pet collars to roach spray. Between 1965 and 1989, Dow was responsible for all research, testing, marketing, manufacture, and sale of Dursban products in the United States.

In 1981, Dursban became subject to the registration requirements of the Federal Insecticide, Fungicide, and Rodenticide Act ("FIFRA"), which provides that no pesticide may be sold or distributed in the United States unless the EPA has first registered it.[23] We alleged in our complaint that Dow, to get its Dursban product registered with the EPA, engaged in a racketeering conspiracy and fraudulent scheme to mislead the public and consumers (as well as the EPA) about the safety of Dursban.[24] We further alleged that Dow was part of a racketeering enterprise that included numerous pesticide applicators across the United States, such as Terminix,

Although Cirque du Soleil Canada is the primary Company in the Cirque family of related companies, Cirque Du Soleil America, Inc. is the primary Cirque operating company in the United States.

By June of 2007, John Goodwin was transferred to Cirque Du Soleil America to join the production of Quidam as a Director. Quidam was touring in Asia at the time, where it had a longstanding run of performances in Shanghai, China. John's office was in a newly constructed, semi-permanent structure designed and built by Cirque with a contractor under the supervision of Cirque.

This central office area, where Goodwin worked, was defectively constructed in that there were no thresholds under the doors to prevent water from entering the office in the event of a rainstorm. The electric cables that supplied power to the office equipment ran through a hole cut into the exterior wall, approximately six inches in diameter and about eight inches above the floor. The main electrical cables then ran along the floor where there was frequent foot traffic. An electric distribution box was the primary power source for the office. There were no warning or danger signs in the office that would warn people regarding the dangers posed by the electrical equipment.

In addition, the electrical equipment in the office where John worked was not equipped with Ground Fault Interrupt (GFI) breakers designed to detect water infiltration between connections or to detect a ground fault. Nor was there an RCD breaker present in the distribution box. Some electrical equipment, including a 30-amp load center and one 30-amp twist-lock connector, were not placed high enough to avoid being flooded should water come into the office. Significant rainstorms were not uncommon in Shanghai, and the electrical setup was precarious.

In mid-June 2007, a Shanghai rainstorm not surprisingly led to water leaking into the office through the hole in the exterior wall and underneath the office door. Shortly after that, on June 28, 2007, a second severe rainstorm hit Shanghai. The water again started leaking into the office through the same openings, mainly the hole in the exterior wall and underneath the office door. In response to this, John Goodwin began to remove bags and other items from the office floor to avoid getting them wet. After picking up a plastic bag from behind one of the desks in the office, John picked up the electrical distribution box, which was also on the floor, with both hands. The distribution box had a metal handle

Orkin, and Pelican Pest Control, who distributed false and misleading pamphlets and informational materials provided them by Dow.[25]

Dow's elaborate attempts to avoid making complete and truthful disclosures to the federal regulators were not, however, entirely successful. In August 1995, after Dow failed to provide "adverse incident reports" to the EPA required under FIFRA, the EPA hit Dow with an $876,000 fine for failing to inform it about reports of 249 Dursban poisoning cases it had received.[26] Even when Dow submitted adverse incident reports to the EPA about Dursban poisonings, our research indicated that many if not most of these disclosures were inaccurate or misleading.[27]

By 1999, enough adverse incident reports and scientific data about products containing chlorpyrifos had come to light. The EPA entered into negotiations with pesticide manufacturers, including Dow, to compel them to voluntarily withdraw or phase out the use of products containing chlorpyrifos in the United States.[28] On June 8, 2000, the EPA reached an agreement with Dow to restrict virtually all residential usage of Dursban and phase out the product's residential and commercial sales. As part of that agreement, the EPA canceled the FIFRA registration of several Dursban products, effective December 1, 2000.[29] However, the settlement left a massive loophole in that it did not order retail products containing Dursban to be pulled from store shelves. This substantial loophole allowed Pelican Pest Control to use Dursban on the Williams house, with disastrous consequences.

After Dow filed a motion to dismiss our complaint, District Court Judge Richard M. Berman issued his opinion on March 21, 2003, granting Dow's motion in part and denying it in part.[30] Concerning our civil RICO claims against Dow, the district court found that the civil RICO statute only allows for the recovery lost money or property. It "does not provide recovery for physical and emotional injuries."[31]

In addition, Judge Berman's decision found that the fraudulent statements and concealments we alleged in our complaint were directed by the Dow defendants at the EPA, not the Williams family or other consumers. It thus did not constitute "racketeering activity" within the meaning of the RICO statute.[32] Judge Berman's decision also held that plaintiffs' allegations of fraud on the EPA could not be considered racketeering activity. He concluded that the alleged scheme was designed to obtain

EPA regulatory approval of Dursban, not to deprive the EPA of "money or property" as required by the RICO statute.

Although Judge Berman dismissed plaintiffs' RICO, Lanham Act, and express warranty claims, he ruled that plaintiffs' misrepresentation and injunction claims should only be dismissed in part, which meant that these causes of action substantially survived. We also prevailed as to our argument that the court should grant an injunction requiring disclosure by Dow of "medical research and toxicology information" about Dursban. The court found that this requested injunctive relief would survive the motion to dismiss because this relief would not necessarily "conflict with, and therefore be preempted by, the labeling provisions of FIFRA."[33]

Judge Berman further noted that the defendants' motion did not challenge many of the plaintiffs' claims, including our claims for public nuisance, civil conspiracy, negligent testing, design and formulation; strict liability-ultra-hazardous activity; and violation of the New York State General Business Law, Section 349. As a result, when the dust finally settled, much of our case still survived, and we were ready to move the case forward to trial.

Faced with a formidable set of claims still pending against it, Dow quickly entered into settlement discussions with us. Shortly after that, a confidential settlement was entered into between plaintiffs and Dow. However, Dow insisted on calling it a "resolution" rather than a "settlement" so that it could continue to publicly claim that the company had never "settled" a Dursban claim. But no matter what you call it, plaintiffs and their counsel felt that it brought this complex litigation to a satisfactory conclusion.

Chapter 14
The Cirque du Soleil Case

John Goodwin was born in Manchester, England, to Irish parents, who moved the family back to their native county Mayo in the 1980s. By the time he graduated from Oxford, he had already made a name in the theatrical production field. John's creative talents came as no surprise since he came from a highly creative family. His grandparents owned the famous Goodwin's dance hall in Bonniconlon, County Mayo, and his father was an award-winning traditional Irish musician with the Boifiled Ceili Band.

In 1995 John was hired by Cirque de Soleil Europe. Headquartered in Montreal, Cirque de Soleil is the most prominent contemporary circus producer globally. The Company was founded in June 1984 by former street performers Guy Laliberté and Gilles Ste-Croix. Originating as a performance troupe, they toured Quebec in various forms between 1979 and 1983. The pair received significant financing in 1983 through a government grant from the Canada Council for the Arts to perform as part of the 450th-anniversary celebrations of Jacques Cartier's voyage to Canada. Their first official production- Le Grand Tour du Cirque du Soleil- was a success in 1984. After securing a second year of funding Laliberté hired Guy Caron from the National Circus School to recreate Cirque as a "proper circus." Its theatrical, character-driven approach and the absence of performing animals helped define Cirque du Soleil as contemporary circus ("nouveau cirque") that it remains today.

Cirque du Soleil expanded rapidly through the 1990s and 2000s, growing from one show to 19 shows in over 300 cities on six continents. The Company employed 4,900 people from 50 countries and generated approximately $1 billion annual revenue by 2017. The multiple permanent Las Vegas shows alone played to more than 9,000 people and 5% of the City's visitors. Over 100 million people have seen Cirque du Soleil productions worldwide.

attached to the top structure of the box, which made it easy to pick up and suggested, to John and others, that it was designed to be picked up for ease of movement from one place to another.

The result of this well-intentioned attempt to protect equipment from damage led to John receiving a massive electrical shock. It was so intense he couldn't let go of the box. Another person working in the office hit John's elbow and eventually jarred his arm enough to break the grip on the electric distribution box. In so doing, this person also received a shock, as the electricity moving through John's body was quite powerful.

According to an eyewitness, Shauna Fitgerald, "John seemed to me to be dazed and in a mild state of shock. He appeared very pale and was shaking." Similarly, another witness, Lucy Ifrah, Cirque's Transport & Lodging Coordinator, reported that she saw John "collapsed onto his knees." Ifrah further noted: "He was conscient but very pale and shaky. It seems like he was on the verge of passing out, but he kept patting his chest, fingers, and holding his head in his hands." John told Ifrah "that he felt the shock go through his body and that his hands and arms were numb; he also mentioned the pain inside his chest."

There was no first aid box or equipment on site. In Shanghai, Michael Cummings, Cirque's Head of Security, caused unnecessary delay and confusion by telling those present that "a Chinese lady [would] take care of John because she was a doctor." When Lucy Ifrah and the other witnesses finally realized that the "Chinese lady" was *not* a doctor, John was sent to a local hospital in a private automobile. According to the Incident Report, "Mr. Goodwin was kept in overnight [for observation] due to the result of an irregular heartbeat."

The doctors who treated Goodwin at Shanghai East International Medical Center advised him that the electrical shock caused problems with his heartbeat, and it was likely that he had also suffered some neurological damage caused by the electrocution. They advised him that he would need further medical attention and treatment. He spent approximately 24 hours in the hospital, where he was diagnosed as having an "Abnormal ECG," namely an "Abnormal left axis deviation."

On August 24, 2007, John traveled to the United States for further treatment, first seeing doctors at John Hopkins Medical Center in Baltimore, Maryland. According to the medical notes, John reported having "a generalized numbness, which affected both arms and legs on both sides and subsequently this numbness gradually diminished to a point where he still has some numbness in the fingertips and the toe tips. He also still feels generally weaker."

The Johns Hopkins "Clinic Note" found the following:

> One of his greatest complaints which did not improve since the incident was that he is unable to perform his duties because of apparent cognitive difficulties. He has low levels of energy. He feels 'drained' and 'dazed' and 'energy and power sucked out of him. Apparently, Mr. Goodwin's post-electric-shock syndrome is not recovering or improving at the pace he was hoping for. He has not had much in terms of neurological workup and assessment as far [as] he is concerned. It is well known that patients can experience cognitive changes after electric shocks.

The following day John underwent a battery of tests. Based upon this testing, Dr. Schrenen of Johns Hopkins Medical Center concluded that he had "a cognitive disorder" with "selective impairments of sustained attention, choice reaction time, word list generation and learning/memory for both verbal and visual material. He also showed mild psychomotor slowing and borderline working memory on some tasks."

Upon his return to New York, John underwent extensive testing and long-term treatment for brain injury rehabilitation. For example, on November 14, 2007, he underwent EMG testing at Rehabilitation Medicine Associates in Manhattan, who found his EMG test results to be "Abnormal" and "consistent with some literature after electrical injury."

John also participated in an extensive treatment program at Mt. Sinai Hospital, which lasted 26 weeks, five days per week. As outlined in a letter dated April 25, 2008, by Dr. Wayne Gordon of Mt. Sinai, "the treatment is intended to improve attention, executive functions, and management of emotions in individuals with brain injuries." Dr. Gordon compared John's condition to a patient who suffered from Traumatic Brain Injury ("TBI") from a concussion or similar head injury.

Dr. Gordon further noted that John was, in his professional opinion, "totally disabled":

> [John Goodwin] continues to experience physical and cognitive deficits that interfere with task performance and render him totally disabled. His physical problems include debilitating headaches and neurologic pain in the limbs, vision problems,

and significant fatigue. His cognitive deficits include problems with attention and multitasking, especially in high-stimulation environments. Diminished attention, pain, and fatigue interfere with Mr. Goodwin's decision making, planning, and organizational abilities in his daily life and would affect his work performance negatively. Given the extent of his deficits, Mr. Goodwin is unable at present to return to work and perform material and substantial duties on a full-time basis in his prior position.

The Investigation

Although we served Cirque with a discovery demand seeking all relevant documents immediately after filing and serving the Complaint in the case, and followed up these with additional written demands on December 6, 2010, Cirque ignored these discovery requests for over a year. Finally, we brought a motion to compel discovery, which Judge Judith J. Gische granted in a written decision dated May 14, 2012.[1] Soon after that, we received from Cirque the "smoking gun" that John Goodwin had told us all along that Cirque had been hiding. There was an "Incident Report" prepared by a Cirque employee, basically admitting responsibility for the negligent design and construction of the electrical system for the Shanghai show. Entitled "Report on the electric shock incident of Mr. John Goodwin [on June 28, 2007]" prepared by Yannick Chapidos, a Senior Electrician employed by Cirque, the Incident report confirmed that the electrical equipment was defectively designed and installed. It was not equipped with Ground Fault Interrupt (GFI) breakers designed to detect water infiltration between connections or to detect a ground fault. In the section of the Report entitled "Possible causes of the incident," the electrical investigator concluded as follows:

> After I put all the results of all the tests together and the statements of the witnesses at the scene, I believe that the incident was caused by water infiltration inside the 30-amp twist lock connector sitting on the floor in a puddle of water. The water possibly reached the level of the plug where the water can short between phases and the ground, making the load center "live."

The Report also found the cause of the incident was that "the entire electrical infrastructure . . .is not equipped with Ground Fault Interrupt breakers." In addition, the report noted that "[w]e discovered that there is no protection system against water infiltration in electrical connections." Further, although there was a "breaker" in place that would "trip if the load goes higher than 30 amps, this breaker is not made to detect water infiltration between connections or to detect a ground fault."

In addition, Cirque was finally forced to produce to us a "Project Postmortem" prepared in October 2007, succinctly summarizing Cirque's negligent construction of the Shanghai tour facilities, concluding that "it was doubtful that the structures could withstand, without constant care, the [wear and tear] resulting from an operation to the scale of a touring show."

The Litigation

Although Cirque du Soleil vigorously defended the action filed in New York State Supreme Court, they could not overcome our core argument, which was that Cirque was responsible for the negligently installed electrical system that was directly responsible for John Goodwin's injuries. Cirque's own "Incident Report" supported the argument.

When Cirque was finally forced to turn over their documents to us, they provided further evidence that Cirque failed to fulfill the duty that was owed to John. Under the law of almost all jurisdictions, employees are entitled to a reasonably safe working environment, free of the risk of electrical shocks and other hazards that may cause serious injury. Cirque had violated this duty of care to John and its other employees by failing to follow the electrical safety guidelines its touring shows were required to follow. Because of this, we were able to establish that there was a serious risk that the electrical system would malfunction every time the leaking water reached the electrical equipment.

We also gathered evidence indicating that Cirque senior personnel were on notice that water had flooded into the office during previous rainstorms and posed a severe health and safety risk, especially given the presence of live electrical equipment on the office floor. Nevertheless, the evidence clearly showed they had failed to take any action to correct this dangerous situation. In particular, it was clear that the electrical equipment sitting on the floor was risky and inferior, a problem that became extremely hazardous given the presence of water whenever it rained.

Despite the overwhelming evidence of negligence against it, Cirque made a last-ditch effort to have our Complaint dismissed by filing a motion for summary judgment. They argued that the case – involving an injury to a U.K. national injured halfway around the globe from New York - should not be tried in the New York courts. Cirque further argued that, since John had been injured on the job, his claims should have been brought under the Worker's Compensation Law, not New York common and statutory law.

On May 14, 2012, Judge Judith Gische denied Cirque's motion for summary judgment, finding that "plaintiff's choice of forum [in the New York courts] is entitled to great deference," and that Goodwin had established that his residency was in New York for at least the past several years. Even though the incident in question was in China, it would make more sense to require Cirque to defend the case in New York and pay for the travel expenses of out-of-state and out-of-country witnesses, than to require John Goodwin to prosecute the case in China. Judge Gische found that Cirque was "guilty of laches," in that it had waited over three years from the filing of the plaintiff's Complaint to make the motion for a change of venue, so it had forfeited its right to claim that New York was an "inconvenient forum."

Cirque's argument that John's claim should have been brought in a workers' compensation court was also rejected by Judge Gische. The court's opinion recognized that, generally speaking, New York's Workers' Compensation Law was the exclusive remedy whenever an employee sustained a work-related injury. However, Cirque had not provided workers' compensation coverage to Goodwin, so it could not now claim that he was barred from suing Cirque in a court of law.

Mediation and Damages

Even though the case dragged on for several years, John's medical care and therapy on a nearly continuous basis did not significantly improve his condition. He continued to suffer from pain in the joint areas, debilitating headaches, diminished cognitive and mental capacity in the form of confusion, inability to focus, loss of memory, extreme exhaustion, and fatigue. His doctors also advised him that his "synaptic response" had been permanently damaged, and he continued to suffer from "peripheral nerve/

muscle damage." Whenever I met with him, John wore dark sunglasses since he was highly light-sensitive, and I noticed that he was having difficulty focusing on any subject matter for more than a couple of minutes. His mind tended to wander, and he frequently became too exhausted to continue without a long break.

Increasingly, I became worried that John's condition was so fragile that he would not be able to undergo an extended trial in court before a jury. Therefore, I recommended that we explore the possibility of settling the case with the assistance of a professional mediator, which is usually a retired judge or well-respected attorney with mediation experience. While mediation is "non-binding," in the sense that neither party has to agree to settle, mediations are often successful since both parties have to agree to it and come to the table with at least, theoretically, some motivation to settle the case out of court.

When John agreed to my proposal, I contacted the attorneys for Cirque, who consulted with their client and got back to me with a positive response. The mediation group we chose was JAMS, formerly known as Judicial Arbitration and Mediation Services, Inc., which was (and still is) a U.S.–based for-profit organization of alternative dispute resolution services, including mediation.

To prepare for the mediation, we had to calculate Goodwin's damages. We retained the services of Smith Economics Group, Ltd., a well-respected national and international economic consulting group that had regularly prepared damages calculations for me and my firm in almost every case we had. Stan V. Smith, Ph.D., based in Chicago, and Stephanie Uhl, his senior staff member, had become pretty good friends and colleagues over the years, having worked closely together on numerous 9/11 and Flight 587 cases, among many others.

It is difficult to put a dollar number on the physical, emotional, and psychological damages. Regardless of what a person suffers as a result of a personal injury from electrical shock or other cause, the law requires that a jury or other factfinder come up with a dollar number of damages if they find that a plaintiff is entitled to such an award. Most plaintiffs would settle for turning back the clock and restoring them to their prior total health, but neither a judge nor any other mortal can do this. As a result, all we can do is to provide a plaintiff with money damages.

Stan Smith and Stephanie Uhl started their analysis by interviewing John Goodwin and finding out that he made about $135,000 in the last year before his injury. He was also entitled to a bonus of between $12,000 and $15,000 based on his performance evaluation. The last paycheck he received was for the pay period ending July 7, 2007. Cirque also paid for his housing when he was traveling, which was 365 days per year as of the time he was injured. He would either have a room in a four or 5-star hotel or a 1 to 2 bedroom apartment. Cirque also paid for his meals when he was touring. In all, his total yearly compensation was computed to be $213,673 a year. Since he was born in December 1970 and injured on June 28, 2007, he was 36.5 years old as of the date of injury. Assuming he would have been employed full-time until age 72, his lost income was, therefore, $7,403,499.00. Since he received $120,000 in disability benefits as of the date of Stan Smith's Report (February 19, 2013), his net loss of earning capacity due to his injuries was $7,283,499.00, taking into account his disability income offset.

If this case had gone to trial in New York, a jury would likely have also been permitted to award him damages for lost "use and enjoyment" of life. Since he could not do everything he had previously done and had fairly constant headaches and other pains, there could be little question that John had suffered damages over and above his lost income. However, arriving at what that number should be can be tricky. Although I usually had Smith Economics Group calculate "reduction in the value of life" for each plaintiff I represented, judges rarely, if ever, permitted an expert economist to testify at trial as to those numbers. Most juries – or at least in New York – are left to their own life experiences and sound judgment to arrive at such non-economic damage numbers without the aid of an expert witness.

Nevertheless, for mediation purposes, in this case, I asked Stan Smith to calculate these "hedonic" (lost enjoyment of life) damages, which he figured to be about $3,136,593.00 throughout John Goodwin's life. This calculation was done by first estimating the total value of a year of full enjoyment of life (economists put numbers on this, believe it or not). Economist T. R. Miller, for example, studied the results of 67 different estimates of the value of life published by economists in peer-reviewed academic journals.[2] Miller concluded that the estimates of the annual value of life ranged from approximately $1.6 million to $2.9 million in

1988 after-tax dollars, with a mean of roughly $2.2 million.[3] Many economists, including Stan Smith, take a much more conservative approach to arrive at this annual figure, as he did in this case.

In calculating the percentage loss of that enjoyment value of life for any particular plaintiff, you would first estimate what percentage that person lost with regard to their enjoyment of life and then make a simple calculation to determine their loss. For example, if a person lost one-half (50%) of their ability to enjoy life, then the loss per year for this category of losses would be 50% of the number you estimate to be the full value of a year's worth of life enjoyment. Many judges consider such calculations to be far-fetched. But, it is important to note that this methodology is employed by the U.S. Government as the standard and recommended approach for the use by all U.S. agencies in valuing life for policy purposes, as mandated in current and part Presidential Executive Orders in effect since 1972.

* * *

At the JAMS mediation in Manhattan, the Cirque representative took a fairly aggressive approach at the start of the mediation. I had told the mediator in confidence that I anticipated that, given the strength of his case and the extensive permanent damages he had suffered, it was unlikely that Mr. Goodwin would settle for a number less than several million dollars. I gave the mediator a specific number, but I cannot disclose the exact settlement numbers discussed or ultimately agreed upon since the mediation was confidential. Apparently, the mediator had shared my number with the other side because the Cirque representatives' first words were not "hello," but "If you think you are going to walk out of here with x millions of dollars, you are sadly mistaken."

This was something of a tactical error on Cirque's part since I took it (correctly as it turned out) to be an unintended signal that the Company would be willing to go to that number – albeit painfully. At the end of the day of mediation, the settlement agreed upon was precisely the number that Cirque said it would never pay.

* * *

John eventually recovered sufficiently to use some of the settlement funds to start his own production company based in Dublin. He also purchased a spectacular three-bedroom penthouse apartment in the Dockside area of Dublin, with a panoramic view of the harbor. The apartment was featured in the hit U.S. show, "House Hunters International."

In September 2021, after deciding to relocate back to his native county of Mayo in the west of Ireland, John used his creative juices to develop a unique way to sell his apartment. He set up a lottery system, whereby anyone could buy a lottery ticket for 58 euros (about $65), with the winner getting title to the apartment. Explaining the inspiration behind the prize draw to the Connaught Telegraph, he said: "Last year during the lockdown, a young Brazilian food delivery cyclist was killed in a hit-and-run close to my home in Dublin. The tragic circumstances hit me hard and led me to realize that life can end in a flash."[4] John set up a fundraiser online and raised almost €14,000 to donate to the young man's fiancé, helping her and his family with the funeral costs.

* * *

As fate would have it, I myself experienced what it was like to receive a substantial jolt of electricity while sailing with my family on Long Island Sound. I received a massive shock when I touched a metal fitting during an electrical storm. I later learned that the ship's electrical system had malfunctioned due to what is known as "reverse polarity," causing an electrical current to run through metal parts of the ship. I was able to pull my hand away and never lost consciousness, so I considered myself fortunate not to have experienced what John Goodwin had gone through.

However, my sense of relief was short-lived. When we returned to our home port in Mamaroneck, New York, I experienced a complete cardiac arrest. My wife's attempts to get an EMT or ambulance service to come were painfully slow since there had been several other emergencies in the area. About twelve minutes later, a police car arrived, fortunately with a defibrillator, but the officers could not revive me during their first few tries. One of the officers guided my wife out of the room and asked her to call a family member since my prognosis was looking rather bleak.

Finally, the officers succeeded in jump-starting my heart, but my breathing was shallow and very weak. I was still unconscious and would remain so for the next three days. I was transported by ambulance to Sound Shore Hospital in New Rochelle. Fortuitously, a hypothermal unit had been anonymously donated to the hospital only a couple of weeks earlier. I was the first patient to be placed in the unit, which lowered the body temperature. The theory is that, by lowering the body temperature, the deterioration and loss of brain cells is slowed since the brain starts to shut down, and brain cells tend to start dying off when deprived of oxygen and blood flow for an extended period. To keep the body from shivering and shaking, I was given a paralytic drug so that I could not move, even involuntarily.

As the cardiologists later explained to me, the electrical charge had caused a chunk of plaque in one of my arteries to break loose, and when it found its way to my heart, it got stuck in my heart valve, causing the total cardiac arrest. As the doctors explained to my wife Susan, there was about a 50-50 chance that I would never recover consciousness, and if I did, I might well be in a semi-vegetative state. But she never believed it, staying by my bedside non-stop for three days and refusing to have me given "last rights" by a priest, since she was sure I would miraculously recover.

Since I was always a big believer in organ donation, the hospital had already put out an alert as to my condition, and there was a growing list of potential recipients for my more prized body parts. But, it was not to be. I could not accommodate any of these worthy recipients. Unbeknown to us, I was the first to receive – and then recover – with aid of the hypo-thermal treatment. Because of my unexpected recovery, I became a hospital celebrity. The doctors were rather surprised (and hopefully delighted) by my recovery since I was quickly speaking in full sentences, and was clearly not the drooling, incoherent vegetable they were expecting. My wife wasn't so sure I was "all there," since after I regained consciousness, I couldn't remember her name and, instead, used my first wife's name. This must have been pretty painful for her, after her three-day vigil by my side, but she seemed genuinely pleased to have me back anyway.

One of the doctors suggested that I must have been brought back for a reason. To this, my 95-year-old mother piped up, saying, "Of course he was brought back for a reason – to take care of his old mom!" The fact that we had a four-year-old son at the time was clearly a secondary con-sideration. After being transferred to Columbia Presbyterian Hospital, and after some extensive surgery, I was anxious to get out of the hospital and back to work, but the medical staff refused to release me for at least several days.

In late 2019, to celebrate my full recovery, and just a few months before the Covid-19 pandemic hit and the world went into lockdown, I had the opportunity to return to Ireland to visit with some of my Irish relatives and friends. Although I was born in the Bronx, grew up in Pelham, and lived almost my entire life in the U.S., I had fond memories of the summer trips that my family had made to Ireland. I also wanted to introduce our youngest son, Foard, to the Emerald Isle for the first time. He had developed a keen interest in the Titanic in middle school. The ship had been built in Belfast, not far from where the McCallion Clan originated, and still flourished in County Tyrone. Susan, Foard, and I visited the superb Titanic Museum there and then took a "black cab" tour of the areas of Belfast that had been hardest hit by the sectarian "Troubles" of the late 20th Century. The City was sharply divided between intermittently warring Irish Catholics and Protestant "Orangemen," who vehemently opposed any reunification of Northern Ireland with the Republic of Ireland to its south and west. When I grew up and spent some summers in Ireland with relatives, many of these communities in Belfast were "no-go" areas that I had never been allowed to visit before.

Returning to Dublin, we toured the Four Courts on the River Liffey, where, as a young lawyer, I had briefly had the opportunity to assist some Irish barristers with a significant environmental case pending in those historic courts. This was shortly after Ireland had joined the European Union in 1973. Since my grandparents had been born in Ireland, I had been eligible for Irish citizenship and could also get an E.U. passport. We also visited Trinity College Dublin and its law school, where we had lunch at the faculty dining room there with an old colleague, Professor William Binchy. We then went to the Waterloo Pub on Baggot Street, one of several pubs owned by the Quinn brothers in Dublin. I had gotten to know Frank, Michael, and Sean Quinn quite well when they owned an Irish pub in Manhattan – The Irish Times – and we had kept in close touch over the years.

I had asked John Goodwin if he could join us "for a pint" at the Waterloo, and sure enough, John stopped by with his nephew, who was studying law in Dublin at the time. It was great to spend a few hours with him, learning more about his creative projects and the charitable work he was doing. Not every plaintiff who suddenly comes into some money through a settlement, judgment, or award spends it wisely, despite our best efforts to steer them onto a prudent financial course. But in John's case, it was heartwarming to see that the Cirque settlement had allowed him to get his life back on track.

Chapter 15

The MTBE and KeySpan Cases

Environmental Groundwater Pollution

Since the industrial revolution, manufacturing companies generally released toxic waste into the environment with impunity, with little or no risk of penalty. However, in recent decades, environmental laws and more assertive environmental litigation have held polluters to a more responsible standard.

I and others in my law firm were involved in many of the major environmental pollution cases over the years, including cases involving "coal tar" pollution by Manufactured Gas Plants ("MGP") against KeySpan Corp. and related companies. Another major case we handled involved groundwater contamination by the gasoline additive methyl tertiary butyl ether ("MTBE") produced by gasoline manufacturers.

The KeySpan MGP Cases

From the late 1800s to the mid-1900s, hundreds of manufactured gas plants ("MGPs") across New York State supplied homes and industry fuel for heating, cooking, and lighting. The manufactured gas was produced through the compression of coal. Some less-volatile chemical compounds would condense as the manufactured gas cooled to form a complex oily liquid mixture commonly called "coal tar." Some coal tar residue was used for building materials, but most was discarded. Little thought was given at the time to the catastrophic environmental consequences when this MGP waste contaminated the groundwater and, consequently, the water supplies of thousands of homes and properties in dozens of communities.

KeySpan Corp, the electric and gas utility company servicing most of Long Island,[1] owned and controlled several former Manufactured Gas Plant ("MGP") sites, including one located in Bay Shore, Long Island, a working-class community comprised mainly of modestly priced homes with small yards, as well as small businesses serving the community.

On September 30, 1999, KeySpan entered a Consent Order with the New York State Department of Environmental Conservation ("DEC").[2] It agreed to implement an investigation and Remedial Response Program for the abandoned Bay Shore MGP site. It also agreed to clean up and remediate six other sites on Long Island. However, for the next seven years, KeySpan performed no physical remediation at the Bay Shore MGP site until it started to excavate the contaminated area in 2007.

Also in 2007, attorney Irving Like and his law firm – Reilly, Like & Tenety - started to investigate the matter on behalf of Bay Shore property owners and small businesses impacted by the MGP groundwater contamination. Based on this investigation, evidence was uncovered that KeySpan had known of the contamination and environmental problems posed by the leaking of MGP waste into the groundwater for many years, if not decades, and that it also knew that a sizeable underground plume of MGP waste had silently been spreading throughout the community. For example, documents were obtained indicating that KeySpan's predecessor – the Long Island Lighting Company ("LILCO") - was well aware of reports from its engineering department as far back as 1977 of significant Bay Shore MGP site soil and groundwater contamination.[3] Evidence also emerged that the Malcolm Pirnie engineering firm warned in 1993 that the Bayshore MGP site could be highly hazardous based on its possible risk to the sole source drinking water aquifer. One LILCO witness, Steven Dalton, had also testified at a deposition that it was his company's practice to intentionally dump coal tar residue into a coal tar pit with a dirt bottom. This process caused the contaminants to leak through the soil and into the groundwater.[4] Dalton also admitted that polluted water was discharged from the MGP site into surface waters, violating a permit to release unpolluted water.

Irving Like and his partner, Vincent Tenety, asked my law firm to join them as co-counsel for the plaintiffs in the numerous cases they were filing against KeySpan at the courthouse in Riverhead of the New York State Supreme Court, Suffolk County. The complaints alleged that KeySpan's predecessor (LILCO) had been grossly negligent in the disposal of the MGP waste from the Bay Shore plant and that the groundwater contamination also had contaminated the homes and properties of the homeowners in the path of the toxic underground plumes. This posed a serious risk to the health and well-being of the homeowners and their families. We also alleged in the complaints that the remediation work performed by KeySpan and its contractors substantially interfered with the rights of the homeowners to the quiet use and enjoyment of their properties. These property rights were being violated by the constant noise, vibrations, increased traffic and other activities associated with the clean-up. These activities, we alleged, constituted a public and private nuisance, for which the homeowners were entitled to receive compensation.

As KeySpan and the New York State Dept. of Environmental Conservation ("DEC") developed maps of the location and scope of the underground MGP contaminated "plumes," it soon became readily apparent that the contaminated groundwater plumes were far more widespread than initially estimated. The maps showed that the contamination extended not only to residential properties in the area but also to affordable housing projects, businesses, and places of public assembly, including the St. Patrick's Parish, North Clinton Avenue Synagogue, and a YMCA. There was a realistic fear that the contamination might spread to Suffolk County's sole source drinking water aquifer, which, if contaminated, might require residents to rely on bottled water.

Evidence also began to emerge that KeySpan was engaging in a two-pronged strategy. On the one hand, KeySpan was generally taking the public position that the MGP underground plumes did not present any significant risk to the homeowners and their families in the area. However, at the same time, KeySpan was secretly purchasing several severely contaminated properties and demolishing some of them as part of a preemptive strategy to prevent lawsuits from being filed against it by the owners of the most severely contaminated properties.

As I became more and more involved in these Bayshore MGP cases, I had numerous meetings with the clients, both at the law offices of Reilly, Like & Tenety, which was more conveniently located for the clients in Suffolk County than my Manhattan office. I also made "house calls" to the clients at their homes so I could see firsthand for myself the impact that the MGP contamination and KeySpan's cleanup activities were having on their properties and their lives.

Aristea Mousis

One of the most compelling stories regarding the impact of the MGP contamination was that of a delightful elderly lady – Aristea Mousis – who had resided continuously at 58 N. Clinton Avenue in Bay Shore since she purchased it with her husband in 1979. After her husband died on May 27, 2005, her two daughters, Frenia Arena and Jean Delucca, took on the increasing responsibility of looking after their mother and dealing with the litigation against KeySpan and lawyers such as me. Even though she had been living for many years in the U.S., Mrs. Mousis was still more comfortable conversing in her native Greek. Hence, her daughters had to act as intermediaries between Mrs. Mousis and me, at least when it came to verbal and written communications.

Mrs. Mousis's had a Vapor Intrusion Assessment performed in 2013 following reports of pungent chemical smells from members of the Mousis family. As her daughters recounted it, "there was a strong smell of gasoline that was so strong that it felt as if they were living in a barrel of gasoline." They informed KeySpan and the Suffolk County Dept. of Health Services, which took some air samples.

The Mousis family also reported that KeySpan's remediation activities in the immediate neighborhood caused a continuing nuisance and interfered with their use and enjoyment of the property. There was a well cluster (a group of monitoring wells) installed on the southwest corner of Union Boulevard and North Clinton Avenue, adjacent to their property, as early as 2003. They further reported that the interruption and interference worsened from April 30, 2007, through May 24, 2007, when North Clinton Avenue was closed due to extensive remediation and construction work. The near-constant noise and vibrations were extremely upsetting, particularly to Mrs. Mousis, to the point that her family asked KeySpan to relocate her to other living quarters, at least temporarily. KeySpan, however, refused.

Finally, Mrs. Mousis's daughters helped their 84-year-old mother vacate the premises when KeySpan personnel started testing in the basement of her home. This created so much noise, vibrations, and nuisance that the premises became, at least temporarily, uninhabitable. When asked at her deposition how to describe the noise, Eugenia Delucca – one of Mrs. Mousis's daughters – described the noise from the pile driving as follows:

Boom, boom, boom, boom. And the house was shaking, and a lot of construction work. It's almost like you were right at the site of a big skyscraper going up in New York City. That's how loud and intense it was. It was all the equipment noises that goes with it.

In addition to the noise, cracks started appearing in the plaster inside and outside the house. The damage came from what Jean Delucca described as "mini-earthquakes" and severe vibrations from KeySpan's construction and remediation activities in the neighborhood. When plaster started coming down in large chunks from the kitchen ceiling, Mrs. Mousis's son-in-law Vinny tried to clean and patch up the mess, but it was only a temporary fix. They could not afford to bring in a contractor to do a complete job, which was also the case with the cracks in the house's front stoop.

During one of the tests conducted by a KeySpan contractor in their basement, the technicians cut through the cement slab in the cellar floor, which released a strong chemical odor. At that point, according to deposition testimony, "everyone ran out the door," including the KeySpan and Suffolk County Department of Health personnel. They refused to go back inside without respirators and full protective gear, which Mrs. Mousis's family took as a clear signal for them to vacate the premises themselves. After that, the two daughters took turns caring for Mrs. Mousis at their homes. A local News 12 TV crew took footage of these events, including a group of KeySpan and KeySpan contractor trucks parked outside the home while further outside testing was conducted. It was not until months later that Mrs. Mousis was ever able to return to the familiar home that she knew and loved. By then, her health had deteriorated significantly, so her family had to monitor her on a daily and near-continuous basis.

The Other Bay Shore Homeowner Cases

In addition to Mrs. Mousis, dozens of other Bay Shore homeowners filed cases in New York State Supreme Court against KeySpan, including Jon and Cheryl Tsakis, whose property was located at 20-22 North Clinton Avenue in Bay Shore. At least eight causes of action were brought for each family and homeowner, including claims for negligence, continuing trespass, and public and private nuisance. In essence, Plaintiffs allege that their property had been contaminated by the release and migration of dangerous pollutants into the air, soil, and groundwater near their property from the former MGP facility in Bay Shore. By the time their lawsuit was commenced, the MGP "plumes" of contamination had migrated via the groundwater to both their property and the nearby properties of other residents and property owners in the Bay Shore area.

Instead of trying to deny the impossible - that the toxic MGP plume under or close to the plaintiffs' homes, as well as the construction/remediation activities, were causing a wide variety of damages – KeySpan and its lawyers took the innovative approach of arguing that the plaintiffs had failed to file their complaints in a timely manner. The statute of limitations for most of our causes of action for negligence was three years. KeySpan argued that since the company had been mailing out informational bulletins about the MGP contamination of the groundwater since at least 1999, the lawsuits should have been filed by 2002 or 2003. There also had been a great deal of newspaper and TV coverage on the subject for over a decade. KeySpan's lawyers argued that the plaintiffs should have had their property tested to determine whether it was contaminated or not and should have taken such other steps as necessary to decide whether or not they had viable legal claims against KeySpan. Never mind that most of the "informational mailings" by KeySpan were intended to reassure the homeowners and lull them into a false sense of complacency about the dangers posed by the underground MGP-contaminated plume. KeySpan repeatedly reassured the homeowners in countless mailings and surveys that the contamination presented little or no risk to the homeowners and their families and that the problem would be quickly cleaned up and taken care of. By the time that some members of the community realized that KeySpan had deceived them, and the problem was not going away quickly, it was already too late, according to KeySpan. It argued that the statute of limitations clock for the filing of a lawsuit against the company had already passed.

Much to our surprise, the New York State Supreme Court judges assigned to these cases generally agreed with KeySpan's argument and dismissed dozens of homeowners' complaints on statute of limitations grounds. Virtually the entire Bay Shore community was disenfranchised since most residents were barred from seeking any judicial remedy for their damage. In most cases, the judges hearing the cases accepted Keyspan's claim that the plaintiffs had "sat on their rights" and failed to take legal action quickly enough. They reached this conclusion even though plaintiffs presented numerous sworn affidavits and other evidence indicating that they were not clearly "on notice" of the impact of the contamination on their properties until well within the three year statutory period. The plaintiffs showed in detail how the information about the extent of the contamination and the remediation activities necessary to deal with it had only been slowly emerging over an extended period of time. In addition, some of the "informational" brochures and mailing from KeySpan minimized the risks to the homeowners' health and property, and tended to lull the homeowners into a false sense of complacency as to whether they had actually been damaged or not.

On behalf of the plaintiffs, we argued – unsuccessfully in many cases - that it was unreasonable to shift the burden on the homeowners to have taken the expensive and complex testing required to determine whether their properties and homes were contaminated. In addition, we argued the toxic underground MGP plumes were "dynamic," which means that they moved and expanded over time. One of the causes of this underground movement of the contaminated plumes was that KeySpan personnel were pumping oxygen into these underground plumes to speed up the chemical and organic process by which the MGP chemicals were broken down. The location and shape of the plumes tended to move in response to this oxygen pumping, much as what happens to a balloon when it has air blown into it. So a property that did not have subsurface contamination one year when it was tested could well have contamination showing up in test results in future years.

Jon and Cheryl Tsakis

The trial court even went so far as to dismiss the case brought by Jon and Cheryl Tsakis, who had lived in Virginia from 1993 until about 2013 and had not resided at their Bay Shore property after 1992. After that, they rented out their property in Bay Shore. Nevertheless, even though Mr. and Mrs. Tsakis lived in a distant state, the Judge concluded in his written opinion that "plaintiffs knew facts which would put a reasonable person on notice of the need to undertake further investigation into the contamination events as early as [the] 1999 door-to-door [KeySpan] canvassing."[5] Of course, Mr. and Mrs. Tsakis were not at their premises in Bay Shore when this door-to-door canvassing took place, but this does not seem to have been taken into account in the court's dismissal of their case against KeySpan.

The court also relied on evidence submitted by KeySpan to the effect that one of the tenants in the building owned by Jon and Cheryl Tsakis received mailings from KeySpan. However, it was never explained in the court's decision as to how the tenant's supposed knowledge of what KeySpan was saying it was doing concerning the MGP contamination could somehow be attributed to them as landlords living in Virginia. If Mr. and Mrs. Tsakis had designated their tenant as their legal agent for such notices, then the law might view it differently. However, in this case, we argued that since Mr. and Mrs. Tsakis had not authorized or "deputized" their tenant to act as their agent, so any knowledge of the tenants should not have been legally attributed to the owners.

In dismissing the Tsakis complaint for failing to file their 2008 complaint within the three-year statute of limitations period, Judge Thomas F. Whelan of the New York State Supreme Court, Suffolk County, also noted that KeySpan had "invited" residents to attend public meetings, beginning on January 29, 2003. The court's decision seemed to suggest that that even though there was no evidence that Mr. and Mrs. Tsakis actually received such public meeting notices in the mail, they should have heard about these meetings and should have traveled from their home in Virginia back to Bay Shore to attend these "informational" meetings. The court, in its decision, also bought into KeySpan's argument that the area's remediation activities and construction work were evident from early 2007 until 2009. So, the judge concluded, Mr. and Mrs. Tsakis were on notice that something significant was going on regarding the MGP contamination and that they should have undertaken their investigation at that time.[6]

In reaching the decision that the Tsakis complaint should be dismissed, the court also rejected the affidavit of environmental expert Martin Trent submitted by plaintiffs, concluding that defendants had grossly misrepresented both the scope and extent of the MGP contamination in their mailings to the residents and homeowners and that KeySpan had also provided plaintiffs with misleading representations as to the speed and efficacy of the ongoing remediation efforts, and the length of time that it will take to remediate the contamination fully.

In addition, the court wholly disregarded the testimony of the plaintiffs' second environmental expert, Timothy R. Minnich, who found that KeySpan's repeated representations that there was no contamination on plaintiffs' properties "were false, reckless, and completely without factual or scientific basis."

On October 16, 2019, the Appellate Division, Second Department, sitting in Brooklyn, reversed the lower court's decision in the *Tsakis* case,[7] as well as the lower court's dismissals in several other cases. The court held that the Supreme Court's determination by Judge Whelan that the causes of action to recover damages resulting from contamination were time-barred was in error.[8] The appellate court noted, in particular, that the lower court's decision had not adequately considered the affidavits and deposition testimony of Mr. and Mrs. Tsakis, who explained that they had resided in Virginia continuously since 1992 and visited the subject property only once or twice a year through 2002, and even less frequently after that.[9] The appellate court further noted that plaintiffs denied observing any signs of contamination or receiving any complaints relating to the contamination from their tenants or rental brokers and that Mr. and Mrs. Tsakis also denied receiving any information from the defendants at their home in Virginia.[10]

The appellate court also refreshingly gave some credit to the sworn testimony of the plaintiffs as to when they had first become aware of the MGP contamination. The court noted that Cheryl Tsakis testified she first became aware of the contamination upon receiving a letter from an attorney's office, and that the date of the letter was well within the limitations period.[11] Similarly, Jon Tsakis testified that he first became aware of the contamination during a visit to the subject property in 2006, when he observed an attorney advertisement in the window of a nearby building. The Second Department thus found the plaintiffs' testimony on this issue to be credible, leading to the conclusion that they had filed their complaint well within the three-year statute of limitations period.[12]

The Second Department appeals court concluded that "In view of the conflicting evidence submitted in support of the defendants' motion, the defendants failed to establish their prima facie entitlement to summary judgment since they did not demonstrate that the plaintiffs had an objective level of awareness of the dangers and consequences of the contamination sufficient to place them on notice of the primary condition on which their exposure-related claims for damages were based within the applicable limitations period."

Of equal significance, the Second Department reversed the lower court's dismissal of the causes of action, alleging that the noise, vibrations, and other side-effects caused by KeySpan's remediation activities' constituted a public and private nuisance.[13] The appellate court pointed out that these causes of action were subject to the limitations period set forth in CPLR 214(4) rather than CPLR 214-c(2) since they do not seek "to recover damages for personal injury or injury to property caused by the latent effects of exposure."[14] The impact of this ruling was significant since the three-year statute of limitations recognizes a continuous injury to property caused by a "nuisance" such as KeySpan's remediation activities. Also, the "trespass" of the MGP contaminated plumes beneath plaintiffs' properties meant the statute of limitations could never fully expire until the contamination that was "trespassing" on plaintiffs' properties was thoroughly cleaned up, and KeySpan's remediation activities were concluded.[15]

Based upon the partial reversal of the lower court's dismissal of the Mousis, Tsakis, and other cases by the Appellate Division, Second Department, the KeySpan MGP cases with causes of action still surviving were remanded to Judge Whelan for trial. However, these cases were settled in 2021 before trial, which often happens in complex environmental cases, and was especially true amidst the COVID-19 pandemic, given the difficulties faced in assembling a jury pool at a courthouse, selecting the jury, and actually trying a case before them.

The MTBE Litigation

The gasoline additive MTBE is one of the most pernicious man-made toxins ever released into the environment. Designed to reduce the toxicity of air emissions from automobiles, MTBE also had the unintended consequence of exponentially increasing the risk of groundwater contamination. It is highly soluble and travels faster and farther in water than other gasoline components. As a result, whenever MTBE is released into the environment, it can infiltrate underground water reservoirs and contaminate wells drawing from underground aquifers. MTBE's foul taste and odor render water unusable and unfit for human consumption. The chemical make-up of MTBE also allows it to persist in underground aquifers for decades at a time.

Throughout the 1980s and 1990s, and until it was finally banned, over nine million gallons of gasoline with MTBE escaped each year into the environment during transportation, storage, sale, or use in the United States. Thousands of gallons also entered the ground from gas stations due to consumer overfills of gas tanks, as well as supplier overfills of underground storage tanks ("UST's").

Congress itself inadvertently added to the MTBE crisis by establishing the Reformulated Gasoline Program ("RFG Program") as part of the Clean Air Act ("CAA").[16] The RFG program was enacted to help reduce air pollution caused by ozone-forming volatile organic compounds ("VOCs") and emissions of toxic air pollutants.[17] The RFG program required the use of reformulated gasoline in the nine largest metropolitan areas with the most severe summertime ozone levels.[18] One particular section directed the EPA, the agency charged with overseeing the RFG Program, to issue regulations requiring the greatest reduction in ozone-forming volatile organic compounds and emissions of toxic air pollutants through the reformulation of conventional gasoline.[19]

Gasoline manufacturers added oxygenates such as MTBE to meet the requirements of the federal RFG program. The EPA certified gasoline with MTBE for use in the RFG Program, and MTBE quickly became the oil industries oxygenate of choice. Gasoline manufacturers began manufacturing, distributing, and selling gasoline containing MTBE in the late 1970s. After enacting the RFG Program, manufacturers began adding MTBE to gasoline in much greater concentrations. By the mid-1980s, MTBE was in widespread use in high-octane gasoline. By 2001, MTBE comprised up to 15% of every gallon of gasoline sold in certain parts of the country.

At the same time that manufacturers were expanding MTBE use, they were also becoming increasingly aware of its threat to clean groundwater. They first became aware of specific incidents of MTBE groundwater contamination as early as 1980. By 1984, defendants, including Exxon, Shell, and Chevron, were exchanging information concerning MTBE contamination in Maryland, New York, and Rhode Island dating back to 1978. In March 1987, the defendant gasoline manufacturers became aware of MTBE contamination in six locations along the eastern seaboard. In addition, the defendants knew of two significant pollution incidents in Liberty, New York, and East Patchogue, New York, occurring from 1988 to 1990.

Defendants were also well aware of scientific studies describing the dangers of MTBE. For example, in 1986, Peter Garrett and Marcel Moreau of the Maine Department of Environmental Protection authored an environmental report on MTBE as a Ground Water Contaminant (the "Garrett Report"). The report detailed the threat posed to groundwater by MTBE and recommended that MTBE be banned as a gasoline additive, or at the very least, be stored in double-contained facilities. A draft of this report was circulated throughout the oil industry. On December 23, 1986, a staff employee with the Groundwater Technical Task Force ("GTTF") forwarded the Garrett Report to its members, including representatives of Shell, Arco, and Exxon, seeking their comments. The comments from the GTTF members culminated in a letter sent to the National Well Water Association. This organization argued against the Garrett Report, disputing the Garrett Report's findings and recommendations. However, although the gasoline manufacturers publicly disputed the conclusions of the Garrett Report, they privately acknowledged the report's validity. In a letter dated February 4, 1987, Arco Chemical, at the time a division of Arco, stated that it had no data refuting the findings of the Garrett Report. That same year, concerns regarding the dangers of MTBE were published in memoranda prepared by Mobil and Chevron. In 1992, Shell employees prepared a memorandum entitled the "MTBE WHITE PAPER: the Impact of MTBE on Groundwater," which acknowledged that MTBE was nearly 25 times more soluble than benzene (another chemical component of gasoline). It also confirmed that MTBE did not biodegrade in the subsurface environment, and the increased use of MTBE would increase the risks associated with accidental gasoline releases in the future. Another Shell document dated June 1997 noted the difficulty in removing MTBE from groundwater compared to other gasoline components. In May 1999, Chevron employees further discussed concerns relating to the use of MTBE in a report entitled "Solving Problems From MTBE Contamination It's Not Just Regulating Underground Tanks."

Although the defendants were aware of the dangers associated with MTBE, they conspired to mislead the EPA and the public to convince them of the desirability of increasing concentrations of MTBE in gasoline. In 1986, the federal Interagency Testing Committee ("ITC") recommended that the EPA conduct testing of MTBE to assess MTBE's health and environmental risks. The ITC invited written comments on this subject. The defendants mobilized to convince the EPA that additional testing of MTBE was unnecessary. On or about December 12, 1986, Arco, speaking on behalf of the other defendants, responded to the ITC's recommendation by discrediting the information relied upon by the ITC and intentionally downplayed the risks associated with MTBE, falsely stating that MTBE is only *slightly* soluble in water. At a public focus meeting held a few days later, Arco and Exxon made presentations supporting the industry that additional medical testing was unnecessary.

In early 1987, defendants formed the MTBE Committee to address MTBE's environmental, health, safety, legislative, and regulatory issues. Members of the MTBE Committee included Amoco, Arco, Chevron, Citgo, Exxon, Shell, Sunoco, Texaco, and Conoco. Defendants also formed the MTBE Technical Subcommittee to coordinate the oil industry's response to EPA concerns relating to MTBE. However, defendants were not forthcoming in their responses to the EPA's inquiries concerning MTBE. For example, on February 27, 1987, the MTBE Committee provided information to the EPA representing that MTBE was only slightly soluble in water, potential environmental exposure to MTBE was low, and that MTBE had excellent biodegradation characteristics, all of which defendants knew to be false or misleading. In addition, the MTBE Committee submitted written comments to the EPA stating that there was no evidence that MTBE posed any significant risk of harm to public health or the environment. One year after successfully convincing the EPA that further testing of MTBE was unnecessary, the MTBE Committee disbanded.

The defendants also misled the public. In April 1987, George Dominguez of the MTBE Committee presented at a Conference on Alcohol and Octane. He withheld information relating to MTBE and stated that MTBE gasoline spills had been dealt with effectively. In 1994, the API responded to an article raising questions about MTBE's environmental and health benefits by stating that there was no basis to question the continued use of MTBE. In an April 1996 pamphlet distributed by the Oxygenated Fuels Association ("OFA"), the OFA expressed confidence that federal regulations and industry practices made MTBE contamination "a thing of the past." It even went so far as to suggest that MTBE groundwater contamination could provide a public service, as it "can serve as an early indicator of gasoline contamination in groundwater, triggering its cleanup and remediation, and limiting the probability of harm from the usual constituents of gasoline."

MTBE's groundwater pollution reached such epidemic proportions in the 1980s and 1990s that hundreds if not thousands of cases were brought on behalf of private well-owners seeking monetary damages for the pollution by MTBE of their well-water. These cases, including several class action cases, were consolidated through the multi-district litigation process into the U.S. District Court for the Southern District of New York and assigned to District Court Judge Shira Scheindlin, a well-respected and scholarly judge on that court.

Although the allegations of each action were somewhat different, the common charge was essentially the same: that the defendant petroleum companies doing business throughout the United States knowingly caused the widespread contamination of groundwater as a result of their use of MTBE. In addition to seeking compensatory and punitive damages, the plaintiffs in these lawsuits also sought a court-supervised program of MTBE testing, monitoring, education, and, where appropriate, remediation.

One of the cases consolidated with the other MDL cases *was Berrian v. Amerada Hess Corp. et al.,*[20] which dealt with the plaintiff-homeowners represented by my law firm. The named plaintiffs, Colleen and Robert Berrian, Barbara and James Hayes, and Felicia Ritters, were all residents of Hyde Park, New York, whose wells had tested positive for MTBE. The defendants named in the *Berrian* action include Arco, BP Corp., Amoco, Citgo, Chevron, Exxon-Mobil, Equilon, Phillips, Shell, Shell Oil, Texaco, Texaco Refining, El Paso, Amerada Hess, Sunoco. Motiva, Tosco, United Refining, and Valero. The Plaintiffs in the *Berrian* action also sought to represent a class of private well owners in New York whose wells were contaminated with MTBE. Since it was virtually impossible to remove the MTBE from the well water once it was contaminated, these homeowners had to be connected to the municipal water system, which was a laborious and costly process.

The defendant companies moved to dismiss the class action complaints by arguing, among other things, that they were "preempted" by federal law since they conflicted with Congress's federal Clean Air Act and the RFG Program. Judge Scheindlin, however, denied their motion to dismiss, finding that the Clean Air Act ("CAA") and the RFG Program were enacted by Congress to regulate motor vehicle emissions and that plaintiffs' complaints did not interfere with that goal.[21] The court explained that the plaintiffs were only concerned with groundwater contamination caused by spills and gasoline leakage containing MTBE and were, therefore, outside the scope of the preemption provision of those federal statutes.[22]

Judge Scheindlin further denied the defendants' request to exercise her judicial discretion to abstain from hearing these cases based upon the "primary jurisdiction doctrine." This doctrine states that a federal court may exercise discretion to stay the action and defer it to an administrative agency with more specialized expertise in complex technical issues.[23] The district court found that deference to an administrative agency was unnecessary in these cases since plaintiffs' common law state claims were grounded in state tort law, not federal law.[24]

In denying the defendants' motion to dismiss, Judge Scheindlin also found that the mere fact that some plaintiffs were unable to identify which defendant manufacturer of MTBE caused their injury was not a fatal impediment. Although such specific identification was impossible in many cases, the court applied generally recognized collective theories of liability - such as market share liability, alternative liability, and collective action/conspiracy liability - as a basis for imposing liability upon all defendants.

The "collective liability" theory first arose in a 1948 California case, *Summers v. Tice*.[25] A hunter was injured when shot by one of two companions, who each fired in his direction simultaneously. This theory then became widely applied when the conduct of two or more actors toward a plaintiff was tortious, and the harm to the plaintiff was caused by only one of them, but there was uncertainty as to which one caused the injury. The burden of proof as to causation was reversed and placed upon each defendant to prove that it did not cause harm.[26]

Similarly, "market-share liability" was first recognized by the California Supreme Court in a case involving an injury caused by the drug diethylstilbestrol (DES), a generic drug some pregnant women took to help prevent a miscarriage.[27] In these cases, it was impossible to trace the specific drug ingested back to the manufacturer when the plaintiff manifested an injury, often years after the product was consumed. Under market-share liability, then, when a plaintiff cannot identify the specific manufacturer of a fungible or generic product that caused her injury, the plaintiff may recover damages from a manufacturer or manufacturers in proportion to each manufacturer's share of the total market for the product.[28]

Judge Scheindlin further found that the legal theory of "enterprise liability" was potentially applicable,[29] as well as the theory of "conspiracy" or "concert of action." Under the legal theory of conspiracy, a defendant may be held jointly and severally liable if it commits a tortious act in concert with another or if a defendant gives substantial assistance to another, knowing that the other's conduct constitutes a breach of duty.[30]

In denying the defendants' motion to dismiss the complaints, the district court further found a sufficient legal and factual basis to hold defendants liable under the theory of "strict liability for design defect" and negligence. Plaintiffs alleged in their complaints that the design of MTBE was defective at the time of sale or distribution and that the foreseeable risks of harm posed by the product could have been reduced or avoided by adopting a reasonable alternative design.[31] Plaintiffs further alleged that defendants knew of the unreasonable dangers associated with gasoline containing MTBE, actively conspired to conceal these dangers, and safer alternatives to MTBE were known and available to the defendants for use in gasoline.

Judge Scheindlin also denied the defendants' motion to dismiss plaintiffs' "failure to warn" claims, noting that "a manufacturer must warn against latent dangers resulting from foreseeable uses of its product of which it knew or should have known."[32] The court found that the allegations in these MTBE complaints were sufficient to show that the harm suffered by the plaintiffs was a foreseeable result of the defendants' placement of gasoline containing MTBE in the marketplace.

In addition, Judge Scheindlin held that plaintiffs had sufficiently pled a "public nuisance" cause of action, which is defined as "an unreasonable interference with a right common to the general public."[33] In so holding, the district court rejected defendants' argument that they could not be held liable for public nuisance because they had no control over the product when it was "released" onto the plaintiffs' property. The court noted that plaintiffs had sufficiently alleged that defendants had extensive knowledge of all phases of the petroleum business, from the extraction of crude oils to the refining, distribution, marketing, and retail sale of gasoline, including the design and manufacture of gasoline containing MTBE. The district court judge found that the available evidence supported the claim that defendants added MTBE to gasoline and marketed and distributed gasoline containing MTBE, all with the knowledge of MTBE's dangers to groundwater. In addition, the court noted that plaintiffs alleged that defendants failed to warn the downstream handlers, retailers, gasoline purchasers, government officials, and well owners of the dangers associated with MTBE.

Judge Scheindlin's decision also reaffirmed the principle that the public has a right to soil and water free from environmental contamination.[34] Plaintiffs' reliance on the use of wells for their drinking and household water distinguished them from the rest of the homeowners in the area, which were tied into municipal water systems and did not have to rely on well water. Therefore, the court found that plaintiffs' injuries were distinct in both degree and kind from the injuries suffered by the public at large, which qualified them to assert a public nuisance claim.

Judge Sheindlin also denied that portion of the defendants' motion seeking to dismiss plaintiffs' "civil conspiracy" claims to market a defective product. She found that, under a civil conspiracy theory, defendants may be held jointly and severally liable for committing tortious acts under a common design, or if a defendant gives substantial assistance to another knowing that the other's conduct constitutes a breach of duty.[35] The example that the district court judge used was the case involving a drag race between two cars. One driver was the cause-in-fact of the plaintiff's injury. Still, the other racer could also be held liable for the damage because their joint misbehavior contributed to the accident.[36] Applying these principles to the MTBE litigation, the court held that the plaintiffs' strict liability claim for design defect was sufficient to support the conspiracy claim.[37] Thus, the court found that Plaintiffs had adequately alleged that defendants conspired to market a product they knew to be dangerous to the environment and intentionally failed to warn downstream handlers, government officials, and the public about the threat from MTBE.

* * *

The KeySpan MGP cases and the multi-district MTBE litigation highlight how both state and federal courts can provide homeowners and property owners at least some modicum of justice in complex environmental pollution cases, even though the large multi-nationals and utility companies are prepared to aggressively defend these cases over the course of many years. For those intrepid plaintiff lawyers who are willing to stay the course and expend the financial and human resources necessary to prosecute these cases, a satisfactory conclusion for their clients in these cases can often be achieved.

Chapter 16

Germany's Attempted Extermination of the Ovaherero and Nama Peoples

The First Genocide of the Twentieth Century

The Ottoman Empire's campaign of genocide against the Armenian people from 1915 to 1917 was a horrific episode in world history, deserving universal condemnation. However, it was not – as is generally believed – the first genocide of the Twentieth Century. That tragic label belongs to Imperial Germany's extermination campaign against the Ovaherero and Nama peoples in what was called German South West Africa, now part of Namibia. Up to 80% of these indigenous peoples were wiped out in only a few short years. Those that survived were enslaved and imprisoned in concentration camps under terrible conditions. They were forced to perform grueling labor for the German occupiers, usually leading to death by starvation, overwork, beatings, or a combination of the above.

Incredibly, even though I had considerable experience as an international human rights lawyer, I learned about this tragedy relatively recently. I had virtually no knowledge of this genocide until I was asked by a colleague of mine, Professor Richard Weisberg of Cardozo Law School, to attend a conference in 2017 sponsored by the Holocaust Foundation of Long Island, New York. I was told that the conference's subject matter would be an African genocide that Germany had perpetrated in the early 1900s, but I did not have any more information at that point.

When I arrived at the Holocaust Center for the conference, I was immediately struck by the colorful uniforms worn by the men and the bright red dresses and hats worn by the women in attendance. They were all members of the affected communities. Several of the representatives of the Ovaherero and Nama indigenous communities had traveled all the way from Namibia to attend the conference, and others present were representatives of the U.S.-based organizations for the Ovaherero and

Prisoners from the Herero and Nama tribes during the 1904-1908 war against Germany.
Unknown author - Public domain. Wikimedia Commons

Nama peoples who had emigrated to the U.S. since the time of the geno-cides. During the conference, I learned much more about the history of the genocide and the efforts that these groups had undertaken to gain acknowledgement, an apology, and restitution from the German govern-ment for the incalculable damage that Imperial Germany had inflicted on their ancestors.

At the end of the conference, I attended a smaller meeting with some of the group's leaders. They asked me to explore the possibility of bringing a genocide case against Germany in the U.S. courts. I agreed to research the matter, and in the weeks after that, I took a crash course in the history of the genocide. I and others in my law firm also researched the possible legal remedies available to the impacted communities.

Little did I suspect at the time that I would be spending much of the next several years working to assist the Ovaherero and Nama peoples win some degree of recognition and restorative justice from Germany for this often forgotten first genocide of the Twentieth Century. As part of the legal journey, I travelled with my wife Susan and youngest son, Foard, to Namibia, South Africa, and Botswana to attend a conference on the genocide and to meet with leaders and members of the Ovaherero and Nama communities in those countries. It seemed as if we drove at least 1000 miles crisscrossing those vast countries to visit their welcoming towns and villages. We also were shown the notorious landmarks where many of their ancestors had made a stand against the Germans, been held captive, or slaughtered.

The van we drove in was large enough to accommodate three of our closest Ovaherero colleagues – Veraa Katuuo, Vepuka Kauari, and Ngondi Kamatuka – who, by then, had become our good friends and travelled with us from the U.S. Veraa was a distinguished New York architect, and his wife, Vepuka, was a head nurse at New York's Columbia Presbyterian Hospital. Ngondi was a distinguished professor at the University of Kansas. All of them had grown up in Namibia before emigrating to the U.S., and all of them had worked tirelessly for decades, seeking justice for their communities and their people. Our van was followed by several cars filled with Ovaherero men assigned to be our guides and "protectors" during our stay in Namibia. The leader of our security detail was Bob Vezera Kandetu, a charismatic community activist, media personality, and author of the book, "Namibia in Perspective." At each of our stops we were met by large groups of Ovaherero and Nama people. Each time, we gave them a briefing on the status of the litigation and other efforts to gain direct Herero and Nama participation in the ongoing talks between the Namibian Government and Germany.[1] Ovaherero Paramount Chief ("P.C.") and Advocate Vekuii Rukoro was present at all of the Ovaherero community events, along with other Ovaherero leaders and lawyers such as Festus U. Muundjua, Lazarus Kairabeb, Sam Kauapirura and Mutjinde Katjiua, who was later elevated to the position of Paramount Chief after the untimely and tragic death of P.C. Rukoro. At each of the Nama community events we were joined by Sima Luipert and Chief (Goab) Johannes Isaack, as well as other Nama leaders and community members. In addition to speeches and the answering of countless questions, most of these events also involved some traditional dancing, singing, storytelling, feasting and even some drinking. In Botswana, we were greeted by one community with a huge outdoor pig roast and bonfire, complete with traditional dances, singing and ceremonies. It was a night to remember. At another event, my wife Susan was honored with a traditional native gown, and my son received a youth corps shirt and matching hat. As for myself, I received a walking stick emblazoned with my new Ovaherero name and title, "Nokokure," or "Noko" for short, which literally translates as "kin folk" or "family." As I was told by Paramount Chief Rukoro at the conference where he conferred the name on me, the Ovaherero people believe that even in faraway places, there will always be a friend, kin folk, or family member who will be there to help you out. I was honored to be considered as a member of the Ovaherero family.

* * *

As I quickly learned, Germany's dealings with the indigenous peoples of southwestern Africa started well but ended tragically.[2] By the late 1800s, Germany – newly unified and seeking its "place in the sun" – aimed to compete with other European empires by establishing colonies in Africa and elsewhere. Imperial Germany established its colony in southwestern Africa in 1883 and then signed a treaty with the Chief of the Ovaherero tribe on October 21, 1885. The treaty was signed on behalf of Imperial Germany by Heinrich Ernst Göring, the Colonial Governor and father of Nazi Luftwaffe commander Hermann Goring.

Germany's impetus to expand into Africa in the 1880s was fueled mainly by the concept of *Lebensraum* ("living space"), coined by German geographer Friedrich Ratzel in 1897, which relied upon the misguided belief in German biological and racial supremacy. Germany was undergoing exponential population growth in the late 19th century, leading to urban squalor, mass unemployment, and immigration (mostly to the U.S.). Germany's "Volk ohne Raum" ("people without space") had an obligation, in Ratzel's view, to colonize other lands to create the extra "living space" needed to cure Germany's urban overcrowding. Ratzel's belief in the racial superiority of the German people justified taking land from "uncivilized" people (i.e. non-Europeans) who were not sufficiently exploiting natural resources or industrializing their economies. Although Adolph Hitler later expanded this concept with deadly consequences during the Third Reich, it first took root in Germany's colonization of South West Africa.

The Herero are a Bantu ethnic group who speak the Otjiherero language. They arrived in South West Africa in approximately the 15th century, bringing cattle and establishing themselves there as herdsmen. Before being virtually annihilated by German forces, the Ovaherero people had evolved from a confederation of chieftaincies into a complex unified sovereignty under the leadership of the Maherero dynasty. The region's arid climate limited large-scale agriculture, and so the Ovaherero prospered as nomadic cattle herders. Ovaherero families privately owned their cattle but held collective property and ownership rights over Hereroland as a collaborative people.

The Nama people, who resided in Great Namaqualand in Southwestern Africa and South Africa for many centuries, are a Khoikhoi-speaking people spread between a confederation of tribes across the southern portion of South West Africa. Although originally from the Cape of modern South Africa, like the Ovaherero, the Nama were prosperous cattle herders. Yet Dutch colonial expansion in the cape and the attendant violence led a confederation of Nama under the leadership of David Witbooi to migrate across the Orange River into South West Africa in the 1840s. Like the Ovaherero, over the 19th century, the Nama people evolved from a confederation of chieftaincies into a unified sovereignty under the Witbooi dynasty. By the start of the 20th century, the Nama population of Namaqualand had grown to approximately 20,000 people, with cattle herds numbering about 100,000.

Nama migration into South West Africa led to conflict with the Herero there over grazing territory. Between 1884 and 1892, German colonial officials exploited Herero-Nama tensions. By posing as potential allies, the Germans signed treaties with both peoples that they cynically never intended to honor. They hoped to divide and conquer the region by keeping the Ovaherero and Nama quarrelling amongst themselves.

In 1885, Germany hosted the Berlin West Africa Conference, attended by the European powers who were vying for control of portions of West Africa. In Articles VI and IX of the Conference's General Act, Germany and the other participants attempted to justify their annexation of African territories with the high-minded pledge to "support the native population [of Africa] and improve their moral and material situation." They also promised to end the slave trade. Thus, under the guise of humanitarianism and with the full backing of the other leading European powers, Germany began its racist and imperialist expropriation of the African territories known as "German South West Africa."

That same year – 1885 – Germany dispatched Imperial Commissioner Goring to Southwestern Africa. He successfully negotiated a "protection treaty" with Chief Kamaherero of the Ovaherero people. This treaty, dated October 21, 1885, promised the "absolute highest level of protection" to the Ovaherero people and promised that all Germans would respect the customs and laws of Hereroland, which belonged to the Ovaherero people. In exchange, the Ovaherero people gave Germany certain mineral and easement rights and promised that German settlers and merchants could work in peace in Hereroland.

Germany, however, had no intention of honoring the terms of the treaty and only used it as a ruse to seize Ovaherero wealth without compensation. Throughout the 1885–88 period, Germany continually breached the letter and the spirit of this treaty. Germany and its agents permitted German settlers and companies to steal Ovaherero cattle, exploit mineral rights without compensation, abuse and injure Ovaherero men and laborers, and rape Ovaherero women and children.

Germany also started taking military action against the Ovaherero. In 1889, German Captain Curt von François established Fort Wilhelmsfeste on the road connecting Swakopmund to the major Hereroland settlement of Otjimbingwe. He also blocked the import of arms into Hereroland, thereby depriving the Ovaherero people of the ability to defend themselves.

In November 1892, to prevent the Ovaherero and Nama from joining forces under a peace treaty between these two peoples, Germany sent colonial "protection troops" (*Schutztruppe*) reinforcements to re-instigate war between the Ovaherero and Nama. On the night of April 12, 1893, Captain von François troops furtively encircled the Nama settlement of Hoornkrans and assumed fortified positions. Von François gave the firing orders at dawn. Within thirty minutes, sixteen thousand rounds of ammunition were fired at the sleeping Nama of Hoornkrans, including women, children, and elders.

Under surprise attack, Nama Chief Hendrik Witbooi ordered his men to retreat to the far side of the valley to draw German fire away from the women and children. But instead, the German colonial troops ignored the men and concentrated on killing as many women and children as possible. Seventy-eight Nama women and children were killed. Chief Witbooi's 12-year-old son, Klein Hendrik, born with crippling partial paralysis, was killed while fleeing. He crawled unarmed in a riverbed where a German soldier found him and executed him with a point-blank shot to the head.

Germany continued to commit similar atrocities against the Nama people from 1893–1895, during which time German troops and settlers stole Nama cattle and other valuable property, including gemstones and precious minerals. German settlers were able to establish lucrative plantations by exploiting the labor of the local indigenous Ovaherero and Nama. Since the German colonial authorities and the German colonists considered Africans to be *Untermenschen* ("subhuman"), Ovaherero and Nama tribeswomen were subjected to constant rape and other abuses. Then their men were frequently killed for attempting to defend them.

Major-General Theodor Gotthilf Leutwein arrived in South West Africa in 1895 to continue the scorched-earth campaign against the Nama. He approved the use of artillery and machine guns against tribal members armed with only spears and other rudimentary weapons. Finally, Chief Witbooi was forced to surrender. As Governor Leutwein later candidly admitted, "divested of all ideals and talk of humanity, the aim of all colonization lies ultimately in profit."[3] By 1903, Germany had seized over a quarter of Ovaherero and Nama lands (originally over 50,000 square miles).

As a result of Germany's unlawful taking of livestock and an epidemic of *Rinderpest* cattle plague, the Ovaherero and Nama herds had dwindled to just 50,000 head of cattle by 1903, down from an estimated several hundreds of thousands of cattle in the 1880s. With their cattle (and therefore their livelihood) gone, the Ovaherero and Nama herders were forced into wage labor, slavery, and servitude, which was accelerated by usurious and fraudulent loans foisted upon many Ovaherero and Nama herders by German agents, banks, and traders. Under the 1903 Credit Ordinance, German creditors' claims against Ovaherero and Nama debtors were due within twelve months. When the Ovaherero and Nama were unable to pay back these usurious loans, armed agents of the German creditors responded by immediately descending upon impoverished Ovaherero and Nama debtors on horseback, enforcing their claims through violent theft of all remaining Ovaherero and Nama cattle and other valuable property.

In December 1903, *Schutztruppe* Lieutenant Zürn summoned Ovaherero leaders to his fortification in Okahandja and demanded that they sign a contract handing over vast tracts of ancestral land. When the leaders refused, they were physically removed from Zürn's office. Zürn subsequently forged their signatures and on December 8, 1903, Zürn announced new northern borders to Hereroland. Lt. Zürn and other German agents also dug up the holy graveyards of the Maherero dynasty, thus defiling the corpses of the royal clan's ancestors – a flagrant violation of customary Ovaherero law.

In early January 1904, false rumors began to spread among the German settlers and troops about a coordinated Ovaherero uprising. German traders spread the false rumors that the Ovaherero were buying goods on credit to stock up in preparation for an attack. On January 10, 1904, one trader, Alex Niet, falsely reported to Lieutenant Zürn that he witnessed 300 armed Ovaherero poised to attack Okahandja. Zürn telegrammed Okahandja and hid in his fort with the German settlers, traders, and newly arrived *Schutztruppe* reinforcements.

Lieutenant Zürn sent out numerous scouts over the next two days, all of whom returned with no indication of a threat. Nonetheless, the Germans had begun gossiping, spreading rumors, and preparing for what they ultimately desired: an opportunity to kill their African neighbors and take their remaining property under the guise of an Ovaherero "revolt."

On January 12, 1904, Germany began its war against the Ovaherero people. Lieutenant Zürn ordered his soldiers to open fire on any Ovaherero people who happened to be in the fort's proximity. Forced to defend themselves from this unprovoked violence, the Ovaherero surrounded the town of Okahandja in early 1904, cutting all links to Windhoek, the colonial capital. Under the explicit humanitarian directives of Chief Maherero, the Ovaherero forces were directed not to harm any German woman, children, or missionaries, and no violence was to be conducted against the English, the Boers, or any other tribes. Fewer than 150 German settlers and soldiers lost their lives in this initial Ovaherero military action. In response, German troops brutally lynched any Ovaherero civilian men they found to incite fear and terror among the native population.

Frustrated with Governor Leutwein's slow progress in subduing the stalwart Herero and Nama warriors and embarrassed by Leutwein's retreat at the battle of Oviombo, the Kaiser replaced Leutwein with Lieutenant-General Adrien Dietrich Lothar von Trotha in May 1904. Lothar von Trotha was an experienced colonial fighter who had previously been sent by the Kaiser to brutally repress East African and Chinese attempts to resist German colonization.[4] General von Trotha's orders were to "end the war by fair or foul means," and command was entrusted in him with "fullest confidence in his insight, energy, and experience."

The German Extermination Proclamations and Orders

On June 11, 1904, von Trotha arrived with an expeditionary force of 14,000 troops. Von Trotha immediately made clear his intentions to crush the resistance and annihilate the Ovaherero and Nama peoples, leaving the land free to fulfill the German dream of Lebensraum. Before the Battle of Waterberg on August 11-12, 1904, where his troops cornered and finally defeated the Ovaherero, General von Trotha issued the following proclamation: "I believe that the [Ovaherero] nation as such should be annihilated, or, if this was not possible by tactical measures, have to be expelled from the country."[5] Von Trotha further wrote: "It is my intention to destroy the rebellious tribes with streams of blood and money." He repeatedly used the German word "Vernichtung," meaning "to exterminate" or "to annihilate." Von Trotha's extermination orders were extraordinary; even during Germany's campaign to annihilate the Jewish population of Europe in the Holocaust, the genocidal orders were never put into writing.

By August 1904, over 60,000 Ovaherero people had fled von Trotha's massacres and gathered at Waterberg, including the elderly, handicapped, unarmed men, women, and children. They planned to surrender. General von Trotha's troops descended upon Waterberg, encircling the Ovaherero camp with a battalion of 4,000 men, 1,500 rifles, hand grenades, thirty heavy artillery pieces, and twelve state-of-the-art machine guns, split into six divisions in a star-shaped formation. It was a deadly firing squad intended to almost completely encircle the Herero encampment.

General von Trotha, however, left one exit open to the Ovaherero: a valley leading to the Omaheke Desert to the east, which he intended to use as a death trap. After an artillery barrage targeted the Herero civilians, Chief Maherero led his men in multiple attempts to break through the German encirclement. After suffering heavy losses to the high-tech German forces, Chief Maherero was left with no option but to lead an escape into the Omaheke. The tens of thousands of Ovaherero men, women, and children that were not killed in the assault were forced to abandon all their belongings and herds and escape into the waterless desert. As one German officer described it: "the entire national wealth of the Herero was left by the wayside." The German troops carefully gathered up any valuables, which were confiscated and shipped back to Germany.

The Omaheke Desert is a vast sandvelt with extreme desert temperatures, virtually no rainfall or vegetation (typically under 5 millimeters fall from August to September), dried arroyos, and sparse, extremely limited sources of water. Its ecosystem, perhaps too grand a term for such a desolate tract of land, does not support much life. Nevertheless, some of the Ovaherero, including Chief Samuel Maherero, survived the arduous trek across the desert to the British protectorate Bechuanaland—today, Botswana—where they took refuge. Others fled to Ovamboland, and others to South Africa. But the vast majority of the Ovaherero who entered the desert perished.

Following his victory, von Trotha issued Imperial Order No. 3737, dated October 2, 1904, which was unquestionably an Extermination Order:[6]

> I, the Great General of the German Soldiers, send this letter to the Herero people. The Herero people are no longer German subjects . . . The Herero people must now leave the country. If they refuse, I will force them to leave with my Big Cannon. Every Herero found inside the German border, with or without

a gun or cattle, will be shot. I shall spare neither women nor children: send them back to their people or shoot them. These are my words to the Herero people.

Von Trotha further explained that his campaign to annihilate the Ovaherero peoples "is and remains the beginning of a racial struggle." The extermination actively continued for months, with German troops roving the countryside and killing any survivors they found. Von Trotha also ordered a perimeter established at the border of the Omaheke, to prevent any Herero from reentering their land, including women and children who approached the perimeter of the desert surrendering and seeking aid.

The rhetoric von Trotha used to justify the extermination of the Ovaherero and Nama peoples eerily presaged the language later used by Hitler to justify the mass extermination of the Jewish people as an "ethnic cleansing" necessary for the resurrection of a New Germany. While Leutwein had sought a détente with the Herero and Nama, viewing them as necessary for German development of the region, von Trotha saw the utter destruction of the Ovaherero and Nama peoples as serving a higher purpose and establishing a new world order. He said: "I destroy the African tribes with streams of blood... Only following this cleansing can something new emerge, which will remain."

Germany's Attempted Extermination of the Nama People

While von Trotha's forces were in the process of exterminating or enslaving the entire Ovaherero population, Germany craftily negotiated with the Nama, biding its time until prepared to handle both fronts.

Ultimately convinced that extermination, genocide, and total expropriation were required to secure the wealth of Great Namaqualand for itself, two companies of German soldiers and an artillery battery were sent to Great Namaqualand in April 1904 to begin staging an assault.

On May 25, 1904, an Imperial Officer in the town of Keetmanshoop informed the Governor that a revolt was likely. He noted that several hundred lawsuits had been brought in recent months against Nama debtors by German firms and traders in Keetmanshoop. Creditors had been enforcing their (often fraudulent) judgments against the Nama by stealing the only possessions they had left: their cattle, gemstones, and any other valuables.

In July 1904, Chief Jacob Morenga of the Bondelszwart Nama tribe sought to liberate his people from Germany's violent and oppressive policies and practices. Morenga, who earned the title "the Black Napoleon" and colleagues began an uprising by robbing German farmers of their ammunition and arms. In response, a German force was sent to capture Morenga but failed. Morenga soon commanded a guerilla force of 400 Nama soldiers, supplemented by Herero men seeking revenge against the Germans.

General von Trotha placed Colonel Berthold von Deimling in command of the Nama war, provided for reinforcements of 4,000 men, and began construction of a railway into Great Namaqualand for logistical support. Colonel von Deimling vowed to "destroy" the Nama before they had a chance to escape. Deimling, however, was poorly equipped to confront a tactical mastermind like Morenga and suffered embarrassing defeats and heavy losses.

In April 1905, General von Trotha took personal command over the Nama campaign. As his first order of business, General von Trotha set about drafting a second Extermination Order, using the Ovaherero Extermination Order as a template. He issued the Extermination Order to the Nama people in the city of Gibeon on April 22, 1905:[7]

> Those few refusing to surrender will suffer the same fate suffered by the Herero people, who, in their blindness, believed that they could successfully wage war against the mighty German Emperor and the great German People. I ask you: Where are the Herero people today? Where are their chiefs today?

The Extermination Order made clear that the genocide would continue until every Nama man, woman, and child were either enslaved or murdered: "The Nama who chooses not to surrender and lets himself be seen in German territory will be shot until all are exterminated."

Most Nama tribes were forced into surrender by mid-1906. The Germans enslaved approximately 2,000 Nama men, women, and children taken prisoner during the war and the ensuing surrender. They were placed in concentration camps with the Ovaherero, and all of their land, livestock, and other property was confiscated.

Germany Herds the Ovaherero and Nama Survivors Into Concentration Camps

By the end of 1904, German colonial forces belatedly realized that they had acute labor shortage, primarily due to the killing of potential Ovaherero and Nama laborers. To solve this problem, all surviving Ovaherero and Nama peoples were herded into concentration camps. They were then counted as "heads" like cattle and made available for contracting out to colonists and private companies as slave labor, or for purposes of medical and eugenic experimentation. The camps were established at Okahandja, Omaruru, Karibib, Keetmanshoop, Lüderitz Bay, Swakopmund, Windhoek, and elsewhere. Approximately 2,000 Nama and 14,769 Ovaherero people —primarily women and children — were enslaved in the concentration camps.[8]

All prisoners were first divided into two categories: those who were fit to work and those who were not. For administrative purposes, pre-printed death certificates uniformly gave the cause of death as "death by exhaustion following privation." The inmates were housed in atrocious conditions, given dilapidated tents surrounded by walls, barbed wire, and guards. German forces also permitted private concentration camps to be erected at the industrial facilities of firms that purchased slaves. Ovaherero and Nama people of all ages and gender were treated uniformly and housed without distinction. Those who surrendered and those who were captured received the same merciless fate.

The Ovaherero and Nama had been accustomed to a varied diet of dairy, meat, and fruit. Due to food deprivation and the absence of normal nutrition, the prisoners suffered numerous illnesses, including scurvy, bronchitis, and chickenpox. Pneumonia was also commonplace. Despite rampant illness, German policy and practices were for the camp Medical Offices to leave the Ovaherero and Nama peoples untreated.

The widespread rape of Ovaherero and Nama women and children had a profound negative effect on the individual victims themselves and for generations to come. Diseased German soldiers and civilians caused physical damage to the reproductive organs of the Ovaherero and Nama women and children. They spread venereal disease to Ovaherero and Nama women and children, rendering many of them sterile. The Ovaherero and Nama birth rates plummeted in the years following the genocide.

German colonial authorities were well aware of this gruesome effect and saw it as an effective means to sterilize the Ovaherero and Nama peoples, furthering its policy and practice of total annihilation by preventing the birth of new generations.

The most notorious of the concentration camps was the Lüderitz Bay concentration camp, which was located on Shark Island, a small island — and now peninsula — just off the coast. Here, German forces practiced prison techniques later employed at similarly structured death camps in the 1930s and 1940s. The annual mortality rate from disease, exhaustion, and malnutrition at Shark Island was perhaps 74 percent. By 1907, out of thousands sent to Shark Island, fewer than 30 camp inmates were capable of physical labor. Despite these harsh conditions, all Ovaherero men, women, and children who could stand were taken outside the camp every day as forced laborers. At the same time, the sick and dying were left without medical assistance. Shootings, hangings, and beatings of the forced laborers were widely reported by eyewitnesses, in the press, and in Germany's well-maintained Imperial records. One eyewitness reported that "cartloads of their bodies were every day carted over to the back beach, buried in a few inches of sand at low tide, and as the tide came in the bodies were out, food for the sharks."

Before the Ovaherero genocide, approximately 100,000 Ovaherero people lived in Hereroland. Following the genocide, the Germans had hunted down so many that the Ovaherero population was only around 14,769 in South West Africa, with a few thousand living in exile. The Nama population was similarly decimated. A 1911 census found an Ovaherero population of only 15,130 and a Nama population of only 9,781.

Germany's Plunder of Ovaherero and Nama Lands and Other Property

In addition to the mass killings and genocide, German authorities also confiscated and expropriated Ovaherero and Nama lands and other property without compensation. The native peoples who survived and remained on the land were only permitted to do so if they were working on farms now owned by German settlers. By stripping the Ovaherero and Nama of lands and livestock, they deprived them of all their political and economic power and their means to resist.

In addition to unjustly enriching themselves with revenue derived from concessions, taxation, and customs rights that previously generated revenue for the Ovaherero and Nama peoples, Germany and its colonial authorities also made a substantial fortune through the industrial export of copper ore, diamonds, gold, cattle, hides, artifacts, and ostrich feathers. After forcibly seizing Ovaherero and Nama copper deposit concession rights, taxation rights, and customs rights, Germany obtained immense revenues by selling these concession rights to copper mining firms and taxing the firms' profits, and by charging customs, tariffs, and duties on the exported copper.

German diamond dealers and speculators also greatly benefited from to Germany's illegal occupation and confiscation of Ovaherero and Nama lands. These lands became home to diamond mining operations, which increased significantly when additional diamonds were discovered in 1908 in portions of the Namib Desert traditionally owned by the Ovaherero and Nama. By 1913, diamond production in South West Africa accounted for a quarter of total global diamond exports.

Germany's Medical Experimentation and Sale of Skulls and Body Parts

At Shark Island, 778 Ovaherero and Nama bodies were dissected in post-mortems for German medical research. The Pathological Institute also requested Ovaherero and Nama skulls for Berlin and the University of Breslau for experimentation, display, and scientific research in the eugenics-adjacent *Rassenlehre* (Race Theory), a field of scientific study in Germany that espoused the superiority of the white race.

The German troops and colonial authorities decapitated an estimated three hundred Ovaherero men at Shark Island by ax, machete, or saw. The severed heads were then boiled in water, and Ovaherero women and girls were forced to clean the boiled heads of flesh with shards of glass. This routine required the women and girls to strip off the noses, faces, scalps, and neck tissue and then remove the inner tissue, tongues, and brains from the boiled heads of their husbands and fathers, leaving only the polished skulls. Once so cleaned, the German forces packaged the skulls for transport by ship to Germany.[9]

Some heads of Nama women and children were treated likewise, including the head of a one-year-old Nama girl. In late 1906, a German eugenicist named Dr. Bofinger decapitated an infant girl then removed and weighed her brain before placing her head in preservatives, sealing it in a tin, and sending it for further examination at the Institute of Pathology at the University of Berlin.

In 2011 – after years of denial – Germany's Museum of Medical History at the Charité in Berlin returned twenty skulls of Ovaherero and Nama people to Namibia. These included eleven Nama and nine Herero skulls, which had belonged to four women, fifteen men, and a boy. In April 2017, Professor Philipp Osten, the Museum Director of the Museum of Medical History at the Medical School of Hamburg-Eppendorf, announced that seventy-three skulls were newly discovered. The Museum had purchased them between 1917–33.

Hamburg University Professor Jürgen Zimmerer, who is also President of the International Network of Genocide Scholars, and several doctoral students analyzed the origins of approximately 5,000 objects from Africa, including skulls, body parts, and other mortal remains of victims murdered by German authorities. Some of the bodies taken and shipped back to Germany by German authorities included the exhumed bodies of Ovaherero and Nama holy ancestors, previously resting in sanctified cemeteries. Some of the robbed graves held the bodies of the royal Maherero clan.

Germany Finally Acknowledged the Genocide, But Refuses to Include the Ovaherero and Nama Leaders in Negotiations

In 1985, the United Nations "Whitaker Report" classified Germany's massacres as an attempt to exterminate the Ovaherero and Nama peoples of South-West Africa, and therefore the earliest cases of genocide in the 20th century. In 1998, German President Roman Herzog visited Namibia and met with Ovaherero leaders. Chief Munjuku Nguvauva demanded a public apology and compensation, but Herzog stopped short of an apology, only expressing "regret."

Thereafter, on August 16, 2004, at the 100th anniversary of the start of the genocide, a member of the German government, Heidemarie

Wieczorek-Zeul, Germany's Minister for Economic Development and Cooperation, apologized and expressed grief about the genocide:[10]

> We Germans accept our historic and moral responsibility, and the guilt incurred by Germans at that time . . . The atrocities committed at that time would have been termed genocide.

However, the German government quickly made it clear that her speech could not be interpreted as an "official apology" by Germany or a basis for paying any compensation, reparations, or restitution.

Minister Wieczorek-Zeul also has explained that Germany's 2004 admission of liability was tied to the equally implicit admission that "there exists a continuing injury against the living descendants."[11] Minister Wieczorek-Zeul and other prominent members of the German government admitted that the living descendants of the Ovaherero and Nama peoples suffer a continuing intergenerational injury due to the expropriation of their ancestors' lands, personal wealth, and valuables. The current generation of Ovaherero and Nama continue to suffer the lack of adequate educational and social support systems that would be available to them but for the wrongful taking of their people's lands, wealth and personal property.

In 2015, Germany inched further towards an explicit recognition of the atrocities as a genocide when the German Foreign Ministry guidelines began referring to the killings as a "genocide." At or around the same time, Germany acknowledged the "Armenian genocide" for the first time. The Armenian genocide, like the Ovaherero-Nama genocide, was marked by large-scale genocidal expropriation. In September 1915, the Ottoman parliament passed the "Temporary Law of Expropriation and Confiscation," taking all property and land of the Armenians.

Like the Ovaherero and Nama peoples, the Armenians died through numerous causes, including but not limited to targeted killings, thirst, and hunger, whether in concentration camps or slave labor. A strong argument was made that Germany could not logically or morally consider the Ottoman/Turkish mistreatment of the Armenians as genocide without also acknowledging that the same or similar actions it took against the Ovaherero and Nama were also genocidal.

In 2015, the President of Germany and the former Foreign Minister Frank-Walter Steinmeier also admitted that Germany's actions in South

West Africa amounted to a "war of annihilation and constitute a war crime and genocide." This followed a formal declaration by the German federal government, apologizing for the genocide.

Germany Excludes the Ovaherero and Nama in Talks with Namibia

Instead of dealing directly with the Herero and Nama communities, which were the direct victims of the genocides, Germany sought to negotiate solely with the Namibian Government, which was focused almost entirely on the hope and expectation of a financial bail-out of the government and the failing Namibian economy in general, rather than the urgent needs of the long neglected Ovaherero and Nama communities. Both Germany and the Namibian Government thus steadfastly refused to even consider the issue of restitution or direct compensation to the Ovaherero and Nama peoples for the losses that had been inflicted upon them.

Germany's refusal to negotiate directly with the victim communities violated the rights of the Ovaherero and Nama peoples under international law, particularly its obligations under the U.N. Declaration on the Rights of Indigenous Peoples, which explicitly provides, at Article 11 (2): "States shall provide redress through effective mechanisms, which may include restitution, developed in conjunction with indigenous peoples, with respect to their cultural, intellectual, religious and spiritual property taken without their free, prior and informed consent or in violation of their laws, traditions and customs."

In addition, Article 18 of the U.N. Declaration provides: "Indigenous peoples have the right to participate in decision-making in matters which would affect their rights, through representatives chosen by themselves in accordance with their own procedures. . .."

In short, Germany's exclusion and violation of the U.N. Declaration perpetuated the imperialist policies manifested in 1884–85 at the Berlin West Africa Conference. In 1884, Germany — in a typical manifestation of the prevailing racist perspective of European colonial powers —did not view the Ovaherero and Nama peoples as "sovereign equals," but rather as belonging to a lesser, uncivilized object race lacking agency over its people or fate. The irony of this perspective was lost on Germany, since

Germany had negotiated numerous treaties with the Herero and Nama sovereign entities, at least when it was convenient for them.

This dismissive, and frankly racist, attitude continues through the present, with Germany refusing to include the Ovaherero and Nama peoples in its discussions with Namibia, again treating the Ovaherero and Nama peoples as lesser, uncivilized objects without "sovereign equality." Germany thus continued to ignore, objectify, and marginalize the Ovaherero and Nama peoples, just as it did in 1884 in Berlin.

The German "Bone Trade" and the Discovery of Ovaherero and Nama Human Remains at the American Museum of Natural History in New York

In September 2017, the American Museum of Natural History ("AMNH") in New York City confirmed to representatives of the Ovaherero and Nama peoples that it was in possession of human remains relating to the 1904-1908 German genocide of the Ovaherero and Nama. These were part of a collection of Herero, Nama, and other human remains, books, and materials, which compose the so-called *Lehrmittelsammlung* ("Teaching Collection") assembled by Felix von Luschan over decades of employment at the *Königliches Museum für Völkerkunde* ("Royal Museum of Ethnology") and the Friedrich Wilhelm University, now Humboldt University. Importantly, both of these institutions which profited from the collection were Imperial institutions in Berlin.

As of its sale in 1924, the Teaching Collection was an "anatomical collection comprising 5,000 human crania, 200 complete skeletons, a study collection, and a private library."[12] The Herero and Nama remains in the Teaching Collection found their way to New York in connection with Germany's role in the international commercial trade in bones, which grew in the late 19th century to supply eugenicists with "research" material. After von Luschan died in February 1924, his Teaching Collection was sold to the AMNH. The purchase price of $41,500 was paid on the AMNH's behalf by New York philanthropist Felix Warburg.[13]

Of the eight human remains from Namibia at the AMNH, at least two appear to be genocide victims, including one from Shark Island, and one from Windhoek, where the German colonial authorities also maintained a concentration camp for the Ovaherero and Nama prisoners. For the Herero, who practice ancestor veneration, the mistreatment of their ancestors' remains is a continuing affront.

Discovery of Copy of "Blue Book" in New York Public Library

In our efforts to demonstrate that the U.S. courts had jurisdiction over this 1904-1908 genocide, we also discovered that a rare copy of the "Blue Book," published in 1918, was located at the New York Public Library's main branch on Fifth Avenue in Manhattan. The book, formally titled "Union of South Africa – Report On the Natives of South-West Africa And Their Treatment By Germany," was prepared by South African officials in Windhoek as they took over administration of the colony at the end of the First World War. It was published in the United Kingdom by His Majesty's Stationery Office (HMSO) and presented to both Houses of Parliament that year.

This invaluable Blue Book included testimony to the German atrocities from genocide survivors. The very presence of a Blue Book copy in New York was extraordinary, since between the two World Wars Great Britain briefly considered Germany an ally and attempted to suppress records of Germany's genocide of the indigenous peoples of South West Africa by, among other things, destroying all copies of the Blue Book. The copy located at the New York Public Library is one of the few surviving copies.

The Lawsuit

On January 5, 2017, we filed a class action lawsuit in the United States District Court for the Southern District of New York.[14] The named plaintiffs were Vekuii Rukoro, Paramount Chief of the Ovaherero people and representative of the Ovaherero Traditional Authority; Johannes Isaack, Chief and Chairman of the Nama Traditional Leaders Association; the Association of the Ovaherero Genocide in the USA, Inc.; and Barnabas V. Katuuo, an officer of that association. These named plaintiffs sought to represent all descendants and members of the Ovaherero and Nama peoples, for damages and other relief arising from Germany's genocide of Ovaherero and Nama civilians and the unlawful taking of their property in violation of international law in Hereroland and Great Namaqualand, sovereign entities now part of the Republic of Namibia. We argued that the case could properly be maintained as a Class action pursuant to Rule 23, Federal Rules of Civil Procedure, since all the members of the class had common interests, and the prosecution of separate actions by individual members of the Class would create a risk, since resolving individual claims could preclude other Nama or Herero members from seeing justice. We argued, therefore, that a Class Action would serve to best protect the interests of all class members.

In the Complaint, Plaintiffs sought damages for the genocide pursuant to the Alien Tort Statute,[15] federal common law, and the law of nations (also referred to as customary international law). We also sought damages for conversion of various property rights, damages for unjust enrichment, an accounting, the establishment of a constructive trust, and declaratory relief recognizing Plaintiffs as the "legitimate successors to sovereign nations" and declaring that the exclusion of Plaintiffs from negotiations between Germany and the Namibian Government was unjust.

In the factual portion of the Complaint, we briefly explained the history of how, between 1884–94, Germany (then the German Empire) made numerous treaties with the Ovaherero and Nama Chiefs, who maintained their sovereignty and promised to protect German citizens wishing to settle in their lands in exchange for Germany's promise of an alliance to protect them against outside forces. We further explained that Germany breached these treaties and, through its colonial authorities, pursued policies of fraud, plunder, exploitation, and violence against the Ovaherero and Nama peoples. We further alleged that, between 1884–1903, Germany unlawfully took, and aided and abetted the taking of, Ovaherero and Nama land and livestock. For peoples whose economies relied on cattle herding, this was tantamount to stealing the food from their mouths. Nonetheless, we noted that, by early 1904, Germany had only limited sovereign control over any land, as the Ovaherero and Nama sovereignties still reigned over most of the territory of modern-day Namibia.[16]

The Complaint further alleged that, under the guise of quelling "uprisings" in 1904, Germany dispatched Lothar von Trotha and 14,000 soldiers with the true goal of expropriating the lands of these indigenous peoples and annihilating them. We further explained in the Complaint that German forces drove the Ovaherero into the desert, the Nama into the mountains, and both into death or exile. Finally, provided details in the Complaint about the approximately 100,000 Ovaherero and Nama victims who lost their lives at the hands of the German government: at least 80% of the Ovaherero and 50% of the Nama.

On February 14, 2018, we filed an Amended Complaint,[17] providing further factual allegations based upon our continued investigation, including the discovery of Ovaherero and Nama skulls and other body parts at the American Museum of Natural History in New York.

Germany's Extermination Campaign As A Violation of International Law

The first thing that we had to legally establish in our federal case was that the conduct of the German colonial forces was a violation of international law, both at the time that the conduct took place and under international law today. Therefore, we set forth in our complaint references to publications by German legal scholars during the 1800s, establishing that the German government knew at the time that its taking of property without compensation and exterminations unquestionably violated existing binding prohibitions under customary international law. We specifically quoted from one of the foremost legal scholars at the time, Johann Kasper Bluntschli, who wrote: "Wars of extermination and annihilation against peoples and tribes capable of life and culture are violations of international law."[18] We, therefore, argued that Germany's illegal takings and genocide were also, without question, a violation of international law at the time they occurred, as well as a violation of contemporary international law.

Federal Jurisdiction Under the Foreign Sovereign Immunities Act (FSIA)

Proving that Germany's reprehensible conduct towards the Ovaherero and Nama peoples was a recognized violation of customary international law was, however, the easy part of our case. In order for a U.S. court to take jurisdiction over our claims, we also had to prove that Germany's conduct fell under one or more of the recognized exceptions of the Foreign Sovereign Immunities Act ("FSIA").[19] Under the so-called "takings exception,"[20] we alleged that the FSIA grants subject matter jurisdiction to the U.S. courts where a foreign state takes human remains in violation of international law and then processes, commercializes, ships, and causes such remains to be sold in the United States as part of a course of commercial activity in and substantially contacting the United States. In other words, we argued that when Germany sold the Herero and Nama remains to the AMNH, they engaged in commercial activity "substantially contacting" the U.S., and therefore lost protection granted to sovereign nations under the FSIA.

We also argued that the FSIA's "expropriation" or "takings" exception applied to the Ovaherero and Nama skulls stored at the AMNH in New York, which are "present" in the U.S. "in connection with a commercial activity carried on" by a foreign state (Germany), even though the activity "carried on" (i.e., the sale of bones and body parts) was in the past, and not currently being "carried on" in the U.S.

We further argued that, under the "takings exception," Germany's real estate that it owned in New York was "property exchanged for property" within the meaning of the FSIA, since the bones and body parts of the Ovaherero and Nama victims of the genocide had been sold by German Imperial institutions, and the money derived from such sales was used by the German treasury to purchase real estate in New York that Germany used for commercial purposes, such as for exhibitions and various other events.

As anticipated, Germany's legal counsel filed a motion to dismiss our Complaint, arguing that it failed to fall within the scope of any of the exceptions to the FSIA. We fully briefed the issues, arguing, amongst other things, that the District Court had jurisdiction over the case under the FSIA's "commercial activity" exception. To meet the requirements of this exception, we had to show that Germany's actions caused a "direct effect" in the United States. In support of our argument that there was a direct effect in the U.S., we pointed out the following factors: (1) members of the class who were injured by the genocide currently resided in the United States, (2) certain genocide victim remains collected by German anthropologist Felix von Luschan were present at the AMNH, (3) a copy of the "Blue Book" was located in the New York Public Library, and (4) New York had become a leading research and conference center for the study of the genocide. We, therefore, argued that the FSIA's "takings exception" applied.

An oral argument was held before District Court Judge Laura Taylor Swain in the U.S. District Courthouse in lower Manhattan. Paramount Chief Rukoro and other leaders of the Ovaherero and Nama traditional authorities were in attendance, dressed in their colorful and distinctive uniforms. There were also numerous Ovaherero and Nama women present, decked out in their colorful gowns and distinctive headdresses. Some had travelled all the way from Namibia to attend the court hearing and oral argument, underscoring the importance that these communities placed on their struggle for justice. There was some significant national and international press coverage of the event, and after the hearing was over, we were all treated to a marching demonstration outside the courthouse by a para-military group of highly trained and disciplined Ovaherero men.

On March 6, 2019, we received the disappointing news that Judge Swain handed down a decision[21] granting Germany's motion to dismiss our Amended Complaint, finding that we had failed to establish that our case fell within either the "commercial activity"[22] or the "takings exception"[23] of the FSIA. In particular, the court was unpersuaded by our efforts to establish that Germany's genocidal conduct caused a "direct effect" in the United States. Even though we presented evidence during the briefing process on Germany's motion to dismiss that the bones came into the possession of the AMNH through a sale by the Royal Museum of Ethnology in Berlin, and not from von Luschan's private collection as originally thought, the district court still concluded: "Plaintiffs have thus failed to demonstrate that the alleged transfer of the remains was the result of any act by a foreign state, or that it flowed directly from Germany's conduct in South West Africa."

As for the "takings exception" to the FSIA, the district court found that, even though Plaintiffs alleged sufficiently that the expropriated property, or property exchanged for the expropriated property, was present in the United States, the Amended Complaint failed to allege that the expropriated property was present "in connection with a commercial activity" carried on by Germany. Of particular note was the court's view that we had alleged facts sufficient to support their theory that property expropriated by Germany in the early twentieth century was either sold or leased, and that the proceeds of those transactions were commingled into the German treasury and used to purchase the New York properties owned by the German government. However, the court concluded that the "takings exception" did not ultimately apply since the court found that the single commercial transaction involving the sale of the bones by the Museum in Berlin to the AMNH was not substantial enough to constitute a "commercial activity carried on in the United States by a foreign state" as that term is defined in the FSIA.[24]

The Appeal to the Second Circuit Court of Appeals

Since we obviously disagreed with the district court's findings that neither of the two available exceptions to the FSIA applied to our case, we appealed the decision to the Second Circuit Court of Appeals, an intermediate court between the U.S. district courts and the U.S. Supreme Court.

After fully briefing our appeal and arguing before the three-judge panel assigned to consider the appeal,[25] the Second Circuit issued a decision and order on the appeal on September 20, 2020, affirming the lower court's dismissal of our case on jurisdictional grounds.[26]

Although the Second Circuit Court of Appeals agreed with the district court's conclusion that neither the commercial activity nor the takings exception applied to this case, it disagreed with the district court's opinion to the effect that property taken by Germany from plaintiffs were then converted into currency and comingled with other monies in Germany's general treasury account, and that those monies could be traced to Germany's purchase of property in New York.

In concluding its opinion, the Second Circuit did acknowledge, however, that plaintiffs had suffered as a result of the "terrible wrongs elucidated in Plaintiffs' complaint," but that such wrongs "must be addressed through a vehicle other than the U.S. court system."[27]

Negotiations and Joint Resolution Between Germany and Namibian Government

In 2015, Germany communicated to the Namibian Government a willingness to negotiate a resolution of issues related to its colonial crimes, particularly the Ovaherero and Nama genocide. However, the official representatives of the Ovaherero and Nama traditional counsels and other recognized leaders of these communities were inexplicably excluded from the negotiations. In addition, the negotiations were generally sealed off from the public and the press, despite the fact that the subject matters of the negotiations were highly relevant to the citizens of both countries, as well as the descendants of the Ovaherero and Nama in Botswana, South Africa, and elsewhere throughout the world.

In June 2021, after years of closed-door negotiations between representatives of the two countries and hand-picked "representatives" of the Herero and Nama (who were not, in fact, the legitimate representatives of the affected communities), the German and Namibian governments announced a Joint Declaration that, to the surprise of many, used the format of a "declaration," rather than that of an "agreement." In this declaration, the German government vaguely acknowledged its responsibility for the "events of 1904-1908" and deemed it genocide only from "today's perspective," leading merely to a "moral responsibility" but not a legal one. As a consequence, the term "reparations" was not mentioned whatsoever.

In this declaration, the German government agreed to make available the amount of 1.1 billion Euros over many years as a grant to implement projects as part of reconstruction and development programs.

The Joint Declaration ignited protests on the part of a wide range of indigenous organizations, including the Ovaherero Traditional Authority (OTA), the Nama Traditional Leaders Association (NTLA), the Nama Genocide Technical Committee (NGTC), and the Ovaherero Genocide Foundation (OGF). The Declaration also triggered a strong negative reaction from the Namibian parliament and civil organizations across Namibia and around the globe.

In addition to the exclusion of the legitimate representatives of the affected communities, the Declaration was fatally flawed as a matter of law since it continued to reflect Germany's refusal to acknowledge its responsibility in terms of international human rights law, or to provide for reparations to the damaged parties.

Along with the European Center of Constitutional and Human Rights (ECCHR), our law firm protested the Declaration – which still had not been officially signed by the representatives of both countries or approved by their respective legislative bodies – to the relevant United Nations committees and related international bodies. For example, in October 2021, we helped draft the "Alternative Report to the 7th Periodic Report submitted by the Federal Republic of Germany under Article 40 of the International Covenant on Civil and Political Rights (ICCPR)." This document challenged Germany on the claim made in its filing to the UN Human Rights Committee in its 133th Session in 2021 that it had complied with its obligations under ICCPR. We submitted this "Alternative Report" on behalf of the alliance of the Nama Traditional

Leaders Association (NTLA), the Ovaherero Traditional Authority (OTA), the Botswana Society for Nama, Ovaherero and Ovambanderu (BOSNOO), and the Berlin Postkolonial organization, pointing out that the exclusion of the indigenous community representatives in the negotiations culminating in the German-Namibian Declaration specifically violated Article 1 of ICCHR, which declares: "All peoples have the right of self-determination. By virtue of that right they freely determine their political status and freely pursue their economic, social and cultural development."

We also argued that the Declaration violated Article 25 of the Covenant, which declares: "Every citizen shall have the right and the opportunity . . . to take part in the conduct of public affairs, directly or through freely chosen representatives." We argued – I think persuasively – that not only did the Namibian government fail to adequately represent the affected indigenous communities within Namibia, but that it most certainly could not represent the affected communities outside Namibia, who chose the leaders of their Traditional Authorities to represent their interests, yet were pointedly excluded from participation in the negotiations.

* * *

As of this book's publication, the legal and human rights struggle by the Ovaherero and Nama communities continues in the U.N.; the courts and legislative proceedings in Namibia; and in the press and court of public opinion in Germany and around the globe. Just as the settlement with Germany of all Holocaust claims came only after stinging defeats of the plaintiffs' claims in U.S. courts, the Ovaherero and Nama communities, and their legal and human rights advocates worldwide – including our law firm – have a realistic hope and expectation that these affected communities will eventually receive the restorative justice and reparations they so richly deserve.

"There can be no settlement about us without us," has been the rallying cry of these proud peoples for more than a decade. Their resolve to continue the fight until justice is achieved remains undiminished. So does that of their legal team. The struggle continues. . ..

Chapter 17

The Legal Struggle for Human and Political Rights in Ukraine

Perhaps the highest-profile client I ever represented was Yulia Tymoshenko, the iconic co-leader of Ukraine's Orange Revolution in late 2004 and early 2005,[1] and the first (and so far) only woman prime minister in the history of Ukraine. As the leader of the Batkivshchyna ("Fatherland") political party, she strongly supported Ukraine's integration into the European Union and NATO. She placed third in *Forbes* magazine's list of the world's most powerful women in 2005. But by the time I started representing her, she was languishing in a Ukrainian prison with serious and life-threatening health issues. She was a victim of a political vendetta conducted by the pro-Russian president, who was misusing Ukraine's corrupt judicial system to punish and destroy the pro-democracy political forces in the country.

Tymoshenko's legal problems started in 2010 when she lost a close election to Viktor Yanukovych in the 2010 Ukrainian presidential runoff. Yanukovych promptly ordered a politically motivated criminal investigation against her. She was soon arrested on a series of trumped-up criminal charges and thrown into prison, where she remained as a political prisoner with serious medical problems from August 2011 to February 2014. She was also subjected to a political show trial of meritless charges during this time.

My involvement with the case started with a call from Peter Borisow, a Ukrainian-American colleague working closely with Yulia Tymoshenko and other pro-Western political leaders in Ukraine. During my years in the federal government, I established a relatively comprehensive network of contacts with officers and agents in the U.S. law enforcement and intelligence communities, particularly those dealing with Eastern Europe and Russia. I maintained those contacts long after leaving the government, so it was not unusual for a former colleague with close ties to the pro-democracy movement in Ukraine to contact me about a potential human rights case involving a prominent Ukrainian political figure.

Tymoshenko's Ukrainian legal team asked me to investigate allegations that the mistreatment and prosecution were part of a broader scheme to destroy Tymoshenko and, eventually, all other political opposition leaders in Ukraine. Evidence had been gathered indicating the campaign to prosecute and destroy Tymoshenko was financed through a vast money-laundering enterprise involving President Yanukovych. One of his chief political advisors was U.S. lawyer Paul Manafort, and much of Yanukovych's financing came from Dimitri Firtash, a Ukrainian billionaire close to the Russian power elite.

Tymoshenko's Ukrainian legal team may have asked me to join their efforts because it was relatively well known I had worked on several cases with international dimensions involving the global reach of the civil RICO statute. These included Holocaust-related and other human rights cases where the wrongful acts took place primarily overseas but had a substantial and direct impact in the U.S. I also maintained excellent contacts in the U.S. State Department, U.S. Department of Justice, and the CIA, so I touched base with as many of them as possible to get myself up to speed on what was happening in Ukraine in general, and Tymoshenko in particular. I got a generally enthusiastic response from these contacts, so I had reason to believe that the U.S. government would at least tacitly support our legal efforts to help release Tymoshenko from prison and allow her to receive the medical attention she needed. I also felt that the U.S. government would support our efforts to expose the corruption and money laundering activities of Yanukovych, Firtash, Manafort, and other insiders who exerted considerable influence on the pro-Russian Yanukovych government.

Both my Ukrainian legal counterparts and I knew that the struggle over Tymoshenko's fate, as well as that of Ukraine itself, was part of a more significant geopolitical battle between Russia and the West. The question was whether Ukraine and other former Soviet vassal states would remain in the Russian orbit or whether they could successfully realign themselves with Western European democracies. Since the pro-democracy forces in Ukraine were asking me for my legal assistance in this struggle, I did not hesitate in taking up the challenge, even though I knew it would put a strain on our financial resources. A David and Goliath battle ensued,

Ukrainian Prime Minister Yulia Tymoshenko on March 23, 2009
Wiktor Dabkowski/ZUMA Press, Inc. / Alamy Stock Photo DR5KKC.

with the odds firmly stacked against us. Yet this was precisely the kind of case that had drawn me to the practice of law in the first place. There was never a serious question of whether I would jump in with both feet and take my chances.

Quite frankly, I was also genuinely offended that Paul Manafort, a prominent American lawyer, played a significant role in steering Ukraine closer to Moscow and attempting to destroy a true Ukrainian patriot in the process. I thought it highly suspect – indeed treasonous – for an American citizen to promote Russian interests in Eastern Europe, directly undercutting U.S. interests and democracy in general.

Long before Donald Trump tapped him to be Campaign Chairman for his 2016 quest for the White House, Manafort worked overseas for a series of dictators, autocrats, and human rights violators. In addition to Ukrainian President Viktor Yanukovych, Manafort's dubious rogue's gallery of clients included President Marcos, who was eventually forced to flee the Philippines. Over the years, he also worked for despotic leaders of the Dominican Republic, Nigeria, Kenya, Equatorial Guinea, and Somalia. These men held onto power through violence, terror, the conscription of child soldiers, the sale of blood diamonds, and the torture and murder of political opponents. A 1992 report from the Center for Public Integrity listed the consulting firm of "Black, Manafort, Stone, and Kelly" as one of the charter members of "The Torturers' Lobby," a list of firms that profited the most by doing business with foreign governments that violated human rights.[2]

Just as he had done for numerous other despots, Manafort remade Viktor Yanukovych. Manafort molded this rough-hewn apparatchik into a cosmopolitan and contemporary-looking statesman. Under Manafort's tutelage, the Yanukovych regime also ratcheted up its anti-Western European rhetoric as part of a campaign to prevent Ukraine from pursuing membership in the European Union.

When Yanukovych followed Manafort's advice and denounced the NATO naval exercises in the eastern Mediterranean as an infringement on Ukrainian sovereignty, American Ambassador William Taylor urgently requested a meeting with Manafort at the U.S. Embassy in Kyiv. At the meeting, Manafort was told that his work for Yanukovych and his anti-NATO rhetoric were counter to U.S. interests. In a State Department cable that later became public, Ambassador Taylor further expressed his concern that a Yanukovych and Manafort-aligned Ukrainian oligarch – Dimitri Firtash – was closely associated with Russian organized crime chief Semion Mogilevich.[3] Manafort ignored Taylor's warnings and continued to advise the Ukrainian pro-Russian political forces to do everything in their power to keep Ukraine out of the EU and NATO. All other appeals to Manafort's patriotism by U.S. officials were equally rebuffed.

Following Yanukovych's ouster in a popular, pro-democracy uprising in Ukraine in February and March of 2014, new evidence emerged showing just how much Manafort had been a critical player in propping up this corrupt, pro-Russian autocrat's regime. In August 2016, for example, The New York Times reported that a secret handwritten ledger maintained by the Yanukovych Administration in Kyiv, Ukraine listed Manafort as the intended recipient of $12.7 million in "off the books" and undisclosed cash payments from 2007 to 2012.[4] The money was from Yanukovych's pro-Russian political party, the Party of Regions, for Manafort's work on their behalf.[5] Government investigators in Ukraine described the ledger as evidence of a corrupt network within the Yanukovych Administration designed to loot Ukrainian assets and influence election results illegally.[6]

In addition, on August 17, 2016, The Associated Press reported that, in 2012, Manafort and Rick Gates, then-deputy in the Trump campaign, helped The Party of Regions secretly route at least $2.2 million in payments to two prominent Washington lobbying firms: Podesta Group Inc. and Mercury LLC.[7] Among other things, these lobbyists leveraged their considerable political influence in Washington to defeat a proposed Congressional resolution condemning the pro-Russian Yanukovych government for its human rights violations, including the imprisonment of former Prime Minister Tymoshenko.

After Yanukovych fled Kyiv amidst the popular "Maiden" uprising of February- March 2014, Manafort landed an even more prominent pro-Russian politician with autocratic tendencies: Donald J. Trump. Manafort was hired by the Trump Campaign specifically for his close Russian connections and his promises to hook Trump up with the real power players in Russia. Trump wanted contacts who could clear away any "red tape" delaying the Trump Tower Moscow project. Manafort almost immediately contacted his longtime associate in Kyiv, a known GRU (Russian military intelligence) officer named Konstantin Kilimnik.[8]

Manafort was also one of the intermediaries between the Trump Campaign and WikiLeaks, which became closely linked to the GRU and the FSB (formerly known as the KGB). On November 27, 2018, *The Guardian* reported that Manafort met with Julian Assange inside the Ecuadorian embassy in London in 2013, in 2015, and in March 2016.[9] If accurate, this information provided further proof of the link between the Trump Campaign and Russian intelligence operatives through WikiLeaks. They were collecting illegally hacked documents to damage the Hillary Clinton Campaign.[10] By the time Trump's campaign was in full swing in March 2016, Russian intelligence operatives already had close ties with Wikileaks and Assange. After WikiLeaks released a treasure trove of documents hacked from the Clinton Campaign and Democratic Congressional Campaign Committee (DCCC) in late March and early April 2016, U.S. intelligence agencies confirmed that Wikileaks had essentially become an arm of Russian intelligence.[11]

Manafort successfully navigated the Trump Campaign through the Republican National Convention into the general election. Then a series of news articles started appearing in mid-August 2016, disclosing disturbing details regarding the extent of Manafort's ties with the pro-Russian Yanukovych Administration and the millions that he had allegedly received in "off-the-books" cash payment. Manafort's role in the Trump campaign was quickly downgraded before he was finally cut loose entirely on August 9, 2016.[12] However, his faithful deputy, Rick Gates, stayed on to maintain the close working relationship between the Trump campaign and pro-Putin forces in Russia and Ukraine, primarily through Kilimnik, their GRU-affiliated associate.

Although Manafort no longer held any official position in the Trump Campaign, he continued to stay in touch with Trump directly and indirectly through his longtime deputy, Rick Gates. After all, Trump and Manafort had much in common. They were both enamored with money, and all things Russian, primarily since Russian money had provided both of them with the lavish lifestyles they had become accustomed to and which they would never give up.[13]

The Money Laundering and Racketeering Investigation

Based on our investigation's information, the funds used to harass and prosecute Tymoshenko were primarily being laundered through complex bank transfers around the globe, including transfers involving banks in New York and other U.S. banking centers. Much of these funds came from RosUkrEnergo AG (RUE), one-half of which was controlled by Dimitri Firtash through his company Centragas Holding AG. The other half of RUE was owned by Gazprom, the Russian government-owned natural gas monopoly.

Russian organized crime was another major player in this international money laundering scheme. This seemed inevitable since Firtash had already admitted that he had started his gas trading business with Semion Mogilevich, the Ukraine-born Russian organized crime boss. At the time, Mogilevich was the subject of a 45-count racketeering and money laundering indictment in the United States District Court for the Eastern District of Pennsylvania, located in Philadelphia. He was accused of masterminding an elaborate stock fraud using a web of shell companies in Europe. He was in the FBI's "top 10" most wanted list, and he was also at the top of Interpol's list. Undeterred by the U.S. and international law enforcement agency's efforts to apprehend him, Mogilevich concocted with Firtash an elaborate scheme whereby they could siphon millions of dollars from RUE and then launder the money through a byzantine series of banking transactions.

During our investigation, we discovered that Firtash, through his company Group DF, did business in New York and elsewhere in the U.S. through Manafort's CMZ Ventures. We found a paper trail showing that Group DF had wired $25 million of a $112 million commitment to one of CMZ Ventures' New York bank accounts. The money was supposed to be used as a down payment to buy the Drake Hotel in New York as part of a real estate development project. However, the real estate was never purchased, and the transactions were never completed. This left millions of dollars in the middle of a transaction that could then be siphoned off and used for illicit purposes, such as political payoffs to prosecutors and others pursuing the bogus criminal charges against Tymoshenko.

Once we completed our investigation, we filed a civil RICO action against Yanukovych, Firtash, Manafort, and others, detailing the intricate scheme they concocted to launder money skimmed from RUE through the U.S. and international bank accounts and business transactions. [14] The federal complaint asserted that the defendants formed a labyrinth of companies with similar names. If one of these companies were subjected to an investigation or sued by a victim of fraudulent activities, they would close down the company (or "bust out," as they referred to it). Then they would transfer its operations to another "clean" company with a similar name, thus confusing government regulators and making it more difficult for their operations and financing to be traced.

Tymoshenko's problems with the Kremlin and its corrupt cronies in Ukraine started in January 2009. As the Ukrainian Prime Minister, she successfully eliminated RUE as the middleman in the natural gas transactions between Russia and Ukraine. She won Russia's agreement that Gazprom would transfer RUE's debts to Naftogaz, Ukraine's state-owned natural gas utility. Naftogaz then agreed to pay Russia the $1.7 billion owed by RUE to Firtash, RUE's largest shareholder. In return, under the new agreement between Russia and Ukraine, Naftogaz would receive access to the 11 billion cubic meters of gas that Firtash and RUE had in Ukrainian government storage tanks.

Most significantly, the agreement, which Naftogaz Deputy Chairman Ihor Didenko signed upon instructions from Tymoshenko, provided that the governments of Russia and Ukraine would conduct their gas dealings directly with each other in the future. They eliminated RUE as the middleman/broker and cut it off from the billions of dollars in "royalties" that was used as a slush fund to pay off corrupt Russian and Ukrainian officials. The money was also used to finance Russia's campaign to undermine political efforts in Ukraine and other former Soviet satellite countries to loosen their traditionally close ties with Russia and to realign themselves with Western Europe and the U.S.

Naftogaz kept its side of the bargain by transferring $1.7 billion for the 11 billion cubic meters of natural gas. Naftogaz also complied with all other provisions of the agreement. However, Putin and the Kremlin elite started having second thoughts about the deal when it was celebrated as a tremendous victory by Western European countries, the major recipients and users of the natural gas transported by pipeline through Ukraine. The

U.S. Embassy, which had described Firtash as a "questionable character" in cables to Washington, expressed the view that the elimination of RUE could introduce "transparency and accountability" into the gas trade.

Firtash himself was understandably outraged by the January 2009 agreement, which eliminated one of the most lucrative aspects of RUE's business with the stroke of a pen. He complained to the U.S. Ambassador to Kyiv that the agreement was "criminal" and that if anyone other than Tymoshenko had made the agreement, "he would have already been hanging from the streetlights." One Firtash ally, Yuriy Boyko, energy minister in Ukraine's pro-Russian opposition's shadow cabinet and a former member of the coordinating council of RUE, called the agreement a "betrayal of national interests."

Firtash and his associates promptly filed an arbitration claim with the Arbitration Institute of the Stockholm Chamber of Commerce, claiming that the agreement between Russia and Ukraine was illegal. However, Tymoshenko and the rest of the pro-Western Ukraine Government were confident they would win the arbitration. Since Naftogaz, not RUE, had paid for the natural gas in question, there was no monetary consideration for RUE's claim to ownership of the gas.

However, while the arbitration proceedings in Stockholm were still ongoing, the Ukrainian government changed hands. In February 2010, Tymoshenko's s pro-Russian rival, Victor Yanukovych, became President. Since Firtash (who had been distributing large amounts of cash to opponents of Tymoshenko) was one of the key financial backers of the new President, he was immediately elevated to Yanukovych's inner circle. At the same time, many of Firtash's associates were appointed to government posts in the new Yanukovych administration. Two of his close friends and associates, Yuriy Boyko and Serhiy Lyovochkin, became energy minister and the President's chief of staff, respectively. In addition, Firtash's confident, Valeriy Khoroshkovsky, owner of the InterMedia empire, in which Firtash owned a purchase option at the time, was named the chief of the SBU, the Ukrainian state security system and successor to Ukraine's KGB.

With the ascendence of Yanukovych to the Ukraine presidency, the entire management team of the state-owned Naftogaz was replaced with managers loyal to Yanukovych, Firtash, and the rest of their inner circle. One of the removed managers was Igor Didenko, who had signed the

January 19, 2009, agreement. After that, he was the target of a politically motivated investigation that led to his arrest and imprisonment.

Since the entire management team at Naftogaz reported to the Yanukovych administration (and indirectly to Firtash), the two parties facing each other in the Stockholm arbitration were now friends and allies. Indeed, there was only one side. Firtash was negotiating in the interest of RUE and himself. At the same time, the Ukrainian government, which was supposed to be representing the Ukrainian people on the other side of the table, was represented by Energy Minister Boyko, a longstanding friend and ally of Firtash.

Once the Ukrainian government changed hands, it immediately reversed its position in the Stockholm arbitration proceedings by 180 degrees. The Yanukovych administration was now "admitting" that RUE had always owned the gas in dispute and that Naftogaz had no legal reason to acquire the disputed quantity of natural gas from RUE.

Since the Ukraine government and Naftogaz had withdrawn their opposition to RUE's claim on the gas, the Stockholm Arbitration Tribunal was left with no alternative but to grant RUE's claim. In June 2010, the Tribunal ruled that Naftogaz owed its former gas supply intermediary, RUE, 11 billion cubic meters of natural gas, which RUE claimed was illegally confiscated in January 2009. In addition, the Tribunal fined Naftogaz an additional 1.1 billion cubic meters for a total award of 12.1 billion cubic meters of gas. When Yanukovych and his pro-Russian allies in control of the Ukraine government sold out Naftogaz in the Stockholm Arbitration, they also sold out the Ukrainian people, who have suffered untold hardship throughout history. The transfer of the natural gas ordered by the Tribunal represented more than 50% of the total volume of natural gas annually extracted in Ukraine from the country's resources and 50% of the country's annual needs.

The Stockholm arbitration panel ruling gave Firtash and his associates an even greater ability to illegally fund the pervasive system of corruption and racketeering that encompassed every level of government in Ukraine. At the same time, they could carry on suppressing political dissent through intimidation, racketeering, and other violations of fundamental human and political rights. Moreover, the vast windfall obtained from the Stockholm arbitration ruling gave Firtash and his associates an even greater reservoir of cash to invest their unlawfully obtained funds both in Ukraine and internationally, including in the U.S.

The resulting transfer of vast amounts of natural gas from Naftogaz to RUE had a dramatic and immediate impact on Ukraine's economy and the well-being of its citizens. Although the Tribunal award was technically against Naftogaz, since that company was state-owned, the payments were made with natural gas that was, in essence, owned by Ukraine and its citizens. This proved to be a colossal disaster. The gas now transferred to RUE had been paid for through a transfer of $1.7 billion from Naftogaz to Gazprom. In addition, Ukrainian citizens were now being deprived of a considerable amount of gas needed within Ukraine, critical to the well-being of the people. To fill this shortfall in gas supply for domestic consumption, Naftogaz had to purchase gas from foreign sources; however, the price of the 12.1 billion cubic meters of gas had increased dramatically since the pricing at the time of the original transaction, which averaged out to $1.7 billion. It was now worth at least $3.5 billion.

Firtash and one of his companies – DF Group – used a significant percentage of their $3.5 billion in windfall profits through RUE to increase offshore money laundering activities in the U.S. and elsewhere through CMZ Ventures, the investment fund Paul Manafort and others set up in the U.S. However, CMZ and its related companies came under increasing scrutiny by federal and state law enforcement agencies. Manafort, Brad Zackson, and Arthur Cohen began using various offshore "shell" companies, which had been in place in December 2007. These companies created an intentionally complex trail of paperwork distributed across multiple legal venues to make it more difficult for investigators to follow the money. These offshore companies used to hide the "money trail" included DVN Eleuthera Development, Inc., Dynamic-Vulcan Eleuthera, Inc., and Greywold Enterprises Inc, all of which were Panamanian companies.

Under U.S. law, they were required to file Foreign Bank Account Reports (FBARs) for these offshore bank accounts but failed to do so. Through information provided by some former CMZ Venture employees, we obtained "smoking gun" evidence in the form of emails between Manafort and Firtash associates discussing the wire transfer of funds for money laundering and corrupt financial activities. For example, Manafort sent one email, dated June 8, 2009, to Brad Zackson discussing Manafort's recent trip to Kyiv, where Manafort met with Firtash and some of his associates. Manafort reported to Zackson in the email: "[Firtash] is still totally on board, and a wire will be forthcoming either the end of this week or next week." One of the New York bank accounts used for their wire transfers was a CMZ Ventures account with Metropolitan National Bank, and a second bank account was a law firm account with Capital One bank.

Meanwhile, in Ukraine, the deprivation of fundamental human rights and erosion of the rule of law there reached such epidemic proportions that the European Union felt compelled to issue a Resolution on June 9, 2011, noting:

> [S]ince the launch of the investigations on December 15, 2010, Yulia Tymoshenko has been interrogated 44 times, a travel ban has been imposed on her, both domestically and internationally, for nearly six months, she has been prevented by the Ukrainian authorities from traveling inside Ukraine on four occasions, as well as from traveling to Brussels in February and June, and she was summoned and questioned on May 25, 2011, for several hours before being released. [15]

The EU Resolution concluded that "corruption and abuse of power remain widespread in Ukraine." The Resolution claimed there was an urgent need for "a comprehensive reform of the judiciary and measures to ensure respect for the rule of law in criminal investigations and prosecutions, including the principle of fair, impartial and independent judicial proceedings, [which] has not yet been implemented in Ukraine."

The Amended Complaint

We filed an amended complaint on behalf of Tymoshenko and other opposition leaders in the federal district court in Manhattan on December 19, 2011, adding Paul Manafort and several other U.S. defendants to the complaint.[16] We continued to gather additional information on the international racketeering and money laundering enterprise that Firtash, Manafort, and their associates were overseeing and amended the complaint against them with further details of their corrupt activities.

The Amended Complaint charged Firtash, Manafort, and the other defendants with engaging in a vast international money laundering scheme involving illegal funds. We asserted that the defendants obtained the funds from unlawfully "skimming" hundreds of millions of dollars. Those funds that would otherwise have been used for legitimate purposes and the benefit of Ukraine's people came from natural gas transactions, the money improperly received by Firtash and RUE through the Stockholm Arbitration Award, and from other acts of racketeering.

Our Amended Complaint further explained that the U.S.-based defendants then laundered a substantial portion of these funds through a labyrinth of New York-based shell companies and bank accounts. Now appearing "clean," the money was next moved into Ukrainian and other European accounts to make illegal kickbacks and bribes to corrupt Ukrainian officials. With their palms sufficiently greased, those officials campaigned to persecute and destroy Tymoshenko and other political opposition leaders. Among the tools they used were politically motivated investigations, prolonged arbitrary detentions under cruel, inhumane, degrading, and barbaric conditions, and other violations of fundamental human rights.

We identified Manafort as the primary U.S. architect of this racketeering scheme. The Amended Complaint explained in great detail how Manafort invited defendant Firtash to join their scheme to move some of his illicit funds to the United States, where the money could then be "laundered" through ostensibly legitimate real estate transactions. Much of the laundered funds were then funneled back to the Ukraine-based defendants.[17]

Some of the causes of action asserted in our Amended Complaint related to the well-documented allegations that the defendants had violated Tymoshenko's fundamental human rights.[18] We also alleged in the Amended Complaint that the defendants had engaged in a civil racketeering (RICO) conspiracy to illegally launder funds to, among other things, finance their campaign to suppress the pro-democracy forces in Ukraine.[19] Specifically, it was alleged that the Yanukovych administration, aided and abetted by the defendants and other co-conspirators, launched a wave of arrests and investigations aimed at Tymoshenko and her political allies in a concerted campaign to eliminate political opposition in Ukraine.[20]

In addition to the civil RICO statute, the complaint also contained allegations under the Alien Tort Statute (ATS), a section in the United States Code that gives federal courts jurisdiction over lawsuits filed by foreign nationals for torts committed in violation of international law.[21] The ATS is one of the oldest federal laws, having been enacted in 1789 as part of the First Judiciary Act. However, for the next two centuries it was rarely used, until some enterprising human rights lawyers started employed it on behalf of victims of human rights violations in various countries.[22]

The March 26, 2013 Decision

On March 26, 2013, U.S. federal judge Kimba Wood granted the motion to dismiss brought by Manafort and the other U.S. defendants but permitted plaintiffs to file another amended complaint. We were allowed to expand on the allegations of arbitrary detention and political persecution by the Ukrainian government headed at that time by Viktor Yanukovych and masterminded by Firtash.[23] The court accepted as true the complaint's allegations that Manafort and other defendants participated in a "complex racketeering scheme," by which the Ukrainian Defendants laundered money through a series of U.S.-based "shell companies." Judge Wood's decision also accepted as accurate for purposes of the motion the allegations in the complaint that Tymoshenko was detained for interrogation on approximately forty-four occasions, including one incident when Tymoshenko was surrounded by "25 to 30 militia guards wearing face masks and black uniforms."[24]

The court also recognized that Tymoshenko and other Ukrainian opposition leaders were detained under inhumane conditions at the notoriously overcrowded Lukyanivska prison in Kyiv, which housed almost 50% more prisoners than it was designed to accommodate.[25] Although Tymoshenko became ill while incarcerated, the Ukrainian judge overseeing her case repeatedly denied requests to allow Tymoshenko's physician to conduct a physical examination. Tymoshenko refused to be treated by prison doctors close to the Yanukovych administration because she justifiably feared for her life.[26] Her physical condition deteriorated so significantly that the Ukrainian regime ultimately relented, concerned about the political and diplomatic repercussions if she died in prison.

The Tymoshenko case received intense international press attention. The German government and its EU allies pressured Ukraine to win her release to the care of a team of German doctors who were standing by to perform life-saving surgery on her if given the opportunity. When the Ukrainian government finally relented, Tymoshenko was flown by medical transport to Germany. She underwent surgery and a brief recovery period before being handed back to Ukrainian authorities.

At first blush, the concern by Tymoshenko and her advisers that Ukrainian government doctors might try to kill her seemed far-fetched. However, I got a personal taste of the extreme skepticism (some would say verging on paranoia) that Ukrainian opposition leaders and their followers had about the government-run health care system. During one of my trips to Kyiv, some opposition members of parliament (MPs) and I got in the middle of a reasonably commonplace shouting and shoving match with plainclothes government security officers. These government officers shadowed our every move in Kyiv during the increasing tension and violence leading up to the Maidan Revolution in early 2014, which ultimately resulted in the overthrow of the Yanukovych regime. When I fell to the ground during a brief shoving match with some government officers, I instinctively tried to break my fall with my right arm. This, however, was a grave mistake on my part since a prior injury made me very susceptible to dislocating my right shoulder for the umpteenth time. This time, the dislocation was far worse than any I had experienced before, and I could not manipulate it back into place. The pain was excruciating. I asked the MPs to take me to the nearest hospital. Still, they refused, saying that a few Ukrainians known as leaders of the opposition movement had gone into government hospitals but never resurfaced. In my case, they did not want a repeat of this, resulting in a long car ride around the city until we found a trustworthy doctor on the far side of town. By then, my shoulder had become "frozen" in its dislocated position, requiring that the doctor administer an anesthetic to loosen up my shoulder enough for him to manipulate it back into place. Several MPs assisted by holding me down. When I was finally released with my arm in a sling and a generous supply of painkillers, I had to move up my departure from Kyiv to undergo emergency surgery in New York. However, as I was transferring planes in Warsaw, Poland, I had to remove the sling and bandages at an airport checkpoint to convince the Polish security personnel that I was not hiding any weapon or bomb in the sling. It was a painful and agonizing process, but I kept telling myself it was better for all of us that they took their jobs seriously, no matter how unlikely it was that an aging lawyer from New York fit the terrorist profile.

The ATS and Civil RICO Claims

In dismissing the ATS claims outlined in the Amended Complaint, Judge Wood found that, while arbitrary detention is actionable under the ATS, we failed to plead facts sufficient to show that the U.S. Defendants had aided abetted the Ukrainian Defendants' violations of the ATS.[27] The court noted that, under the ATS, "arbitrary detention occurs when a person is detained without warrant or articulable suspicion, is not apprised of charges against him or her and is not brought to trial."[28] The court found that Tymoshenko's detention was not technically "arbitrary" since her detention was accompanied by legal process. She had been apprised of charges against her, and she had the opportunity to challenge them at trial, albeit in a kangaroo court. Judge Wood pointed out that counsel had represented Tymoshenko at each stage of the proceedings against her. Judge Wood characterized Tymoshenko's claims as not so much that she had been denied legal process, but rather that the process afforded rested on factual inaccuracies and was legally insufficient.[29]

The court ultimately dismissed Plaintiffs' civil RICO allegations because money laundering allegations in the complaint primarily related to the foreign aspects of the international racketeering enterprise, and most of the acts alleged that formed the pattern of racketeering activity took place abroad. In short, the court found that civil RICO does not provide a cause of action for extraterritorial offenses, requiring dismissal of Plaintiffs' civil RICO claims against the U.S. Defendants.[30] The Court found that the scheme alleged by Plaintiffs to be primarily foreign, involving the bribery of Ukrainian officials and the use of politically-motivated trials and incarcerations, with the connection to the United States to be incidental, mostly involving money laundering and the investment of money in U.S.-based corporations.

The Second Amended Complaint

Although the district court dismissed our amended complaint, we were permitted to amend our pleadings again with a Second Amended Complaint. We redoubled our efforts to obtain additional evidence to flesh out our money laundering and racketeering claims against Firtash, Manafort, Gates, and the rest of their co-conspirators. In addition, some investigative reporters started chasing down leads disclosed in our court proceedings, and some significant investigative reporting began appearing in the media. As a result, we were contacted by former employees of Manafort, Brad Zackson, and their corporate labyrinth.

Two of these former employees – Scott Snizek and Christy Rullis – joined Yulia Tymoshenko as named plaintiffs in the Second Amended Complaint against the defendants. Manafort and his cronies had duped and deceived these employees into believing they were engaged in legitimate business ventures in New York. However, in truth and fact, defendants operated their various U.S.-based companies solely to provide a veneer of legitimacy to their money laundering and other racketeering activities. The defendants even failed to pay the salaries and commissions owed to these employees. The few payments that Snizek, Rullis, and others received were often disguised as "reimbursements of expenses" so that the defendants could illegally avoid making tax withholding and other required deductions.

Snizek, Rullis, and other former employees of the defendants provided us with some additional critical information, including emails and documents. They gave us more granular detail of the far-flung racketeering conspiracy that Firtash, Manafort, and the rest of their co-conspirators hatched and carried out for years.

Although our Second Amended Complaint provided significant additional factual support to Tymoshenko's case, Judge Kimba M. Wood still found that it fell short of what was legally required. However, Judge Wood permitted plaintiffs to amend once again, especially since the Second Circuit had recently come down with an important decision discussing the extraterritorial impact of the civil RICO statute.[31]

The Maidan Revolution and the Treasure-Trove of New Documents

And then the unexpected happened, changing everything. A national revolution led to a sudden change of fate for Tymoshenko and the rest of Ukraine.

During my frequent trips to Ukraine, I heard some political opposition members predict that if the Yanukovych regime continued to stifle pro-democracy and pro-Western voices, there would have to be a revolution. I considered this talk to be largely rhetorical, but in November 2013, pro-democracy demonstrators in Ukraine successfully launched the Euromaidan revolution, also known as "The Revolution of Dignity." Pro-Western protesters occupied the Maidan Nezalezhnosti Plaza in the center of Kyiv and repulsed attempts by riot police and government sharpshooters to oust them. The protests were triggered by the Ukrainian government's decision to suspend the signing of an association agreement with the European Union. Instead, the Yanukovych government sought closer ties to Russia and the Eurasian Economic Union.

Finally, following months of increasing protests, in February 2014, Yanukovych and members of his inner circle fled the country, seeking the safety of Moscow. However, in his haste to depart Kyiv, Yanukovych left many incriminating documents, giving investigative reporters and human rights lawyers a bonanza of new information. Numerous nylon bags of documents were retrieved from the riverbed near Yanukovych's palatial compound. Another trove of documents was found in the comedically opulent residence of the deposed prosecutor general, Viktor Pshonka, including records found in his sauna. Many waterlogged documents had to be dried out and posted on an internet website named "Yanukovychleaks. org." In addition, certain former operatives affiliated with the Yanukovych Administration agreed to cooperate with the Ukraine Ministry of Justice and General Prosecutor's Office, now staffed with appointees of the interim government. These former officials provided valuable information regarding governmental corruption by the Yanukovych Regime and their private, non-governmental sources of money, such as Dimitri Firtash and the numerous companies he controlled.

On April 4, 2014, I filed a supplemental memorandum with the court, attaching some "smoking gun" documents relating to the case retrieved following the fall of the Yanukovych Regime and the re-emergence of liberal democracy in Ukraine. One of the documents recovered from the former Prosecutor General Pshonka's sauna was an email/memo dated August 24, 2012, from Gregory B. Craig to Paul Manafort. Craig, at the time a partner at the Skadden Arps law firm, was working on the not-so-independent investigation and report regarding the Tymoshenko criminal prosecutions. The document suggested that Manafort was communicating directly with Craig, Yanukovych, and other co-conspirators to fully inform them of what Skadden was looking for and where the "investigation" was headed. This and other documents cast a pall over the Skadden law firm investigation by showing that Manafort was clearly orchestrating and manipulating the Skadden's investigation from behind the curtain. He was leaving nothing to chance as to the outcome of the investigation - the conclusion that the Tymoshenko prosecution was reasonably fair and not politically manipulated.

Other "smoking gun" documents uncovered following the Maidan Revolution were drafts of the Skadden Report edited by Ukrainian government officials in the Yanukovych administration. The inference was that the Report's contents were being cleared with Ukrainian officials and that the public statements about the Report being "independent" were a hoax. [32]

Among the other critical documents that came to light following the 2014 revolution was evidence confirming our suspicions that the amount paid to the Skadden law firm was much more than the $12,000 that the Ukraine government publicly said it was paying for the "independent" investigation. We had previously suspected that some fraud was afoot between the Skadden firm and Manafort. Even before discovering these additional documents, an email was sent by Tymoshenko's Ukrainian counsel, Sergiy Vlasenko, to Gregory Craig and Alex Haskell, two Skadden partners who visited Ukraine during the investigation. In this email, the Skadden Firm was asked how two "highly ranked" partners of Skadden and a large team of associates could have worked for more than five months (May through October 2012) on the investigation for only $12,000. Their travel and lodging expenses alone for their time in Kyiv would have exceeded that sum. Mr. Vlasenko never received a response from the Skadden Firm to his questions. The blatant political motivation behind the sham "investigations" and "prosecutions" of Tymoshenko and other political opposition leaders were excised entirely from the Skadden final report. The report, in effect, was merely an expensive whitewashing of Yanukovych's corruption.

Tymoshenko's Release

One of the primary goals of our federal court litigation was to add pressure on the Yanukovych Regime to release Tymoshenko from prison. On February 22, 2014, this was accomplished when Tymoshenko was released and joined the victorious protesters in downtown Kyiv at the Maidan (Independence Square). Meanwhile, Yanukovych fled to Moscow.

After her release, Tymoshenko and her pro-democracy allies concentrated their efforts on rebuilding a viable democracy in Ukraine and helping it face the existential threat posed by Russia's *de facto* annexation of Crimea and portions of eastern Ukraine known as the Donbas. She, therefore, asked us to discontinue our efforts to pursue her case. Most of our objectives had already been achieved. Not only was she now a free woman, but the litigation had exposed the corruption, money laundering, and racketeering activities that Manafort and his U.S. and Ukrainian co-conspirators had engaged in over the years.

* * *

Perhaps more than any other case I had worked on, the Tymoshenko case took me in directions that I never expected it to go. It became much more than just a human rights case on behalf of one high-profile and persecuted woman political leader and ended up ripping off the lid of political corruption both in Ukraine and in the United States.

Chapter 18

The Manafort and Guiliani Investigations

With the end of the Tymoshenko litigation and her release from prison, I thought that my work regarding Ukraine-related matters was over. This, however, proved not to be the case.

As soon as the Special Counsel's office was established in May 2017, under the leadership of Robert S. Mueller III, it took over the federal investigation of Manafort and Gates, which had been ongoing for several years. The investigation had been handled by the FBI and the U.S. Attorney's Office for the Southern District of New York (SDNY). A part of the federal investigation of Manafort and Gates was based on their money-laundering activities, detailed in a civil RICO case filed in the U.S. District Court, SDNY, by my law firm on behalf of Yulia Tymoshenko.[1] Prosecutors in the U.S. Attorney's Office – and later the Special Counsel's office – followed up on leads we provided in the civil RICO case. They issued subpoenas for the records of CMZ Ventures as part of their investigation of Manafort's Russian and Ukrainian ties and his money laundering efforts involving the U.S.[2]

Of particular interest to federal agents were documents that my law firm filed on April 4, 2014, relating to the civil RICO case. These documents showed the depth of Manafort's relationship with Putin and his entire inner circle, particularly the Russian oligarch Oleg Deripaska, who was considered to be the closest of the Kremlin inner circle to Putin. Later, court documents relating to Manafort's indictment revealed that he had taken a $10 million loan from Deripaska in 2010, which was forgiven once Manafort established himself as Trump's go-between with Deripaska and others in Putin's inner circle.[3]

One of the documents left behind when Yanukovych and his cronies fled Kyiv in late February 2014 was a Russian translation of an email/memo dated August 24, 2012, from Gregory B. Craig to Paul Manafort.

Craig was a partner at the Skadden Arps law firm, working on an allegedly "independent" investigation and report regarding the Tymoshenko criminal prosecutions.[4] The clear inference of the document was that Manafort orchestrated and "coordinated" Skadden's so-called "independent" investigation with the Ukrainian government. The intention was for Yanukovych and his racketeering co-conspirators to be kept fully informed of what the Skadden team were looking at, and where the "investigation" was headed. For example, an early draft of Skadden's report annotated by Ukrainian government officials appeared to push the Skadden lawyers to revise their conclusions and take a more pro-government and pro-Russian view of the case against Tymoshenko.

Unsurprisingly, after apparently being heavily edited by Manafort and his pro-Russian clients in Kyiv, the final draft of the Skadden report released to the press concluded that the Tymoshenko prosecution by the Ukraine government – although slightly flawed – was not politically motivated.[5]

Indictment and Arrest of Manafort and Gates

On July 25, 2017, the FBI and other federal agents executed a search warrant at Manafort's private residence in Northern Virginia in the early morning hours.[6] They carted off Manafort's personal computer and documents believed to be tax and foreign banking records. They also took photographs of his vast wardrobe. The pictures were later used to support government claims that Manafort had millions in illegally laundered funds from Russian oligarchs and the Ukraine government. The raid was Special Counsel Mueller's way of getting Manafort's attention and impressing upon him the seriousness of the federal investigation.

On October 29-30, 2017, government prosecutors filed a 12-count grand jury indictment in the District of Columbia against Paul Manafort and Trump's ex-Deputy Campaign Chairman, Rick Gates. Prosecutors charged them with numerous federal crimes, including conspiracy to launder money, conspiracy against the United States, acting as unregistered agents of a foreign principal, and false and misleading FARA statements. The indictment also charged them with hiding tens of millions of dollars received from former Ukrainian President Viktor Yanukovych, his Party of Regions, and the Opposition Bloc between 2006 to 2015.

Former Trump campaign chairman Paul Manafort arrives to the courtroom as he is arraigned at the New York Supreme Court in New York, U.S., June 27, 2019.
REUTERS/Eduardo Munoz/Alamy Stock Photo 2CKT53C

These payments occurred before, during, and after March 2014, when a popular uprising caused Yanukovych to flee Ukraine, ultimately landing him in Moscow under Putin's protection.

The indictment further charged Manafort and Gates with funneling millions of dollars into the U.S. through various offshore bank accounts without paying U.S. taxes. In addition to funding their lavish lifestyles, Manafort and Gates also used this money to conduct lobbying efforts in Washington for Yanukovych, his political party, and the Government of Ukraine. However, they never took the trouble to register or provide the necessary disclosures as foreign agents under FARA. The indictment also alleged that Manafort and Gates lobbied multiple members of Congress and their staffs about Ukraine sanctions, the validity of Ukraine elections, and the propriety of Yanukovych's imprisoning his presidential rival, Yulia Tymoshenko.

Although the indictment was substantially accurate, a portion of the charge erroneously refered to Tymoshenko's background as a former Ukraine president. This minor error triggered a Russian-orchestrated campaign to discredit the indictment and the entire Special Counsel's investigation. Although Tymoshenko served twice as Ukraine's prime minister, U.S. prosecutors inadvertently misstated that she had served as Ukraine's president in their indictment.[7] On October 31, 2017, shortly after the Manafort and Gates indictment was publicly released, Russia's foreign ministry seized on this parenthetical factual error as proof the allegations were "cooked up" and not part of a "serious investigation."[8]

Manafort's legal troubles were far from over. On February 22, 2018, a federal grand jury in Alexandria, Virginia, filed a new set of charges against him and Gates, charging them with 32 counts of tax, financial, and bank fraud charges.[9] Buried among the many other charges was the allegation that Steve Calk, the chief executive of Chicago's Federal Savings Bank, had "expedited" approval of $16 million in loans for Paul Manafort. Crucially, the loan was approved *after* Manafort mentioned a possible role for Calk in the Trump Campaign and administration.[10]

This second indictment proved too much for Gates to bear. The heat placed on Gates by the Special Counsel's office, combined with the financial strain of his rapidly mounting legal fees, broke his will to fight. As a result, on February 23, 2018, Rick Gates pleaded guilty to one count of conspiracy against the United States and making false statements to the

FBI.[11] In exchange for an agreement to plead guilty and to cooperate with federal prosecutors, the government dropped the other charges relating to money laundering, acting as an unregistered foreign agent, and making false statements.[12] On November 14, 2018, Special Counsel Mueller's office pushed back the sentencing of Gates, representing in federal court that Gates was now cooperating on "several ongoing investigations."[13]

On June 8, 2018, the grand jury returned a superseding indictment charging Manafort and his longtime associate, GRU agent Konstantin Kilimnik, with obstruction of justice and conspiracy to obstruct justice for their alleged efforts to contact and influence potential witnesses.[14]

After an 11-day federal jury trial in Alexandria, Virginia, on August 21, 2018, Manafort was found guilty on eight of eighteen counts of financial fraud.[15] He continued to face the additional charges pending in federal court in Washington, D.C., and the counts in the Virginia federal case where the jury could not reach a verdict. This proved too much for Manafort. So a few weeks later, on September 14, 2018, he entered into a plea agreement. Manafort agreed to plead guilty to two of the many indictment counts and fully cooperate with the Special Counsel's ongoing investigation.[16] He even agreed to forfeit to the government his $7.3 million mansion in the Hamptons and his $3 million Trump Tower condo.[17]

In connection with Manafort's guilty plea, the government released substantial new evidence of a 2012 dirty-tricks campaign that Manafort orchestrated to smear Yulia Tymoshenko and label her as an anti-Semite.[18] At that time, Tymoshenko was still in a Ukrainian prison, and then-Secretary of State Hillary Clinton was one of the leading international voices calling for her release.[19] Manafort and Gates were actively working for then-President Yanukovych's Party of Regions, facing off against Tymoshenko's All-Ukrainian Union "Fatherland" party in the 2012 Ukrainian parliamentary elections. According to the documents released by the Special Counsel's office, Manafort bragged that he could "plant some stink" on her by spreading false rumors that she espoused anti-Semitic views.[20] Although Tymoshenko's party lost many seats in the 2012 elections (likely due in part to electoral fraud), Manafort's plan to tarnish Tymoshenko's reputation in the U.S. failed. The Obama Administration continued to criticize Yanukovych and call Tymoshenko's prosecution "unfair."

On Monday, November 26, 2018, the Special Counsel's office filed a report with the U.S. District Court in Washington, D.C., stating that Manafort had lied to federal investigators and violated his plea agreement.[21] The prosecutors concluded in this report that, due to Manafort's breach of the plea agreement, the Special Counsel's office was no longer bound to recommend a reduced sentence for him based upon his cooperation and "acceptance of responsibility." It was disclosed that Manafort was secretly communicating with the White House when he was supposedly "cooperating" with the government. It soon became apparent that Manafort was a double-agent who passed valuable information about the investigation to the Trump administration. [22]

This was not the first time Manafort was accused of breaching his plea agreement and committing additional crimes. In June 2018, Manafort was charged by the prosecutors with witness tampering, which led U.S. District Court Judge Amy Berman Jackson to revoke Manafort's $10 million bond and sending him back to jail.[23]

Rudy Giuliani

With Manafort in prison, the Trump Team in the White House quickly found a replacement lawyer to keep alive their pro-Russian connections in Ukraine. The former U.S. Attorney and New York City's Mayor, Rudy Giuliani, stepped into Manafort's shoes. He became President Donald Trump's new "back channel" liaison with various Ukrainian and Russian figures seeking "dirt" on then-Senator Joe Biden, considered by many to be the leading potential Democratic candidate for the U.S. presidency in November 2019. There were media reports that the FBI and U.S. Department of Justice had opened an investigation into Giuliani's activities in Ukraine, so I was not surprised when I received some phone calls from the FBI and U.S. Justice Department attorneys. It was relatively well known that I remained in close contact with the Ukrainian members of the Tymoshenko legal team and had developed well-placed Ukrainian contacts while working on the Tymoshenko case. The reason for these calls was to find out whether my associates or contacts could provide them with any information about Giuliani and his cohorts in Ukraine.

In response to these inquiries, I provided the names and contact information for at least three people in the Ukrainian business community

Rudy Giuliani on December 5, 2020 in Boca Raton, FL
Hoo Me/Media Punch/Alamy Live News 2DFTKAE

and the newly formed Ukrainian government who had been contacted by Giuliani or one of his associates. This was part of Giuliani's continuing efforts, on behalf of Trump, to collect derogatory information about Hunter Biden's supposedly corrupt association with Burisma Holdings Limited, one of the largest natural gas providers in Ukraine. At the same time, Giuliani and his cohorts were also promoting business "opportunities" for these Ukrainians to invest in, all of which turned out to be investment scams by Giuliani and his group of shady operators. Based partly on this information we provided, both Lev Parnas and Igor Fruman – two of Giuliani's primary contacts with Russian intelligence and organized crime operatives – were indicted by the U.S. Attorney's Office for SDNY.

Years before, I had worked closely with Giuliani when we were both federal prosecutors working in New York. He was based in Manhattan with the U.S. Attorney's Office for the SDNY, and my office was across the East River in downtown Brooklyn. But neither organized crime nor Russian intelligence operatives in New York respected the jurisdictional dividing lines between the two U.S. Attorney's Offices in New York, so we were forced to work together on many vital cases. I then saw Giuliani's become "America's Mayor" after September 11, 2001, terrorist attacks on the World Trade Center and the Pentagon.

Now, during the moral squalor of the Trump Era, I watched in sadness and dismay as Giuliani seemed intent to now earn the title of "America's Traitor" for actively assisting Russia's campaign to undermine American democracy in the 2020 election.

On Tuesday, March 16, 2020, a U.S. intelligence report was released detailing attempts by Russia and other countries to influence the 2020 election. As one very notable passage in the report stated, "A key element of Moscow's strategy this election cycle was its use of people linked to Russian intelligence to launder influence narratives — including misleading or unsubstantiated allegations against President Biden — through U.S. media organizations, U.S. officials, and prominent U.S. individuals, some of whom were close to former President Trump and his administration."

As Trump's lawyer and chief conduit to Moscow, Giuliani was clearly at the top of the U.S. Intelligence community's list of White House insiders who were knowingly spreading Kremlin disinformation designed to call into question the legitimacy of the 2020 election and our country's entire democratic electoral system. Federal investigators were also probing whether, and to what extent, Giuliani, Parnas, and Fruman were acting in concert with Russian intelligence operatives such as Andrii Derkach, a Ukrainian lawmaker sanctioned by the U.S. Treasury Department as a Russian agent.

Meanwhile, Giuliani had his own legal troubles. He successfully avoided any criminal indictments, at least through the end of 2021. However, his professional reputation was essentially shredded, and he remains under scrutiny for his prominent role in the January 6, 2021 insurrection at the U.S. Capitol, where he urged the crowd to engage in "trial by combat."

Conclusion

Do not go gentle into that good night,
Old age should burn and rave at close of day;
Rage, rage against the dying of the light.

– Dylan Thomas

After 50 years of practicing law, perhaps a wiser man would be fully retired. But for me, what's past is prologue. Not a day goes by when I don't get a call asking for legal advice or representation. And when violations of civil or human rights are involved, or when a former client or dear friend is seeking some additional legal assistance or advice, it is virtually impossible for me to say no. So, as long as I continue to be in good health and my mind is reasonably sharp, the practice of law will be what keeps me going and the blood flowing. Hopefully, a second volume of this book is in my future, if I am so fortunate.

The passion and intensity with which I have approached the practice of law – as well as everything else in life – has, however, not been without sacrifice. The long hours and weeks or months of separation from those I loved took its toll. While Alaska was an extraordinarily wonderful venue for me during the Exxon Valdez litigation, the separation from my first wife and young children for weeks on end left me fighting bouts of loneliness and depression. This all quickly disappeared when I was able to return to New York for at least a few days or when they flew to Anchorage or Seattle so that we could spend some quality time together.

It has been an exciting roller coaster ride, to be sure. I supported myself and my family (with difficulty at times) while doing what I loved and doing what I felt was important. Doing good and doing well at the same time is a tricky business, but I am living proof that it is possible. As my father used to tell us, the law is not just a job, it is a noble profession. Every lawyer has a duty and sacred trust to represent the interests of the client and the community with the utmost dedication and zeal, within the bounds of the law and ethics.

I have also met some of my closest and lifelong friends through the practice of law, including some of my longstanding legal colleagues and clients. I have had the honor to represent some truly amazing people and to help them rebuild their lives and obtain some modicum of justice. For example, after their home was rendered uninhabitable by toxic pesticides, Tina and John Williams were able to use the monies they received from the judgment against the defendants to buy a new home to live and raise their family. Similarly, the men and women of the Ovaherero and Nama tribal communities I represented are living examples of how perseverance in the face of hardship and adversity could finally force Germany and the world to acknowledge the full extent of the genocidal tragedy they had suffered.

It has been a life worth living and will hopefully continue to be for some time – if the Good Lord's willing and the creek don't rise.

Endnotes

Chapter 1

1   John L. Hess, *"Nursing Homes Fight Subpoena By State's Special Prosecutor," New York Times, May 8, 1975*

2   ibid.

3   ibid.

4   ibid.

5   ibid.

6   Staff, "Nursing Homes Under Fire", *Time*, February 3, 1975.

7   Rasenberger, Jim. "Shadows on the Wall", *The New York Times*, January 23, 2005.

8   Staff, "Nursing Homes Under Fire", *Time*, February 3, 1975.

9   Hess, John L. "Bergman Given 4 Months; BERGMAN DRAWS A 4-MONTH TERM", *The New York Times*, June 18, 1976.

10   ibid.

11   Sullivan, Ronald. "BERNARD BERGMAN, NURSING-HOME FIGURE, IS DEAD", *The New York Times*, June 22, 1984.

12   Roberts, Sam. "Metro Matters; Bergman Legacy: $1,376,032 Check And 110 Auditors", *The New York Times*, February 13, 1989.

13   New York Times, June 22, 1984, Section B, Page 6 of the National edition.

14   Sullivan, Ronald. "BERNARD BERGMAN, NURSING-HOME FIGURE, IS DEAD", *The New York Times*, June 22, 1984.

15   New York Times, "A Nursing Home Must Repay US," November 21, 1975, Page 25

16   ibid.

17   ibid.

18   ibid.

19   *New York Times, "Medicaid Billed For Trip Abroad,"* John L. Hess, Jan. 9, 1975

20   *New York Time, "Nursing Homes' Gifts to Charities Under Study by Special Prosecutor,"* Richard J. Meislin, Oct. 21, 1976

21   ibid.

22   ibid.

23   ibid.

24   *"History". National Association of Medicaid Fraud Control Units.*

25   ibid.

Chapter 2

1   Ronald Goldfarb, *Perfect Villains, Imperfect Heroes.*

2   Jacqueline A. Schmitz. "Hoffa, James Riddle". libraries.psu.edu. Archived from the original on May 15, 2013.

3   "Robt. Kennedy Stands Firm Against Hoffa". *Chicago Tribune.* July 8, 1961.

4   "Threw Robert Kennedy from Office: Hoffa". *Chicago Tribune.* September 8, 1962.

5   *"United States v. Hoffa, 367 F.2d 698; Casetext".* casetext.com.Brill, Steven. *The Teamsters.* Paperback ed. New York: Simon & Schuster, 1979. ISBN 0-671-82905-X; Sloane, Arthur A. *Hoffa.* Cambridge, Mass.: MIT

6   "3 Teamster Boss Pals Face Term; Dorfman Freed". *Chicago Tribune.* March 5, 1964.

7   18 U.S.C. § 371.

8   *United States v. Fatico*, 441 F. Supp. 1285, 1289 (E.D.N.Y.1977).

9   *United States v. Fatico*, 579 F.2d 707 at 708 (2d Cir. 1978).

10 *United States v. Fatico*, 458 F. Supp. 388 (E.D.N.Y 1978).

11 *United States v. Fatico*, 458 F. Supp. 388 (E.D.N.Y. 1978).

12 https://www.courthousenews.com/cult-and-sex-ring-werent-synonymous-heiress-in-nxivm-case-insists/

13 18 U.S.C. 1961 et seq.

14 *Special Report". Usdoj.gov. Retrieved September 22, 2012.*

15 https://www.nytimes.com/1982/12/02/nyregion/cody-sentenced-to-5-year-term-as-a-racketeer.html

16 https://www.nytimes.com/1979/05/06/archives/suffolk-scandal-exposes-a-sewer-of-corruption.html

17 ibid.

18 https://www.nytimes.com/1979/06/01/archives/supplier-of-pipe-for-li-sewers-guilty-of-fraud-us-jury-returns.html

19 United States of America v. Vincent Delillo, David Francis and Clearview Concrete Products Corporation, 620 F.2d 939 (2d Cir. 1980); https://www.nytimes.com/1979/06/01/archives/supplier-of-pipe-for-li-sewers-guilty-of-fraud-us-jury-returns.html

Whelton, In Guards We Trust, N.Y. Times, Sept.19, 1976, § 6 (Magazine), at 20.

20 ibid.

21 Wall St. J., July 24, 1980, § I, at 1, col. 7.

22 https://www.nytimes.com/1982/09/01/nyregion/mob-alliance-to-share-casino-riches-reported.html

23 https://www.nytimes.com/1982/07/20/nyregion/us-links-union-chief-to-2-unsolved-slayings.html

24 https://www.nytimes.com/1982/07/30/nyregion/the-city-guards-president-gets-prison-term.html

25 https://www.nytimes.com/1982/09/29/nyregion/judge-revokes-bail-of-li-union-chief-in-racketeering-case.html

Chapter 3

1   *Chernobyl Nuclear Accident". www.iaea.org. 14 May 2014;* Burgherr, Peter; Hirschberg, Stefan (2008). *"A Comparative Analysis of Accident Risks in Fossil, Hydro, and Nuclear Energy Chains". Human and Ecological Risk Assessment: An International Journal. 14 (5): 947–973.*

2   NSAG-7: The Chernobyl Accident: Updating of INSAG-1" (PDF). *IAEA.* 1992. Archived (PDF) from the original on 20 October 2018.

3   McCall, Chris (April 2016). "Chernobyl disaster 30 years on: lessons not learned". *The Lancet.* 387 (10029): 1707–1708. doi:10.1016/s0140-6736(16)30304-x. ISSN 0140-6736. PMID 27116266. S2CID 39494685.

4   Mettler Jr., Fred A. "Medical decision making and care of casualties from delayed effects of a nuclear detonation" (PDF). *The National Academies of Sciences, Engineering, and Medicine.* Archived from the original (PDF) on 12 July 2018.

5   Peplow, M. (1 April 2006). "Special Report: Counting the dead". *Nature.* 440(7087): 982–983. Bibcode:2006Natur.440..982.. doi:10.1038/440982a. PMID 16625167.

6   628 F. Supp. 654 (E.D.N.Y. 1986).

7   Newsday, Susan Benkelman, *LILCO Crisis Plan Flawed,* March 12, 1987, at 3.

8   Los Angeles Times, John S. Goldman and David Treadwell, "At Least 40 Killed As Jet Crashes on Long Island: 158 Aboard," January 26, 1990, at A1, Column 3.

9   *N.Y. Pub. Serv. Law § 4(1)* (McKinney 1989).

10 ibid. § 66(12).

11 The plaintiffs also alleged that the LILCO defendants testified falsely about the projected commercial operation date of two nuclear power stations at Jamesport, New York. However, at the trial of *Suffolk v. LILCO et al.* these allegations were rejected by the jury, and no

aspect of LILCO's alleged misconduct in the Jamesport-related proceedings is at issue on this appeal.

18 *U.S.C. § 1961 et seq. (1988).*

12 *18 U.S.C. § 1961 et seq. (1988).*

13 Newsday, Robert Fresco, *Judge Raps LILCO Trial Testimony,* October 18, 1988 at 23.

14 Newsday, Robert Kessler, Kathleen Keir and Susan Benkelman, *U.S. Atty: LILCO Belongs to Eastern District,* March 29, 1988, at 5.

15 18 U.S.C. § 1961 et seq.

16 18 U.S.C. § 1964

17 Newsday, Robert Fresco, *The No Nonsense Judge,* December 7, 1988, at 25.

18 ibid.

19 ibid.

20 ttps://www.nytimes.com/1988/03/11/nyregion/suffolk-suit-accuses-lilco-of-lying.html

21 *County of Suffolk v. Long Island Lighting Co., 710 F. Supp. 1405, 1406 (E.D.N.Y. 1989)* (quoting *Fed. R. Civ. P. 23(a)(4)).*

22 MDL 381 Docket Document No. 0033.

23 Newsday, Robert Fresco, *LILCO Denied Delay in Fraud Trial,* September 28, 1988, at 25.

24 ibid.

25 Newsday, Robert Fresco, *Witness: PSC Was Misled,* October 27, 1988, at 38.

26 Newsday, October 26, 1988.

27 ibid.

28 Newsday, Robert Fresco, *Shoreham Jury Gets a Tour of Plant,* November 3, 1988, at 25.

29 Newsday, Susan Benkelman, *Shareholders Say Yes,* November 5, 1988, at 3.

30 ibid.

31 Newsday, Lisa Ruppel, *Sharing a Sense of Resignation,* November 5, 1988, at 3.

32 ibid.

33 ibid.

34 The jury also concluded that the other defendants – Charles R. Pierce, who served at various times as a Senior Vice-President, President, and then Chairman of LILCO's Board of Directors; Charles J. Davis, a LILCO Vice-President; and Andrew W. Wofford, also a LILCO Vice-President during pertinent time periods herein – had not committed fraud in any of the eight PSC proceedings.

35 New York Post, December 6, 1988, at 15.

36 Wall Street Journal, Bill Paul, *Jury Rules LILCO Lied to Win Rate Boosts, Complicating Firm's Plans for Shoreham,* December 6, 1988, at A4.

37 ibid.

38 *710 F. Supp. at 1389-90.*

39 ibid., 710 F. Supp. at 1393.

40 ibid. *at 1393.*

41 ibid., *at 1400, 1402-03.*

42 ibid. at 1395.

43 ibid. at 1405.

44 Wall Street Journal, Bill Paul, *County May Offer to Settle with LILCO, Proposal Would Slash Firm's Book Value,* December 8, 1988, at A14.

45 Long Island Newsday, *Time-Out on Shoreham: Verdict Against LILCO Put Talk of Deal on Hold,* December 7, 1988, at 5.

46 ibid.

47 New York Times, Dennis Hevasi, *After LILCO: A Future for RICO against Regulated Industries?,* February 12, 1989, at 42.

48 ibid.

49 Manhattan Lawyer, *LILCO Ruling My Limit RICO Actions,* February 21-27, 1989, at 4.

50 ibid.

51 ibid.

52 *710 F. Supp. at 1424.*

53 New York Times, John Rather, December 18, 1988, *Shoreham's Ratepayers Enter the Fray*, at 12.
54 ibid.
55 ibid.
56 ibid.
57 ibid.
58 *710 F. Supp. at 1424.*
59 Memorandum and Order of Judge Weinstein, dated March 22, 1989, 10-11.
60 *See 710 F. Supp. at 1452-66.*
61 Transcript of Fairness Hearing, March 3, 1989.
62 ibid.
63 ibid. at 7455.
64 ibid.
65 ibid.
66 *710 F. Supp. 1428.*
67 Memorandum and Order, March 22, 1989, at 5-6.
68 ibid.
69 ibid.
70 ibid.
71 ibid. at 7546.
72 *710 F. Supp. 1477.*
73 *County of Suffolk v. Long Island Lighting Company*, 907 F. 2d 1295 (2d Cir. 1989)
74 ibid.
75 *City of Detroit v. Grinnell Corp.*, 560 F.2d 1093, 1098 (2d Cir. 1977) (quoting *Trustees of the Internal Improvement Fund v. Greenough*, 105 U.S. 527, 536, 26 L. Ed. 1157 (1881)).
76 *County of Suffolk v. Long Island Lighting Company*, 907 F. 2d 1295 (2d Cir. 1990)
77 Long Island Newsday, Rita Ciolli, *Verdict Rekindles Debate over Racketeering Law*, December 12, 1988, at 3.
78 ibid.
79 ibid.
80 ibid.
81 Although lobbying records are not readily available for 2007, SCANA spent a total of $1.5 million lobbying South Carolina legislators since 2009. SCANA also spent $63,000 in campaign contributions during the 2006 South Carolina state election cycle, making it the eleventh largest overall contributor that year. In 2008, that number more than doubled to $168,605, making SCANA the sixth largest donor in the state. SCANA has been in the top-ten South Carolina state election spenders in every election cycle since—most recently spending $224,644 in the 2016 cycle. (data compiled from https://www.opensecrets.org).
82 http://www.thestate.com/news/politics-government/articlel 6564 1762.html
83 Direct Testimony of Kevin B. Marsh on Behalf of South Carolina Electric & Gas Company, Docket No. 2008-196-E, https://www.nrc.gov/docs/ML0910/ML091060781.pdf
84 Docket No. 2013-150-E at 6.
85 ibid. at Ex. A, p. 2.
86 *Lightsey et. al. v. South Carolina Electric and Gas, et. al.*, 2017-CP-25-335.
87 TIMOTHY GLIBOWSKI v. SCANA CORPORATION et al, Civ. No. 18-273.
88 3:17-cv-02563-TLW.
89 Glibowski, Delmatter et al v. SCANA et al, Civ. No. 9:18-273-TLW.
90 473 U.S. 479, 496 (1985).
91 *Palmetto State Med. Ctr., Inc. v. Operation Lifeline*, 117 F. 3d 142, 148 (4th Cir. 1997).
92 *Hemi Group, LLC v. City of New York*, 559 U.S. 1, 9, 130 S.Ct. 983 (2010).
93 *Friends of the Earth, Inc. v. Gaston Cooper Recycling Corp.*, 204 F. 3d 149, 154 (4th Cir. 2000).
94 *Allstate Ins. Co. v. Plambeck*, 802 F. 3d 665, 676 (5th Cir. 2015).
95 *United States v. Schmuck*, 489 U.S. 705, 710-11; see also ibid. at 714-15 (1989).

96   *United States v. Gillion*, 704 F. 3d 284, 296 (4th Cir. 2012); see also *Neder v. United States*, 527 U.S. 1, 25 (1999).

97   492 U.S. 229 at 239 (1989).

98   *Lightsey* settled for between $2.175 and $2.2 billion, depending on the ultimate monetization value of the transferred property. It included a cash payment of $115 million, the transfer of real estate to the class with an estimated value between $60 and $85 million, and up to $2 billion in rate relief to be administered through the PSC.

99   *See Lightsey, et al. v. South Carolina Electric & Gas, et al.*, "Order On Class Counsel's Motions For Final Settlement Approval And For An Award Of Attorneys' Fees And Costs" at 33.

100 Bland, David Travis, and Avery G. Wilkes. "SCANA Settles $2 Billion Lawsuit over VC Summer Project's Failure." The Greenville News, 26 Nov. 2018, https://www.greenvilleonline.com/story/news/2018/11/26/scana-settles-2-billion-lawsuit-over-vc-summer-projects-failure/2116059002/.

Chapter 4

1   270 F. 3d, at 1246–1247.

2   *In Re the Exxon Valdez*, 296 F. Supp. 2d 1071 (D. Alaska 2004)

3   ibid.

4   472 F. 3d 600, 601, 625 (9th Cir. 2006) (per curiam), and 490 F. 3d 1066, 1068 (2007).

5   Exxon Shipping Co. v. Baker, 554 U.S. 471 (2008)

6   ibid.

7   See Kizzia, Tom (May 13, 1999). "Double-hull tankers face slow going". *Anchorage Daily News*.

Chapter 5

1   Bano v. Union Carbide Corp., 99 Civ. 11329 (U.S.D.C., S.D.N.Y.).

2   See *In re Union Carbide Corp. Gas Plant Disaster at Bhopal, India in December 1984*, 634 F. Supp. 842 (S.D.N.Y.1986).

3   See *In re Union Carbide Corp. Gas Plant Disaster at Bhopal, India in December 1984*, 809 F.2d 195 (2d Cir.), cert. denied, 484 U.S. 871, 108 S.Ct. 199 (1987).

4   Union Carbide Corp. v. Union of India, 1989 [Supplement] S.C.A.L.E. 89, 90.

5   In Re Union Carbide Corporation Gas Plant Disaster, 1992 WL 36135, 1992 U.S. District LEXIS 1909 (S.D.N.Y. February 18, 1992).

6   Bi v Union Carbide, 984 F. 2d 582 (2d Cir.), cert denied, 510 U.S. 862 (1993).

7   *Bano v. Union Carbide*, 273 F.3d 120 (2nd Cir. 2001).

8   ibid.

Chapter 6

1   No. 96 Civ. 4849 (E.D.N.Y. Apr. 1997).

2   *In re Holocaust Victim Assets Litig., No. CV 96-4849 (ERK) (MDG) (E.D.N.Y.); h*ttps://www.cbsnews.com/news/holocaust-claims-settled/

3   ibid.

4   *In Re Holocaust Victim Assets Litigation*, 105 F. Supp. 2d 139 (E.D.N.Y. 2000)

5   ibid.

6   Fed. R.Civ.P. 23(e).

7   No. 98 Civ. 3938 (SWK) (S.D.N.Y.)

8   https://law.justia.com/cases/federal/appellate-courts/F3/317/91/484332/; In re Austrian and German Bank Holocaust Litigation, 317 F.3d 91 (2d Cir. 2003).

9   ibid.

10 *See In re Nazi Era Cases Against German Defendants Litigation*, 198 F.R.D. 429, 431 (D.N.J. 2000) ("*Nazi Era Cases*").

11 Stern v. Generali, No. BC185376 (Cal., Los Angeles County Super. Ct. Nov. 23, 1999).

12 http://www.bbc.co.uk/history/worldwars/genocide/jewish_deportation_01.shtml

13 ibid.

14 «Pétain a durci le texte sur Les Juifs, Selon un document inédit». *Le Point.* 3 October 2010.

15 ahil, Leni (1990). *The Holocaust: The Fate of European Jewry, 1932–1945.* New York: Oxford University Press. ISBN 0195045238.

16 See report by the *Mission d'étude sur la spoliation des Juifs*

17 https://www.theguardian.com/world/1999/mar/28/theobserver7

18 ibid.

19 ibid.

20 ibid.

21 Nos. 97 CV 7433(SJ).

22 No. 98 Civ. 7851.

23 https://www.nytimes.com/1998/12/24/business/chase-and-morgan-sued-over-jewish-assets.html

24 28 U.S.C. 1350.

25 https://www.nytimes.com/1998/12/24/business/chase-and-morgan-sued-over-jewish-assets.html

26 Matteoli Commission, 1st Report at 3-4, 116

27 Final Report at 15.

28 https://www.wsj.com/articles/SB951271524654360876

29 ibid.

30 ibid., citing *Brown v. Cameron-Brown Co.,* 652 F.2d 375, 378 (4th Cir. 1981). *Presidential Life Ins. Co. v. Milken,* 946 F. Supp. 267, 280 (S.D.N.Y.1996).

31 ibid., citing *See Continental Cas. Co. v. Diversified Indus.,* 884 F. Supp. 937, 961 (E.D.Pa.1995).

32 *See e.g., In Re NASDAQ Market-Makers Antitrust Litigation,* 169 F.R.D. 493, 508 (S.D.N.Y.1996) (reasoning the injury to one plaintiff by a particular defendant as a result of the conspiracy confers standing to represent a class of plaintiffs injured by any of defendants› co-conspirators, even where only twenty-three of thirty-three defendants were alleged to have traded on behalf of plaintiffs); D*uPont Glore Forgan Inc. v. American Tel. & Tel.,* 69 F.R.D. 481, 486 (S.D.N.Y.1975) (finding standing exists where plaintiffs dealt with only two of twenty-three defendant companies).

33 *See Piper Aircraft Co. v. Reyno,* 454 U.S. 235, 102 S. Ct. 252, 70 L. Ed. 2d 419 (1981).

34 *See R. Maganlal & Co. v. M.G. Chem. Co., Inc.,* 942 F.2d 164 (2d Cir. 1991).

35 *Gulf Oil Corp. v. Gilbert,, 91 L. Ed. 1055* 330 U.S. 501, 508, 67 S. Ct. 839 (1946).

36 ibid., citing *See Cerbone v. International Ladies' Garment Workers' Union,* 768 F.2d 45, 48 (2d Cir.1985).

37 ibid.

38 *Bodner v. Paribas,* 202 F.R.D. 370 (E.D.N.Y. 2000), Decided Dec 21, 2000, citing *Aerospatiale and Compagnie Francaise d'Assurance Pour le Commerce Exterieur v. Phillips Petroleum,* 105 F.R.D. 16, 29 (S.D.N.Y. 1984).

39 Bush v. Gore, 531 U.S. 98 (2000).

Chapter 7

1 After Iran Air Flight 655.

2 After the 9/11 attack and American Airlines Flight 191.

3 Younge, Gary (November 10, 2006), "Flight to the Death," The Guardian.

4 *"Families dedicate Flight 587 memorial on 5-year anniversary".* The International Herald Tribune, Associated Press, November 12, 2006.

5 For example, the cases filed in Texas state court were timely removed by American Airlines to the Northern District of Texas pursuant to 28 U.S.C. § 1331 and 1441 on the basis of the Convention for the Unification of Certain Rules Relating to International Transportation by Air, October 12, 1929, 49 Stat. 3000, T.S. no. 876, 137 L.N.T.S. 11 (1934), as amended by the Protocol done at The Hague, 1995 and by Protocol No. 4 of Montreal, 1975, reprinted

in S. Exec. Rep., No. 105-20 pp. 21-32 (1998) (the "Warsaw Convention") and the Federal Aviation Act of 1958, Pub.L. No. 85-726 (recodified as amended in 49 U.S.C. § 40101 et seq.) (the "Aviation Act"). The complaint does not specifically refer to the Warsaw Act or the Aviation Act. See In re Air Crash at Belle Harbor, MDL No. 1448 (RWS), 02 Civ. 8411 (RWS) (S.D.N.Y. Jan. 15, 2003)

6   ibid.
7   *"Judicial Panel on Multidistrict Litigation".* *Federal Judicial Center.*

Chapter 8

1   Civ. No. 5:11-cv-1374.
2   See Naples News article, *"Study Recent Virginia Tech Settlement Bring Spotlight to College Suicide,"* January 1, 2012.
3   *"Lethal Beauty/The Allure: Beauty and an easy route to death have long made the Golden Gate Bridge a magnet for suicides,"* Edward Guthmann, SF Gate, October 30, 2005.
4   ibid.
5   ibid.
6   ibid. at 27.
7   Howard I. Ginsburg, as Administrator of the Estate of Bradley Marc Ginsburg v. The City of Ithaca and Cornell University, United States District Court for the Northern District of New York, Civ. No. 5:11 cv 01374.
8   *Ginsberg v. City of Ithaca et al,* 839 F. Supp. 2d 537 (N.D.N.Y. 2012).
9   The district court based its decision on the established law that a landowner (or anyone else who "controls" property) "has a duty to exercise reasonable care under the circumstances in maintaining its property in a safe condition," citing In re Kush v. City of Buffalo, 59 N.Y. 2d 26, 29 (1983). See also, Pearce v. Holland Property Management, Inc., 2009 U.S. Dist. LEXIS 47723*12 (N.D.N.Y. 2009) (the primary focus in the inquiry on duty concerns "whether the defendant's conduct created a foreseeable zone of risk, not whether the defendant could foresee the specific injury that actually occurred," citing Stanford v. Kuwait Airways Corp., 89 F. 3d 117, 125 (2d Cir. 1996); and DeVeau v. United States, 833 F. Supp. 139, 142 (N.D.N.Y. 1993) (a plaintiff must demonstrate "that there was a dangerous condition and that either the defendant affirmatively created . . . or had notice [of it] . . ., after [such] knowledge or notice was received, the defendant had a reasonable opportunity to correct the dangerous condition . . ., and that the defendant . . . failed to correct the condition within a reasonable time thereafter").
10   See National Research Consortium of Counseling Centers in Higher Education, *"New Data on the Nature of Suicidal Crises in College Students: Shifting the Paradigm,"* Dunn et al, Professional Psychology, Research and Practice, Vol. 40, No. 3, 213-222.
11   See *"Ithaca Is No Longer Fences,"* by Alex Bores, The Cornell Daily Sun, 11/29/11; see also, in the "2006 National College Health Assessment," it was found that 10% of students are contemplating suicide at any given time, with 1.3% reporting that they actually attempted suicide. *"A Public Health Approach to Campus Mental Health promotion and Suicide Prevention,"* Gregory T. Ells, PhD, Director of Counseling and Psychological Services, et al, Harvard Health Policy Review, Volume 13.
12   See article written by Timothy C. Marchell, PhD, M.P.H. Cornell's Director of Mental Health Initiatives, for the *Ithaca Journal* on June 27, 2011, entitled, *"History, research and responsibility show the need for safer bridges."*
13   *See* Rob Fishman, "Cornell Suicides: Do Ithaca's Gorges Invite Jumpers?" *Huffington Post,* 3/11/10.
14   See guest editorial in *the Ithaca Journal* entitled, "Moral Concern: Safe Bridges," dated April 15, 1978, written by Nina Miller, the founder of the Suicide Prevention and Crisis Services (SPCS) of Tompkins County, and W. Jack Lewis, Director, Cornell United Religious Work, calling for means restriction on Ithaca's gorge bridges.
15   See *Huffington Post* article, Rob Fishman, *"Cornell Suicides: Do Ithaca's Gorges Invite Jumpers?",* 12/16/2010, reporting on the suicide of Bradley Ginsburg in February 2010; three weeks

later, William Sinclair, and the very next day, Matthew Zika. See also, *Inside Higher Education*, "Does 6 Deaths in 6 Months made Cornell A 'Suicide School?"

16   See *"Means Restriction on Ithaca's Bridges: A Key Element of a Comprehensive Approach to Preventing Suicide,"* prepared by Dr. Tim Marchell (updated: April 14, 2011).

17   See New York Times ("NYT") article dated 11/5/94, *"Another Fatal Plunge has Cornell Asking Whether Its Gorges Inspire Student Suicides."*

18   See *Inside Higher Ed.* (updated 3/16/2010, "Does 6 deaths in 6 months make Cornell 'suicide school?", Jennifer Epstein, reprinted in USA Today.

19   Dr. Tim Marchell, Paper, *"Means Restriction on Ithaca's Bridges, A Key Element of a Comprehensive Approach to Preventing Suicide,"* (updated April 14, 2011), at 5-9.

20   "The Final Leap: Suicide on the Golden Gate Bridge," John Bateson, at p. 141.

21   See www.mhrsonline.org at 1. See also, Gannett Health Services: website section "Notice & Respond," Cornell website (http://gannett.cornell.edu/notice/resources/suicide.cfm), at page 4 of 5.

22   See Article, SF Gate, 11/03/05, by Carolyn Zinko.

23   ibid.

24   New York Times, "Suicides Mounting, Golden Gate Looks to Add a Safety Net, Carol Pogash, March 26, 2014.

25   New York Times, March 26, 2014, "Suicides Mounting, Golden Gate Looks to Add a Safety Net," Carol Pogash.

26   ibid.

27   ibid.

28   ibid.

29   Public opinion also seems to have changed in favor of suicide prevention since 1995, when the number of bridge suicides was approaching 1000 and a radio disc jockey offered a case of Snapple to the family of the 1000th jumper. ibid.

30   ibid.

31   Howard I. Ginsburg, as Administrator of the Estate of Bradley Marc Ginsburg v. The City of Ithaca and Cornell University, United States District Court for the Northern District of New York, Civ. No. 5:11 cv 01374.

32   Cornell University North Campus Circulation Study, prepared for Cornell University by Sasaki Associates, Inc., dated May 2002 ("Sasaki Report").

33   Cornell's expert report submitted in the district court directly contradicted the Report that Cornell commissioned shortly after Bradley's death, which pointed out that the gorges are iconic spots and that "means restriction is critical to preventing suicides by jumping and individuals almost always do not find a second method when they are obstructed from using the first . . . that most individuals who would jump from iconic spots are ambivalent, act impulsively, choose a specific site, and if thwarted from an attempt at that site at a particular time, will survive."

34   *Ginsberg v. City of Ithaca and Cornell University*, 5 Supp. 3d 243 (N.D.N.Y. 2014).

35   *Ginsberg v. City of Ithaca and Cornell University*, 5 Supp. 3d 243 (N.D.N.Y. 2014).

36   ibid.

37   ibid.

38   See Nieswald, 692 F. Supp. at 1469, where the court found that an "implied contract" existed between Cornell and its students since Cornell had assumed responsibility to maintain effective security measures on campus. Cornell was slo on notice that "the problem of propped open doors was well known," and that "the University failed to take steps to resolve the problem. " Nieswand, at 1471.

39   *Nguyen v. Mass. Inst. of Tech.*, 479 Mass. 436 (Mass. 2018)

Chapter 9

1   Klarman, Michael J.,*Brown v. Board of Education and the Civil Rights Movement* [electronic resource] : abridged edition of *From Jim Crow to Civil Rights: The Supreme Court and the Struggle for Racial Equality*, Oxford; New York : Oxford University Press, 2007, p. 55.

2   Brown v. Board of Education of Topeka, 347 U.S. 483 (1954)

3   Boyle, Kevin (November 21, 1995). *The UAW and the Heyday of American Liberalism, 1945–1968*. Cornell University Press. p. 121. ISBN 978-1-5017-1327-9.

4   Risa L. Goluboff, *The Lost Promise of Civil Rights*, Harvard University Press, MA: Cambridge, 2007, pp. 249–251

5   Mary L Dudziak «Brown as a Cold War Case»*Journal of American History*, June 2004Archived December 7, 2014,

6   Brown v. Board of Education of Topeka, 347 U.S. 483 (1954).

7   379 U.S. 241 (1964)

8   388 U.S. 1 (1967)

9   «*Civil Rights Act of 1964 – CRA – Title VII – Equal Employment Opportunities – 42 US Code Chapter 21 – findUSlaw*». *Archived from the original on October 21, 2010.*

10   See *Pajarito Plateau Homesteaders, Inc. v U.S*, 346 F. 3d 983 (10th Cir. 2003).

11   ttps://news.yahoo.com/school-safety-officer-charged-murder-221039191.html

12   Case 1:15-cv-04844-AMD-LB

13   *Concepcion v. City of New York*, 2019 U.S. Dist. LEXIS 76601(E.D.N.Y. May 6, 2019)

14   ibid. , citing *Crenshaw v. City of Mount Vernon*, 372 F. App'x 202, 205-06 (2d Cir. 2010).

15   ibid., citing *Crenshaw*, 372 F. App'x at 205-06 (a person is guilty of committing disorderly conduct if he refuses to obey an officer's order to move, unless the order was arbitrary and "not calculated in any way to promote the public order." (quoting *People v. Galpern*, 181 N.E. 572, 574 (1932))); N.Y. Penal Law § 240.20.

16   See *Kass v. City of New York*, 864 F.3d 200, 206, 213-14 (2d Cir. 2017) (dismissing federal and state law false arrest claims, and holding "an officer is entitled to qualified immunity from a federal false arrest and imprisonment claim if he had arguable probable cause to arrest the plaintiff for any offense, regardless of the offense with which the plaintiff was actually charged.").

17   ibid., citing *Lombardi v. Whitman*, 485 F.3d 73, 79 (2d Cir. 2007).

18   ibid.

19   *Concepcion v. NYC Dept. of Education*, 19 cv 1693, 836 Fed. Appx. 27 (2d Cir. 2020), citing *Amnesty Am. v. Town of W. Hartford*, 361 F.3d 113, 123 (2d Cir. 2004).

20   ibid.

21   ibid.

22   *Prince McCoy, Sr.v. Alamu*, 950 F.3d 226 (5th Cir. 2020).

23   555 U.S. 223 (2009).

24   A Gratuitous Defense: Qualified Immunity and the Path to its Abolition — COLUMBIA POLITICAL REVIEW (cpreview.org)

25   595 U.S. ____ (2021).

Chapter 10

1   See *Manning v. Niagara Mohawk Power Corp.*, 501 N.Y.S.2d 218 (3d Dep't 1986); *Manning v. Niagara Mohawk Power Corp.*, 603 N.Y.S. 2d 214 (3d Dep't 1993); *Manning v. Niagara Mohawk Power Corp.*, 650 N.Y.S. 2d 431 (3d Dep't 1996).

2   MSP, 42 U.S.C. § 1395y(b) (2000).

3   The district court's first decision ("Manning I") dismissed Count Two (defendants' fraud claim for bad faith refusal to pay for his medical expenses and other workers' compensation benefits in a timely manner)." See *Manning v. Utilities Mut. Ins. Co.*, No. 98 Civ. 4790 (RCC), 1999 WL 782569 (S.D.N.Y. Sept. 30, 1999) ("Manning I").

4   See *Manning v. Utilities Mut. Ins. Co.*, No. 98 Civ. 4790 (RCC), 2000 WL 1234591 (S.D.N.Y. Aug. 31, 2000) ("Manning II").

5   *Robert Manning v. Utilities Mutual Ins. Co.*, 254 F3d 387 (2d Cir. 2001).

6   The Second Circuit held that the six-year statute of limitations applicable to private rights of action under the False Claims Act ("FCA"), see 31 U.S.C. § 3731(b)(1) (2000), should be applied to private rights of action under the MSP.

7   *Agency Holding Corp. v. Malley Duff & Associates*, 483 U.S. 143 (1987)

Chapter 11

1   The New York State Human Rights Law (Executive Law § 296 [1] [a]).
2   The New York City Human Rights Law (Administrative Code of City of NY § 8-107 [1] [a]).
3   Order, Supreme Court, New York County (Geoffrey D. Wright, J.), entered July 19, 2011.
4   ibid. at 432).
5   ibid. at 432–433.
6   ibid. at 433.
7   See ibid. at 433–437.
8   ibid. at 435–436.
9   See ibid. at 436.
10   ibid.
11   ibid. at 437. See Phillips, 66 AD3d at 176; see *Parker v. Columbia Pictures Industr.*, 204 F3d 326, 338 (2d Cir2002) (holding that an employee's proposal of a reasonable accommodation "triggers a responsibility on the employer's part to investigate that request and determine its feasibility," and "(a)n employer who fails to do so, and instead terminates the employee based on exhaustion of leave, has discriminated 'because of' disability within the meaning of the federal Americans with Disabilities Act)"; see also Kinneary v. City of New York, 601 F3d 151, 156 [2d Cir2010]; Morton v. United Parcel Service, Inc., 272 F3d 1249, 1256 n 7 [9th Cir.2001], overruled in part on other grounds by Bates v. United Parcel Service, Inc., 511 F3d 974, 998 (9th Cir2007); *Barnett v. U.S. Air, Inc.*, 228 F3d 1105, 1116 (9th Cir2000).
12   *Jacobsen v. NYC Health and Hospitals Corp.*, 2014 N.Y. Slip Op 02098 (2014).
13   See Administrative Code of the City of N.Y. § 8–107.
14   See Executive Law § 296.
15   *Jacobsen v. NYC Heath & Hospitals Corp.*, 97 A.D.3d 428; 948 N.Y.S.2d 586 (1st Dept. 2012).
16   New York Executive Law § 290[3].
17   Letter from Governor's Office of Employee Relations [June 22, 1979], ibid. at 18 [stating that, under the amended State HRL, adverse employment actions against an individual could not be justified based upon a mere relationship between the disability and the employee's ability to perform certain job duties but rather were warranted only "based upon an insurmountable 'disability' which would prevent a particular individual from performing the tasks which are inherently involved in a particular job "] [emphasis added]).

Chapter 12

1   "DSM-5 criteria for dementia,*" Diagnostic and Statistical Manual of Mental Disorders, Fifth Edition (DSM-5)*, (web), American Psychiatric Association.
2   See *Djavaheri – Saatchi v. Djavaheri- Saatchi*, 236 A.D. 2d 583, 654 N.Y.S. 2d 653 (2d Dept. 1997).
3   See *In re Will of Djavaheri-Saatchi*, 2018 N.Y. Slip Op. 32754 (N.Y. Surr. Ct. 2018).

Chapter 13

1   "Social Movements: Environmental movement," Civil Service India. Accessed January 6, 2022, https://www.civilserviceindia.com/subject/Political-Science/notes/social-movements-environmental-movements.html.
2   *The National Environmental Policy Act*, 42 U.S. Code (1969), § 4332
3   Editors of Encyclopaedia Britannica, "Earth Day," *Encyclopedia Britannica*, March 31, 2020. Accessed January 6, 2022, https://www.britannica.com/topic/Earth-Day.
4   Thomas J. Prohaska, "After a year of wrangling, federal judge refuses to handle Love Canal lawsuits," *The Buffalo News*, January 26, 2021. Accessed January 6, 2022, https://buffalonews.com/news/local/after-a-year-of-wrangling-federal-judge-refuses-to-handle-love-canal-lawsuits/article_5905647e-5fe5-11eb-991b-57290158ada6.html.

5   J. Raloff, *"Agent Orange and Birth Defects Risk,"* Science News 126, No. 8, (1984): 117;
     "Agent Orange - Anzac Portal," Australian Department of Veterans Affairs, *March 6,*
     2020. Acceessed January 6, 2022, https://anzacportal.dva.gov.au/wars-and-missions/viet-
     nam-war-1962-1975/events/aftermath/agent-orange.

6   *In Re "Agent Orange" Product Liability Litigation* MDL No. 381, 597 F. Supp. 740
     (E.D.N.Y. 1984).

7   *In Re "Agent Orange" Product Liability Litigation* MDL No. 381, 818 F.2d 187 (2d Cir. 1987).

8   App. A "Settlement Agreement," *In Re Agent Orange*, 597 F. Supp. at 862-866.

9   *In re "Agent Orange" Product Liability Litigation,* 597 F.Supp. 740,at 747. (E.D.N.Y.1984).

10   Agent Orange I Opt-Out Op., *In re "Agent Orange"* 818 F.2d at 189 (internal cita-
     tions omitted).

11   *In re Agent Orange,* 818 F.2d at 150.

12   ibid.

13   I had no involvement as class counsel at any point in this litigation.

14   *In re Agent Orange,* 818 F.2d at 152.

15   See *Burke v. Dow Chemical Co.,* 797 F. Supp. 1128 (E.D.N.Y. 1992) ("[Dow] may also be
     liable under New York law for injuries caused by [its product] Rid-A-Bug if plaintiffs can
     prove that Xylene or the mixture of Dursban and Xylene is teratogenic, that Dow knew or
     should have known this and that Dow failed to transmit this knowledge to its own indus-
     trial customers or to the ultimate users," citing *In re Agent Orange*, 597 F. Supp. 830-32, *aff'd,*
     818 F.2d 145, *cert. denied,* 484 U.S. 1004 (1988).

16   It was eventually rebuilt by a purchaser who had bought it dirt-cheap.

17   *Williams v Pelican Pest Control,* 11 A.D. 3d 454 , 782 N.Y.S. 2d 748 (2d Dept. 2004), citing
     Nicastro v Park, 113 AD2d 129, 134 (2d Dept. 1985), quoting *Delgado v Board of Educ.,* 65
     AD2d 547 (2d Dept. 1978).

18   ibid.

19   ibid.

20   *Williams v. Dow Chemical Co.,* 255 F. Supp. 2d 219 (S.D.N.Y. 2003).

21   *Racketeer Influenced And Corrupt Organizations Act,* 18 U.S. Code (1970), § 1961 *est seq.*

22   *The Lanham Act,* 15 U.S. Code (1946) § 1051 *et seq.*

23   *Federal Insecticide, Fungicide, and Rodenticide Act,* 7 U.S. Code (1996) § 136.

24   See *Williams v Dow Chemical Company,* 255 F. Supp. 2d, Dkt. No. 13, Second Amended
     Complaint ("SAC") at ¶ 7.

25   SAC ¶ 105(d).

26   SAC ¶ 164.

27   SAC ¶ 77.

28   SAC ¶ 82.

29   "As part of the Agreement, the signatory registrants that hold the pesticide registrations of
     manufacturing-use pesticide products containing chlorpyrifos have asked EPA to cancel
     their registrations for these products. In addition, these companies asked EPA to cancel or
     amend their registrations for end-use products containing chlorpyrifos." *Chlorpyrifos; Cancel-
     lation Order,* 65 Fed.Reg. 76233 (December 12, 2000).

30   *Williams v Dow Chemical Company,* 255 F. Supp. 2d. at 221.

31   ibid., at 225.

32   ibid.; see also *Corcoran v. American Plan Corp.,* 886 F.2d 16, 20 (2d Cir.1989) (fraudulent
     scheme directed at state insurance regulator «did not allege acts of mail fraud which could
     support a claim under RICO»).

33   ibid., *citing Abdu-Brisson v. Delta Airlines, Inc.,* 128 F.3d 77, 84 (2d Cir. 1997) («Delta,
     therefore, would seem to bear the burden of overcoming the initial presumption against pre-
     emption by establishing that enforcing the state and city laws would frustrate the purpose
     of the ADA.»).

Chapter 14

1   See *Goodwin v. Cirque du Soleil,* NYS Supreme Court, New York County, Index No. 117151/09.
2   "Plausible Range for the Value of Life," T.R. Miller, Journal of Forensic Economics, Vol. 3, No. 3, Fall 1990, pp. 17-39.
3   ibid.
4   /www.con-telegraph.ie/2021/09/12/mayo-man-raffling-dublin-penthouse-for-e58-per-entry/

Chapter 15

1   KeySpan was purchased by National Grid
2   Index No. D1-0001-98-11.
3   See, e.g., *Mauro v. KeySpan,* NYS Supreme Court, Suffolk County, Index No. 10-42289.
4   The Dalton and other deposition transcripts of key LILCO/KeySpan employees were included in the judicial record relating to *Nicholson, et al. v. KeySpan, et al.,* New York State Supreme Court, Suffolk County, Index No. 17458/06.
5   *Tsakis v. KeySpan,* Index No. 08-5022, NYS Supreme Court, Suffolk County, Opinion and Order, January 7, 2016.
6   Leaving aside the fact that Mr. and Mrs. Tsakis were not in Long Island during those years so that they would not have seen KeySpan's ongoing remediation activities, they did file their complaint in 2008. Since the three-year statute of limitations would have stretched back to 2005 in their case, the fact that remediation activities were ongoing in the vicinity of their property from 2007 to 2009 would hardly be evidence favoring KeySpan's statute of limitations argument.
7   *Tsakis v Keyspan Corp.* 2019 NY Slip Op 07436 (2d Dept. October 16, 2019).
8   ibid.
9   ibid.
10   ibid.
11   ibid.
12   ibid.
13   ibid.
14   ibid., citing *Sullivan v Keyspan Corp.,* 155 A.D.3d 804, 64 N.Y.S. 2d 82 (2d Dept. 2017); *Scheg v Agway, Inc.,* 229 A.D. 2d 963, 964 (2d Dept. 1996).
15   ibid.; see also, *Suffolk County Water Auth. v. Dow Chem. Co.,* 2014 NY Slip Op 05420, 121 A.D. 3d 50 (2d Dept. 2014)
16   See Clean Water Act, 42 U.S.C. §§ 7401 et seq., at in section 211(k), 42 U.S.C. § 7545(k),
17   See 42 U.S.C. § 7545(k) (1).
18   See 42 U.S.C. § 7545(k) (6) and (10) (D).
19   Section 7545(k) (1).
20   U.S.D.C., S.D.N.Y., MDL No. 01 Civ. 1076.
21   *In Re Methyl Tertiary Butyl Ether ("Mtbe") Prod. Liability Litigation,* 175 F. Supp. 2d 593 (S.D.N.Y. 2001)
22   ibid. citing *Oxygenated Fuels,* 2001 WL 958793, at *3-4, 158 F. Supp. 2d 248.
23   ibid., citing *Far East Conference v. United States,* 342 U.S. 570, 574, 72 S. Ct. 492 (1952).
24   ibid.
25   *Summers v. Tice,* 199 P.2d 1 (Cal. 1948) (en banc).
26   *New Jersey Turnpike Auth. v. PPG Indus., Inc.,* 197 F.3d 96, 106-07 (3d Cir.1999).
27   *Sindell v. Abbott Labs.,* 26 Cal. 3d 588, 163 Cal. Rptr. 132, 607 P.2d 924 (Ca.1980).
28   See, e.g., *Hymowitz v. Eli Lilly & Co.,* 73 N.Y.2d 487, 509-513, 541 N.Y.S.2d 941, 539 N.E.2d 1069 (1989) (DES); *Sindell,* 163 Cal. Rptr. 132, 607 P.2d at 936-38; see also *Richie v. Bridgestone/Firestone, Inc.,* 22 Cal. App. 4th 335, 27 Cal. Rptr. 2d 418, 421 (1994) ("Under the market share theory of liability, a plaintiff harmed by a fungible product that cannot be

traced to a specific producer may sue various makers of the product if the plaintiff joins a substantial share of those makers as defendants.").

29   ibid., citing *Hall v. E.I. DuPont De Nemours & Co.*, 345 F. Supp. 353, 374-78 (E.D.N.Y.1972).

30   ibid., citing *Smith*, 148 Ill. Dec. 22, 560 N.E.2d at 329, and Restatement (Second) of Torts § 876.

31   Restatement (Third) of Torts: Products Liability § 2(b) (1998); See *Marilyn Merrill v. Navegar, Inc.*, 110 Cal. Rptr. 2d 370, 28 P.3d 116 (2001) (a product is defectively designed if it has failed to perform as safely as an ordinary consumer would expect when used in an intended or reasonably foreseeable manner, or if the benefits of the challenged design do not outweigh the risk of danger inherent in such design); *Lamkin v. Towner*, 138 Ill. 2d 510, 150 Ill.Dec. 562, 563 N.E.2d 449, 457 (1990) (same); *Voss v. Black & Decker Mfg. Co.*, 59 N.Y.2d 102, 108, 463 N.Y.S.2d 398, 450 N.E.2d 204 (1983) (adopting risk-utility test for design defect claims).

32   ibid., citing *Liriano v. Hobart Corp.*, 92 N.Y.2d 232, 237, 677 N.Y.S.2d 764 (1998); *DeLeon v. Commercial Mfg. & Supply Co.*, 148 Cal. App. 3d 336, 195 Cal. Rptr. 867, 871 (1983) ("A duty to warn or disclose danger arises when an article is or should be known to be dangerous for its intended use, either inherently or because of defects."); *Sollami v. Eaton*, 319 Ill. App.3d 612, 254 Ill.Dec. 335, 747 N.E.2d 375, 380-81 (2001) ("A duty to warn exists where there is unequal knowledge, actual or constructive, and the defendant, possessed of such knowledge, knows or should know that harm might or could occur if no warning is given."); *Brown v. Glade and Grove Supply, Inc.*, 647 So. 2d 1033, 1035 (Fla. Dist.Ct.App.1994) ("a manufacturer … who knows or has reason to know that the product is likely to be dangerous in normal use has a duty to warn those who may not fully appreciate the possibility of such danger.").

33   ibid., Restatement (Second) of Torts § 821B(1).

34   ibid., citing *State v. Schenectady Chemicals, Inc.*, 117 Misc.2d 960, 459 N.Y.S.2d 971, 978 (1983) ("The common law rule has long been that water, like air, is an element in which no person can have an absolute property, yet, it is also, like air, free for the use of all, and the law has been diligent and rigorous to maintain it in its natural purity.")

35   ibid., citing Restatement (Second) of Torts § 876.

36   ibid., citing *Marshall v. Celotex Corp.*, 691 F. Supp. 1045, 1047 (E.D.Mich.1988).

37   ibid., citing *Sackman v. Liggett*, 965 F. Supp. 391, 395-96 (E.D.N.Y.1997)

Chapter 16

1   The Herero and Nama peoples are minorities in Namibia, respectively making up 7% and 5% of the national population. This has resulted in continuing political disenfranchisement and stymied their access to negotiations between Namibian and German government officials, despite the specific targeting of these tribes by German Imperial extermination decrees. "Africa: Namibia," The World Factbook, Central Intelligence Agency, January 5 2020, https://www.cia.gov/the-world-factbook/countries/namibia/.

2   *See* David Olusoga and Casper W. Erichson's *The Kaiser's Holocaust,* (London: Faber & Faber, 2011), for a well-written and exhaustively sourced account of Germany's colonial motivations, policies, and eventual genocide in modern Namibia.

3   Susanne Kuss, *German Colonial Wars and the Context of Violence* (Cambridge: Harvard University Press, 2017), 38.

4   The Kaiser dispatched von Trotha and his men to China with the following exhortation: "Just as a thousand years ago the Huns under their King Attila made a name for themselves, one that even today makes them seem mighty in history and legend, may the name German be affirmed by you in such a way in China that no Chinese will ever again dare to look cross-eyed at a German." *Quoted in* Manfred Görtemaker, "Deutschland im 19. Jahrhundert. Entwicklungslinien (Germany in the 19th Century. Paths in Development)," *Schriftenreihe der Bundeszentrale für politische Bildung* 274 (1996), 357. *Translation by Thomas Dunlap.*

5   *Quoted in* Mahmood Mamdani, *When Victims Become Killers: Colonialism, Nativism, and the Genocide in Rwanda* (Princeton: Princeton University Press, 2020), 11.

6   Von Trotha's command became known as a *"Vernichtungsbefehl,"* i.e., an "extermination order."

7   *Quoted in* Jeremy Sarkin-Hughes, *Germany's Genocide of the Herero* (Woodbridge: Boydell and Brewer, 2011), 118.

8   Germany called the camps *"Konzentrationslager"* (Concentration Camps), as early as January 1905, in a telegram sent from the German Imperial Chancellery.

9   The details of the methods used to obtain these skulls were recorded in the "Health Report of the Imperial *Schutztruppe* for South West Africa during the Herero and Nama Rebellion during January 1, 1904 to March 31, 1907," (*Sanitätsbericht über die kaiserliche Schutztruppe für SWA während des Herero und Hottentottenaufstandes für die Zeit vom 1/1/04 – 31/3/07*) (1909), as well as the letter from the State Secretary of the Imperial Ministry of Colonies (*Reichs-Kolonialamt*) to the Imperial Governor in Windhoek, dated July 31, 1908.

10   *Quoted in* Andrew Meldrum, "German minister says sorry for genocide in Namibia," *The Guardian*, August 15, 2004.

11   "... *eine fortdauernde Verletzung der Nachfahren der Opfer.*" *See* Forward by Heidemarie Wieczorek-Zeul *in* Reinhart Kößler and Henning Melber, *Völkermord – und Was Dann?* (Frankfurt: Brandes & Apsel, 2017), 9.

12   *See Rukoro v. Federal Republic of Germany*, 363 F. Supp. 3d 436 (S.D.N.Y. 2019), Dkt. 45-2, Accession Card and Accession Record, Declaration of Barnabas Veraa Katuuo, at ¶ 8 & Exhibits 1–2.

13   ibid.

14   *See Rukoro v. Federal Republic of Germany*, 363 F. Supp. 3d.

15   *Alien Tort Claims Act*, 28 U.S. Code (1948), §1350.

16   *See* Hermann Hesse, *Die Schutzverträge in Südwestafrika - Ein Beitrag Zur Rechtsgeschichtlichen Und Politischen Entwicklung Des Schutzgebietes* (Berlin: Süsserott, 1905).

17   *Rukoro v. Federal Republic of Germany*, 363 F. Supp. 3d, Dkt. 39.

18   *See* Johann Caspar Bluntschli, *Das Moderne Völkerrecht Der Civilisirten Staten* (1878), *supra* note 2, at 299. For a detailed discussion of anti-genocide international law contemporary to the Herero-Nama genocide *see also* Rachel J. Anderson, "Redressing Colonial Genocide: The Hereros' Cause of Action Against Germany," *Scholarly Works* 288 (2005). Accessed January 13, 2022, https://scholars.law.unlv.edu/facpub/288.

19   *The Foreign Sovereign Immunities Act*, 28 U.S. Code § 1603, *et seq.*

20   *The Foreign Sovereign Immunities Act,* § 1605(a)(3).

21   *Rukoro v. Federal Republic of Germany*, 363 F.Supp.3d.

22   The commercial activity exception provides, in pertinent part, that a foreign state shall not be immune from jurisdiction in any case in which the action is "based ... upon an act outside the territory of the United States in connection with a commercial activity of the foreign state elsewhere and that act causes a direct effect in the United States." *The Foreign Sovereign Immunities Act,* § 1605(a)(2).

23   The takings exception provides, in pertinent part, that a foreign state shall not be immune from jurisdiction in any case "in which rights in property taken in violation of international law are in issue and that property or any property exchanged for such property is present in the United States in connection with a commercial activity carried on in the United States by the foreign state; or that property or any property exchanged for such property is owned or operated by an agency or instrumentality of the foreign state and that agency or instrumentality is engaged in a commercial activity in the United States." *The Foreign Sovereign Immunities Act,* § 1605(a)(3).

24   *The Foreign Sovereign Immunities Act,* § 1603(e).

25   Circuit Judges Pooler, Winter and Park.

26   *Rukoro v. Federal Republic of Germany*, 976 F.3d 218 (2d Cir. 2020). On June 9, 2020, the U.S. Supreme Court denied our petition for certiorari in *Vekuii Rukoro, et al. v. Federal Republic of Germany*, No. 20-1454.

27   ibid.

Chapter 17

1   The Orange Revolution was a series of protests and civil resistance efforts that took place in Ukraine from late November 2004 to January 2005, in the immediate aftermath of the run-off vote of the 2004 Ukrainian presidential election. Opposition politicians claimed the election was marred by massive fraud in favor of one of the candidates, Viktor Yanukovych. The protests succeeded when the results of the run-off were annulled, and a second run-off took place. The final results showed a clear victory for Viktor Yushchenko, who was then inaugurated on January 23, 2005.

2   Pamela Brogan, *The Torturers' Lobby: How Human Rights-Abusing Nations Are Represented in Washington*, (Washington, D.C.: *The Center for Public Integrity*, 1992).

3   Peter Stone, "Trump's new right-hand man has history of controversial clients and deals," *The Guardian*, April 27, 2016.

4   Andrew Kramer, et al., "Secret Ledger in Ukraine Lists Cash for Donald Trump's Campaign Chief," *The New York Times*, August 14, 2016.

5   Andrew Higgins and Andrew Kramer, "Archrival Is Freed as Ukraine Leader Flees," *The New York Times*, February 22, 2014.

6   Andrew Kramer, "How a Ukrainian Hairdresser Became a Front for Paul Manafort," *The New York Times*, September 15, 2018.

7   ibid.

8   Kilimnik was indicted with Manafort on June 8, 2018, on obstruction of justice charges relating to witness tampering. *See* Jeff Horwitz and Maria Danilova, "Russian Charged with Trump's Ex-Campaign Chief Is Key Figure," *US News*, July 2, 2018; *see also* Andrew Prokop, "Mueller just added more charges to Paul Manafort – and indicted Konstantin Kilimnik," *Vox*, June 8, 2018.

9   Luke Harding and Dan Collyns, "Manafort held secret talks with Assange in Ecuadorian embassy, sources say," *The Guardian*, November 27, 2018. Assange himself publicly confirmed this on June 12, 2016, during a BBC interview.

10 Kenneth McCallion, "How much the borscht just thickened: The Trump-Russia connections are getting impossible to explain away," *New York Daily News*, November 29, 2018.

11 Kathryn Watson, "How did WikiLeaks become associated with Russia?" *CBS News*, November 15, 2017.

12 Maggie Haberman and Jonathan Martin, "Paul Manafort Quits Donald Trump's Campaign After a Tumultuous Run," *The New York Times*, August 19, 2016.

13 Manafort's weakness for expensive clothing seemed to capture the public imagination, particularly the revelation that Manafort had bought a $15,000 ostrich leather jacket with his ill-gotten gains. *See* Robin Givhan, "Paul Manafort's ostrich Jacket pretty much sums up Paul Manafort," *The Washington Post*, August 2, 2018.

14 *Tymoshenko v. Firtash et al.*, 57 F.Supp.3d at 315-316.

15 European Union: European Parliament, *European Parliament resolution on Ukraine: the cases of Yulia Tymoshenko and other members of the former government*, June 9, 2011, P7_TA-PROV (2011)0272.

16 *Tymoshenko v. Firtash et al.*, 57 F.Supp.3d.

17 *See Tymoshenko v. Firtash et al.*, 57 F.Supp.3d. at 318.

18 *Alien Tort Claims Act*, 28 U.S. Code (1948), §1350.

19 *Racketeer Influenced And Corrupt Organizations Act*, 18 U.S. Code (1970), § 1961 *est seq.*

20 Other political opposition leaders jailed and/or prosecuted for criticizing defendants and their co-conspirators for "skimming" gas contract monies under the guise of "commissions" were: Yuriy Lutsenko, an important ally of Tymoshenko during her second term as Prime Minister, who was jailed for "failing to cooperate with the prosecution; Valeriy Ivashchenko, another Plaintiff Class Member and former Acting Minister of Defense during Tymoshenko's premiership, was arrested on August 21, 2010 on politically motivated charges of "abuse of power of official position;" Ihor Didenko, Naftogaz's former CEO who signed the 2009 gas contracts on behalf of Naftogaz, was arrested in July 2010; Yevhen Korniychuk, the

former First Deputy Minister of Justice in the Tymoshenko administration, was arrested and jailed on December 22, 2010 on politically-motivated charges that courts had twice concluded to be without merit; Anatoly Makarenko, the Customs Chief of Ukraine in the Tymoshenko administration; Mykola Petrenko, a member of Ukraine's executive administration during Tymoshenko's term as Prime Minister and Director of UkrMedPostach, the state-run enterprise through which Ukraine's Ministry of Health was attempting to improve the health of Ukraine's rural population; Taras Shepitko, who served as Deputy Head of the Department of the Kyiv Regional Customs Office in the Tymoshenko administration; Mykola Synkovsky, former Deputy Head of the State Committee of State Material Reserves under Tymoshenko; Mykhailo Pozhyvanoy, former Chairman of the State Committee of State Material Reserves and Deputy Economy Minister; Bogtdan D0anylyshyn, the former Minister of the Economy under Tymoshenko; Viktor Bondar, former Minister for Transport and Communications and Deputy Head of the State Customs Service; Vitaliy Nikitin, who served as Acting Head of the State Committee of State Material Reserves under the Tymoshenko Government; Tetyana Slyuz, former head of the State Treasury of Ukraine; Tetyana Grytsun, former First Deputy Head of the State Treasury; Victor Kolbun, former Deputy Pension Fund Board Chairman; and Oleksandr Danyevych, former State Treasury Deputy Chief.

21 *Alien Tort Claims Act*, § 1350.

22 The ATS permits a federal suit to be filed "by an alien for a tort only, committed in violation of the law of nations or a treaty of the United States." *Alien Tort Claims Act*, § 1350. In 1980, the U.S. Court of Appeals for the Second Circuit decided *Filártiga v. Peña-Irala*, which the Center for Constitutional Rights brought on behalf of two Paraguayan citizens, who were residents in the U.S. *Filártiga v. Peña-Irala*, 630 F.2d 876 (2d Cir. 1980). These plaintiffs brought suit against a Paraguayan former police chief also living in the United States, alleging that he had tortured and murdered a family member. Plaintiffs asserted that U.S. federal courts had jurisdiction over their suit under the ATS. The district court dismissed the complaint for lack of subject-matter jurisdiction, holding that the "law of nations" – which is how international law is described in the ATS – does not regulate a state's treatment of its citizens. The U.S. Court of Appeals for the Second Circuit reversed the district court›s decision. They held that the ATS, which allowed jurisdiction in the federal courts over a suit between two aliens, was a legitimate constitutional exercise of Congress›s power because "the law of nations ... has always been part of the federal common law." Thus the statute fell within federal-question jurisdiction. The Second Circuit further held that the current law of nations had expanded since the ATS's enactment to prohibit state-sanctioned torture. The court found that multilateral treaties and domestic prohibitions on torture evidenced a consistent state practice of proscribing official torture. The court similarly found that United Nations declarations prohibited official torture, such as the Universal Declaration on Human Rights. The court, therefore, held that the right to be free from torture had become a principle of customary international law. In addition to torture, federal courts had found that the ATS also covers other international law crimes, including cruel, inhuman, or degrading treatment; genocide; war crimes; crimes against humanity; summary execution; and prolonged arbitrary detention.

23 *Tymoshenko v. Firtash et al.*, 57 F.Supp.3d. 311 (S.D.N.Y. 2013)

24 ibid., citing Amended Complaint ("AC") at ¶ 189.

25 *See* AC ¶¶ 196, 253.

26 ibid., ¶¶ 256-58.

27 ibid.

28 ibid., citing *Kiobel*, 456 F. Supp. 2d at 466 (quoting *Wiwa*, 2002 WL 319887, at *7).

29 *See* AC ¶¶ 6

30 See *Norex Petroleum Ltd. v. Access Indus., Inc.*, 631 F.3d 29, 32-33 (2d Cir. 2010) (per curiam).

31 *European Commission v. RJR Nabisco, Inc.*, 764 F. 3d 129 (2d Cir. 2014).

32 *See* Andrew Kramer, "Prize Catch for Ukrainians at Boat Harbor: A Soggy Trove of Government Secrets," *New York Times*, February 26, 2014.

Chapter 18

1   *Tymoshenko v. Firtash et al.,* 57 F.Supp.3d 311 (S.D.N.Y. 2014).

2   Christian Berthelsen and Greg Farrell, "Robert Mueller Subpoenas Paul Manafort Bank Records in Russia Investigation," *Time,* August 10, 2017; *see also* Christian Berthelsen and Greg Farrell, "With Bank Subpoenas, Mueller Turns Up the Heat on Manafort," *Bloomberg,* August 10, 2017.

3   "Manafort had $10 million loan from Russian oligarch: court filing," *Reuters,* June 27, 2018; *see also* Stephanie Baker and David Voreacos, "Manafort Reported $10 Million Loan From Russian Oligarch in 2010," *Bloomberg,* June 28, 2018.

4   Kenneth Vogel and Matthew Goldstein, "How Skadden, the Giant Law Firm, Got Entangled in the Mueller Investigation," *The New York Times,* February 24, 2018.

5   Kenneth Vogel and Andrew Kramer, "Skadden, Big New York Law Firm, Faces Questions on Work With Manafort," *The New York Times,* September 21, 2017.

6   Michael Schmidt and Adam Goldman, "Manafort's Home Searched as Part of Mueller Inquiry," *The New York Times,* August 9, 2017.

7   The author and his law firm, McCallion & Associates LLP, served as U.S. counsel for Tymoshenko while she was incarcerated and tried on bogus, politically motivated charges by the pro-Russian Yanukovych Regime. While still incarcerated in Ukraine, McCallion & Associates LLP filed a civil RICO complaint against Manafort, Gates, and others in the U.S. District Court for the Southern District of New York on behalf of Tymoshenko and others. The details of this complaint, and the document attached to it, became part of the source material for the federal investigation resulting in the indictments of Manafort, Gates, and van der Zwaan. *See Tymoshenko v. Firtash et al.,* 57 F.Supp.3d.

8   Alan Kaytukov and Alexander Smith, "Mistake in Manafort Indictment Shows Case Was 'Cooked Up,' Russia Says," *NBC News,* October 31, 2017; *See also* Andrew Prokop, "Read: Mueller's new indictment of Paul Manafort and Rick Gates." *Vox,* February 22, 2018.

9   Prokop, "Read: Mueller's new indictment."

10   Kevin Johnson, "Paul Manafort trial: Bank fast-tracked loan as Trump chairman discussed cabinet posts for CEO," *USA Today,* August 10, 2018.

11   Andrew Prokop, "Robert Mueller just flipped his third former Trump aide," *Vox,* February 23, 2018.

12   ibid.

13   Darren Samuelsohn, "Mueller delays sentencing for ex-Trump aide Gates over ongoing cooperation," *Politico,* November 14, 2018. Accessed January 11, 2022, www.politico.com/ story/2018/11/14/rick-gates-sentencing-mueller-probe-990758.

14   Prokop, "Mueller just added more charges to Paul Manafort."

15   Kevin Johnson, et al., "Paul Manafort trial: Jury finds former Trump campaign manager guilty on 8 counts in tax fraud case," *USA Today,* August 21, 2018.

16   Anna Gearan, "'Bada bing bada boom': Paul Manafort's attempt to smear a jailed Ukrainian Politician," *The Washington Post,* September 14, 2018.

17   Hadassa Kalatizadeh, "Govt to Seize Manafort's Hamptons Home & Trump Tower Condo in Plea Deal," *The Jewish Voice,* October 10, 2018.

18   ibid.

19   ibid.

20   ibid.

21   Christine Wang, et al., "Ex-Trump campaign chief Paul Manafort broke plea deal, lied to prosecutors, Mueller says," *CNBC,* November 26, 2018.

22   Brett Samuels, "Manafort attorney relayed info about Mueller probe to Trump lawyers: report," *The Hill,* 27 November, 2018. Accessed January 11, 2022, https://thehill.com/ policy/national-security/418600-manaforts-attorney-relayed-info-about-mueller-investigation-to-trump.

23   Sharon LaFraniere, "Judge Orders Paul Manafort Jailed Before Trial, Citing New Obstruction Charges," *The New York Times,* June 15, 2018.

CPSIA information can be obtained
at www.ICGtesting.com
Printed in the USA
BVHW030114270622
640641BV00009B/62/J